The Management of Sales and Customer Relations

Contents

PART 6 – TELEMARKETING AND TRADE FAIRS

Acknowledgements

The editors would like to thank the authors and publishers who have agreed to the readings being reproduced. They appear in full. A special thank you to Neil Rackham, Kevin Wilson, Adrian Palmer, Sue Reynard, Professor Noriaki Kano and Professor David Kerridge for their assistance.

The ideas and comments expressed in the introduction to each section are the sole responsibility of the editors. We sincerely hope that we have not misquoted or wrongly interpreted the work of others; if we have, please accept our apologies and let us know.

Introduction

In the West we have become obsessed with finance, competition, downsizing and free markets, yet the performance of many organizations is disappointing. We seem to have lost focus or forgotten where revenue and consequently profit comes from. Why is this? Where have we gone wrong? Professor Robert Grant and colleagues refer to two emerging and contrasting management paradigms namely the 'Economic Model of the Firm' and 'Total Quality Management' (TQM).[1] The organizational objectives of the former are maximizing profit, i.e. shareholder wealth. TQM's organizatioal objectives are, 'serving customers by supplying goods and services of the highest possible quality'.

Professor Kosaku Yoshida[2] compares the relationship between Japanese and American automobile manufacturers and their suppliers,

> Those involved in the group transaction tend to develop long-term relationships between suppliers and customers. Because of the co-ordination natural to such long-term relationships, parts produced by different companies within the group fit together very well so that, together, they tend to produce better quality products with low costs. In contrast, the relationship between auto producers and suppliers within the U.S. is relatively short-term, price is a major concern, and suppliers are considered as replaceable parts within the overall system.

A company is a system consisting of several components or departments, i.e. sales, production, administration, and so on, that all need to work together to satisfy customer's needs. Instead of working together we set up different departments as separate cost centres that all compete against each other. Within 'sales' we may have the Northern region competing against the Southern region. Professor Yoshida states, 'The entire Japanese establishment and all management practices are aimed at eliminating competition.'

The link between an organization and its customers in most business-to-business relationships is the sales professional, area sales manager, key account manager or whatever title he or she happens to have. To the customer *they are the company.* The management of this relationship is of *strategic importance*. Successful organizations realize this, think long-term and take great care how they manage and develop this relationship. Relationships are not built over night: 'one night stands' or 'pseudo relationships' do not last. It takes time to develop a bond and trust between two organizations. Once this develops then the business conducted between the two tends to increase.

Their less successful counterparts do not see the importance of a relationship, fail to appreciate that customers represent future revenue flows. They believe the link is more of a day-to-day *operational management issue*. Thinking will typically focus on meeting 'this month's quota', blaming employees for a fall in revenue or mistakes in deliveries. Top management will never for a moment think that they themselves could be wrong, that it might be the system itself at fault or that there might be 'better ways' to do things. '*Short termism*' is their forté. These champions of short-term thinking have caused the downfall of so many companies and industries in the West. They never look in the mirror. They do not provide proper training for their sales people, expect them to sink or swim, have a high turnover of sales staff and are the most valued customers of recruitment and selection companies.

It is often said that people are a company's most important asset. While we would not want to downgrade their importance, surely it is the customer who represents the most important asset. Revenue comes from customers. Without them there is no revenue and assets such as buildings, cars, computers, work in progress and inventory serve no purpose. This means that we have to work with our customers, nurture them and look after them. The readings in this book focus on various aspects that can help contribute to better relationships between customers and suppliers.

Sales is still treated as a Cinderella subject and is not seen to be as sexy as marketing. It is considered by many to be rather seedy, not a worthy academic subject and certainly not a 'blue chip' career. This is not surprising considering:

- the methods that some organizations resort to in order to get a sale
- many marketing academics have no real practical experience or understanding of the sales field and continue to regurgitate the same outdated models in their textbooks and lectures
- some of the dubious sales training programmes offered.

Many books on sales management cover the traditional topics extensively. These include the role of the sales force, territory structure and design, size of the sales force, the selling process, evaluation and control and personnel issues such as recruitment, remuneration and motivation. For this reason, these topics are not covered directly in this collection of readings. A review of eight major textbooks on sales management[3] (six published since 1990) gave rise to concern over the topics which appeared to have been overlooked. From an analysis of the contents pages of eight books the following was noted:

Number of books with:

Topic	*Full chapter*	*Part chapter*
Relationship marketing	0	0
Customer care	0	1
Negotiation	1	1
Major accounts	1	2
Agents and distributors	0	2
Telesales	2	4
Trade shows	0	2
Sales administration	2	0
Computer aided sales	0	3

This book of readings remedies some of these failings and provides some of the latest thinking in the area of the 'Management of sales and customer relations'. Building customer relations is an underlying theme common to all the readings and particularly those dealing with database marketing, sales negotiation and customer service. In selecting these readings, we are attempting to differentiate between 'sales management' and 'management of sales'. The term sales manager has traditionally been associated with management of the field sales force, resulting in a rather narrow approach. By using the term 'management of sales' it is hoped to convey a rather wider meaning:

> Management of sales is the integrated approach to the management of all functions and activities involving customer relationships including selling, order processing, fulfilment, and service with the aim of not merely satisfying customers but delighting them.

It may be argued that traditional approaches to the organization of sales and marketing functions, are becoming too much of a constraint on the development of effective mechanisms for serving customers. The effective integration of marketing, sales, distribution, and service is a very real challenge. For organizations which are reliant on large customers (key accounts) these issues become critical. One of the difficulties in discussing the organization required for effective management of sales and customer relations is that it cuts across functional boundaries: the field sales force, telemarketing, direct mail, dealers, order processing, customer service, and the management of the physical distribution function. In addition, computerized information and communication systems now impact heavily in all these areas. Perhaps it is this last development which is driving all these functions closer together. Significant opportunities for improving sales effectiveness, organizational efficiency and customer service now present themselves. However, this challenge can only be met if a strategic view is taken of customer contact management in order to build appropriate relationships.

The readings presented in this book have all been previously published. They are divided into six specialist subsections. Each is provided with a short introduction by the editors to set the scene and place the readings in context. They range from the theoretical to the practical 'how to do' approach. Some contain case histories by way of example. The six parts are:

Part 1: Changing Nature of Sales and Customer Relations

In Part 1, we have included three readings that reflect on the changing nature of sales and customer relations, all taken from the first three years of the decade. They summarize important changes which are affecting the way sales and customers are managed and discuss the impact on organization structure, systems and culture. Issues covered range from managing the industrial sales force, organizing for key accounts, and the impact of information technology on sales support and direct marketing.

Part 2: Selling and Negotiation

Part 2 covers the field of selling and negotiation. The old traditional adversarial approach to selling and negotiating with customers is changing. This part includes five readings that reflect these changes. Traditional remuneration systems with a heavy emphasis on commission are counter-productive to fulfilling and exceeding customer's expectations. Identification and management of key accounts, the importance of negotiation in the major sale, and building long-term relationships with customers are all discussed in some depth.

Part 3: Database Marketing

In Part 3 there are five readings that examine how database marketing is contributing towards building profitable relations with customers. The term, which is often misunderstood, is explained and its relationship to direct marketing, sales support, and customer service is discussed. Tips on how to build and manage a database are offered and the strategic implications examined.

Part 4: Customer Service and Relationship Marketing

Part 4 includes four readings in the important field of customer service. Many products are now so similar that customer service is one area where organisations can differentiate themselves from their competitors. The traditional focus in sales and marketing used to be on acquiring customers. Now greater attention is given to retaining existing customers. However, satisfying existing customers may provide a false feeling of security as even satisfied customers may defect.

Part 5: Managing Agents and Distributors

In Part 5 there are six short readings on managing agents and distributors. Sales agents (or manufacturers' representatives) and distributors are a frequently used means of serving the market. Manufacturers and service providers both large and small use independent agents and distributors. Little has been written on the use of sales management, and most books on agents assume that the selling organization employs all sales people and managers directly. This part discusses the use of agents, the services they perform, their selection, and how to form a strategic alliance and build long-term relationships.

Part 6: Telemarketing and Trade Fairs

Part 6 contains two readings on telemarketing and two on trade fairs. There has been an enormous increase in the use of the telephone over the last two decades, both in supporting the field sales force and also in direct response marketing. Trade fairs provide a convenient and cost-effective way of meeting existing and potential customers. Both telemarketing and trade fairs are an important way of generating sales leads.

These readings provide guidance on how companies can improve relationships with their customers. They do not provide the definitive solution. There will always be a need for continuous improvement in every aspect of this relationship. Complacency must not prevail. The survivors will be those that are the most creative in developing links with their customers to mutual benefit.

References

1 Grant, R.M., Shani, R. and Krishnan, R. 'TQM's challenge to management theory and practice', *Sloan Management Review*, Winter 1994, pp. 25–35.
2 Yoshida, K. 'New economic principles in America – competition and cooperation: a comparative study of the U.S. and Japan'. *The Columbia Journal of World Business*, Vol. XXVI, No. IV, Winter 1992.
3 Hartley, R.A. 'Sales management or management of sales', *Marketing Education Group (UK), Conference Proceedings*, June 1994, pp. 467–76.

Part 1

The Changing Nature of Selling and Customer Relations

INTRODUCTION

Part 1 sets the scene with three readings from the first three years of the decade. At the time these papers summarized some important changes in the business environment. All tried to look ahead and identify crucial developments which would influence sales methods and customer relations in the coming decade. The issues identified then are now usually referred to as 'relationship marketing'. What was certain at the time was that traditional methods of managing the sales force, organizing promotions to provide incentive for the buyer, using direct mail, and running customer service departments were fast becoming outdated. The reasons why are discussed in these readings, but may be summarized as:

- rising cost of field sales activity
- traditional focus on opening new accounts rather on customer retention
- changes in purchasing practice and buyer expertise
- concentration of buying power in many industries
- reinforcement of the 80:20 rule, 80 per cent of sales from 20 per cent of customers
- recognition of the importance of key accounts
- growing importance of reliability, quality and customer service
- intense international competition and globalization of markets
- fragmentation of some markets (micro marketing) and increasing sophistication of segmentation
- media fragmentation and reduction in the impact of television advertising
- growth of direct marketing (direct mail and telemarketing) and database marketing
- technological developments in computing and telecommunications.

What was not so certain at the time was the magnitude of the changes or the speed with which they would be adopted. With the continuing rise in the cost of running the field sales force, a real fall in the cost of computing, data handling and communications, and the recession of the late 1980s running on much longer than expected intensifying competition still further, the changes predicted in these readings gathered pace.

The first reading, 'The shape of things to come' by William O'Connell and William Keenan, is based on a survey of sales force productivity. This identifies some of the environmental changes mentioned above and the changing nature of the sales manager's role. In particular it questions traditional approaches to opening new accounts which may be at the expense of the retention of existing accounts. The paper comments on the integration of new technology into sales, levels of pay and its effect on sales, training, introducing new products to customers, and on systems selling techniques. The authors suggest that the scrutiny of the board room will fall increasingly on the line items that comprise general sales administration costs. The sales executive will need to justify these costs. Their survey results suggest that the cost of 'a business-to-business sales call has been increasing at an annualized rate of just over 11 per cent'. However, they report that participants in the survey have only been able to raise prices 5 per cent over the preceding three years.

'Managing the industrial sales force of the 1990s' by Kevin Wilson provides the second reading. The author details the changes which have taken place in the business-to-business sales environment. The emerging role of the sales executive is identified as:

- customer partner
- buyer/seller team co-ordinator
- customer service provider
- buyer behaviour expert
- information gatherer
- market analyst and planner
- sales forecaster
- marketing cost analyser
- technologist.

The growing importance of key account management and team selling are discussed, as are the implications for training. Traditional methods of selling and associated training are criticized as being inappropriate for major sales, and support is expressed for the work of Neil Rackham (see Part 2 – Rackham has developed an approach for dealing with major sales and building customer relationships). Wilson goes on to discuss the management of customer relations and managing the activities of the sales force. It is suggested that this activity needs to be integrated with marketing strategy. While this is 'widely recognized' in sales management literature, little discussion occurs about what the link between marketing strategy and sales strategy should be. The issues affecting integration with reference to building better customer relations with key accounts in business-to-business sales are identified. In measuring sales force performance in this context he questions the validity of quantitative systems which reward sales volume and measure activity rates such as calls, conversions, new accounts opened, and so on. Wilson concludes with the need for:

- integration of the sales function into the organization's strategy
- training of the sales force in managing customer relationships
- recognition of customer relations as a strategic issue
- improvements in the professionalism of the sales force and integration of new technology
- measurement of the potential long-term exchanges with customers.

Reading 3 from Keith Fletcher, Colin Wheeler and Julia Wright examines the term database marketing (DBM). This paper asks 'what is database marketing?', suggests distinctions between direct marketing (DM) and DBM and identifies the factors related to the successful introduction of DBM. In conclusion, it is suggested that marketing orientation is required and that the decision to introduce DBM needs the support of top management. DBM should be seen as a long-term development and investment decisions should be considered over the long term. Starting in a small way and allowing the system to evolve is recommended as this allows the organization to change and adjust to the new systems and ways of working.

These three readings provide an introduction to the main themes covered in this collection. Part 2 looks at selling and negotiation, Part 3 concentrates on database marketing, Part 4 on customer service and relationship marketing, Part 5 on managing agents and distributors and Part 6 on telesales and trade fairs. It may be argued that traditional approaches to the organization of sales and marketing functions are becoming too much of a constraint on the development of effective mechanisms for serving customers. The effective integration of marketing, sales, service, and distribution is a very real challenge. For organizations which are reliant on large customers (key accounts) these issues become critical. Computerized information and communication systems (CICS) linked to a modern relational database, present significant opportunities for improving sales effectiveness, organizational efficiency, and customer service. However, the design and implementation of such systems is a strategic issue and will present a significant challenge to the organization's culture and structure.

Reading 1

The shape of things to come

What you need to know to make your sales effort more productive – and your company more profitable

William A. O'Connell and William Keenan Jr

Reprinted from *Sales & Marketing Management*, January 1990, pp. 36–41.

This survey on Sales Force Productivity was a joint project of Sales & Marketing Management and Personnel Corporation of America. Results are based on responses from 192 companies representing a total of nearly 10,000 sales representatives. The average company participating in the survey had a sales force of 61, an average annual sales volume of $86.5 million, and profits of 11.8%.

In the coming decade, not only will the sales executive preside over some radical changes in selling, he will also be under a microscope as never before.

Most sales executives, in fact, will already have had a taste of the changes that will affect their work in the next decade – just-in-time production and purchasing, sophisticated computer-based materials planning, and the growing concentration of buying points for companies selling in any number of industries. Added to these are changes arising out of the way goods and services are marketed and sold, with new distribution options, telemarketing, computer-aided target marketing, and more.

It's an evolution the outlines of which are just beginning to emerge, and when it has run its course, the typical sales executive is likely to find himself or herself presiding either over a field sales force that has lost its traditional power, effectiveness, and prestige or over a more powerful sales organization that integrates the best efficiencies of direct marketing, data-base marketing, telemarketing, and a whole arsenal of automated sales tools.

Efficiency and effectiveness, as you might guess, are the key words in this evolution and should key the decision making of sales executives in the decade to come.

A new survey, conducted jointly by *Sales & Marketing Management* and

Personnel Corporation of America, suggests that, in the nineties, the scrutiny of the boardroom will fall increasingly on the line items that comprise general sales administration costs. And, of course, it will be the sales executive who will be asked to justify those costs.

It won't be easy. The average cost of a business-to-business sales call has been increasing at an annualized rate of just over 11%. At the same time, survey participants report that they've been able to raise prices by an average of only 5% over the past three years. The result is that the overall cost of a sale amounts to an average of 14.5% of sales volume, according to our survey, but it can range as high as 30%–35% at some companies. Given that improvements in sales productivity will drop straight to the bottom line, many CEOs will be knocking on the sales manager's door looking for changes.

THE 80/20 REALITY

A change in purchasing practices – just-in-time inventory control, for instance, computer-based purchasing, or preferred vendor relationships – can have a profound impact on a firm, especially if it affects your sales relationship with a key account. And the fact is that while the 80/20 rule – the general rule that 80% of your sales will come from 20% of your customers – may not be literally true, it's true enough that the unexpected loss of a key account can radically alter a company's fortunes.

Our Sales Productivity Survey indicates that the top 20% of accounts contributed a median 75% of sales volume for participants (see Figure 1.1) – a sort of 75/20 rule – but also that 50% of a typical company's sales volume came from the top 10% of its customers, and a full 90% of all firms' sales volume came from the top 50% of their accounts. The sales manager who ignores – or is ignorant of – that sort of distribution among his customers does so at his own risk.

It's no surprise, then, that the majority of sales managers believe that the most important objectives of their sales forces ought to be: 1) retaining existing accounts, and 2) gaining share with existing accounts (see Figure 1.2). What *is* striking about the results overall, however, is the fact that sales managers' perceptions of their present performance in these key areas of selling effectiveness fall far short, in virtually all cases, of their rating of their importance.

For example, while 76% of participants rated retaining existing accounts as very important, only 63% rated themselves as very effective at doing it. Similarly, while gaining share within existing accounts was rated as important by 68% of respondents, only 39% saw themselves as very effective at accomplishing that goal. That's clearly no vote of self-confidence.

Part of the reason for that lack of effectiveness, we suspect, may be the

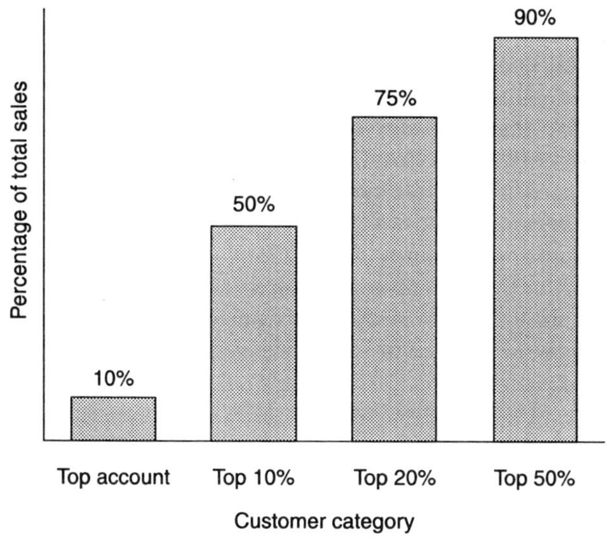

Figure 1.1 Pareto variations

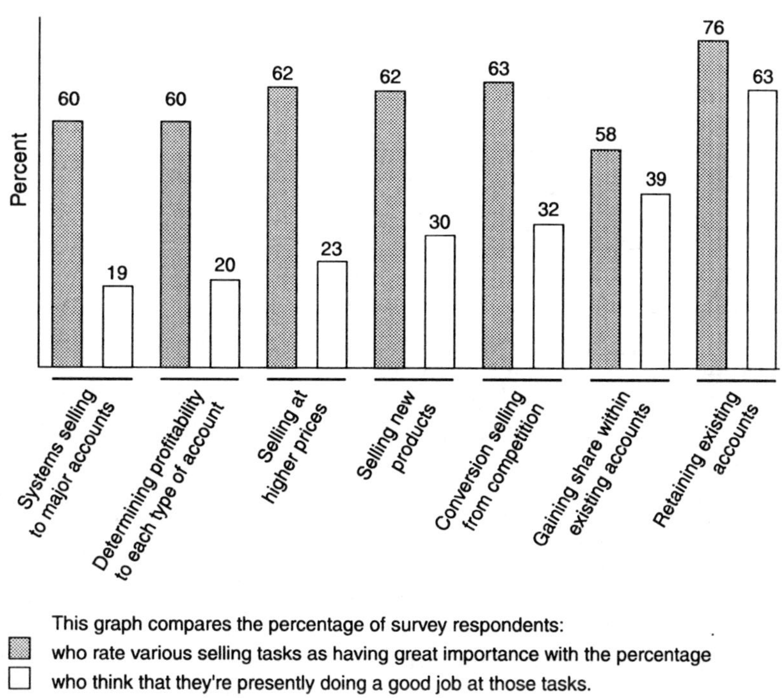

Figure 1.2 How you rate yourselves

amount of time and resources companies are committing – whether as a strategic goal or simply out of habit – to finding new customers and opening up new accounts. Just how tough it can be for those whose sales performance depends on gaining new accounts can be calculated by reviewing what managers say an average sales call costs and also how many calls are required to close first sales in contrast to subsequent sales.

Specifically, survey respondents reported that it took *an average of seven calls to close a first sale* compared to only three calls to close a subsequent sale with an existing customer.

By multiplying the difference of four sales calls by the average cost of a sales call or $239, we can see that it's more than twice as expensive to land a new account as to penetrate an existing account.

Type of Account	*Number of calls Required to Close*	*Cost of a sale Call*	*Cost of a Sale*
New	7	$239	$1,673
Existing	3	239	717
Difference			$956

That amounts to a whooping 133% premium on the cost of a new sale over one to an existing account. And while it should be no surprise that breaking a new account costs more (companies spend an average of 53% more on T&E alone on new accounts, as we saw in last May's T&E survey, "Are You Getting Your Money's Worth?"), the level of those costs should give companies a better perspective on how their sales efforts should be distributed among new and existing accounts.

In fact, survey participants report that an average of only 17% of their companies' total sales volume comes from sales to new accounts. That figure isn't surprising when we consider that managers at most firms indicate that the margins accepted 'to get a foot in the door' are often lower than those for subsequent sales – making new account business the least profitable as well as the most costly.

Given that survey respondents indicate that the average number of active accounts per sales representative is 99, we can also profile the return on annual time investment of the average American sales force by calculating that 17% of 99 accounts (or 17 × 7 sales calls) equals 119 sales calls and comparing that to the 246 calls per year (82 accounts × the 3 calls required to close) that remain. The inescapable and depressing conclusion: the average sales force seems to be spending 33% of its selling time gaining the least profitable 17% of its revenue.

You might want to keep some of those numbers in mind the next time a salesperson is transferred to a virgin territory or a new sales representative is sent out into the field without a base of existing accounts.

Evolution of a Sales Manager

One of the most surprising things that turned up in our survey is how many different sales positions, goals, market segments, sales skills, pricing issues, and ROI expectations will have to be managed by top sales executives in the 1990s in contrast to the relatively simple management challenge of the past.

The degree of complexity (and stress) found in a managerial job can be measured by estimating the extent of differentiated tasks and interpersonal relationships that must be integrated toward one objective by the sales manager:

	1950s–1970s	1990s
Volume sold by	Direct Sales force	75% through direct sales 5% through telemarketing 11% through distributors wholesalers/VARs 6.6% through outside sales agencies 2.4% through others
Kinds of sales jobs	Territory sales reps District managers Regional managers	Territory sales reps Key or major account reps National account managers Sales support reps Telemarketing reps Administrators Sales trainers District managers Industry specialists
Marketing approach	Mass marketing techniques targeting one type of customer	Market segmentation techniques targeting several "niches"
Performance expectations	Increase in overall sales volume Minimize turnover	Increase in sales volume in strategic markets, strategic products Increase margin contribution Decrease cost of sales Attract top sales performers

PRODUCTIVITY PRESCRIPTIONS

Our survey results suggest that some sales managers have already started to respond to the challenge of improving sales force productivity. Table 1.1 suggests some of the options that will receive greater attention.

In particular, it reveals that sales managers are leaning toward two productivity levers to regain lost ground:

- *Integrating new technology into the sales force.* The sales force of the 1990s will be making greater use of such technologies as laptop computers, E-mail, faxes, car phones, and other electronic or computer-based tools.

Table 1.1 Weighing the options

The table below ranks sales productivity improvement options in terms of the percentage of companies that rate them as important now and *in the 1990s*. Those options growing most significantly in importance are asterisked.

NOW

Rank:		
1.	Increasing incentives for strategic accounts	60%
2.	Increasing incentives for strategic products	57%
3.	Increasing incentives on volume	53%
4.	Improving motivation programs	50%
5.	Integrating new technology	47%
6.	Sales alternatives: direct mail	41%
7.	Sales alternatives: telemarketing	35%
8.	Increasing reliance on independent reps	35%
9.	Sales alternatives: catalogues	34%
10.	Increasing reliance on distributors	34%
11.	Increasing reliance on VARs	23%

1990s

Rank:		
1.	Integrating new technologies	69%*
2.	Increasing incentives for strategic accounts	69%
3.	Increasing incentives to strategic products	68%*
4.	Improving motivation programs	57%
5.	Increasing incentives on volume	56%
6.	Sales alternatives: telemarketing	45%*
7.	Sales alternatives: direct mail	45%
8.	Sales alternatives: catalogues	41%
9.	Increasing reliance on independent reps	40%
10.	Increasing reliance on distributors	37%
11.	Increasing reliance on VARs	23%

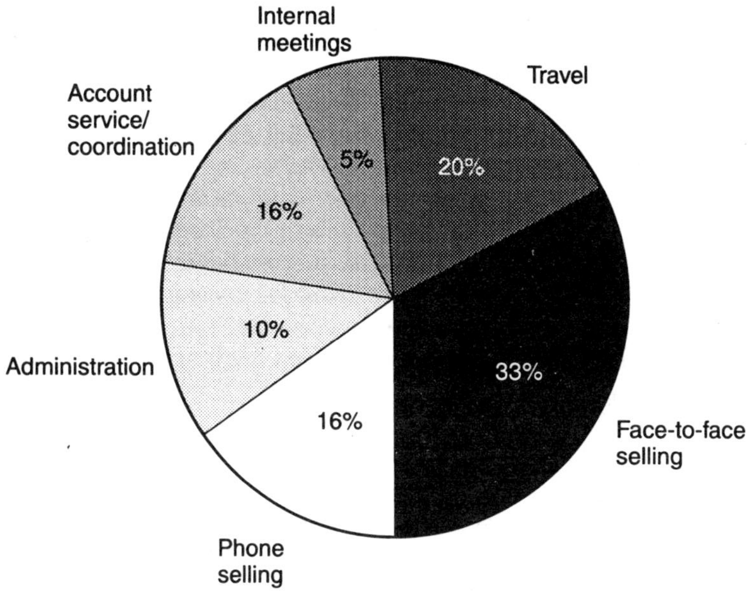

Figure 1.3 How salespeople spend their time

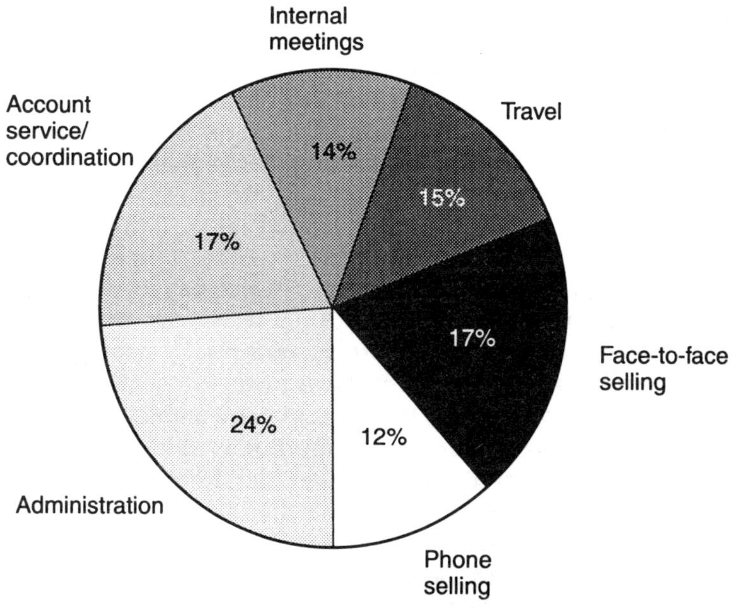

Figure 1.4 And sales managers

While 47% of top sales managers believe that integrating new technology is important now, fully 66% believe that integrating new technology will be a critically important productivity lever in the 1990s.

• *Increasing sales force incentives.* The single most favored productivity lever both now and in the next decade is using incentives to focus sales efforts on strategic accounts and products.

The trouble is, while these measures may be favored, we don't necessarily know that they will work. Through a closer look at some of the better-performing sales forces in the survey, however, we can offer some concrete prescriptions for sales managers seeking to develop a more productive sales team over the next decade.

To accomplish that analysis, we first defined the best performing sales forces by arraying the survey responses for each firm's cost of sales by quarters from high (low performance) to low (high performance). We then correlated the level of sales force investment or input measures for the firms in the high-performing quarter to the level of investment indicated by the overall result and firms in the lowest performing quarter.

The conclusions (displayed in the table below) should arm sales managers with some of the information they need to make their sales efforts more productive and their companies more profitable (and their top management happier).

	Average Annual Total Cash Compensation per Rep Paid by the Firm	*Sales Rep Annual Turnover Rate For Those Firms*
TOP QUARTER	$76,435	24%
3RD QUARTER	$47,957	26%
2ND QUARTER	$40,913	29%
1ST QUARTER	$30,087	37%

• First, there is a distinct relationship between pay levels and sales force turnover. Over several decades, sales rep turnover has been the highest of all white collar professions. Many are the sales managers who have argued for higher pay and who have moaned about the high cost of turnover. The survey results (which combine voluntary and involuntary turnover) provide one more strong argument for these sales managers: as the chart above indicates, the higher the firm's average total cash compensation for sales reps, the lower their likely turnover.

• Second, the survey shows that the more a firm pays a sales rep or manager, the more he or she will produce for it. According to the survey, firms that have a low cost per sale pay their sales managers an average total compensation of $71,286 and their sales reps an average total

Table 1.2 Sales management practices: productivity indicators for those who rate themselves highly effective vs. overall survey average

Practice	*% Who Consider Themselves Very Effective or Quite Effective*	*Profitability*			*Cost of Sales*		
		Overall Survey	*Effective Firms*	*% Difference*	*Overall Survey*	*Effective Firms*	*% Difference*
Systems selling to major accounts	18	11.8	15.2	28.8	14	11.8	(15.7)
Determining the profitability of sales to each account	20	11.8	21.8	84.7	14	13.6	(2.9)
Selling at higher prices	27	11.8	8.4	(28.8)	14	12.8	(8.6)
Gaining share within existing accounts	37	11.8	32.7	177	14	12.5	(10.7)
Selling new products	32	11.8	34.4	192	14	16.3	16.4
Retaining existing accounts	62	11.8	22.6	91.5	14	13.1	(6.4)

Note: Profitability is given as the ratio of profits to total sales; cost of sales as the ratio of reported sales costs to total sales.

compensation of $53,069. In comparison, the overall survey average total compensation for sales managers was $67,926, and for sales reps $49,158. Firms with a high cost of sales, on the other hand, paid sales managers an average of $62,357 and sales reps an average of $43,310. The implication is clear – better paid sales forces sell more per rep.

• Third, top performance sales forces invest in their sales force by spending an annual average of $5,361 per sales rep on training, while firms in the lowest performance group spend $279 per sales rep in their annual training budget.

What's more, the annual meetings budget of top performance sales forces averages $4,563 per sales rep in contrast to the lowest quarter sales organizations, whose annual meetings budget averages $232 per sales rep.

To get another angle on what areas to target for productivity improvement, we can also look more closely at the profit gains achieved by companies that gave themselves a high rating for effectiveness in specific aspects of their sales efforts. Table 1.2, for example, suggests once again that the big gains are to be made through an effective focus on existing accounts and on introducing new products.

The prescriptive conclusions for sales managers looking to join the ranks of top performance sales organizations are quite clear:

• Concentrate sales efforts on new products, particularly to existing accounts. Firms that are effective in accomplishing these objectives are three times more profitable than the overall survey average for those measures. In addition, firms that are effective at gaining share within existing accounts are able to maintain cost-of-sale levels 10% lower than the average for the survey as a whole.

• Be wary of systems selling. Systems selling to major accounts does seem to correlate to a lower cost of sales (11.8% compared with 14% for the survey overall). However, be aware that only a few companies have focused on this effort, and these for a relatively short period of time. Thus far, there is no indication that it results in a higher level of profitability.

William A. O'Connell is a partner in the sales force management practice for Personnel Corporation of America, a Norwalk, CT-based management consulting firm. William Keenan is the journal's Senior Editor.

Reading 2

Managing the industrial sales force of the 1990s

Kevin Wilson

Reprinted from Journal of Marketing Management, 1993, Vol. 9, No. 2, pp. 123–39 by permission of the publisher.

This article is concerned with the changes which have affected the personal selling function in industrial markets in recent years. It reviews research findings from the UK, Europe and America, and discusses the implications for sales force management and sales training. It concludes that industrial marketing must focus upon key account relationship management, rather than the manipulation of the four Ps in order to create competitive advantage, and that radical new approaches are needed in sales training which reflect the changing nature of the sales person's role, and which may be demonstrated to have a positive affect on selling effectiveness.

INTRODUCTION

Recent studies in the UK (Abberton Associates 1991), America (Anderson and Rosenbloom 1982; Filipczak *et al*; 1991; Yovovich 1992), and Western Europe (Hakansson 1982; Ford 1990), have identified a number of factors which have had a significant impact upon the personal selling function, and the ways in which sales forces will need to be managed throughout the 1990s. One consequence of this is that there is now a growing recognition that in many markets the major potential for strategic advantage available to companies lies with the sales force (Baker 1987; McDonald 1989), and the long-term relationships that they forge and sustain with organizational customers. The role of the sales force is therefore changing and now extends beyond the context of the sale to encompass a wider set of activities which demand not only more of the individual sales person, but also of their managers.

Despite this recognition on the part of some academics, companies and research organizations, that changes have occurred, most appear still to take a largely traditional view of sales force management, with personal selling still being viewed by many as a mere sub-set of the promotional element of the marketing mix, with little real attempt being made to integrate it into the wider marketing activities of the firm.

This article will review the major developments which have been observed in industrial and organizational markets, outline the effects of these developments upon the sales force and consider what changes are required in attitudes and practice in the field of sales force management as well as sales and sales management training.

THE HISTORICAL PERSPECTIVE

The majority of marketing texts have traditionally viewed the role of face to face selling as a sub-set of the promotional element of the marketing mix. Historically, the role of the sales force has been perceived as adversarial and confrontational (Churchill *et al.* 1990), their job being to persuade customers to buy what manufacturers make (Baker 1987) and tied largely to the context of discreet exchange transactions. Such phrases as "marketing isn't selling" and "the aim of marketing is to make selling superfluous" (Drucker 1974), whilst they may not have been intended to do so, have also served to undervalue the importance of personal selling within the marketing discipline.

Jones and Monieson (1990), in tracing the growth of marketing theory from foundations in the German historic school of economics, suggest that the influence of individual behavioural and sociological phenomena have been largely ignored in favour of the development of generalized theories applicable to "markets". This focus upon the general rather than the particular in marketing theory appears to reflect a concentration on consumer marketing, where generalized theories have undoubted value, whilst largely ignoring the nature of inter-organizational markets, where exchange is largely facilitated through the medium of personal contact and the tailoring of bespoke solutions to customer problems (The IMP Group 1982, 1990).

Kotler (1984) suggests that if the marketer "does a good job in identifying customer needs, developing appropriate products, and pricing, distributing and promoting them effectively, these products will sell very easily". Whilst the essence of this may well be true, the observation fails to recognize the fundamental reality that in many markets it is the sales person who identifies customer need, that products are often developed jointly with customers, that price is often a matter for negotiation, and that distribution is facilitated by personal contact. In organizational and industrial markets it is also often the case that few other forms of promotion are used besides personal selling.

The traditional view, that the role of the sales person is tied to the context of the sale, is reinforced by the contents of many sales training courses which reflect a narrow view of the sales person's role. The focus upon the acquisition of context-specific skills such as questioning, objection handling and closing techniques, presents the sale as a discrete event which occurs in isolation from any ongoing process of relationship interaction.*

In industrial and organizational markets sales people span the boundaries between buying and selling organizations. They are largely, though not exclusively, responsible for creating and sustaining the long term exchange relationships which many writers view as the key to strategic competitive advantage (Gummesson 1987) in industrial markets. Gummesson describes industrial marketing as "relationship management; creating, developing, and maintaining a network within which the firm thrives". Dwyer Schur and Oh (1987) suggest that long term interactive relationships are the primary area upon which marketing activity should focus, whilst Frazier *et al.* (1988) claim that they should provide the core phenomenon for study in the marketing discipline.

Despite the growing recognition that personal selling is viewed as the "key to success in the 1990s – more so than at any time in the past" (Ingram 1990), little attention is paid to the development in sales people of the marketing, strategic management skills and relational skills which would enable them to manage the relationship with key customers which are so important to the survival of their firms.

CHANGING TIMES

In the United States . . . ,

Several recent studies serve to highlight the changes which have occurred in the field of personal selling. In the United States, for example, in an article entitled "The Sales Manager: Tomorrow's Super Marketer" (Anderson and Rosenbloom 1982), the authors identify eight "megatrends" which have generated both change in consumer and industrial selling.

1 Buyers are more expert and demanding.
2 Customer expectations are rising.
3 There have been revolutionary advances in telecommunications and computer technology.

---

* A review of recent editions of the UK publications "Sales and Marketing Management" and "Sales Direction" suggests that most sales training organizations still focus upon the acquisition of context-specific selling skills, rather than upon the creation of long term customer relationships within the broader context of an overall marketing strategy.

4 Consumer products sales forces are shrinking.
5 Women and minority groups are increasingly represented in sales forces.
6 Domestic markets are undergoing micro-segmentation.
7 Competition from foreign companies is intensifying.
8 Markets are becoming increasingly international.

More recently, Rackham and Wilson (1990) identified four trends which have emerged to affect sales force management and training in the late 1980s, and which will continue, in their view, to have significant effects in the 1990s:

1 Sales training will increasingly focus upon what the authors call the larger sale, which requires a greater emphasis on strategy, an understanding of buying cycles, and a greater move toward team selling and account management systems.
2 Product and skills training will become increasingly integrated as markets become more dynamic and product life cycles shorten.
3 Sales force structure will reflect market segmentation based upon relational considerations. Major key accounts will be viewed as strategic partnerships, strategic team selling will be employed to serve other important customers, individual sales people will work with middle market customers, and alternative forms of promotion and distribution will be employed on the least important groups of customers.
4 Training will extend beyond traditional classroom training.

Filipczak *et al.* (1991) identified six major trends that would help to shape the work of sales into the 1990s, which reflect many of the findings already reported.

a Relationships will be important.
b Better educated customers will demand better educated sales people.
c The selling function will become increasingly important.
d Training will become more widespread and improvements in communications systems will affect both the way in which sales people sell, and the way in which they are managed.

In addition to these factors, O'Connell (1988), writing in *Sales and Marketing Management*, identified an increase of 11% per annum in the cost of maintaining a sales force in the United States, whilst sales revenues were seen to be growing at only 5% per annum. Some of the reasons for increased selling costs were identified by the *Wall Street Journal* as the following.
1 An increasing emphasis on market segmentation.
2 A greater use of national account selling.

3 Growing demands for increased levels of customer service.
4 Increased transportation costs.
5 More professional buyers.
6 Increasing distributor (channel) power.
7 Increases in approved vendor and single source purchasing systems. (*The Wall Street Journal*, Nov. 25, 1986, p. 1).

In consumer markets particularly, cost increases, perhaps more than any other factor, have led companies to explore new ways to serve their customers, turning to telesales, the use of outside contract sales organizations, agents, part time sales staff and a variety of direct marketing methods including catalogues, automatic vending machines and television home shopping (Anderson 1991). Despite these factors, and even with a reduction in the number of sales people employed by companies operating in consumer markets, costs have still risen by 11%.

In industrial and organizational markets the picture is somewhat different. In their 1982 article, Anderson and Rosenbloom observed that the role of the sales person had expanded beyond that of a mere seller of products towards a concept of consultative selling. The sales person was perceived as performing a number of roles which extended beyond the context of the single sale and encompassed areas of far greater strategic significance to the selling organization (Table 2.1). In America, at least, the role of the sales person is seen as increasing in strategic importance. Peters and Waterman (1982) "suggest that personal selling is at the 'heart of marketing'", whilst Ries and Trout (1988) imply that selling is the critical organizational function, and that the primary role of marketing is to provide support to the sales force.

. . . in the UK,

A recent survey (Abberton and Associates 1991), carried out in the UK and focusing largely upon industrial and organizational markets, reflects many of the findings that have been observed in the United States. Whilst it is recognized that this work is a commercial study, it is nevertheless valuable in the absence of detailed academic research into the area, within the UK, and in its focus upon the practical problems facing sales force managers.

The survey, conducted by Abberton Associates, on behalf of CPM Field Marketing Ltd, looked at changes in sales force management between 1985–91 and highlighted a number of major trends.

1 The total number of sales executives in the UK declined between 1985–91, but the greatest decline is in the repeat consumer and consumer durable sectors.
2 In all sectors, repeat consumer, consumer durable, repeat industrial and capital equipment markets, an average increase of 91% in the

Table 2.1 The roles sales people now perform

"Customer Partner" working with customers to create strategic advantage in the buyer's market.

"Market Analyst and Planner" monitoring changes and devising strategies to adjust to them.

"Buyer Seller Team Co-ordinator" managing the buyer-seller relationship using back up specialists from both the buyer and seller organizations to solve client's problems.

"Customer Service Provider" adding to the product offering through technical advice, financing, deliveries and after sales service.

"Buyer Behaviour Expert" who knows about the customer's buying unit and decision making processes.

"Information Gatherer" gleaning and passing back market information to head office.

"Sales Forecaster" providing information upon which senior management can base strategic planning and quota setting.

"Market Cost Analyser" focusing upon profitable sales rather than sales volume.

"Technologist" adopting new technologies to improve a performance.

Adapted from Ralph E. Anderson and Bert Rosenbloom, "Eclectic Sales Management: Strategic Responses to Trends in the 1980s", *Journal of Personal Selling and Sales Management*, November 1982, pp. 41–46.

number of key account managers employed, was reported by the 154 companies surveyed (adjusted to reflect UK total), and major accounts were perceived by many respondents as becoming more important with the growth of buyer sophistication.

3 The role of the sales executive has changed since 1985, whilst changing relationships with key accounts have resulted in new order and call mechanisms being adopted and new activities such as marketing research (see Table 2.1) being added to their function.

Two orders of factors were identified as having generated change in the selling profession: reactive factors and proactive factors.

Reactive Factors are those variables which are external to the sales organization and require management in order to enhance sales and profitability. They include:

i changing customer needs;
ii increasing customer sophistication;
iii the evolution of new customer supplier relationship;
iv increases in the demands suppliers make on sales people;
v increasing internationalization.

Proactive Factors are those variables which can be controlled within the sales force in order to enhance sales and profitability and reduce selling costs. The most significant are the following.

i An increasing emphasis upon sales force effectiveness is being sought through the optimization of market coverage and the deployment of resources according to profit rather than sales potential.
ii Increasing costs are driving companies to seek more efficiency from their sales forces.
iii New methods of customer contact are increasingly being employed to supplement face to face selling by the company's field sales force. (Direct mail, telesales, merchandizers, third party sales support companies.)
iv New technology "in all its guises" was seen as a major catalyst for change in the 1990s.

Perhaps the most significant change, both in the United States and in the UK, has been the growth in importance of key account management and the resultant demand for higher levels of expertise and professionalism of sales forces who must work within the context of increasingly complex customer relationships.

. . . and in Europe

The theme of changing buyer-supplier relationships has been extensively explored by the IMP Research Group (Hakansson 1982; Ford 1990). They suggest that in industrial organizational markets, strategic advantage is best gained through forging and sustaining long term, mutually beneficial relationships with customers, rather than through judicious manipulation of the four Ps of the marketing mix. Recognition of this suggests that within the context of organizational exchange relationships the sales person plays a central role, not only in forging and sustaining links with the customer's buying decision unit, but also in determining buyer product, manufacturing and business process need, and in tailoring the total market offering to meet those needs (Wilson 1992).

The Effects of Change

The trends observed in both the United States, in Western Europe, and in the UK herald an era of change in the selling profession which will demand the adoption of radical new approaches to marketing and the personal selling function, particularly in industrial and organizational markets.

The result is that the role of the sales person has moved towards the taxonomy outlined in Table 2.1. The implications of this are outlined below.

Customer Partner

New relationship structures, the growing importance of long term relationships, the incidence of joint developments, the complexity of the decision making unit within class frameworks, all focus upon the sales person's role as key account manager. Sales people will be required to develop deeper knowledge about their customers' businesses and their value adding and decision making processes, in order to help them achieve strategic advantage in their markets.

Buyer-Seller Team Co-ordinator

The increasing centralization of the buying function both in consumer channel markets and in industrial markets demands far greater recognition of the strategic importance of supply chain management. The growing complexity of the organization buying centre also requires a complementary development of organizational selling centres.

Buyers demand high levels of investment by sellers in terms of organizational adjustment, product and process changes, technical knowledge, and the commitment of personnel at managerial and functional levels. Faced with this, there is a need for companies to manage customer relationships in order to allocate resources to those relationships which offer greatest potential for profit or strategic advantage (Cunningham and Homse 1986).

Sales people, standing at the centre of inter-organizational relationships, will increasingly be called upon to take operational decisions about resource allocation within the context of team selling. It is therefore essential that sales and marketing management must take a strategic view, segmenting and targeting customers and directing the activities of the sales force on the basis of relational potential.

Customer Service Provider

In industrial and organizational markets buyers have a range of needs that are only partially met by the basic product offering. The salesperson will be required to develop and provide additional services such as technical assistance, product applications knowledge, financing, individualized delivery, packaging and after sales service which will tailor the total market offering to customers' specific needs in terms of product, manufacturing process and organizational process need.

Buyer Behaviour Expert

With the widening of the organizational buying centre (Hutt *et al.* 1985), the sales person needs to understand in far greater detail not only how buying decisions are reached, but also the nature of the organizational structure; the personal and private motivations of the various functional specialists within the buying group; and the varying influence of professional buyers, users, specifiers and functional specialists upon the nature of the purchasing decision (Robinson *et al.* 1967). There is also a need for the sales person to understand the need to network with the buyer organization, rather than focusing upon one key player in the decision making process.

Information Gatherer

Strategic and operational decisions require information to be fed back by sales people about customer need, buying centre structure, process requirements, market changes and competitor activity. This information can be used in three ways, by the sales manager for strategic decision making, as a management tool to direct and control the efforts of sales people, and by sales people in account management.

Market Analyst and Planner

Sales people must monitor change in the market place in order to identify competitor activity, structural change, and new product development opportunities. This requires a move away from "comfort" or habitual call patterns, and the acquisition of analytical and planning skills which recognize the importance of understanding the buyers' markets and strategic positioning (Campbell and Cunningham 1983). It also requires that companies acknowledge the importance of their sales people and involve them in the strategic decision making process.

Sales Forecaster

One implication of the movement towards the greater involvement of sales people in marketing planning is the expectation that sales forecasts will increasingly be based upon the future plans of customers rather than the corporate objectives of sellers. As part of the information gathering process sales people will be increasingly expected to provide projections of customer product and service need upon which senior managers will base sales targets and individual quotas.

Marketing Cost Analyzer

Sales people and their managers will need to be aware of the costs involved in account management. Resource allocation and call pattern decisions will increasingly be made on the basis of profit rather than sales volume potential. Decisions about call patterns, which customers to cultivate, and which contacts to make within the buyer organization, are increasingly strategic in nature and cannot be left to individual sales people to make on the basis of personal preference.

Technologist

Technology has fuelled many of the changes which are affecting the selling function. Computer literacy is only one demand that will be made of sales people and their managers. Far more fundamental will be the demand for a radical change in attitude and work patterns.

Telecommunications and computerization will also facilitate the growth in team selling and no longer will the sales person be "a man way out there in the blue, riding on a smile and a shoe shine" (Arthur Miller). Instead, (s)he will increasingly be integrated into the total marketing effort of the selling organization. Customers will no longer be the "property" of the salesperson, their buyer details, transaction histories, and call records will increasingly be stored centrally and companies will assume ownership of their most important asset, their customers.

IMPLICATIONS FOR MANAGERS

That growth in the number of key account managers over the last decade suggests that companies have begun to recognize the importance of long term exchange relationships. The role of the sales force is clearly seen as having expanded beyond the generation of sales, to the management of customers. This fundamental change in perception about the role of sales people must be matched by changes in training and management practice.

Implicit in this contention is the suggestion that the traditional criteria for training and managing sales people are incompatible with the effective performance of the sales person's new role. If it is also accepted that in industrial and organizational markets, long term exchange relationships have long been the norm rather than the exception (Gummesson 1987), although they may only recently have begun to receive attention from marketing practitioners, long steeped in the religion of the four Ps, then a further suggestion is unavoidable. That is, that popular views about sales people, the traditional methods of training them, and the focus of management attention, have been wrong.

The Implications for Training

That sales people operate within the context of ongoing relationships rather than discrete sales events, does not of itself invalidate traditional training methods. What must be considered is whether the skills which much sales training claims to deliver are actually supportive of the roles performed by sales people and whether they lead to the successful creation of profitable exchange, or instead act as a block to effective selling.

Many of the basic selling skills taught by sales trainers are based on models developed in the 1920s by E. K. Strong (Rackham 1991), who introduced such ideas as the use of open and closed questions, the presentation of features and benefits, objection handling methods, and closing techniques. Alessandra and Wexler (1988) suggest that "three topics have dominated the sales training field over the years: how to give 'razzle dazzle' sales pitches, 101 ways to close a sale, and power techniques for overcoming objections". These themes are still strongly in evidence, both in sales training courses,* and in many recent texts (see for example Kurtz 1991, Futrell 1991, Pederson *et al.*, 1991, Kurtz and Dodge 1991). In some texts the distinction is made between selling to customers and selling in industrial markets, although this is done largely in terms of the differences in buyer behaviour and the nature of decision making unit, rather than in terms of the different skills required to sell into those markets.

Within the UK perhaps the best indicator of the weight attached to the E. K. Strong model is given in the "Draft Standards for Vocational Qualifications in Sales" (1991) recently issued by the Lead Body for Vocational Qualifications in Sales (now the Sales Qualification Board). Within the context of the sale the skills required of the sales person suggested in the draft focus upon matching customer need to the benefits offered by the product, the recognition of "buying signals", handling objections and upon the use of appropriate closing techniques. Key account management is treated as a separate issue but again, as in the texts mentioned earlier, there is no suggestion that these might require a different range of selling skills.

Subsequent revision of the draft standards have taken account of some of the more advanced skills needed, but the point I make is none the less valid, in that the focus of the document is upon the acquisition of traditional, rather than relational selling skills, at a time when evidence suggests a move away from the sales person's traditional role.

With such a strong body of support for traditional selling methods and the tacit, though hopefully decreasing, acceptance that they are applicable to all selling situations, large or small, discrete or long term, re-buy, modified re-buy or new task, the obvious conclusion might be that they actually work. Why else would companies continue to spend large sums in training sales people in the acquisition of context specific selling skills?

* For one example among many see Spearhead Training's 1991–2 open course programme "Improving Business Performance".

Part of the answer is that the effects of sales training are extremely difficult to gauge accurately (Still *et al.* 1981). Increases in productivity may be effected by the impact of advertising, competitor activity, economic factors, and fluctuations in customer's markets as well as by changes in the sales person's behaviour caused by training. Despite exhortations to evaluate training, few writers suggest reliable and objective methods which will achieve this (Comer 1991), and recent studies suggest (Erffmeyer *et al.* 1991, Peterson 1990, Honeycutt and Stevenson 1989) that most sales training evaluation methods are still relatively simple, relying upon trainee–supervisor evaluation rather than upon learning, behaviour or results measurement.

Faced with the difficulties of evolving objective, effective and quantifiable measures of performance improvement much sales training has evolved on the basis of what top performers claim has been successful behaviour for them. Rackham (1991) warns against trusting the validity of expert practitioner opinion, suggesting that what people think they do often bears little relationship to what they actually do, to achieve success in their chosen field.

In what is claimed to be the only research project of its kind, Rackham (1991) identified that, whilst effective in smaller sales where the buying decision can be made during a single meeting between sales person and buyer, "traditional selling strategies just don't work in the fast moving and complex environment of today's major sale". It is the nature of the major sale and changes in customers' perceptions and behaviour which make major sales different from smaller sales.

Major sales take place within the context of an ongoing relationship, may take many months to complete, tend to involve more people in the decision making process, and, by definition, demand decisions of a higher order from customers, decisions which involve higher levels of risk for the buyer, and which are often taken in the absence of the seller.

In these circumstances the use of classic open and closed questions, linking direct product benefits to customer need, presentations which stress benefits which answer only implied rather than explicit needs, and applying commonly taught closing techniques, whilst useful in the smaller, discrete sale, were found to be counter productive in the major sale.

The employment of traditional objection handling skills, whilst promoted as being of paramount importance in closing sales by many practitioners, were found by Rackham's research to be non-productive in the major sale.

The differences between small and major sales demand a radically different approach in the use of questions. In larger sales there is often no straightforward relationship between the product and the problem it solves because of the way in which the major purchase will impact upon a range of processes within the buyer's organization. Questions must not only uncover need, but explore their implications to the customer, making the needs explicit in order to create a positive desire for a solution. Rackham has labelled these techniques the SPIN®* strategy because of the use of questions which focus upon Situation, Problem, Implication and Need Pay-off.

These views are supported by the findings of other behavioural research. Hersey (1988), for example, states that "questions tend to evoke only surface needs from clients (Situation and Problem Questions). By combining encouraging (Implication) and guiding responses with questions (Need Pay-off), the top performer probes beneath the surface to gather in depth needs". (Author's brackets.)

Objections are viewed by some researchers as being caused by early and frequent closing (Hersey 1968). "Some people are still looking for tricks and gimmicks; they think that if you have a catchy presentation, 101 power closes, and 40 new ways to overcome objections, you will be a success" (Alessandra and Wexler 1988). Rackham identified a negative relationship between the use of closing techniques and successful completion of sales, particularly in larger sales and with professional buyers.

In the light of recent research and changes in sales force structure, there is an obvious need for sales trainers to revise the content of many training courses, and to base their prescriptions on the acquisition of skills which are relevant to the needs of the selling profession, rather than upon untested preconceptions largely based in erroneous folk lore.

For managers charged with spending training budgets the task is even more straightforward, to demand proof from training organizations that the skills they impart actually work.

The Implications for Management Practice

For sales managers the changes that have occurred within the selling profession demand that attention be paid to three areas: the integration of marketing and sales force strategies; the management of customer relationships; and the management of the activities of the sales force.

The Integration of Marketing and Sales Strategies

> The heart of marketing is not computer based segmentation. Much as we have ignored it in the last twenty-five years, the heart of marketing is selling. (Peters and Austin 1985.)

* The acronym SPIN® is a registered trademark. European trademarks for SPIN® are held by Huthwaite Research Group Limited. North American and certain other trademarks for SPIN® are held by Huthwaite, Inc.

This does not argue for a return to sales led market strategies. Indeed, it argues for a recognition of the importance of the selling function in forging and sustaining customer relationships, and an increase in the level of customer orientation.

Marketers require to get close to their customers, and in industrial and organizational markets often the best conduit through which to approach them is provided by the sales force. Marketing strategies in the 1990s must focus upon developing and sustaining strong key account relationships. In achieving these ends the gathering of market information, the strategic development of the sales force, the choice of customers to target, and the use of alternative approach methods will become the primary tasks of the marketing and sales departments. To achieve success their efforts will require high levels of integration.

Strahle and Spiro (1986) observe that, while the need to integrate sales force activity with marketing strategy is widely recognized in sales management literature, little discussion occurs about what the link between marketing strategy and sales strategy should be, and that "the lack of research on the linkages between marketing and sales reflects a more general lack of research on the linkages between marketing and the other functional areas of the firm". (p. 11.)

From a review of existing theory and research, taken from product life cycle and portfolio literature, Strahle and Spiro developed a range of hypothesised sales strategies to support the strategic marketing objectives of "build", "hold", "harvest", and "divest" (Table 2.2). They argue that it is critical that the decisions and activities of functional departments are integrated with marketing strategy, otherwise when business area strategies become uncoupled from functional area strategies, there is a loss of competitive position within the market place, and the firm's resources in terms of both capital and manpower are wasted.

In making their recommendations, Strahle and Spiro recognized that none had been tested empirically, and expressed the hope that they would serve to stimulate managers to examine the consistency of sales and marketing strategies, and marketing scholars to empirically examine marketing and sales strategy linkages.

In the light of the growing recognition of the increasing strategic importance of key account management, discussed earlier, one criticism of the Strahle, Spiro recommendations might be that they focus upon the management of single products throughout their life cycles, without any consideration being given to how the strategies adopted might effect the long term relationship between buyer and seller. The focus both for managerial and scholarly attention, so far as organizational markets are concerned, may better be placed upon the management of the firm's portfolio customers, rather than upon the management of individual products through their life cycle.

Table 2.2. Sales strategy related to marketing strategies

Marketing strategy	*Sales strategy*	*Sales tasks*
Build	– Build sales volume. – Secure distribution. – Provide high service levels. – Product/market feedback.	– Call on prospective and new accounts.
Hold	– Maintain sales volume. – Consolidate market position by focus on targeted segments. – Secure additional outlets.	– Call on targeted current accounts. – Increase service levels. – Call on new accounts.
Harvest	– Reduce selling costs. – Target profitable accounts. – Reduce service costs and inventories.	– Focus on profitable accounts.
Divest	– Minimize costs. – Clear inventory.	– Dump inventory. – Eliminate service.

Adapted from Strahle and Spiro (1986) "Linking Market Share Strategies to Sales Force Objectives, Activities, and Compensation Policies", *Journal of Personal Selling and Sales Management*, August, pp. 11–18.

The Management of Customer Relationships

The changes which have been observed in the United States, in Western Europe, and in the UK, support Gummesson's (1987) claim that the management of long term customer relationships, in industrial and organizational markets, should be the primary concern of marketing strategists. This requires a recognition by managers that strategic advantage is achieved through the medium of relational interaction, the management of the relationship life cycle, rather than the product life cycle.

Ford (1980) outlined the developmental stages of buyer–seller relationships as the preliminary, early, developmental, long term and final stages. The problem facing the sales manager is still to achieve integration, between marketing and functional strategies, but within the context of the developing relationship.

The high cost of sales people has already been noted, what is less often realized is the high cost of other resources allocated to sustaining customer relationships. In industrial and organizational markets buyers value personal contacts and interpersonal communications channels, the ease of contact and the availability of technical advice reduces their perceived risk (Turnbull 1979). The network of contacts between organizations is often complex and can involve large numbers of people from different functions performing a wide range of communication and exchange roles (Cunningham and Homse 1986). Without a system to control customer contact patterns based upon the strategic orientation of the firm and the potential representated by the customer, there is an obvious danger that scarce resources are dissipated.

Cunningham and Homse (1986) identified that whilst call frequency is often prescribed for sales and marketing staff, rarely is such control exercised over technical, manufacturing, research and development staff, or over senior general management. Some of the factors which influence the level of resource allocation to a specific customer are under the control of the seller, others are the result of environmental and competitive forces. The requirement is for sales and marketing managers to identify these factors and take strategic decisions which allow key account managers to direct appropriate levels of resources towards the defence of vital relationships.

Detailed customer and market information is essential for effective strategic decision making, and much of that information is collected by sales people. Turnbull (1979) makes the distinction between "hard" and "soft" data. Hard data relates to price, specification and terms of contract and as such is bound to the context of a specific transaction. Soft data concerns the exchange of information about commercial, technical and organizational matters which may be seen as relating more to the ongoing relationship.

Whereas hard information, because it relates directly to the completion of the sale, may be transferred back to the selling company via customer records or formal customer or sales force requests, it is less certain that the soft elements are communicated as effectively. Much soft information may be collected in an ad-hoc fashion during face to face exchanges between buyer and sales person, and as such, the selling firm relies upon the sales person to record and communicate that information in customer records and market reports, when there is no immediate personal benefit for the sales person to do so. Indeed there are strong reasons why the sales people may prefer to keep such information to themselves. Several studies have cast doubt on the willingness of the sales force to provide information about customers (Lambert *et al.* 1990) which may be due to the high levels of role ambiguity and conflict which are inherent in their position. Control over information about clients and the market place may be one way in which sales people can protect their own interests, creating and nurturing a body of knowledge about customers which they may carry with them from job to job. Companies must ensure, therefore, that customer records and market information systems remove data from the exclusive control of the sales person, and make it available for strategic decision making.

The range of information will also need to expand from an understanding of customer product need and volume requirements if decisions are to be made about which customers offer the most attractive long term prospects of profitable exchange. Some of those information needs are set out below:

- the structure of the decision making unit;
- the nature and focus of the decision making process;
- the strategic orientation of the customer;
- the nature of the customer's market, its rate of growth and the customer's market share;
- the manufacturing, process and organizational needs of the customer; and
- the customer's level of technological dependence and process knowledge.

To illustrate the importance of this type of information, which goes beyond the simple identification of product need, consider the consequences of seeking to develop a key account customer with a radically different strategic focus from the seller. If the seller produces highly differentiated products for incorporation in the seller's product, and adds value through the provision of technological and process knowledge, so long as the buyer is a low cost producer manufacturing for mass consumption, then they are likely to be incompatible. The high investment by the seller in differentiating the product offering is likely to be wasted in the face of continual price reduction pressure from the buyer. The seller is faced with the choice of varying the product offer, thus compromising their strategic stance, or seeking other customer.

A marketing focus upon the analysis of individual customers in this way will facilitate the integration of marketing and selling strategies, allowing decisions to be made as to which customers have the potential to demand the attention of key account managers, and which should be approached in less costly, and perhaps more efficient ways.

In the light of the relational development pattern suggested by Ford (1980), and the recommendations for marketing and sales strategy integration suggested by Strahle and Spiro (1986), a fruitful area for empirical observation may be the exploration of marketing and sales strategies throughout the relational life cycle, which takes account of both the complexity of inter-organizational relationships and the nature and importance of intelligence gathering within that context.

Managing the Activities of the Sales Force

If the focus of selling in the 1990s is to be upon key account management, then management systems will need to highlight the qualitative rather than the quantitative aspects of sales force performance. Profitability rather than sales volume must become the measure of performance and this will require a move away from "tick box" activity monitoring systems which only measure call rates, conversion ratios, mileage and volume sales.

The expansion of computerization will enable increasing levels of accountability to be demanded of the sales force. Without a focus upon quality rather than quantity this will in itself cause resentment and de-motivation. Computer systems must not only facilitate lead tracking, but also profitable account management which takes account of the increasing professionalism demanded of sales people, and the information that they will need to collect, collate and pass back to their company. Computer Aided Sales and Marketing Tools (CASM) must also be shown to be relevant needs of the sales force themselves in helping to create sales and foster relationships with customers, otherwise they will meet resistance from sales people.

SUMMARY

The nature of the role performed by sales people, particularly in industrial and organizational markets, has altered radically during the 1980s and will continue to develop in scope and strategic importance into the 1990s. It follows, therefore, that the role of those who manage them has also changed from that of overseeing the implementation of marketing strategy, to that of strategy formulation, planning and execution.

If companies operating in industrial and organizational markets are to prosper, they must recognize the importance of the long term key account relationships and develop marketing and sales strategies which facilitate their pro-active and profitable management.

1 The sales function must be fully integrated into the company's strategy and recognized as the core activity in the industrial marketing discipline.
2 Sales people must be trained in the management of ongoing customer relationships and not only in the acquisition of context specific selling skills.
3 The management of customer relationships must be recognized as a strategic issue. In industrial markets it is not the manipulation of the four P's which creates strategic advantage, but the management of inter-organizational alliances. The role of marketing and sales management in industrial markets is to identify those customer relationships which hold the most potential for profit and strategic advantage, and to plan the allocation of resources to those relationships in the most effective and efficient way.

4 The management of the sales force must become increasingly professional and sophisticated, employing the potential offered by new technology to expand the use of sales force control and record systems.
5 Management systems should focus, not upon what is merely easy to measure, such as call ratios, mileage and raw sales volume, but upon what is important to measure, the potential for profitable long term exchange, the nature of the customer's decision making process, strategic orientation, and the product, process, knowledge and organizational needs of customers.

The sales force will provide the central focus for marketing management in industrial and organizational markets in the 1990s. The sales manager's essential role will be to direct the sales force in forging and sustaining a portfolio of client relationships through which strategic advantage may be wrested from the market place.

Kevin Wilson is Senior Lecturer in Marketing, Sheffield Business School

References

Allesandra, A. and Wexler, P. (1988), "The Professionalisation of Selling", *Sales and Marketing Training*, February, pp. 37–38, 42–43.
Abberton Associates (1991), *Balancing the Sales Force Equation: The Changing Role of the Sales Organization in the 1990s*, CPM Field Marketing Ltd.
Anderson, R. E. (1991), "Professional Personal Selling", New Jersey, Prentice Hall.
Anderson, R. E. and Rosenbloom, B. (1982), "Eclectic Sales Management: Strategic Responses to Trends in the 1980s", *Journal of Personal Selling and Sales Management*, November, pp. 41–46.
Baker, M. J. (Ed) (1987), *The Marketing Book*, London, Heinemann.
Campbell, N. C. G. and Cunningham, M. T. (1983), "Customer Analysis for Strategy Development in Industrial Markets", *Strategic Management Journal*, **4**, pp. 360–380.
Churchill, G. A., Ford, N. M. and Walker, O. C. (1990), *Sales Force Management*, 3rd Ed. Boston, Unwin.
Comer, J. M. (1991), *Sales Management*, Allyn and Bacon.
Cunningham, M. T. and Homse, E. (1986), "Controlling the Marketing-Purchasing Interface: Resource Development and Organizational Implications", *Industrial Marketing and Purchasing*, **1**, 3–27.
Drucker, P. F. (1974), *Management: Tasks, Responsibilities, Practices*, New York, Harper Row.
Dwyer, F. R., Schurr, P. H. and Oh, S. (1987), "Developing Buyer Seller Relationships", *Journal of Marketing*, 51, pp. 11–27.
Erffmyer, R. C., Russ, K. R. and Hair, J. F. (1991), "Needs Assessment and Evaluation in Sales Training Programs", *Journal of Personal Selling and Sales Management*, 11, pp. 17–30.
Frazier, G. L., Spekeman, R. E. and O'Neil, C. R. (1988), "Just in Time Exchange Relationships in Industrial Markets", *Journal of Marketing*, **XXIII**, pp. 261–270.
Filipczak, R., Geber, B. and Thompson, B. L. (1991), "Training Today: Six Signs of

the Future; Get in Line Soldier!; Focus Shifts to 'Core Skills'", *Training*, **28**, January 1991, pp. 12–16, 95–96.
Ford, D. (1980), "The Development of Buyer–Seller Relationships in Industrial Markets", *European Journal of Marketing*, **14**, pp. 339–354.
Ford, D. (Ed.) (1990), "Understanding Business Markets: Interaction; Relationships; Networks", London, Academic Press.
Futrell, C. (1991), *Fundamentals of Selling*, Illinois, Irwin.
Gummesson, E. (1987), "The New Marketing–Developing Long Term Interactive Relationships", *Long Range Planning*, **20**, pp. 10–20.
Hakansson, H. (Ed.) (1982), *International Marketing and Purchasing of Industrial Goods*, Chichester, John Wiley & Sons.
Hersey, P. (1988), *Selling: A Behavioral Science Approach*, New Jersey, Prentice Hall.
Honeycutt, E. D. and Stevenson, T. H. (1989), "Evaluating Sales Training Programs", *Industrial Marketing Management*, **18**, August, pp. 215–222.
Hutt, M. J., Johnston, W. J. and Ronchetto, J. R. (1985), "Selling Centers and Buying Centers: Formulating Strategic Exchange Patterns", *Journal of Personal Selling*, May, p. 333.
The IMP Group: see Hakansson (1982); Ford (1990).
Ingram, T. N. (1990), "Sales Force Productivity", *Review of Business* (Summer), St. John's University, New York.
Jones, D. G. B. and Monieson, D. D. (1990), "Early Development of the Philosophy of Marketing Thought", *Journal of Marketing*, January, pp. 102–113.
Kotler, P. (1984), *Marketing Management: Analysis, Planning and Control*, New Jersey, Prentice Hall, p. 20.
Kurtz, D. L. (1991), *Professional Selling*, Irwin.
Kurtz, D. L. and Dodge, H. R. (1991), *Fundamentals of Professional Selling*, Illinois, Irwin.
Lambert, D. M., Marmorstein, H. and Sharma, A. (1990), "Industrial Salespeople as a Source of Market Information", *Industrial Marketing Management*, **19**, pp. 144–148.
McDonald, M. H. B. (1989), "Marketing Plans: How to Prepare them. How to Use them", Heinemann CIM.
O'Connell, W. (1988), "A 10 Year Report on Sales Force Productivity", *Sales and Marketing Management*, December, pp. 33–36, 38.
Pederson, C. A., Wright, M. D. and Weitz, B. A. (1991), *Selling: Principles and Methods*, Illinois, Irwin.
Peters, T. and Austin, N. (1985), *A Passion for Excellence*, New York, Random House.
Peters, T. and Waterman, R. H. (1982), *In Search of Excellence: Lessons From America's Best Run Companies*, New York, Harper and Row, pp. 91–92.
Peterson, R. T. (1990), "What Makes Sales Training Programs Successful?", *Training and Development Journal*, **44**, August, pp. 59–64.
Rackham, N. (1991), *Making Major Sales*, Aldershot, Gower.
Rackham, N. and Wilson, J. (1990), "Sales Training in the 1990s", *Training and Development Journal*, **44**, August.
Ries, A. and Trout, J. (1988), *Bottom-up Marketing*, New York, McGregor Hill.
Robinson, P. J., Faris, C. W. and Wind, Y. (1967), *Industrial Buying and Creative Marketing*, Boston, Allyn and Bacon, p. 28.
Still, R. R., Cundiff, E. W. and Govoni, N. A. P. (1981), *Sales Management: Decisions, Strategies, Cases*, New Jersey, Prentice Hall.
Strahle, W. and Spiro, R. L. (1986), "Linking Market Share Strategies to Salesforce Objectives, Activities and Compensation Policies", *Journal of Personal Selling and Sales Management*, August, pp. 11–18.

Turnbull, P. W. (1979), "Roles of Personal Contacts in Industrial Export Marketing", *Scandinavian Journal of Management*, pp. 325–327.

Wilson, K. J. (1992), "The Role of the Sales Force in Creating and Sustaining Strategic Competitive Advantage in Industrial Markets", *Marketing Education Group Conference* 1992. Working Paper.

Yovovich, B. G. (1992), "Partnering at Its Best", *Business Marketing*, 77, March, pp. 36–37.

Reading 3

Success in database marketing: some crucial factors

Outlines for four main factors which contribute to successful database marketing

Keith Fletcher, Colin Wheeler and Julia Wright

Reprinted from Marketing Intelligence & Planning, Vol. 10, No. 6. 1992, pp. 18–23.

This article is based on preliminary qualitative research funded by a research grant from the University of Strathclyde. It involved a survey of expert opinion from both suppliers and users of direct/database marketing in the UK. (A total of 29 experts were interviewed following a semi-structured interview guide, selected from across the UK.) The authors would like to thank the many people who, through their time and effort, contributed to the article. The views expressed are, however, those of the authors.

INTRODUCTION

Marketing has developed and changed over the years to reflect the influences and pressures on it caused by changing marketing conditions, changing business experience and skills and the changing nature of customers. This evolution is natural and must continue if marketing is not to become stultified with limited real-life relevance. In recent years two major pressures can be identified which have encouraged further change, the ubiquitous impact of information technology and the fragmentation of markets, which have led to a new development, usually referred to as "database marketing". It has been argued elsewhere that the successful use of database marketing (DBM) can give strategic advantage through the better use of customer and marketing information. This can be used to develop new and unique products and services, change the basis of competition, build barriers to entry and strengthen customer relationships (Fletcher, *et al.*, 1990; Stone and Shaw, 1987). Despite the clear benefits to be obtained from DBM, problems have arisen in its implementation and use which have resulted in firms not obtaining the advantage intended.

The following discussion therefore considers some crucial factors in the successful use of DBM, based on a study of the literature and an exploratory survey of expert opinion, and attempts to answer the questions, "What is database marketing?", and "What are the factors related to the successful use of database marketing?" It argues that there are four main factors relating to success: the degree of marketing orientation, the degree of information orientation, organizational factors and finally the supplier/client interface.

WHAT IS DATABASE MARKETING?

Database marketing capitalizes on one aspect of IT and, as its name implies, draws on the increased power and reduced cost of computers to access and use customer data in a way which was not previously possible.

Direct marketing is the tool most frequently used to exploit the opportunities presented by the computerized customer base, and indeed many direct marketing professionals believe the two are inseparable. However, while direct marketing could be defined narrowly as an interactive system of marketing which uses one or more advertising media to effect a measurable response and/or transactions at any location, this focus only on media is limiting for database purposes.

Stan Rapp (1989) defines database marketing as "the ability of a company to use the vast potential of today's computer and telecommunications technology to drive customer-oriented programmes in a personalized, articulated and cost-effective manner".

It does this by its ability to analyse customer characteristics and purchasing habits, allowing a profile of customers to be created which can be matched to various lists and geodemographic databases, such as *Acorn* and *Mosaic*, and then used to drive marketing strategy. The computer databases thus allows for greater accuracy in targeting and segmentation than is possible with a simple mailing list or general advertising.

Database marketing (DBM) also emphasizes the creation and exploitation of long-term direct relationships, something which has been identified as having significant implications for the strategic and long-range planning of the firm's marketing (Gummerson, 1987). The application of database marketing uses the computerized customer data to support a dialogue between the customer and the firm, both to the customer's benefit and the firm's profit.

While all sectors can benefit from the DBM approach, in different markets the principal benefit (i.e. communication, research and customer service) will have different emphasis. For example, a company in the financial services market needs to have a *service* emphasis; the database needs to be linked to a screen and records must be called up when customers phone in. On the other hand, fast-moving consumer goods

(FMCG) companies will not necessarily receive many customer calls, and so the service element is less strong. The communications element is also less strong because it is expensive (and often uneconomic) to put together a mailing for a low-ticket item. The database, therefore, will perhaps be more *research*-oriented. Indeed, some FMCG companies are using coupons (i.e. "anonymous data collection") to determine purchase behaviour and improve their products.

Database marketing has now been adopted by some major firms, such as the AA, American Express, Time Life, Austin Rover, British Telecom, etc., and numerous case histories of the successful use of DBM exist (Rapp and Collins, 1987), but other studies warn against the uncritical acceptance that IT is transforming marketing, and highlight the problems involved in implementing the necessary information systems and hardware (Fletcher, 1983, 1990). Database marketing thus requires further study of the factors related to successful use to ensure firms achieve its potential benefits, which are many (Shaw and Stone, 1988). Marketing managers are the "internal customers" of DBM, according to Shaw and Stone and, while DBM can greatly increase revenue streams to do this, it must be fully integrated into marketing practice.

FACTORS RELATED TO SUCCESSFUL USE OF DBM

While some companies and sectors have had major successes in using database marketing other firms seem to have difficulty moving beyond its tactical use. The main benefits of DBM come from its use in changing the nature of competition within an industry and in using the technology to exploit opportunities while defending themselves against attack (Fletcher *et al.*, 1991).

To exploit successfully the full potential of DBM we suggest that four main factors need to be considered:

1 *The degree of marketing orientation* of the adopting firm, which includes the role of marketing and level of marketing skills.
2 *The degree of information, orientation,* which includes the technology and skills needed to exploit the opportunity.
3 *The organization climate and structure,* which includes budgeting for DBM and power relationships.
4 *The supplier/client interface,* which includes the role and sophistication of suppliers and client/supplier relationship.

THE DEGREE OF MARKETING ORIENTATION

Although little research has specifically examined the subject, it is nevertheless intuitively attractive to support the proposition that if the marketing concept is to prevail throughout the company, then those primarily responsible for implementing it should be high-profile, senior people (Baker *et al.*, 1986).

This is particularly true in the successful implementation of *database* marketing and in the authors' study several DBM suppliers and practitioners emphasized the importance of a company's commitment at a high level. This is because:

1 The cost of investment in DBM, not only in terms of hardware and software, but also in time, staff retraining, and data collection, needs high level support.
2 DBM has wide ranging implications for traditional organizational roles and structures (which therefore need to be managed at a senior level).
3 The *strategic* implications require a long-term view of corporate strategy and marketing objectives.

If a key objective of DBM is to achieve competitive advantage through building long-term relationships, then the implications for this also needs support at a high level. Respondent firms have reported success through the use of a management "godfather" or "champion", who recognized the uses and role of DBM in the total corporate strategy and initiates the process, is able to sell it to his companions and, most importantly, remains its supporter throughout.

The customer database must be seen as a *corporate* asset, which is more likely if an organization already has the consumer as the focus of its activities and the marketing department integrated into strategic activities. If it is isolated within an organization, or oriented towards sales of products, then successful implementation is unlikely.

Although most experts agree that the concept of direct marketing is common sense, a number of specific marketing skills are nevertheless required which must be allied to the ability to use the necessary computer technology if DM is to evolve into DBM. This includes a knowledge of the specialized techniques involved, such as in list building, creative work, media usage, evaluation and testing and fulfilment. The long-term view of customer sales and the concept of customer life-time value must also be appreciated (Baier, 1985; Bursk, 1966), as must the possibilities for cross selling, etc. and the revenue streams from this.

If, then, the marketing department of the company:

1 occupies a central role within the organization;
2 is able to focus on the value of customer relationships, and the potential of DBM;
3 possesses good knowledge of the direct marketing process and how it works;

4 is able to persuade senior management, and other departments, of the corporate value of database marketing;

DBM implementation has a *better* chance of long-term success.

INFORMATION ORIENTATION

The second major factor is the necessity for an information orientation. Since marketing is an essentially outward-looking function, it relies on the availability of a large quantity of diverse information. There is agreement in this literature that database marketing represents the modern approach to marketing based on data and the use of data. This data is much more manageable than the traditional sources of data for marketing. The tools which were developed in the 1960s and 1970s, when computers were costly and not so agile, were "next best routes", allowing dipstick research . . . Nowadays, the database of a large sample of individuals can be used as both a *research base* and as a *medium of communication.*

If a database marketing system is seen as a subset of the overall corporate information system, then the strength of a company's commitment to information will affect the success of DBM. A company which recognizes the value of information will be more prepared to invest in technology to exploit it, and also be more prepared to encourage the necessary skills required to use the technology.

Many companies decide to build their marketing databases externally (using a computer bureau or consultancy). However, our survey data supported the literature which argues that, in order to maintain *control* over the data, a company should eventually be able to run its database in-house. The correct technology and skills are therefore vital factors in the successful use of database marketing.

TECHNOLOGY

The technology necessary to exploit database marketing successfully will inevitably vary according to the firm's size and the nature of its business. For instance, a small firm may find Dbase III +, Ashton-Tate's best selling relational database package, an adequate basic tool. On the other hand, the size of the Automobile Association (whose corporate database drives a programme of around 26 *million* direct mailings a year, over and above renewal activity) means that the cost of data storage and manipulation on a relational database would be too high.

For practitioners, analytical software is the key to obtaining the full range of benefits from DBM. As one supplier in our study put it: "It all relies on using statistically-related models" – for example in order to predict which customers are going to respond to a campaign.

One respondent in our study went so far as to argue that knowledge of data can best be supplied by staff with a marketing research background (already a prevalent trend in the United States). Market researchers are ideally suited because:

1 they understand the consumer;
2 they have a historic understanding of the application of the computer data in a marketing context;
3 they know how to interpret marketers' requirements from data;
4 they have a statistical and methodological knowledge;
5 in dealing with personal data, they are ethically bound by the Market Research Society Code of Conduct.

It has been argued that the success of database marketing and advanced segmentation depends on several critical factors: good data, a solid segmentation method properly applied, a sound offer, and underlying mailing economies which justify the effort. Clearly, the more sophisticated a company's DBM effort becomes, the more statisticians and analysts will be required. However, for the Marketing Manager simply having an awareness of the techniques which can be used will support better DBM decision-making. (According to one DM supplier in our study at least one good statistical course for marketing managers is currently available!)

ORGANIZATIONAL STRUCTURE

The third factor relates specifically to the existing method of operating. It has been pointed out that if database marketing is to make a big difference to your marketing, then you cannot continue to work through your old organization. As already discussed, any organizational change needs to be carefully managed, with particular attention paid to a number of key areas.

RESPONSIBILITY FOR DATABASE MARKETING

The question of whose budget will fund the development of a DBM system can become a cause for contention between departments. Information Systems, Research and Development or, most commonly, Marketing might be asked to fund the costs. However, many companies have fallen down where they have had to pay for the database out of their marketing budget: marketers then often have a conflict in their own minds about reaching sales targets – when media expenditure for example, may have to be sacrificed. The concept of life-time value suggests DBM should be reviewed as a capital cost to be depreciated over time (Dean, 1966). (Life-time value is the notion that the total revenue flows from a customer over the entire relationship should be considered in evaluating their worth.)

Because of this there is a strong argument for the creation of a *separate* direct marketing budget. One respondent in the survey, a supplier, pointed out, you cannot just call it "advertising" because advertising does not have any capital cost allowances, while another argued that *product-driven* budgeting (assessing direct product profitability) should be replaced by *marketing-driven* budgeting (assessing direct customer profitability). Many also argue that successful DBM requires the creation of a separate direct marketing department (in a large company) or a direct marketing group within the marketing department. Organizations which have gone down this route include the Abbey National and Sun Life; while Andersen Consulting conclude from their own experience, that it is a key factor in successful implementation.

The execution side of direct marketing has already been described as complex; sometimes, therefore, a company may need an internal unit to manage the process. On the other hand, sometimes a company may use external sources instead. Indeed, some argue that there has to be a unified and integrated budget and department in order to merge the additional DM approach with the marketing approach (rather than reinforcing the divisions between the two). One DBM expert believes that marketing departments should move away from the traditional product divisions into a division between customer recruitment and retention. Since recruitment and retention are key disciplines in DBM, it would therefore follow that DBM should be retained within the marketing department and budget in order to ensure a unified customer-oriented approach to the market.

If the DBM system is accepted as a corporate asset, then there may be a better understanding of the need to look for contributions to the budget from other departments which will benefit from the database – in particular, the marketing research department.

It was evident in our study that companies overlook the value of the market research function in ensuring that maximum benefit is obtained from DBM. The database should, in fact, be seen primarily as a research tool; and so market research should be concerned with elevating their responsibility, status and role within the company.

Within an organization, several roles can be identified as crucial to making database marketing survive:

1 *administrative/management role* – (often a traditional systems role) to make sure that all channels of data are being sourced and channelled into the database; and that address updates filter throughout the company;
2 *decision support role* – the interpretative/research side – determine how the data can be used to support management decisions;

3 *campaign/marketing role* – to make DBM campaigns *happen* once it has been decided to use the database as a medium.

In our survey and in the literature it is evident that practitioners and suppliers of DBM agree that one of the major problems involved in DBM usage is a communications failure between marketing and information systems personnel. The two departments often have different priorities, approaches and terminology which (in the words of one supplier) can lead to "suspicion, protection of territory and tribal sniping". Marketers may even ask their agency to talk to their systems department!

In order to ensure that the DBM system developed does actually meet user requirements, the gulf between the two departments needs to be bridged. In our study one practitioner remarked that success often occurs when someone from the systems department moves into a hybrid role – often as a "dataplanner" – since systems people often pick up the logic, value and potential of DBM far more easily than marketing staff.

The marketing architecture of a company defines the main components of a marketing system from a non-technical, managerial perspective (Stone and Shaw, 1987). The concept of the marketing architecture can also be used to bridge the gap between systems and marketing; as well as to ensure that information management is fully integrated with the needs of the business. This architecture will also show DBM systems to evolve coherently, over time, into larger integrated systems, thereby avoiding the problems of inflexibility, incompatibility and fragmentation apparently suffered by many companies.

SUPPLIER/CLIENT INTERFACE

The DBM industry utilizes a diverse set of services provided by agencies, software companies, computer manufacturers, list brokers, mailing houses and the like. This infrastructure of suppliers has expanded and changed radically as direct and database marketing has grown. Direct marketing agencies, of which there are about 70, can, like traditional agencies, be specialist or full service, national or multinational. In some instances they have grown out of well-known agencies like Saatchi and Saatchi, in other cases sales promotion companies have developed their own agencies. Suppliers of DBM technology including computer bureaux, software companies and computer manufacturers now provide a much more sophisticated and comprehensive range of hardware and software meeting the needs of all sizes and companies across industry sectors. List brokers and mailing houses have grown with the expansion of DM and DBM.

Evidence from the study confirmed a concern within the direct marketing industry about the quality of the supply infrastructure. The infrastructure is seen as being "undercapitalized, underinvested and uneducated". Although the situation is improving, many companies still experience the problem of suppliers letting them down in the chain of events. Nevertheless, many agencies and user companies agree that there are certain steps a client can take in order to ensure successful working relationships – and campaigns.

Most importantly, the client needs to have a good understanding of direct marketing, and of its role alongside other media in the overall mix. One supplier remarked that; in many cases, clients have an imbalance in their advertising budget split, "throwing money" at above-the-line advertising, whilst being "parsimonious" with below-the-line. However, in putting in their minimum budget allocation without thinking what can be achieved for that amount, the client is likely to be disappointed by the results of direct marketing. It is critically important that clients understand the potential strategic impact of direct communications.

Good and thorough briefing of suppliers is also critical to successful direct marketing campaigns; and will overcome many of the communication problems commonly experienced between clients and suppliers. If the full value of direct marketing is understood by the client company, then briefing will ideally be done through the marketing director (and not, as sometimes happens by a junior trainee!). In addition, good briefing requires the client to have a good understanding of the work process and procedures of supplier companies.

Many large companies use their agencies on a long-term basis, involving them in the *strategic* use of direct marketing. In general terms, companies making successful use of direct marketing rate individual relationships and knowledge of the client's product area, as more important in selecting an agency than cost.

CONCLUSION

At this stage of development few firms are sophisticated in their use of database marketing. The size of an organization does not seem to be a factor in its ability to use DBM successfully, it seems more a question of orientation. Users must be open minded if they are to cope with the various structural changes involved in creating a DBM system. A marketing orientation is needed to initiate DBM usage, and this must reach or be supported by senior management. This culture needs to be promoted continuously, through training, etc. if it is to survive which highlights the importance of what some have called "internal marketing".

Fundamental to successful use of DBM is a recognition of its long-term nature. The benefits will accrue over time and the investment in developing the system must likewise be considered in the long term. Many experts agree that it is best to start small and allow the system to evolve. A true DBM system will have an impact across many aspects of a firm's activities and the change can be managed better, if gradually implemented. The marketer of the future is likely to need a wider understanding of the problems of organization change, particularly within a systems perspective, and thus have a systems training.

The suppliers will also have a role to play. As experience grows on both sides then the client's demand for increasingly sophisticated services must be matched by an improvement in skills of agencies, etc. The solution probably lies in more educational initiatives, possibly industry sponsored, to ensure the necessary skills and knowledge are included in university and polytechnic marketing curricula, as well as user-oriented seminars, etc. This will then spread throughout industry, benefiting supplier and user alike.

The 1990s will see a continued growth in direct marketing

Shorter-term initiatives can be seen in the promotion of the British Direct Marketing Association Diploma, the creating of the Scottish Direct Marketing Forum (affiliated to the BDMA), and the work of the Direct Marketing Centre. These initiatives are all aimed at the raising of awareness of the role of DBM and educating industry of its role and strengths. It is likely that the 1990s will see a continued growth in direct marketing, and an increasing exploitation of IT to allow its integration into marketing strategy and tactics, as fully fledged database marketing. It remains to be seen whether British industry is ready for the opportunities and threats which this will create in the competitive environment.

Keith Fletcher is a Professor at the Strathclyde Graduate Business School, Glasgow; Colin Wheeler is Senior Lecturer in the Department of Marketing, Strathclyde University, Glasgow, UK; and Julia Wright is based at Andersen Consulting.

References

Baier, M. (1985), *Elements of Direct Marketing*, McGraw-Hill, New York, pp. 35–46.

Baker, M., Hart, S., Black, C. and Abdel Mohsen, T. (1986), "The Contribution of Marketing to Competitive Success: A Literature Review", *Working Paper MWP 86, Vol. 2*, Dept. of Marketing, University of Strathclyde.

Bursk, E. (1966), "View your Customers as an Investment", *Harvard Business Review*, May/June, pp. 91–9.

Dean, J. (1966), "Does Advertising Belong in the Capital Budget", *Journal of Marketing*, Vol. 30, October, pp. 15–21.

Fletcher, K. (1983), "Information Systems in British Industry", *Management Decision*, Vol. 21, No. 2, pp. 25–36.

Fletcher, K. (1990), *Marketing Management and Information Technology*, Prentice-Hall, Englewood Cliffs, NJ.

Fletcher, K., Wheeler, C. and Wright, J. (1990), "The Role and Status of UK Database & Marketing", *Quarterly Review of Marketing*, Vol. 16 No. 1, pp. 7–13.

Fletcher, K. Wheeler, C. and Wright, J. (1991), "Database Marketing: A Channel, a Medium or a Strategic Response", *International Journal of Advertising*, Vol. 10 No. 2, pp. 117–27.

Gummersson, E. (1987), "The New Marketing – Developing Long-term Interactive Relationships", *Long Range Planning*, Vol. 20 No. 4, pp. 10–20.

Rapp, S. (1989), "So What is Direct Marketing Anyway", *Direct Response*, July, p. 27.

Rapp, S. and Collins, T. (1987), *Maxi-Marketing*, McGraw-Hill, New York.

Shaw, R. and Stone, M. (1988), *Database Marketing*, Gower, Aldershot, Hampshire, UK.

Stone, M. and Shaw, R. (1987), "Database Marketing for Competitive Advantage", *Long Range Planning*, Vol. 20 No. 2, pp. 12–20.

Part 2

Selling and Negotiation

INTRODUCTION

Tom Peters[1] states that the typical American corporation needs to achieve pre-eminence in manufacturing, sales and service in order to restore their competitive position. This book is concerned with sales and customer service. In this part the selection of readings covers the fields of selling and negotiation. Peters says,

> The customer game is ultimately won or lost on the front lines where the customer comes into contact with *any* member of the firm. The front line team *is* the firm in the customer's eyes. Therefore, the front-line team must be treated as the heroes they generally are and supported with tools (training and systems) that allow them to regularly serve the customer heroically. Surprisingly all too few firms understand this.

While Peters is referring to American organizations, the position in the United Kingdom is much the same. The importance of the sales function is also undervalued and under-appreciated. This is extremely short sighted, because the sales force generates the revenue for the organization and so plays a key role in determining the overall profitability. It is not only vital that the importance of the sales force is appreciated, it is equally important that it operates in the most appropriate way.

There are other factors that can have a detrimental effect on both the organization and buyer–seller relations. Take commission selling for instance. Many sales managers believe that sales people's reward should be based on performance shown by the volume or value of sales achieved. Thus higher achievers receive more money for their increased effort. However, some territories may have greater or lesser potential than others and consequently this may affect the salesman's income. Sales people can be easily tempted to either oversell or sell the wrong products to customers. The pension and life insurance industry in the United Kingdom has come in for severe criticism recently for not supplying right product for the customer or for not acting in the customer's best interest. Other difficulties[2] that commission selling can cause are:

- the commission process may be manipulated if sales are held back to the next period in order to get more commission in that period;
- orders may be taken which are not always attractive to the business;
- sales people may be remunerated for taking risks that are not in the company's interest. Examples are selling products 1) that might have a safety risk 2) to companies whose credit rating is not good or failing to make a credit check 3) when it may not be possible to deliver on schedule. This clearly has an effect on the company's reputation with the customer.

Many marketing textbooks describe the 'personal selling process' as consisting of a number of sequential elements such as:[3]

- prospecting and evaluating
- preparing
- approaching the customer
- making the presentation
- overcoming objections
- closing
- following up

'Objection handling' and 'closing' are identified as key parts of the process by several writers.[4,5,6]

Many sales training companies offer courses on personal selling or more focused ones on 'overcoming objections' or 'closing techniques'. There is, however, overwhelming evidence that the use of objection handling and closing techniques can be counter-productive and lose business in major sales. Traditional approaches to selling and sales training are largely based on outdated assumptions such as the sale can be opened and concluded in one visit, that objections can easily be handled, that forced closing techniques have no long-term impact on buyer feelings, and that the more presentations a sales representative can squeeze into the day the higher will be the sales revenue. The evidence for these outdated approaches to selling are presented in the first two readings in this part by Neil Rackham and Richard Ruff from the first two chapters of their book *The Management of Major Sales*. They provide a fascinating account of research conducted by Neil Rackham into selling skills involving 35,000 sales calls over 12 years in 23 different countries.

Reading 4, 'The role of the sales manager in major sales', describes why the initial reaction from some existing sales trainers was extremely hostile. The research showed that the selling skills being taught for low value or single call sales are wholly inappropriate for selling in major sales. The article also describes how managing major sales requires special and different skills compared to the small sale. Finally, a brief outline of the SPIN®* questioning model, which helps uncover a customer's explicit needs is included. This should be used at the investigation stage of the sales call. A full explanation of the SPIN® model can be found in an earlier book by Neil Rackham.[7] It is unfortunate that some marketing and sales textbooks still continue to show the same personal selling process as being applicable for both small and large sales. In order to avoid confusion we refer to the personal selling process outlined above as the 'Traditional Model for Personal Selling'. A number of writers now recognize the importance of Neil Rackham's work.[8,9,10] Others talk about consultative selling with no mention of *objection handling and closing techniques*.

In Reading 5, 'Sales efficiency and sales effectiveness', Neil Rackham explores the myth that increased 'productivity' results in increased sales in all cases. By examining sales results and sales executives behaviour in small sales and large sales he is able to illustrate the critical differences between efficiency (working harder) and effectiveness (working smarter). Both, of course, are components of productivity. According to Rackham, 'A fundamental question for improving sales performance is whether your people need to work harder or to work smarter.' In major accounts it is proposed that sales effectiveness generally has more influence. However, it is also proposed that in major accounts, the side effects of sales efficiency measures, such as increasing call rates, become counter-productive, that is they do more harm than good. For instance, trying to increase call rates in major sales is likely to result in a fall in average order value as salespeople go for the quick hits rather than concentrating on the larger strategic sale.

Selling and negotiating are often terms that are used interchangeably or negotiation may be used as a euphemism for selling. Both uses are wrong. Reading 6 by Neil Rackham entitled, 'How to offer concessions and agree terms: sales negotiation' defines negotiation and explains the difference between selling and negotiating. Unskilled negotiators tend to think in terms of fixed point objectives, whereas skilled negotiators plan their negotiation strategy and think in terms of ranges. The later also plan their questions in advance, separate understanding from agreement and test for misunderstanding – otherwise problems are likely to occur later.

Terry Anderson in an excellent reading entitled, 'Step into my parlour: a survey of strategies and techniques for effective negotiation' argues that negotiators 'tend to divide into two groups that are guided by

---

* The acronym SPIN® is a registered trademark. European trademarks for SPIN® are held by Huthwaite Research Group Limited. North American and certain other trademarks for SPIN® are held by Huthwaite, Inc.

conflicting conceptions of the bargaining process: symbiotic and predatory'. The former believe that joint gains are made by relationship building, sharing information, creativity, open communication and being collaborative. Predatory negotiators believe those characteristics display naiveté and weakness. Predatory negotiators believe in tough bargaining where one party's gain is offset by the other's loss. In practice, negotiators may need to use both symbiotic and predatory strategies. However, if both sides in a negotiation chose a predatory strategy the outcome for both sides is likely to be mediocre.

The final article in this section, Reading 8 – 'Gallery Furniture and Dr. Deming', is by Jim McIngvale. He gives a fascinating account of how he transformed Gallery Furniture based on the management principles of Dr W. Edwards Deming. Turnover has continued to rise since 1993, when the paper was written, to $85 million a year in 1996. It still has the highest sales volume per square foot of any furniture store in the US. The Gallery Furniture Company of Houston, Texas like many sales driven organizations used to reward its sales people by paying salary and commission. The prime focus of sales people was on meeting quotas and not meeting customer's needs. Figures were manipulated, deliveries brought forward or postponed in order to meet quota, customers were oversold with sundry items such as furniture polish. One of the first changes was a switch to paying sales people a straight salary. The outcome was a steady increase in sales with sales people selling the most suitable furniture for the customer. Before sales representatives were focusing on making a living, now they focus on customer's needs.

Whether we are talking about selling, negotiation or relationships with customers then organizations that focus on customers needs, trust and cooperation are more likely to be the long term survivors. Those who look for short term gain at the expense of their customers or suppliers, that is a win-lose scenario are more likely to be those that fail to survive. After all according to Dr Deming survival is not compulsory.[11]

References

1 Peters, T. *Thriving on Chaos*, Macmillan, 1987.
2 British Deming Association, *Quality in Sales*, Booklet Number 14.
3 Dibb, S., Simkin, L., Pride, W.M. and Ferrell, O.C. *Marketing Concepts and Strategies*, 2nd European Edition, Houghton Mifflin, 1994.
4 Kotler, P. and Armstrong G. *Principles of Marketing*, 5th Edn, Prentice-Hall, 1991.
5 McCarthy, E.J. and Perrault, W.D. *Basic Marketing*, 10th edn, Irwin, 1990.
6 Adcock, D., Bradfield, R., Halborg, Al and Ross, C. *Marketing Principles and Practice*, 2nd edn, Pitman Publishing, 1995.
7 Rackham, N. *Making Major Sales*, Gower, 1990. (Republished in paperback as *SPIN® Selling*, Gower, 1995.)

8 Donaldson, B. *Sales Management Theory and Practice*, Macmillan, 1990.
9 Wilson, K.J. 'Managing the industrial sales force of the 1990s', *Journal of Marketing Management*, 1993, Vol. 9, pp. 123–39.
10 Winkler, J. *Winning Sales and Marketing Tactics*, Butterworth Heinemann, 1993.
11 *LA Times*, 31 March 1987.

Reading 4

The role of the sales manager in major sales

N. Rackham and R. Ruff

Reprinted from *The Management of Major Sales*, Gower (England) 1991, Ch. 1, pp. 1–14. Published in the USA by Harper Collins Publishers Inc., 1991.

When we first made public our research on selling skills, we upset many people, particularly in the United States. It didn't matter that our work was based on the largest research study of selling in history – a scientific analysis of the selling skills used in 35 000 sales calls. It didn't matter that it took our team at Huthwaite 12 years, working in 23 countries, to check and double check our data. People were upset. If we hadn't already realized how controversial our findings would be, we were certainly left in no doubt after a national conference we addressed in Los Angeles. At the end of our presentation we were surrounded by a little lynch mob of angry trainers who protested in loud and hysterical terms that we were undermining everything they had been teaching in their sales training programmes. When we finally escaped and collected our overhead projector slides we'd used in our presentation, we found that every one of them had been damaged or defaced. A couple of years later we had a contract with a major publisher in the United States for a book based on this sales research. When the manuscript was sent to reviewers for comments their reaction was a replay of the group in Los Angeles. 'A trash heap,' wrote one reviewer, 'combining arrogance with ignorance.' As a result, the publisher cancelled our contract. What was it, you might ask, that made these ideas so offensive that they couldn't be calmly presented or published?

Our main findings were simple enough. We had shown that the skills which make you successful in small sales can actually hurt your success in larger ones. The small sale normally involves just one face-to-face meeting between a single sales-person and a decision-making customer. This is significantly different from the major sale, which requires a series of meetings spread over many months, involves several people in the selling effort and often allows little or no direct access to the decision maker. Although we use the same word, *'selling'*, to cover both small sales and major sales, in reality we are talking about two very different processes, each needing a different set of skills for success. We found, for example that:

- the closing techniques that succeed in smaller sales will actually *lose* you business as the sale grows larger. Most of the commonly taught closing techniques just don't work in large sales. Our research showed that there were much better and more sophisticated ways to obtain commitments from customers in major sales
- the classic questioning methods of open and closed questions may suffice in smaller sales but are not going to help you much in bigger sales. From the analysis of several thousand sales calls, and from watching some of the world's top salespeople in action, we were able to discover some alternative probing methods that were more business centred and brought better results in major sales
- in major sales, objection handling skills contribute only marginally to sales success. Instead, effective salespeople in larger sales concentrate on objection prevention rather than objection handling. Our research analysed how successful major account salespeople prevented objections from their customers
- traditional wisdom suggests that it's better to sell through benefits than through features. But our research found that some kinds of benefits that succeeded in small sales were actively counter-productive when used in larger sales. From an analysis of the type of benefits offered by successful major account salespeople, we were able to isolate the kinds of benefits that have most impact in the major sale.

Why should innocent-sounding findings like these produce such antagonism? The answer is not unconnected with the vested interests of the billion dollar a year sales training industry – an industry then making a comfortable living from teaching that selling was selling, whether the product was a vacuum cleaner sold door-to-door or to a multi-million dollar computer system. Research like ours was bad news, showing that major sales required different skills. Traditional sales training models, unfortunately, were based on what succeeds in smaller sales. We were raising an awkward point. If our research was right, corporations whose business involved major sales were wasting a great deal of time and money teaching their people models and programmes that, frankly, didn't work for their kind of sale. No wonder we weren't making many friends in the 'one-size-fits-all' climate of sales training that was current at the time.

OUR DEBT TO SALES MANAGERS

But this is a story with a happy ending. Gradually, interest in new models for major account selling grew. The first champions of these newer ideas were practising sales managers who were dissatisfied with the training that their people were getting. Even before our research, thoughtful managers in major sales had been concerned about the relevance of some of the sales training offered to their people. 'Existing training just doesn't apply to our sale,' one of our early supporters told us, 'we send our new people on programmes that teach them selling's about going straight to the decision maker, overcoming a few objections and closing the business. When these kids go out in the field and try to behave that way, they get slaughtered. There's got to be a better way.' Managers like this one found, in research on major sales, data to support the need for more sophisticated and more appropriate selling skills models. Thanks to the encouragement of major sales practitioners, acceptance for these new ideas grew. Our book (rejected in the United States but published in Europe), *Making Major Sales* (Gower, 1990), in true fairytale manner quickly achieved international success in eight languages. Finally, with a new American publisher, it also became a best seller in the United States. Many of the world's leading sales forces began to adopt major sales models based on radically different thinking about what it takes to succeed in major sales.

In just a few years, the climate has changed drastically. It's no longer considered daring to suggest that major sales are different and require different skills and strategies. There are books and training programmes available specifically designed for major account selling. We can't claim much of the credit for this welcome change. It happened because practising major account salespeople and their managers demanded something better. Nevertheless, it's been exhilarating to have played an active part in helping to make these changes happen. We find it very satisfying that we're now on the side of the majority. Few thoughtful people today would quarrel with the once controversial message that major sales are different and that success in major sales rests on a unique set of skills.

IS MAJOR SALES MANAGEMENT DIFFERENT?

But, although the battle over major sales has been won at salesperson level, it still remains to be fought at the level of the sales manager. If selling skills and selling strategies are different in major account selling, isn't it plausible that sales management is different too? During recent years the understanding of what it takes to sell successfully to large accounts has become much more sophisticated. But how well is major account sales management understood? What are the special skills and abilities needed to manage major account salespeople? There's ample evidence that managing major sales *is* different. For example:

- there are many well-documented cases of people who have been outstandingly successful as sales managers with a low-end sales force. When promoted to management positions involving major sales they have failed dismally. Why? The most likely explanation is that the skills that helped them manage small sales well are no longer useful for managing larger sales. It's probable that managing major sales requires some unique skills these people didn't have
- some of the techniques that have proved remarkably successful for increasing productivity in small sales have turned out to be much less effective when used with larger sales. Activity management is a case in point. In most small sales, one of the best tools for increasing productivity is tight management of activity, such as call rates. The same activity management techniques that increase productivity in small sales can often be demonstrated to *reduce* productivity if they are used to manage major sales. Again, the inference is that major sales need to be managed differently
- selling skills and strategies, as research in recent years has so clearly documented, are different in small sales and in large. It's therefore almost inevitable that managing those strategies and skills will be different too.

If the major sale requires different management skills, what are they? Where can major sales managers turn for advice? Not to any of the books on sales management that we've come across. Ten years ago, we were complaining that books on selling failed because they didn't recognize the difference between small sales and large. Exactly that complaint can be made today about books on sales management. The fact is, it's only very recently that researchers and writers have started to realize something which practical sales managers have known for a long time. Managing major sales requires special and different skills. This is the first book which specifically sets out to describe what some of those skills are and what it takes to be a successful major sales manager.

SOME INITIAL RESEARCH

Our research convinced us years ago that managing major sales involves a unique and complex set of skills. We had only to look around us during our research to find examples of some very effective – and some very much less effective – managers in action. What were the effective managers doing differently? Our first thought was that they were using a different *style* of management. We believed that if we could analyse the management style used by successful major account sales managers, then the problem of how to manage major sales would be solved. Full of the certainty and enthusiasm that afflicts the blissfully ignorant, we persuaded a large telecommunications company to let us study their successful major account sales managers to find the magic management style that we believed successful managers were using. Armed with nothing more than questionnaires and structured interview schedules, we set out to explore the management style used by the fifty most successful major account managers in the company. It didn't take long to discover that our quest was, to put it mildly, somewhat naive. Successful managers didn't have just one management style. We found that in this telecommunications company at least, successful major sales managers used widely different styles. Three successful styles stood out, each showing significant differences in how a manager behaved.

Entrepreneurs

These were the successful managers who behaved as if they were running a small company of their own, treating their accounts as a marketplace of business opportunities to be seized and exploited. They tended to use a 'hands on' approach to selling and were more directly involved in face-to-face selling than either of the other successful types of sales manager. They also tended to become particularly involved in face-to-face meetings with customers whenever they felt a blockage was holding up business or where there was an important opportunity to be closed. These managers often competed viciously for internal resources, including stealing sales talent away from other managers in their own company. They built a strong sense of action among their sales teams. Their offices were invariably busy. They had a strong business sense and a good understanding of figures, sales profitability and, in particular, their own contribution to the bottom line compared with other sales managers. One of the Entrepreneur managers we interviewed kept a large wall chart – updated weekly – that showed how much revenue he was generating compared with other sales teams. When he was ahead, the chart was prominently displayed on the wall for all visitors to see. Our visit happened at a point where he had temporarily slipped into third place so, for the time being, the chart was discreetly tucked behind a filing cabinet.

Coalition-builders

Successful managers who built careful networks of contacts and friends, both in customer accounts and within their own company. They were less active in face-to-face selling and spent less time face-to-face with the customer than the Entrepreneurs. Instead, they worked behind the scenes, using their network of contacts to help them and their salespeople to surmount any blockages in the selling cycle. Their meetings with customers were most likely to concentrate on relationship building; such meetings would frequently be outside the formal work environment – at trade shows or on the golf course. These managers always knew somebody who knew somebody who owed them a favour and, as a result, they could quietly make astonishing things happen.

Competitive-strategists

Again, successful managers, Competitive-strategists were particularly skilled at out-thinking and out-manoeuvring the competition. Like the Coalition-builders, they spent less face-to-face time with customers than did the Entrepreneurs. Their strength lay in the way they helped their people plan and form competitive strategies. When they were with customers it was most likely to be during the competitive stages of the sale where, for example, there were competitive capability presentations to be made. Many of the Competitive-strategists we met were clearly bored by 'safe' routine repeat business. 'I'm a hunter,' one of them told us, 'I'd like nothing better than to unload all my safe accounts on a bunch of customer care farmers, so I can go out and kill a few competitors.' In general, Competitive-strategists put great emphasis on the importance of timing. They told us how important it was for a manager to become involved in the selling effort at the right moment in order to gain competitive advantage.

In addition to the differences between these three types, we found an interesting similarity – all the successful managers emphasized the importance of *coaching* as a management tool for building the performance of their people. To them, coaching wasn't just traditional coaching of selling skills; by coaching, they also meant working with their people on account strategy.

Each of these three styles of management is clearly very different, and each has different strengths. These types exist in most successful major account sales operations. If you think of the effective managers you know, you'll probably have no difficulty slotting most of them in to one of these three types. However, interesting as these findings are, they spelt bad news for our attempt to find an 'ideal' style of management for major sales. Long experience as researchers warned us that if we picked out three types of successful managers from a single study in a single organization, we would probably be just scratching the surface. Further work in other places and in greater depth would almost certainly reveal other types and a whole bunch of complications. The only definite conclusion we could draw from this study was a negative one. There is *not* one successful style of management that works best in the major sale. However, this study did give us some important clues about what it takes to be a successful manager in large sales. For example:

- from the *Entrepreneur* we can see that the successful manager in major sales runs a *business*, rather than just manages salespeople
- from the *Coalition-builder* we can see how important it is in major sales to build and use a network of contacts, inside and outside the organization, in order to make things happen
- from the *Competitive-strategist* we can see how useful it is to have a keen awareness of competition and a sense of timing that lets a manager intervene in a sale at the point of maximum competitive advantage.

And, perhaps most important of all, Entrepreneurs, Coalition-builders and Competitive-strategists all agreed on the importance of coaching for successful management of major sales.

HOW MANAGING SMALL SALES IS DIFFERENT

But, for us, the most interesting results of this study were the things we didn't find. Let us for a moment imagine that we were conducting this study in a classic sales organization which was involved in small sales. In all probability, if the traditional theory of sales management is anything to go by, we would find that successful managers had four characteristics. Let us look at these in more detail.

Strong activity management

In small sales it's common to find successful managers who closely manage and monitor their people's activity levels. They introduce and use call reporting systems and they take steps to ensure that their people have a high call rate. They ensure, in other words, that their people are working hard. Before we carried out our study we had assumed that if it was important to manage people's activity levels in small sales, it would be even more important to do so in large ones. After all, we reasoned, in the small sale people are forced to work hard even without close activity management because, if they slacken off, it's immediately visible in their results. In contrast, with larger sales, if someone decides to work less hard, it may take many months before any lessening of activity becomes noticeable in terms of results. For this reason, we had anticipated, it might be more important for managers to give attention to activity levels in large sales than in small. Consequently, we were surprised to find that very few of the successful managers we interviewed made any mention of classic activity management issues such as call rates. At the time, we found this curious but we didn't have any convincing explanation as to why successful managers seemed so uninterested in how hard their people were working.

Since our initial research we've come to understand the reasons much better. In large sales, techniques for making salespeople work harder tend to backfire. Traditional activity management brings with it some crippling disadvantages in major sales; there are well-documented cases that show how, following the introduction of activity management systems in major account sales organizations, sales volume actually falls rather than increases.

Territory management

Most books on sales management have whole chapters devoted to the importance of territory management and stress that its effectiveness is likely to be a key ingredient for success in managing any sales force. Once again, we found a curious absence of concern about territory management among our successful major account sales managers. In this case, at least, the explanation isn't hard to find. In smaller sales it's usual for salespeople to each have several hundred customers and prospects in their territory. Efficient management of sales territories becomes vital to ensure coverage of such large numbers. However, this becomes a non-issue in most major account sales organizations where salespeople usually have fewer customers and sometimes don't even have geographic territories. It's therefore less important to manage coverage efficiently. For this reason, we'll not be giving the usual space to territory management that seems obligatory in books on selling. In fact – and we're sure that many readers will sigh with relief at this – we shan't mention territory management again.

THE MANAGER AS MOTIVATOR

Traditional sales management has put great emphasis on the role of the manager as a motivator. For years, writers on selling have emphasized that selling is the loneliest job in the organization; for example, in manufacturing, administration or finance, people work together with their peers and receive motivation and support from this peer contact. Salespeople, in contrast, not only work alone, they also work in an environment where rejection is a daily fact of life. Under these circumstances, the traditional writers tell us, sales managers have an essential role as motivators. This role is all the more important because, so these writers claim, there's a direct link between motivation and results. By increasing the motivation of salespeople, you increase sales. We therefore expected that our sample of successful major account managers would put great importance on their role as motivators. To our surprise, motivation was rarely mentioned in our interviews. As we'll see later, we had stumbled on a very significant difference between small sales and large. This exploratory study gave us our first clue that traditional approaches to motivation might not be appropriate to major sales.

THE KEY ROLE OF COACHING

As we have seen, coaching was an area where our three types of manager appeared to confirm the conventional wisdom. There was general agreement that coaching played an essential role in their success. In this respect, our results seemed to uncover a common factor between management of both large and small sales. Coaching, despite the fact that it is often neglected or done badly, is perhaps the most important single sales management skill. It is, therefore, hardly surprising that it should emerge so prominently in our study of success. However, our interviews did reveal, in the coaching area, another contrast between large sales and small. In small sales, most coaching is intended to develop people's selling skills. But, in larger sales, coaching often has a different target. In particular, we found that our successful major account managers spent a good deal of time coaching in the area of account strategy. At the time, we regarded this as a relatively minor issue of emphasis rather than a significant difference between small and large sales. After all, we thought, coaching is coaching. It's reasonable to suppose that a manager who is a good skills coach will have little difficulty in putting those same coaching skills to work in the strategy area.

Since then, we've found that it's not so simple. Skills coaching and strategy coaching are very different. We've often found good skills coaches who are mediocre at strategy coaching and *vice versa*. A likely explanation is that different skills are needed for each type of coaching. One factor, of course, is how well the coach understands the subject matter. We recall, for example, one manager who had come into sales from a marketing position. His background gave him an excellent understanding of strategic elements such as pricing or competitive differentiation and, as a result, he was well equipped to coach certain areas of strategy. However, because he hadn't sold before, he knew very little about selling skills, which was a severe disadvantage when it came to skills coaching. But there's much more to being a good skills coach or strategy coach than understanding selling skills or account strategy. For example, you can only coach skills by actually watching how your people sell. That means going out in the field with people, being present with them in customer calls and – yes – letting them do the selling while you observe. Strategy coaching, in contrast, can effectively be carried out without ever going near a customer. (There are several other significant differences that it's important for any effective major sales manager to understand: hence the two chapters on coaching.)

INITIAL CONCLUSIONS

Although our early work on sales management failed in its objective of finding the 'ideal' managerial style, we came away with some conclusions that warranted further study. It was abundantly clear to us that managing the major sale required a different approach from managing smaller sales. Equally clear was that the conventional approach to sales management advocated in books and in training programmes seemed much more relevant to small sales than to large. It was *dèja vu* all over again. Ten years earlier, we had found that approaches to selling skills were derived from small sales and didn't apply to the larger sales we were studying. Now we were finding the same problem in the sales management area. Nobody had recognized the unique set of circumstances which constituted major sales management – or, if they had, they were keeping very quiet about it. In our work we would frequently be asked by sales managers for material they could read which would help them manage large sales more effectively. We knew of nothing. We searched the literature and, as a reward for our efforts, we came up with less than a dozen or so not very helpful articles. In the end we decided to tackle the problem ourselves.

This book is the result of our efforts. It's the first book to look closely at the unique issues that face managers of major sales. Because nothing quite like this has been written before, it may be helpful for us to give you a preview of some of the issues we'll be covering in depth in the chapters ahead.

PRODUCTIVITY IN MAJOR SALES

The methods that achieve sales productivity in small sales generally work much less well in larger ones. Putting the issues at its very simplest, you could say that, in most small sales, you can increase productivity by making people work harder, for example by increasing the number of sales calls, that people make. In larger sales you're much less likely to get an increase in productivity from working harder. Sometimes, a work harder orientation towards sales productivity in major sales can seriously backfire. In one Chicago-based company sales *fell* after measures were introduced to encourage major account salespeople to work harder. So many cases exist where pressure to work harder has failed to improve sales results, or even hurt them, that it's important to understand what goes wrong. Fundamentally, as we'll see, small sale thinking encourages managers to believe in the simple formula: More calls = More sales. There's good evidence to show that this formula holds true in many smaller sales. For example, in one low-end sales force, we found that managers, by pushing the sales force to work harder, were able to double the number of sales calls their people were making. New business sales rose almost in proportion, showing a 90 per cent increase. Clearly, here was a case where the More calls = More sales formula turned out to be valid. However, when we've studied attempts to introduce this kind of thinking to major sales, we've generally seen very disappointing results. Why? There's certainly room for working harder – for making more calls – in most major sales organizations. Surely, even if more calls don't bring a proportionate increase in sales, it doesn't hurt to encourage your people to work hard. As we'll see, it's not so simple. Pressure to work hard usually brings with it some unintended side effects in major sales. To take one example: when salespeople are pressured for higher activity levels, we've found that they tend to focus on making smaller quick-hit sales at the expense of larger strategic ones. We tracked one company that introduced an activity management system to increase their call rates. We found that, after the introduction of the system, calls increased and so did the number of sales. However, the increase was almost exclusively in terms of smaller one-off sales. Larger sales fell after the system was introduced and total sales revenue dropped.

EFFICIENCY AND EFFECTIVENESS

If working harder isn't the answer, what is? At the risk of over-simplifying the points we'll cover in depth later it is true to say that, in major sales, success comes from working *smarter* not harder. Consequently, any attempt to increase sales that focuses only on working harder is likely to have little impact on overall productivity. It's useful to think about sales productivity in terms of two components:

- *sales efficiency*: how to get in front of customers, for the right amount of time at a minimum cost
- *sales effectiveness*: how to maximize sales potential once you're there.

Broadly speaking, though with some important exceptions, efficiency is about working harder, while effectiveness is about working smarter. In smaller sales, a focus on sales efficiency usually brings productivity gains. However, in larger sales, sales efficiency is not normally the answer. Knocking on more doors, for instance, is more likely to lead to increased business in small sales rather than large. In contrast, it's what you do after the door has been opened – what we're defining here as sales effectiveness – that has most influence on your success in major sales. The methods that increase efficiency are very different from the ones that increase effectiveness – many sales organizations have run into severe problems because they have tried to use efficiency solutions to effectiveness problems, and *vice versa*. In particular, we're disturbed at how often major sales managers damage their own success and the success of their people by unintentionally adopting 'selling harder' solutions to 'selling smarter' problems.

THE MANAGER'S SELLING ROLE

Another area in which managing major sales differs from the traditional theory of sales management is the manager's own selling role. A perennial management disease in smaller sales is the manager who, after a successful selling career, is promoted into sales management and continues to behave like a super salesperson. As one sales director of a large insurance company put it: 'We promote salespeople to sales management as if being good at selling qualifies you to be a manager. All we are doing is creating managers who can't let go of the selling role. When will we learn? Selling and managing are two separate professions and, as far as I'm concerned, the further apart we keep them the better.' He speaks a great truth. We carried out a study of successful sales management in a division of a company which sold simple low-end products. We found that:

- the most successful managers did no selling themselves, concentrating instead on managing the activities of their sales teams
- less successful managers, in contrast, played a much more active role in face-to-face selling. It seemed that they couldn't let go of their selling role
- salespeople hated it when their managers became directly involved in selling to customers.

This study, and others like it, convinced us that classic sales management theory was right. Managers should manage, and leave the face-to-face selling to their people. But, although this may be true in smaller sales, it's an unworkable concept for major sales. You can't manage very large sales without playing an integral part in every facet of the sales process, including face-to-face selling. Playing a face-to-face role in major account selling, however, can easily go wrong unless that role is carried out in accordance with some simple but important principles.

PRINCIPLES FOR INVOLVEMENT IN FACE-TO-FACE SELLING

We believe that there are five fundamental principles to guide any sales manager's face-to-face involvement in a major sale.

1 Only become involved in face-to-face selling when your presence makes a unique difference.
2 Don't make sales calls on a customer unless your salesperson is with you.
3 Before any joint call, agree on specific and clear selling roles with your salesperson.
4 Be an active *internal* seller for your salespeople.
5 Always have a withdrawal strategy that prevents any customer from becoming dependent on you personally.

Later we explore these principles in more depth and show how to use them to avoid some of the traps which face-to-face selling creates for the unwary manager.

SALES EFFECTIVENESS MODELS

Most of the basic concepts about how to sell are derived from small sales. In the 1920s, E. K. Strong – a pioneer in our understanding of the one-call sale – introduced such ideas as features and benefits, open and closed questions, objection handling and closing techniques. For more than 60 years, these ideas have played a central role in the way people have thought about selling skills. However, as we now know, simple ideas like these are little help when it comes to complex multi-call sales. In order to understand, manage and coach selling skills in large complex sales, you need to have an effectiveness model. Let us define what is meant by this and also explain why we think it's so important.

An effectiveness model is a simple way to define the elements of a complex real-world problem and to describe how those elements relate to each other. So, for example, economists use econometric models in an attempt to understand the messy and confusing interrelationships that cause them to fail to predict the timing or severity of recessions. Meteorologists use climate models to predict the weather. Doctors, dentists and engineers use models – even lawyers use models. Whenever a profession faces a set of interrelationships that are complex and difficult to predict, it will create a model as a simplified way of understanding the components of the problem and how they fit together. A model becomes an essential tool whenever reality is too complex, or too messy, to easily understand. In the nineteenth century, when engineering, economics, medicine and the other sophisticated professions we know of today were much simpler, it was possible to survive without the simplifying framework that models provide. But, as the professions became more sophisticated, so models came to play an ever more important role in each of them.

In selling, we're now at the point which many other professions reached a hundred years ago. At the simpler end of selling – the one-call sale – it's still possible to survive as a manager without formal models because the sale is not very complex. It's possible, in theory at least, to understand the one-call sale using your own experience without additional help.

However, in larger sales, as the complexity of the sale increases, it becomes much harder to understand what it takes to be effective. The need for a model grows greater with increasing complexity of the sale (Figure 4.1). Since the time of Socrates, people have known that, in order to persuade others, it's more effective to ask questions than to give opinions. In any sale, it's good advice to ask the customer questions. This hardly seems to deserve being called a model, but that's what it is. It's the oldest, and the simplest, sales effectiveness model in existence. In 1925, E. K. Strong gave this model a new twist. He suggested that it's not enough to just ask questions – you have to ask both open and closed questions. Now the model begins to get a little more sophisticated, raising issues such as when it's appropriate to ask each type of question. However, in major account selling, it's clear that just asking open or closed questions isn't an adequate effectiveness model. A major sales-probing model derived from research suggests there are four types of questions that successful people ask:

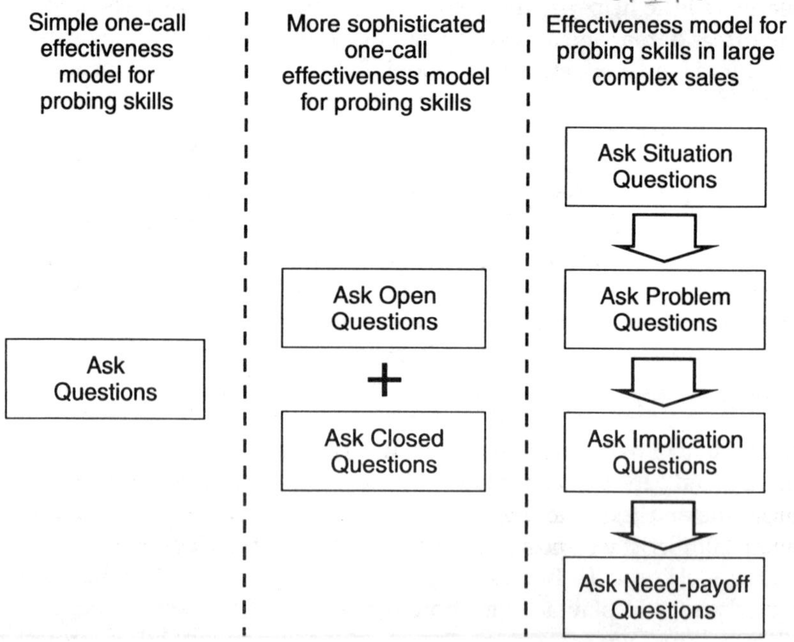

Figure 4.1 Example of an effectiveness model for probing skills

1 *Situation Questions*
About facts and details of the customer's present circumstances. These provide a background that leads to
2 *Problem Questions*
About problems, difficulties and dissatisfactions the customer is experiencing which you can solve with your products or services. These lead to
3 *Implication Questions*
About the consequences or effects of the problems that could make them urgent or severe enough to justify action.
4 *Need-payoff Questions*
About the benefits to the customer from solving the problems.

This model (SPIN®)* together with other examples of effectiveness models for larger sales, is explained in detail in *Making Major Sales*. We include it here as an example of how models for large sales are different, more sophisticated and more necessary, from models for small sales. 'Where does this end?' you might ask. We've gone from simply asking questions to asking two types of questions to asking four types of questions. In really complex sales, aren't there twenty kinds of questions? Or fifty? That brings us to the next point about models. A model is a simplification, it's not meant to be an exact copy of reality. After all, if reality was that great we wouldn't need models. A model exists to delicately balance two factors:

1 *Simplicity*
So that the model contains as few elements as possible. This makes it easy to use, easy to remember and easy to communicate.
2 *Validity*
So that the model is as near to the truth as its simplified elements allow.

There's a desperate need in complex sales for more and better models that combine simplicity with validity.

THE IMPORTANCE OF COACHING

Every major sales manager uses models, whether they come from a manager's own experience and observation, from books or from training programmes. Each individual has a set of ideas about what works and what salespeople should do to be more effective. Whether or not we call

---

* The acronym SPIN® is a registered trademark. European trademarks for SPIN® are held by Huthwaite Research Group Limited. North American and certain other trademarks for SPIN® are held by Huthwaite, Inc.

these ideas effectiveness models, they do play an important role in managing salespeople and in improving their performance. If you have a good model – which we've defined as a set of ideas about effectiveness that combines simplicity and validity – then you have an essential first step for improving sales effectiveness. The next step is to translate those ideas about effective performance into action. That's where coaching comes in. We suggested earlier that there are two distinct types of coaching, skills coaching and strategy coaching, each of which plays a key role in building sales effectiveness. In small sales, skills coaching is the more important, because there's generally little need for strategy and, in consequence, little need for strategy coaching. In major sales, both skills coaching and strategy coaching are equally important.

In coaching, less is more

Coaching often fails because the coach is over-ambitious. Whether improving skills or strategy, coaching is a time-consuming process and it's easy to take on more than you can handle successfully. We've found that the most effective coaches tend to work on fewer things in greater depth. In skills coaching it's important to recognize that people learn skills slowly and in small increments. The good skills coach will:

- choose to coach a few people in depth, rather than specifically coach the whole team
- work with each person on one skill at a time, rather than working on several skills at once.

Good strategy coaching requires a slightly different approach from skills coaching. For example, to ensure the depth of coaching that's needed to have an impact on performance, effective strategy coaches will limit the number of accounts they coach, rather than the number of people. In this way, the coach can get to know each account in the detail that's required to participate in forming and reviewing a workable account strategy.

Strategic coaching is iterative

Another special characteristic of strategy coaching is that its real value comes from the coach having a repeated involvement in the account strategy. Too often, managers put disproportionate coaching effort into initial strategy meetings. They work with their people in great detail, setting account objectives and deciding on elaborate strategic plans for how these objectives will be achieved. Then, once these plans have been created, they have less involvement as the sale progresses. Good strategy coaches, in contrast, don't spend all their time in a long detailed initial planning. Instead, they spread their coaching effort across a number of sessions as events unfold and the seller's knowledge of the account increases. The reason is straightforward. In the initial stages of account planning there are usually too many unknowns to let you form a realistic detailed strategy. It's better to start with a 'quick and dirty' initial strategy and then refine it by repeated iterations as more information about the account, the players and the competition becomes available.

Coaching is a neglected motivational tool

In small sales, salespeople can quickly see the results of their actions. Let's assume, for example, that a seller decides to change some element of selling style. By the end of the week, if the change is a good one, it may already have led to increased sales and to increased income for the seller. In larger sales, however, any changes – even changes that are clearly desirable and effective – may need many months before they lead to a visible impact on sales results. The immediacy of results helps motivate people to change in small sales. It's relatively easy to motivate salespeople to try something new if, within days, they can see tangible effects. It's an entirely different matter asking someone to try something for several months before the change is visibly rewarded by results. This is an area where coaching has an important motivational role to play in major sales.

MOTIVATION IN THE MAJOR SALE

Motivation is a complex area. In general, most motivational tools such as incentive payments, prizes, or motivational speakers, do a much better job of helping people work harder than helping them work smarter. We might, for example, persuade you to put in an additional hour a day, or to make five more sales calls per month, by offering you double your present salary. By using money in this way as a motivational tool, we can probably motivate you to work harder. But whether we double your salary or quadruple it, we're unlikely to cause you to work smarter. Many people could, if they chose, work harder – but most people are already working as smart as they know how. Unfortunately, except in rare cases, working harder isn't the answer to productivity problems in major sales. Because of this, many motivational techniques fail to work in larger complex sales. Yet, there are motivational tools that you can use to help your people to work smarter.

THE FUTURE OF MANAGEMENT IN MAJOR SALES

In the last ten years, selling has become more sophisticated and so has sales management. In major sales we've entered a new era where, perhaps for the first time, the sales job can now truly be said to be comparable in complexity and skill to more established professions. But, if you think that the last ten years have seen advances then, as the saying goes, 'you ain't seen nothing yet'. The changes that will take place during the next ten years will be even more dramatic. Already, we're seeing entirely new concepts of buyer/seller relationships emerging in several markets. Take, for example, the idea of partnering, where two organizations work in such close long-term collaboration that the boundaries between selling and buying organizations have become blurred. Customers work on product-design teams, service people have permanent offices on the customer's premises and joint teams handle issues such as inter-company accounting, administration and installation. What's the role of the sales function in these partnering arrangements? At the moment, because such strategic partnerships are still a new idea, their creation and management has generally been in the hands of top executives from the buying and selling organizations. Too often, the sales function has not played an active role. Yet, where better to manage the interface between two partnering organizations than from the sales function? We see a difficult but exciting role emerging here for the sales management of the future. For some organizations more than half their future revenues will come from partnering arrangements. As the trend to partnering continues, so will the need for sales managers who specifically understand the skills of how to enter into partnering arrangements and how to grow them successfully. Managing strategic partnerships will, almost certainly, require different skills from those we conventionally think of today as 'sales management'.

Sales teams

Already visible at the upper end of major account selling are sales teams. They are becoming increasingly prominent in accounting and consulting firms, in commercial and merchant banks, and sophisticated capital goods companies because the sales task has become too complex for any one individual to handle. As a result, there is a need in such organizations for a strategic sales team to work closely together on the development of a sales strategy and its execution. The skills required to manage these teams are necessarily complex and sophisticated. Simple teamwork skills will be a hopelessly inadequate answer. What's required is altogether more strategic and involves the development of better planning and analysis tools, a common strategic language and mechanisms for helping the team understand and evaluate its strategic options at different points of the selling cycle.

We believe that the models, concepts and ideas which are contained in this book are relevant, not only to sales management today, but also to the exciting and challenging sales management world of tomorrow. In the chapters which follow, we'll share with you our experiences from working for many years with some of the world's top sales organizations. We hope that the insights we've gained from our association with these leading-edge companies, will help you face the demands of the challenges in managing major sales for the future.

Reading 5

Sales efficiency and sales effectiveness

N. Racham and R. Ruff

Reprinted from *The Management of Major Sales*, Gower 1991, Ch. 2, pp. 15–36. Published in the USA by Harper Collins Publishers Inc., 1991.

The 'phone was ringing at 7.30 in the morning. At the other end was a very disturbed client. 'I've got to see you, Neil' he said, 'As you may know, I moved jobs recently and I'm now managing a sales force of 150 people selling industrial equipment. When I took over, sales were in a slump; so, I've started doing some analysis of what's wrong. The first results came in yesterday and I've been up most of the night worrying. I need to talk about them. When can we meet?'

It's hard to challenge the urgency of anything that merits a 7.30 'phone call, so a meeting was hastily arranged for later that day. We assembled four members of our team so that we had a range of experience to hand. Waiting for the troubled client to arrive, the four of us sat around playing the usual consultants' guessing games: 'What's he so worried about?' 'What did he find from his analysis that's keeping him (and us) awake?' Normally these speculations are over and done with in a matter of minutes but, as it happens, the client's plane was delayed for an hour, so our guessing game went on a little longer than usual. One of us suggested that, to pass time, we should play our game with higher stakes. We should each write our answers to two questions about the client's problem and its solution. The person whose answers turned out to be closest to the truth would win a dinner for two paid for by the rest of us. Our questions were:

1 Out of the various sales force problems he's probably analysed, which single one is troubling him the most?
2 Out of the various answers he's come up with, which one will be hardest to talk him out of?

The winner, as it turned out, made the following predictions (and they were so remarkably accurate that the rest of us cheerfully paid for a very expensive meal):

- the most disturbing single fact for this client is that sales force activity levels (call rates) are lower than he or his management had predicted
- we shall try to talk him out of various attempts to increase call activity levels and we shall almost certainly fail

A CLASSIC CASE STUDY

In retrospect, this was an easy bet to win. The client's story was typical of what happens to many sales managers faced with an urgent need for increasing the productivity of their sales force. It was so typical, in fact, that we can take this story – with or without the 7.30 phone call – as a case study of how sales force productivity problems arise, are analysed and dealt with in most organizations.

Poor sales results had prompted the company to look for a new head of sales, which was how our client got his job. Faced with the urgent issue of how to improve sales performance, he had begun by collecting some facts and figures. Among these were analyses of activity levels of the sales force. Management had fondly assumed that salespeople were making three or four calls on customers per day. The figures showed that the true activity level was less than two calls per day. This was startling news and our client, like many sales managers before him, panicked. However, the problem had an obvious solution. Management must find a way to increase sales activity – to push up the call rate. After all, if the sales force were to make twice as many calls, then sales productivity should increase in proportion. In vain we tried to persuade our client that this was another example of a strategy that might work in small sales but was doomed to failure in large ones. Nothing we said could dissuade him from setting up activity management systems and controls aimed at increasing the activity level of his people. He set call rate targets, instituted call reporting systems and began monitoring and evaluating both managers and salespeople in terms of their call activity levels. All this effort certainly succeeded in pushing up call rates. Within a few weeks his people were averaging almost three calls per day. However, sales results didn't show the expected improvement. It wasn't until six months later, with sales still sagging, that he came back to us ready to think about an alternative approach.

Put yourself in his shoes. You've been brought in to increase sales. You find your salespeople are making, at most, two customer calls per day. You'd expected twice that. What would you do? Our client, like most sales managers, had never questioned the basic commonsense productivity formula: More calls = More sales.

He worked on the assumption that because his sales people were now making an average of 9 calls per week, if he could just increase their activity level to 18 or 20 calls per week, then sales would double. 'Well, perhaps not quite double,' he told us when we probed more deeply, 'but certainly increase significantly'. What was wrong with his assumption? Superficially it sounds logical. But, to understand the serious flaw in his logic, we must look more closely at the relationship between call rates and sales.

CALL RATES AND SUCCESS IN SMALL SALES

Let's begin with a case study which seems to support the More calls = More sales notion. A company, based in Florida, manufactured cleaning equipment, such as mops, brushes and scourers. Rather than operate through distributors, the company had a sales force that sold directly to restaurants, offices and small businesses in the major cities of the United States. In the New York area, the company had 12 salespeople who were managed by a relative of the company's owner. This relative, the proverbial sleeping partner, paid little attention to managing the business. Unfortunately, most of his sleeping took place in Florida and not in the New York area where his salespeople were based. Eventually, he overslept the patience of the company's board and left the organization. His replacement, a promising and energetic young woman who had been one of the New York salespeople, was appointed in his place. Before she became manager, the New York salespeople were making an average of 6 new business calls per day in addition to their maintenance calls on existing customers. On average, 2.5 of these 6 calls resulted in a sale. Feeling that this call rate was too low, the new sales manager set about increasing the new business activity level. She set targets of 15 new calls per day. Three months later she was able to show some very impressive figures; she had doubled call rates and, as a result, new business sales volume from the New York area had almost doubled (Figure 5.1).

This increase in sales is dramatic, whether we measure it in terms of sales per day or overall dollar value of these sales.

A dangerous conclusion

What conclusion can we draw from a case like this? The first thing we should ask is whether this is just an isolated example – a rare but lucky chance. Or do cases like this happen regularly when determined sales managers work hard to increase call rates? The evidence here is fairly

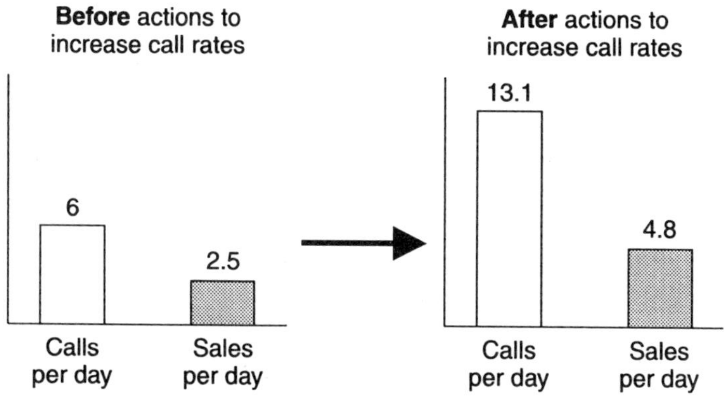

Figure 5.1 Increase in activity levels leads to increase in sales

clear and there are many well-documented cases that show sales increases resulting directly from increases in call rates: a sales force selling cosmetics door-to-door, non-profit organizations 'selling' the merits of the charities they represent, and a variety of sales operations organized along the lines of the cleaning supplies company mentioned above. In each of these cases there's evidence that a manager has greatly increased sales by increasing call rates. With cases like this to back up the notion that more calls equals more sales, it's no wonder that so many sales managers have come to believe that the first step to increasing sales productivity is to increase call rates.

If there's evidence linking call rates to sales volume, why were we advising our client *not* to work on an activity management system to increase his call rates? To understand why we were so critical of his emphasis on more calls, we should look closely at those cases where an increase in call rates has led to an increase in sales. There's an important common factor in these cases. In each one, the sale is very small. Whether we're talking about our cleaning supplies company, cosmetics sales or charities, the average sales is less than $100. What's more, the sales force is often literally knocking on doors. The rule for success in these small sales seems to be that the more doors you knock on, the more sales you will make. This rule has been well understood by generations of knock-on-doors salespeople. One of us had an uncle who, in the 1950s, managed a sales operation selling vacuum cleaners door-to-door. When asked by his children what heaven was like, he replied: 'Heaven is an infinitely long street with doors to knock on both sides.' He certainly understood that in his business there was a direct relationship between knocking on doors and making sales. The link between calls and sales isn't found only in sales forces that literally go knocking on doors. In many small sales, where business can be transacted in just one call, there's a measurable link between the number of calls and the number of sales. Increase your call rate in most small sales and business increases as a result.

However, as we'll see, this relationship breaks down as the size of the sale increases. In major sales, the image of the infinitely long street rarely applies. In fact, in major sales we have to search very hard to find examples where attempts to increase call rates have resulted in an increase in sales volume.

CALL RATES AND SUCCESS IN THE LARGER SALE

Why should increases in call activity bring rich rewards in smaller sales but have little or no positive impact in larger ones? Basically, there are two reasons:

1 Increasing sales activity is a strategy which works well where success can be achieved by selling *harder*. That's often the case in small sales. However, in those sales where success depends on selling *smarter*, increasing call activity generally has only minimal impact.
2 When managers try to increase call activity, their efforts usually create some highly undesirable and unintended side effects. In the small sale, these side effects don't do much damage. However, in large sales, they often cause such damage that sales results actually get worse because of them.

Selling harder or selling smarter?

The first, and most important, question to ask yourself before trying to increase people's activity levels is: 'Do my people need to sell harder or to sell smarter?'.

Most forms of activity management are designed to make people sell harder – to make them increase their call rates. Selling harder is most likely to produce results under these conditions:

- the size of the sale is small
- sales are generally completed in a single call or transaction
- success depends as much on energy and enthusiasm as it does on skill and strategy
- the available and unpenetrated market is very large in comparison to the size of the sales force (in other words, there are lots of doors left to knock on)
- there is distinct evidence that salespeople are not putting enough effort into their selling.

It's clear that in most major account sales, the first three of these conditions don't normally exist. Major account sales are large, multi-call and almost invariably more dependent on skill and strategy than on energy and enthusiasm. But the other two conditions *do* exist in some major sales. It's not uncommon to have a sales force that's too small to penetrate a very large potential market. And many major account sales managers fervently believe that their people are putting insufficient effort into their sales. These were exactly the issues behind our client's 7.30 panic phone call. 'I know all national sales managers *think* their people are lazy underperformers,' he told us, 'but mine *really* are. Some people have been sitting in the sales office so long that there's a layer of dust on them.' His other problem, equally severe, was that his company had produced a new and exceptionally innovative product. 'It's only a matter of months,' he explained, 'before the competition will have an equivalent product. I've got to get these people off their backsides and into customers' offices or we'll lose our precious lead time.' He presented a very logical and persuasive case for activity management. His activity level was low and lots of doors were waiting for his people to knock. No wonder we couldn't talk him out of it.

SIDE EFFECTS OF ACTIVITY MANAGEMENT

But why should we want to talk him out of his plan for activity management if there was evidence it was needed? It wasn't that we completely mistrusted his diagnosis – although we suspected that his people worked harder than he imagined. Our fundamental objection lay in the second reason why activity management fails in major sales. We suspected that his system would result in damaging side effects. In particular, we were afraid that his attempts to increase his people's call levels would lead to four problems, namely:

- a concentration on small sales
- a proliferation of paperwork and administration
- attention to the wrong end of the sales pipeline
- demotivation of top salespeople.

These unintended side effects of activity management are so common, and so deadly, that it's worth examining each in detail.

Concentration on small sales

When managers attempts to increase activity levels, particularly if their attempts are backed up by formal systems such as targets, call reports and call tracking, their people tend to concentrate on quantity rather than

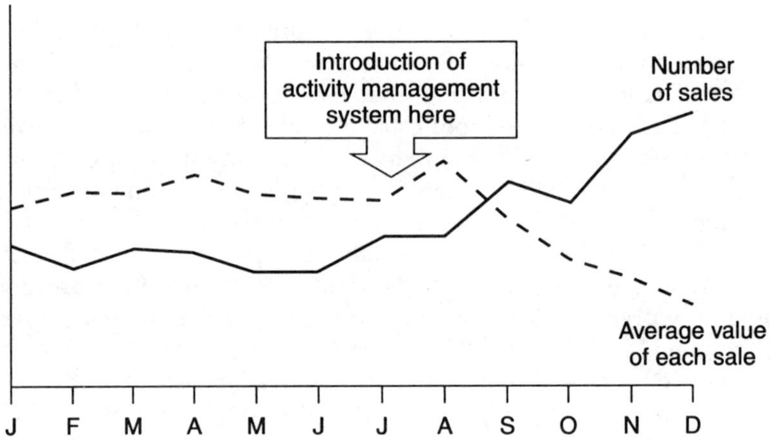

Figure 5.2 More sales means less revenue

quality. As a result, the easy small sale becomes a much more attractive target for salespeople than the complex strategic one. This isn't just a theoretical observation. There are case studies which eloquently illustrate the existence of this small sale concentration and how much damage it can do to an organization's sales.

Consider the case of a large manufacturing company based in Chicago (Figure 5.2). An activity management system was introduced in August as an attempt to boost sales. It was a relatively conventional system. Call reports were beefed up, a tracking form was introduced which had to be filled out weekly, call targets were set. In other words, the company did exactly what most other organizations have done when introducing activity management systems. But look closely at the results. In the five months after the system was introduced, the number of orders increased by 16 per cent, clear evidence that the new activity management system was succeeding in its attempts to increase call activity. But now see what's happened to the average value of each order. There's been an 18 per cent decline. The company's sales revenue *fell* by 1.5 per cent as a result of the new system.

This is not to say that activity management always brings a fall in sales. However, cases like this one should make us very cautious about what happens if an activity management system predisposes salespeople to go after the quick-hits rather than to concentrate on the larger strategic sale. (There are very few studies of the effects of activity management on sales. Most organizations like to keep their sales data confidential and they discourage research. For example, we've only been allowed to use the example of the Chicago company on condition that we don't use the company's name and that we disguise certain aspects of the case.)

Almost every experienced sales manager we've worked with can quote similar examples to the one given here. The sales manager of a corporation that makes packaging machinery recalled: 'When I was younger we had a new boss. He was a real hard driver. "One more call" was his motto. It didn't matter how hard you'd been working – there was always time to fit in one more call. Soon he had us all buzzing around like flies. We worked our tails off but the funny thing was that it didn't make any difference to our sales results. In fact, as I remember it, they might even have gone down a bit.'

Most of us have seen cases like this, where great activity and effort has little or no impact on sales results. Worse still, management pressure for increased activity doesn't just mean that salespeople knock on more doors. It can also mean that they knock on the same door more times. In other words, under pressure to complete more calls, it's easy for salespeople to make real nuisances of themselves by over-calling on existing customers with no clear sales or customer care objective beyond the necessity to demonstrate to management that they are active.

As customers, we were once the victim of over-calling driven by an activity management system. One of our operating companies was served by a bank that had just introduced a new sales activity management system to boost the number of customer visits made by its calling officers. The first visit we received from our friendly neighbourhood calling officer was a pleasant enough opportunity to have a two-hour chat. Three weeks later we had another visit. There was no clear purpose for this second visit and after investing another couple of hours, we were left wondering why we were the chosen recipients of all this free-floating attention. The following month the calling officer phoned us to arrange a third visit. This time we were more reluctant to participate and asked that the meeting should be kept brief. When the meeting began it was clear that the discussion would be no more productive than the others. We asked the calling officer, 'Have you, by any chance, been set some call targets recently?' That's when he confessed and told us about the new activity management system.

In our case, the person who knocked on our door three times in seven weeks didn't have anything to sell. But it would have been equally irritating, from a customer's standpoint, if a salesperson with a clear product objective called on us too frequently when we either didn't have a need or were not ready to discuss next steps.

Activity management can generate an impressive amount of additional sales energy. From a distance, that energy looks to be a step towards greater sales productivity. The senior management of our bank, for example, may have been delighted to see how many more visits their calling officers were making now that a new system was in place. But that energy is often misdirected. We've seen how easily it can lead to a concentration on small quick-hit sales or to a nuisance level of over-calling on existing accounts. Unfortunately, in the 'all heat and no light' atmosphere of such intense activity, few salespeople give enough attention to long term strategic sales that are the key to profitable major account selling.

Proliferation of paperwork

Most activity management systems depend on some form of call reporting and tracking which, in turn, depends on paperwork. Paperwork is an unmitigated evil in many sales organizations. It's not just that salespeople, especially top performers, seem to have an instinctive hatred of paperwork. It's more fundamental than that. You can almost measure the health of a sales organization by the energy it puts into dealing with its customers compared with the energy spent in its internal demands, of which paperwork is a significant component. Over and over again, our advice to clients has been, 'Cut your paperwork in half'. Most call reporting systems are dubiously accurate – which is a charitable way of saying that many call reports are rationalizations or even downright lies. Much time is spent in justifications, cover-ups and explanations of failure. If half the effort that goes into call reporting was put instead into call planning, then there would be fewer failures to report. For this reason there was great rejoicing in the land when IBM abolished its mighty call reporting system recently in favour of a greater emphasis on planning.

Almost every activity management system we have seen has resulted in an increased paperwork demand. In one extreme case we know of, following the introduction of an activity management system, salespeople were spending an additional hour each day on paperwork associated with call reporting. That was more than 10 per cent of their selling time and, in terms of sales productivity, it was a disgrace. In less extreme forms, most activity management has a paperwork component that distracts salespeople from their central task of being with their customers. Our advice is this: if you want to increase sales productivity in the major sale, concentrate your efforts on planning, strategy and the customer. Do your best to minimize reporting, paperwork, justifications and all the assorted nonsense that can cause sales management systems to sink under their own weight.

A word of caution is appropriate here. We've talked with sales managers who assure us that they don't have a paperwork problem any more because they have moved to computerized reporting. 'Now that all our reports are entered directly into the system,' explained a sales manager from a shipping company, 'everything is electronic and we've cut our reporting paperwork down to nothing.' Her salespeople were less enthusiastic. 'Same old junk under a new name,' one of her people told us, 'it takes just as much time to type lies onto a screen as it did to write them down.'

Wrong end of the pipeline

There's a curious phenomenon that often goes with activity management or any other managerial attempts to make salespeople work harder. We're not quite sure why it happens, but it happens so often that it demands some attention. Most organizations institute activity management systems because they are disturbed about sales performance. Their purpose, crudely, is to close more sales. As a result, they give most attention to calls nearest to the decision. Managers scan reports to find which sales are nearest to closing, they help their people plan these closing calls and, if the sale is important, they go out with their people to make the vital final call. Because closing calls get so much managerial attention, there's a corresponding neglect of those calls at an earlier point in the selling cycle. What's wrong with that? If a manager's efforts succeed in closing more sales, then surely attention to closing calls is the best contribution a manager can make to sales productivity. That may be true in simple sales where the number and size of sales closed are the only measures of sales productivity. But, in larger sales, there's another important factor that managers often neglect – the number of calls required to make the sale.

Let's take a case where the number of calls in the selling cycle had a bigger impact on sales productivity than the number of sales. A large multi-national computer company approached us several years ago with such a problem. 'Our new generation of mini-computers,' they told us, 'can do everything a mainframe could do five years ago but at less than one tenth of the cost.' We didn't see why that should be such a problem. 'It's not the price of the machine that's the problem,' they explained, 'it's the way we're selling it. We're using salespeople who started their career selling mainframes. Now they're using the same methods to sell a machine that, although it has the same capabilities, costs only a small fraction of mainframe price. On average it's taking them about 7 calls on a customer to sell a mini. That was fine with a mainframe where we had a fat margin. But on a mini, 7 calls is eating up our profits.' In other words, the productivity issue wasn't the number of sales closed but the resources required to close each sale. We agreed to help and started an investigation of factors that determined the length of their selling cycle.

We correlated the number of calls needed to make the sale with the point in the sale where the manager participated. Those sales where

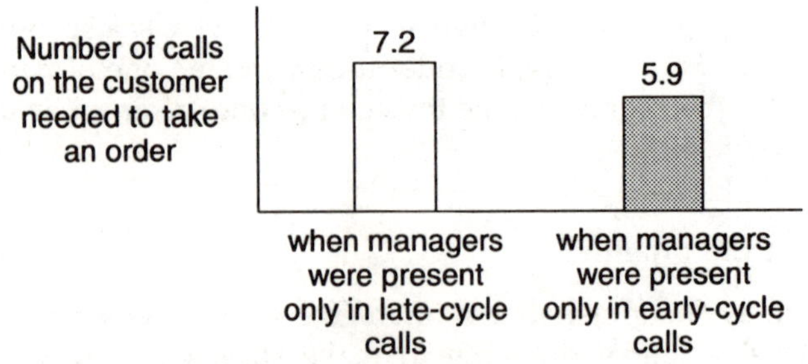

Figure 5.3 Effect of managers' presence in the call

managers were present in late-cycle calls (what we've been calling 'closing calls') had a longer – and therefore less productive – selling cycle than those sales where managers had been present in the early part of the sale. What do results like this mean? Here's how we interpreted them. Manager presence in the call, whether early or late, is a sign of where managers are putting their efforts (Figure 5.3). Those managers who gave their attention to closing calls late in the cycle had longer selling cycles than those who put their attention on early calls. Why? The answer is straightforward. However brilliantly a manager operates late in the cycle, after seven calls have been made on this customer, the best the manager can do is to get the business on the eighth call. You can't rewrite history. Attention to the eighth call will never close the sale in less than eight calls. In contrast, managers who put their attention on the early part of the selling cycle were able to get the sale off to a better start and, because of that, their people had significantly shorter selling cycles. As a manager, the earlier in the selling cycle you put your efforts, the more impact you will have on one of the key components of major account sales productivity – the length of your selling cycle.

It's evidence like this that makes us worried about the tendency of many activity management systems to concentrate effort on calls late in the selling cycle. Of course, it's unfair for us to lay all the blame on activity management. It's possible to design a system that brings equal or greater concentration to calls early in the selling cycle. Unfortunately, that doesn't happen often. When managers take steps to get their people working harder, disproportionate attention usually goes to late-cycle calls.

Demotivation of top salespeople

A final unintended side effect of activity management systems is that they can create serious conflict with top salespeople. Top performers usually chafe against restrictions of any kind. They hate to be told, 'Your target is to make four calls a day', or, 'You must fill in these call reports'. As far as most top performers are concerned, reporting systems are onerous, restrictive, unproductive and, even worse, a sign that their management doesn't trust them or respect their professionalism. Top performers are scarce and, as demand for skilled major account salespeople continues to grow, they are likely to be even more scarce in the future. You can't afford to demotivate them. And, being top performers, they can vote with their feet by moving to a competitor who allows them the freedom they need.

The antipathy top performers have for restrictions is nicely illustrated by a study we did for Xerox Corporation to find why salespeople left the company. We analysed reports of exit interviews, classifying reasons for leaving under five headings:

Compensation
Dissatisfaction with pay.
Job satisfaction
Unhappiness with present job.
Relationships
Problems with management or peers.
Prospects
Opportunities for advancement or growth.
Restrictions
Unproductive or restrictive management systems and controls.

Using these headings, we compared the reasons why top performers and poor performers left. The number one reason why top performers left the company was their dissatisfaction with restrictions (Figure 5.4). The most common restriction mentioned by top performers was the activity management and call reporting system. In contrast, poor performers tended to choose reasons such as compensation, prospects or relation-

Rank	Top performers	Rank	Poor Performers
1	Restrictions	1	Compensation
2	Job satisfaction	2	Prospects
3	Prospects	3	Job satisfaction
4	Compensation	4=	Relationships
5	Relationships	4=	Restrictions

Figure 5.4 Why did you leave the company?

ships. They seemed quite happy to live with the restrictions of the activity management system. It was evidence like this that made us advise our client to be very cautious about introducing any system to increase call rates that could appear restrictive to his top performers.

WORKING HARDER OR WORKING SMARTER?

As we've seen, a fundamental question for improving sales performance is whether your people need to work harder or to work smarter. Generally, in major sales, working smarter is the answer – and that's why it's a central theme throughout this book. But, as in the case of our client, sometimes there's reason to decide on working harder. Our client felt he had evidence that his people were not working hard enough. You may have the same feeling about your salespeople. However, before you introduce methods and controls to make people work harder, pause for a while to review your evidence. Don't plunge unthinkingly into activity management just because you find your people are making fewer calls than you expected. As our old friend Doug McNair says of his work in the telecommunications industry, 'Prospects are a precious commodity. Activity without purpose uses up your prospect base very quickly.' Over the years we've worked with dozens of sales forces who have analysed their salespeople's activity levels or call rates. In almost every case the analysis has created alarm and despondency among management because they had expected a higher level of call activity than they actually found. In fact, we can't think of a single case where management has discovered their people have been making *more* calls than they had imagined. All too often, when sales management is confronted with lower activity levels than anticipated, they have responded by introducing measures that result in one or more of the undesirable side effects we've discussed. They haven't stopped to question the sacred formula More calls = More sales.

TESTING THE FORMULA

How do you know whether or not the More calls = More sales formula applies to your salespeople? As we have seen, in some sales forces there *is* a relationship between call activity and sales results. In other sales forces that link doesn't exist. Is there some way to predict in advance whether your sales force could potentially benefit from activity management? On the face of it, that sounds an unanswerable question. We know of many sales forces who have decided that the only way to tell whether increased activity will mean increased sales is to introduce tighter activity management and to see what happens.

Fortunately, there *is* a way in which you can make a quick and easy test of the More Calls = More sales formula. The simplest method is this:

- take your top performers – not more than about 15 per cent of your sales force – and analyse the number of calls they have made during the last month
- then take the average call rate of the rest of the sales force for the same time period
- look at the differences. If your top performers are making *more* calls than the rest of the sales force, then there's a possibility that better activity management will improve results – that more calls will bring more sales. However, if you find, as often happens in major sales, that your top performers are making *fewer* calls than average, then it's unlikely that activity management will produce a dramatic improvement in sales results.

This is a quick rule-of-thumb method. If you want to carry out a more precise analysis, you can use the method for comparing call rates and business volume shown in Figure 5.5. In a capital goods sales force of 30 people, the top 5 performers all had new business call rates of between 7 and 14 calls a month, compared with the sales force average of 22 calls a month. Management had been contemplating tightening their activity on the assumption that more calls would mean more sales. The evidence here didn't suggest a strong relationship between call rates and success.

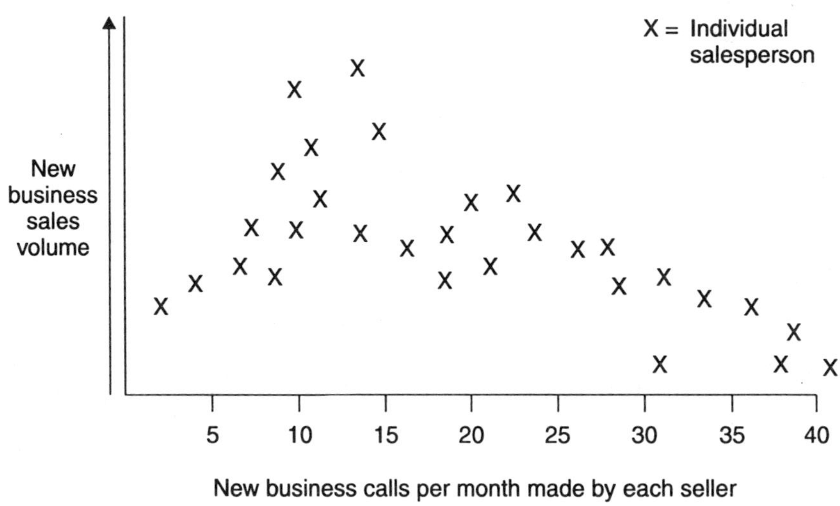

Figure 5.5 Relationship between calls and sales volume in a high value capital goods sales force

We were able to persuade the company to put their effort into helping their people sell smarter rather than sell harder.

WHEN MORE CALLS BRING MORE SALES

In contrast, let's look at some equivalent data from a classic small sale (Figure 5.6). The regional sales force of an office equipment and supplies company provide a contrast to the earlier capital goods example in that:

- on the whole, high performers were making *more* calls than the sales force average
- the top 5 performers out of a sales force of 28 were averaging 70 calls per month compared with an average of 55 calls per month for the rest of the sales force.

In circumstances like these there's a much stronger case to be made for the value of actions to increase overall sales force activity levels. Here, the More calls = More sales equation has the ring of truth.

Analyse the performance of your own people. If you find that your top performers are indeed the ones making the most calls, then you've built a good case for putting energy into activity management. However, even if your analysis shows that you could gain sales by increasing call rates, be

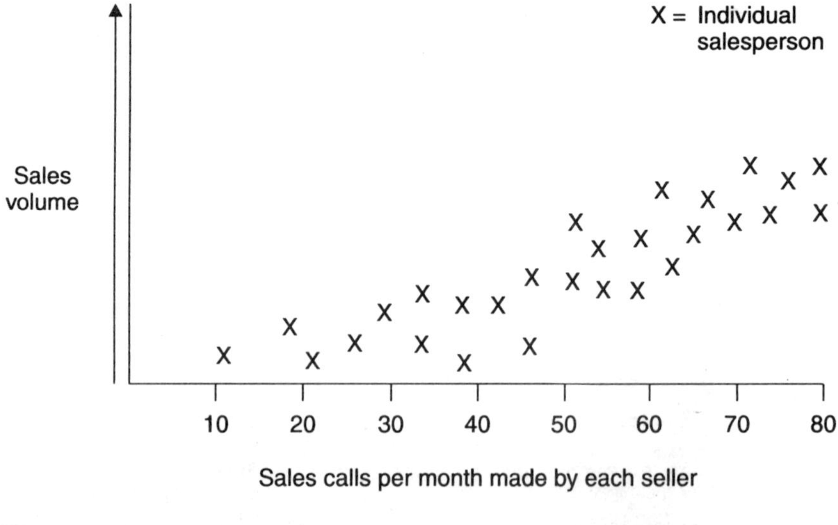

Figure 5.6 Relationship between calls and sales volume of a low value office supplies sales force

careful that you try to minimize the side effects such as small sales concentration or the proliferation of paperwork.

SALES EFFICIENCY AND SALES EFFECTIVENESS

These two company examples illustrate a great truth about sales productivity. The methods that bring you productivity and improve your performance in small sales are generally very different from the ones which work best in large sales. Activity management is a good example and, as we know, in small sales you can often increase performance by increasing call rates. Working harder is a formula for success. But, in large sales, working smarter is likely to be the name of the game. Actions that aim to increase selling effort, such as activity management, have a poor record of success in major account sales. To get a better understanding of why this is, and what sales management must do to improve performance in major sales, we'd like to introduce two important terms, *sales efficiency* and *sales effectiveness*, the two components of sales productivity (Figure 5.7).

These terms have been around for many years in selling, so they may be familiar to you. However, because they have been used with a variety of meanings, we should start with a reminder of the definitions we gave in the opening chapter.

- *Sales efficiency* is about how to get in front of the right customers, for the right amount of time, at a minimum cost.
- *Sales effectiveness* is about how to maximize sales potential once you're there.

The efficiency/effectiveness distinction helps us to understand and improve sales productivity. (It has been the basis of some elegant work

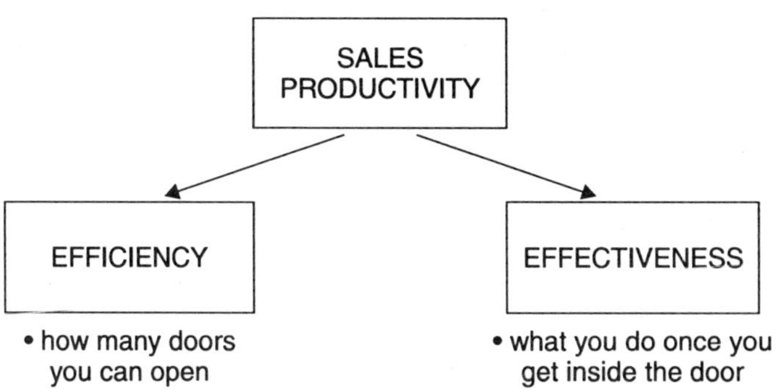

Figure 5.7 The two components of sales productivity

done by McKinsey & Company, which makes this an appropriate point to acknowledge the impact that McKinsey, and in particular John De Vincentis, has had on helping us to clarify our own thinking in this area.)

EFFICIENCY, EFFECTIVENESS AND SIZE OF SALE

It's generally true that a sales force selling lower value products makes many small sales to a large number of customers. A major account sales force, in contrast, tends to have comparatively few customers but the average size of sale is much larger. The number of potential customers in an organization's customer base usually has significant implications for whether a sales force concentrates on efficiency or on effectiveness. To take an extreme example, a manufacturer of commercial aircraft, such as Boeing, has only a few hundred customers worldwide. Efficiency doesn't enter much into the equation – Boeing already knows, and is talking to, just about every potential customer in the world. Their problem is not one of identifying the doors and knocking on them. Success for Boeing depends almost entirely on what they do once they are inside the door – that is on their effectiveness. In contrast, we remember talking to a manufacturer of fax machines in the days when facsimile was a brand new technology. 'What's the market for these things?' we innocently asked. 'The worldwide fax market could easily exceed a hundred million customers,' our client told us, 'the limiting factor of our sales force will be our ability to reach even a tiny fraction of the potential.' If ever a market could justly be described as an infinitely long street with doors on both sides, this was it. Because of the large customer base, the limiting factor for success was efficiency. Tight activity management and improved call rates could well be the secret of success in a market like this. An emphasis on efficiency brings best results in circumstances where each salesperson has many accounts and the size of each sale is small (Figure 5.8). We've already seen one of the reasons why this should be so. For a salesperson who has many potential accounts to cover, efficiency improvement helps open more doors. The other reason why efficiency may be more important than effectiveness in small sales is that small sales demand less skill and strategy from the seller. As a consequence, small sales are easier to make, so improvements in effectiveness, such as better selling skills, have less impact on small sales than they do on large.

IT'S NOT SO SIMPLE

This book is about managing major sales so, naturally, our primary attention is on how to improve effectiveness. We're concerned with how to sell smarter rather than how to sell harder. But we must be careful not

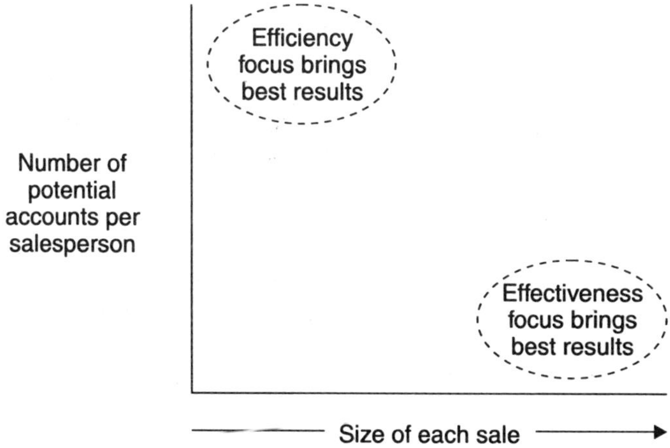

Figure 5.8 Sales effectiveness and account characteristics

to oversimplify things. The idea that in small sales only efficiency matters and in large sales only effectiveness is just not true. Let's examine a couple of cases that illustrate this.

Case 1: increasing face-to-face time with doctors

We worked with a sales force in the pharmaceutical industry, whose business looked, in almost every way, to be the classic small sale. Each of the salespeople called on hundreds of doctors in their territory, trying to interest them in their company's drugs. The average salesperson called on seven doctors a day; not a high call rate when you consider that the average face-to-face time with the doctor in each call was a mere 3 minutes. The drug company was therefore paying their sales force for an alarmingly inefficient use of sales time, getting just 20 minutes a day in front of customers. Even by the luxurious standards of the pharmaceutical industry, this case had all the hallmarks of a serious efficiency problem. There were many small sales: only seven customers a day were being visited. Surely, we thought, by introducing tighter activity management to push up call rates, the company could do better than its present, pitiful 20 face-to-face minutes a day.

On closer examination, the problem was less straightforward. Doctors are very busy people – and even idle doctors like to pretend they are busy. Consequently, salespeople had to wait for an average of almost 30 minutes after arriving on the premises before the doctor was ready to see them. There was nothing salespeople could do to shorten this period. As the seven calls required an unalterable 3½ hours a day of pure waiting, not to mention another 3 hours of travel time between calls, there was little or no latitude to increase productivity by increasing efficiency.

We decided to take an alternative approach. An analysis of the average 3 minute call revealed that its length wasn't the only problem. Conditioned by the general atmosphere of hurry that doctors conveyed, most salespeople sent the allotted minutes blurting out a list of product features and advantages. Then, leaving a trail of samples behind them, they rushed off to their next call and next 30 minute wait. We reasoned that, if we couldn't increase face-to-face time by better efficiency, then we might be able to achieve an improvement by using effectiveness methods. We taught salespeople a different selling approach based on questions rather than on features and advantages. In other words, we tried to increase the effectiveness of the call. Doctors were impressed by the change in selling style. They rated the new style of calls as more informative, more interesting and, better still, they gave more time – an average of 8 minutes rather than 3. In this way, with a constant efficiency level of seven calls a day, we were able to improve call effectiveness to give more than 50 face-to-face minutes a day rather than 20.

Case 2: efficiency problem prevents effectiveness

In the pharmaceuticals case we can see how, even in small sales, apparent sales efficiency problems can contain significant effectiveness elements. The opposite can also be true. Occasionally, in large sales, you'll encounter an apparent effectiveness problem which has its cure in better efficiency. Take the case of a large multi-national computer company. The average size of sale was well into the six figures. The selling cycle was complex. On the face of it, effectiveness was much more important than efficiency. At the time when we were called in, sales had started to sag and competition was eroding market share. Interviews with customers where sales had been lost suggested that the company's products were rated as technically superior and well supported. The most common reason given by customers for lost sales was that the company was outsold by competition. This sounded like an effectiveness problem if ever we saw one.

When we looked more closely, we found a different story. Historically, the company's salespeople made 80 per cent of their calls on data processing managers, who had been the decision makers for their products. However, decision power had been shifting inside many accounts. Functions other than data processing were having a larger say in the acquisition of data processing equipment. Competitors who had realized this early changed their sales strategy. Instead of calling mainly on data processing departments, they called on a wider range of potential influencers in each account. Our client's salespeople, however, were not calling on these important influencers. Why? Not, as it turned out, from lack of willingness or a failure to realize that these influencers were the key to sales success. No, it was purely an efficiency issue. Each salesperson had too many accounts. Management had allocated accounts in the days when the sales job was only to influence the data processing department. There just wasn't the extra time needed to sell to several other functions in each account. The solution didn't lie in typical effectiveness measures such as selling skills or account strategy training. Instead, the company was able to regain sales by reducing the number of accounts each salesperson had to cover. This allowed more time for each account and made it possible for salespeople to call on the new range of influencers. Questions of territory configuration and coverage are typically efficiency issues. In this case, an efficiency solution helped to turn round a situation that, superficially, looked to have all the symptoms of an effectiveness problem.

MORE DIAGNOSTIC TOOLS

Despite these cautionary cases, it's true that the majority of opportunities for increasing productivity in smaller sales will be through efficiency measures. In larger sales, effectiveness will usually be the key to success. But here, as researchers, we feel obliged to introduce one further complication. What if your sales force is somewhere in the middle? What if you're not really making major sales, yet you have relatively high priced products and a multi-call sales cycle, so you're not making small sales either? In the middle sized sale, it's hard to tell whether your productivity improvement opportunities come more through effectiveness or through efficiency. We once faced such a case in a business unit of the Xerox Corporation which sold mid-range copying machines to a customer base that varied from individual purchasers up to divisions of large corporations. The 40-person sales force was geographically organized. The size of each salesperson's territory had been decided when the unit had been set up, about five years before we came on the scene.

Our entry, predictably, was the result of a severe and sustained underperformance by the unit. Equally predictably, before we arrived the unit had gone through an intensive effort to improve its activity management. This effort had resulted in several of the sins we described earlier. Paperwork had proliferated to a point where it was getting in the way of selling. Three of the five top performers had left. Small sales had increased a little, but the overall sales volume was down. The worse the situation became, the more the unit's management put frenetic energy into collecting call reporting information. It was one of the nastiest examples of activity management gone wild that we had ever seen. The call data were collected on an infamous green form, known to the sales force as 'the green weenie'. Stories of sabotage were rife. As one salesperson told us: 'We were convinced that management never read beyond the first few pages, so somewhere about page 7 of the green weenie we started making things up. We'd put in imaginary customers and fake calls. One week, on page 8, I reported a call on the President of IBM and none of the high-ups took any notice. Possibly that's because they were too busy reading the report by one of my colleagues who on the same day had been making a cold call on Ghengis Khan.'

The only good news for us in all this was that vast amounts of data had been collected by the call reporting system. And probably, if we watched out for fake calls and cleaned the data up a little, we had some raw material for an initial test of whether the problem was one of efficiency or effectiveness. We took two immediate actions. First, we persuaded management to suspend call reporting for a month so that people could put some of their attention into other tasks such as selling. This delighted the sales force. Second, we scooped up a truck load of existing call reports and took them back to our offices for analysis. We then took a deep breath and thought about what to do next. 'We must start by deciding whether we've got an effectiveness problem or an efficiency problem,' we decided, 'if we don't get that right, then we'll end up with another wrong solution.' But how could we decide with no better ammunition than a ton of call statistics? After much gloom, more coffee and even more cursing, we came up with two simple diagnostic measure that solved the problem. And, to our discredit as innovators, after all the coffee and curses, these measures weren't even original – we've since seen variations on them used by sales managers all over the world. Our first measure was a way to assess whether an efficiency problem existed. We called it the *suspect/prospect* ratio.

$$\text{Efficiency ratio: } \frac{\text{Suspects} \quad \text{[unknocked doors]}}{\text{Prospects} \quad \text{[doors where you've entered and found an opportunity]}}$$

The suspect/prospect ratio is a guide to the potential of a territory. The more suspects there are compared with the number of prospects, the more evidence that there's inadequate territory coverage. We defined a *suspect* as a potential customer, who had never been called on, where there might be a sales opportunity. Suspects were identified through telephone directories, business directories and similar sources. By the very nature of the identification process, there was no way to know whether or not a suspect really offered a sales opportunity. We only knew there was a door waiting for a knock, we didn't know what was behind it. A *prospect*, on the other hand, was a known quantity. A seller from

Xerox had visited the potential customer so the door had been opened at least to the extent that we could see some sales possibilities behind it. From looking at suspect/prospect ratios we learned:

- in the city centre territories, where general business activity had declined in the five years since territories were drawn up, there were very few suspects compared with the number of prospects. Most doors, in other words, had already been knocked on by Xerox salespeople
- in the suburbs, however, there were three suspects for every prospect. Business growth since the original laying down of territories meant that suburban territories were too large. Salespeople didn't have time to call on all the available opportunities. The suburbs definitely had an efficiency problem
- by redrawing the territories, so that city centre territories were enlarged while suburban territories were reduced, we were able to effect an improvement in efficiency.

In passing, we should note that our method for improving efficiency was territory configuration rather than activity management.

DIAGNOSING EFFECTIVENESS PROBLEMS

The suspect/prospect ratio proved a useful tool for looking at efficiency problems such as those created by uneven territory size. However, we also had reason to believe that efficiency would only be part of the productivity answer. In organizations with mid range sales, like this Xerox unit, there are usually effectiveness problems as well.

$$\text{Effectiveness ratio: } \frac{\text{Calls} \quad \text{[total number of selling calls made by salesperson]}}{\text{Orders} \quad \text{[number of orders resulting from those calls]}}$$

Our diagnostic tool for assessing whether effectiveness problems existed was a *call/order* ratio. From an analysis of call reports, we took the total number of calls made by each salesperson where the objective was to sell, rather than to resolve existing customer problems. We then compared this figure with the total number of orders resulting from these calls. We found an alarmingly wide range of ratios (Figure 5.9). While some salespeople required less than 10 calls to take each order, others were requiring over 30 calls.

We also had some data on how similar sales units were performing in terms of call/order ratios. Compared with other units, the one we were working with needed, on average, 20 per cent more sales calls to take

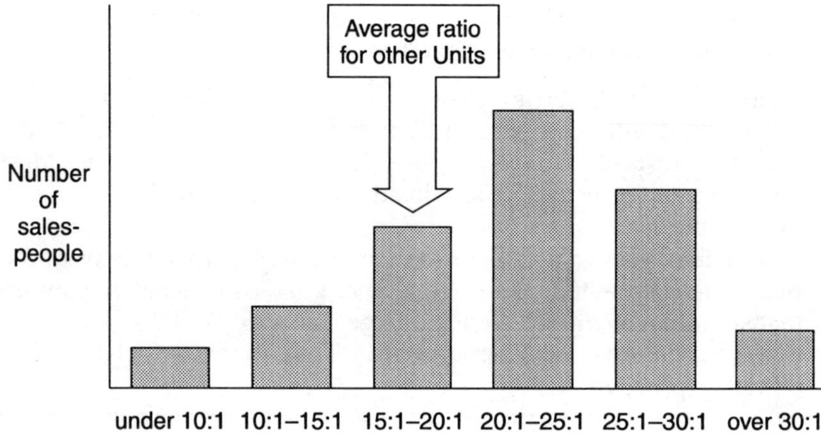

Figure 5.9 Call/order ratios show an effectiveness problem

each order. It looked as if there were some effectiveness problems to be solved. Our solution was to invest in two of the classic techniques for improving effectiveness – coaching and training. We trained managers to coach those salespeople who had a higher than average call/order ratio, using some of the sales effectiveness models we'll be describing later. Within six months, call/order ratios had fallen from an average of 22 calls required to take an order to 13 calls. More important, overall unit performance had improved significantly. Unfortunately we had no way to measure how much of this improvement was due to call/order changes in effectiveness and how much was the result of efficiency improvements and other managerial actions. Establishing the cause of sales productivity changes is a notoriously difficult area, more fully discussed in *Making Major Sales*.

LIMITATIONS OF CALL/ORDER RATIOS

The call/order ratio is a particularly useful diagnostic for effectiveness problems when the following conditions are present:

- the unit size of sale is small enough for each salesperson to be making a significant number of sales each year. There's no exact number here but, to give you a rough guideline, we probably wouldn't want to use call/order ratios where the average number of sales per salesperson per year is less than about 15.

- the value of each sale is within a relatively narrow price band. In our Xerox case, for example, most sales fell within a $15 000–$60 000 range. The average large order, in other words, was about four times the size of the average small order. In general, call/order ratios work well if this range between large and small doesn't exceed 6:1. Above that point, other factors enter into the equation and the call/order ratio has to be replaced by an alternative method reflecting sales volume rather than orders.

Most major account sales fail on one or both of these conditions, which is why the volume based method (Figure 5.5) is generally a better approach when you are dealing with high value sales.

MOVING FROM DIAGNOSIS TO ACTION

Our theme is the major sale, so – when we turn from diagnosis to action – we will look at things that individual managers can do to improve sales effectiveness; we will, too, cover such tools as training, coaching and account strategies that can help develop sales effectiveness. We shall not say much more here about efficiency tools. That's partly because efficiency tools usually have little impact on sales productivity in large sales. But there's also another reason. Efficiency is often an organizational rather than a managerial issue. In the Xerox case, for example, none of the sales managers had individual authority to take the required efficiency actions, such as territory reconfiguration or abolition of the existing activity management system. In contrast, each of them had considerable latitude in the effectiveness area. They could decide how to coach and train their people, they could influence account strategies, they could counsel and motivate. While efficiency can be tackled by decisions from the top, effectiveness lies in the hands of salespeople and their managers. Effectiveness is created at the level where there's most interaction with the customer.

Let's look more closely at this difference, to see why it can sometimes have a profound impact on attempts to improve sales productivity. Most of the actions that influence sales efficiency can be decided on an organizational level and implemented from the top downwards (Figure 5.10). What's more, we can make the decision this afternoon and, by tomorrow morning, we can put it into action. With Xerox, for example, the decision to suspend the activity management system was made at a meeting of ourselves, the Unit Manager and the National Sales Manager. At the same meeting we decided on the territory configuration. Within 24 hours, both those decisions were in full effect. Salespeople had new territories and the call reporting system was gone. In contrast, sales effectiveness decisions can't be made at the top and instantly

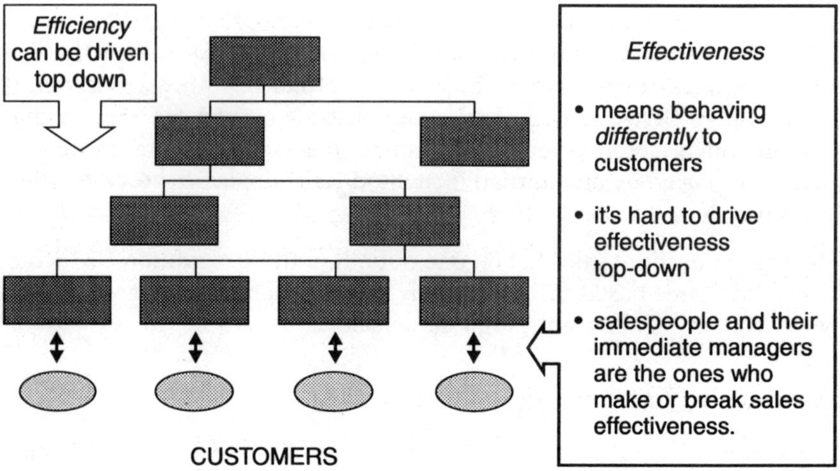

Figure 5.10 Who drives efficiency and effectiveness?

implemented. To be more effective, salespeople must behave differently to customers. That normally requires new skills which take a long time to learn. At Xerox, for example, it took six months of very hard and concerted effort from us, from the sales managers and – most of all – from their salespeople, before we had positive results to show.

Because efficiency measures can be implemented from the top more quickly and decisively than effectiveness measures, it's natural that efficiency strategies should have a greater appeal to most senior managers. And efficiency has another irresistible attraction. It's easier. Often, to increase efficiency, all you've got to do is to work harder – make more calls, knock on more doors, telephone for more appointments. You're doing more of something you already know how to do. Effectiveness, in contrast, is different – you need to do better rather than do more.

We used to joke that most National Sales Managers had a single button on their desk labeled 'The More Button'. When sales figures slumped, they pressed this More Button to get more calls, more activity and – they hoped – more sales. 'Somebody ought to tell them about the Better Button,' we suggested, 'just think what it could do for their results.' Over the years, we saw so many senior sales managers repeatedly pressing their More Buttons that we began to suspect that their Better Buttons had been disconnected. We were once trapped in New York in a blizzard. The city was closed down and we were sitting in an executive suite of the Fortune 100 Company waiting to see an executive vice-president who, because of the weather, had failed to arrive for work. We wandered around the deserted executive suite until we came to the chairman's office. On an irrational impulse we went in, just to see if there was a More Button on his desk. Sure enough, under the desk was a discreet little red button. To be fair, it was probably an unobtrusive way to signal to his secretary to interrupt when a meeting had gone on too long. But we had great delight in telling people that we'd actually seen the fabled More Button. Alas, sales productivity is too often an exercise in pressing the More Button. Sales effectiveness requires the elusive Better Button which, unfortunately, is not located on the chairman's desk.

LAST WORDS ON SALES EFFICIENCY

If we seem less enthusiastic about methods for improving sales efficiency than we are about methods for improving effectiveness, it's because we need to correct an imbalance. Over the years, sales effectiveness has received too little attention from senior sales management. In contrast, efficiency has had more than its just share. We've seen the reasons for this. Efficiency is easier, it can be introduced from the top by management decision and – perhaps most important in this short term age – it can be implemented quickly. No wonder that we so often see inappropriate efficiency measures, like rigid activity management, being introduced as an answer to effectiveness problems. It's our hope that the work of researchers like ourselves will help sales organizations redress this imbalance and find better ways to deal with effectiveness problems. We would like to think that the future of serious selling resides with the Better Button rather than with the More Button. Many sales managers were brought up in the days when pressing the More Button actually worked. Today, pressing the More Button brings disappointing results. In the future, it may become an even less useful sales management tool.

That's not to say that we should judge all efficiency measures as unthinking exercises of the More Button. Clearly they are not. Efficiency tools can have a powerful impact on sales productivity, even in the major sale. We've seen impressive figures from McKinsey, for example, showing the very tangible productivity benefits that can come from taking a thoughtful and systematic approach to sales efficiency. However, as McKinsey would be the first to admit, these results are always more impressive where the sales force is working under the twin conditions of small sales and a large number of potential accounts. In major accounts, effort spent in improving effectiveness almost invariably pays greater dividends.

	Sales efficiency	Sales effectiveness
Definition	How to get in front of the right customers, for the right amount of time at minimum cost	Once there, using skills and abilities to maximise your sales potential
Typical mechanisms for improving performance	Working *harder* mechanisms such as • time management • incentive payments • call reporting • activity management systems • territory design	Working *smarter* mechanisms such as • coaching • selling skills training • account strategy and account reviews • effectiveness models, framework & tools
Typical measures	• penetration • call rates • cost per call	• success rates • repeat business • sustainable margins

Figure 5.11 Sales efficiency and sales effectiveness – more distinctions

SUMMARY

In this chapter, we have made an initial summary of the twin components of sales productivity – sales efficiency and sales effectiveness (Figure 5.11). We have proposed that:

- sales effectiveness generally has more influence on success in major account selling than sales efficiency
- lack of efficiency can inhibit or prevent attempts to improve sales effectiveness
- many efficiency tools, such as activity management, turn out to be counter-productive in the major sale because they have unintended side effects
- efficiency can be influenced quickly and decisively by top management actions. Effectiveness, in contrast, must be developed at the level of the salesperson through longer term mechanisms such as coaching and training
- efficiency is usually an organizational issue; effectiveness is invariably a managerial issue. Top management may set strategies that determine efficiency but it's day-to-day sales management down in the trenches that has most influence on sales effectiveness.

Reading 6

How to offer concessions and agree terms: sales negotiation

N. Rackham

Reprinted from *Account Strategy for Major Sales*, Gower 1988, Ch. 7, pp. 123–47. Reprinted with permission.

On the surface, selling and negotiating may seem very similar. They have the same aim: reaching an acceptable business agreement. They both involve persuasion skills and they both require relationship building. But there's one big difference, and if you don't understand it your entire selling strategy is in trouble. The difference is this: when you're negotiating you have the ability to vary the terms in order to get an agreement. To negotiate, you must first have the authority to change something, such as price, delivery or contract terms. You don't normally expect to negotiate for a can of beans in a supermarket because the check-out person has no authority to change the price. But you do negotiate when you are buying a house, or a used car, because you're dealing with a vendor who has the authority to change the terms and to make concessions. In other words, when you're negotiating you're prepared, if necessary, to give something away in order to do business. That's not true of selling. When you're selling you don't give anything away. Your success rests on persuasion skills alone.

WHY IS THIS DIFFERENCE IMPORTANT?

The most common mistake people make when they're not clear about the difference between selling and negotiating is to begin negotiating too soon. In one large organization I worked with, the sales force was given negotiating authority to offer a discount of up to 10 per cent in order to get the business. Management, when introducing this negotiating authority, stressed to the sales force that negotiation was to be used only if it was absolutely essential to achieving the sale. When this new policy was evaluated six months later, it was discovered that the full discount had been offered in almost every case. The final result was equivalent to an across-the-board price cut of 9.8 per cent. This was, of course, disastrously different from the effect which the company had intended. They had given away their margins and, worse, hadn't even taken a higher sales volume in exchange. A closer analysis showed that the sales force had been offering customers the 10 per cent discount very early in the selling cycle as a means of gaining initial interest. Their salespeople were negotiating – giving away the maximum discount – when they should have been selling. Late in the selling process, when the discount

Negotiating too soon

Ian Gilmore sold document binding machines in the office products market. He was one of his company's most successful salespeople and, because of that, he was given responsibility for several national accounts including an engineering organization which had potential for a very large contract.

At a company sales meeting it was announced that the national accounts representatives, including Ian, would be given the power to negotiate substantial discounts for bulk purchases. And, as often happens at such meetings, management issued dire warnings about how this negotiating authority was only to be used when absolutely necessary. Ian wasn't much concerned about the warnings, he was too delighted at the thought of being able to offer a discount. 'This will make life a lot easier', he thought to himself. One reason for Ian's delight was that he'd just heard that his big engineering customer had decided to produce most of their documents internally and, inevitably, they would need to buy a substantial number of document binding machines. 'What a break,' Ian thought, 'in the same week I find that my biggest customer has finally decided to introduce binders and now I'm given the power to negotiate discounts. This sale is being handed to me on a plate.'

The next day Ian rushed to visit the engineering company buyer. 'Good news,' he told her, 'Because you're a potential national account, I'm able to offer you a special quantity discount which is up to 15 per cent below our published prices.' The buyer was delighted. 'That's really good news,' she told Ian, 'and I'm sure that it will make us much more interested in your machines.'

A month later the engineering company published specifications and invited bids from Ian and three of his competitors. 'I'm glad I was able to offer that extra discount,' Ian told his boss, 'it's helped us get in the door.' The selling cycle progressed until, ultimately, only Ian and one competitor remained. In his final proposal Ian emphasized that, with his special discount, he was almost 10 per cent cheaper than his competition. He was confident that his price advantage would give him the business. The day

> before the decision was due, the buyer called Ian and told him, 'Your competitor has just offered us a price reduction. We'd like you to think about whether you can do the same.' 'But I offered you a price reduction right at the start,' Ian protested, 'you've already had a greatly reduced price from us. I can't offer any more.' 'As you wish,' the buyer told him, 'but I warn you that your competitor's price cut has made a very positive impact on us'. Ian called his boss, 'We've got to reduce our price,' he insisted. 'Impossible,' his boss told him, 'you've already gone to the maximum special discount. We can't do more.' There was nothing Ian could do. The following day he learned that he'd lost the sale.
>
> Ian's mistake was to begin negotiating too soon. He offered his maximum discount as a means of creating interest. He would have been more successful if he'd followed his competitor's example and waited until nearer the decision when his price concession would have maximum impact. Negotiating too soon is the commonest mistake of inexperienced negotiators.

could have been a powerful tool in negotiating for the business, it was no longer available. It had already been given away and its impact lost.

There are many other case studies I could quote of sales organizations which have made the mistake of allowing their people to negotiate price if that was necessary to take the business. Results of this strategy have almost invariably been disappointing. In most cases salespeople have offered the reduced price too soon in the sale and consequently their concessions have had minimal impact or have resulted in giving away more than was necessary.

THE KEY RULE: NEGOTIATE LATE

Cases such as these are not isolated examples. Most people begin negotiating much too soon. Successful sales negotiation depends on a clear understanding of one key rule: NEVER NEGOTIATE BEFORE YOU MUST. The earlier you give concessions, the less impact they will have. Don't begin to modify your terms until it's clear that you have no alternative. Negotiation never has been, and never will be, a substitute for effective selling. There are obviously good business reasons for waiting as long as you can before negotiating and, once negotiation becomes inevitable, for making as few concessions as possible. Why make costly concessions in a negotiation if you can get the same business by using your selling skills without giving so much away?

There are also good psychological reasons for holding back as long as possible before negotiating. By giving things away early, you may create an expectation that even larger concessions will follow later. And as we've said, a concession given early has less impact than the same concession offered late in the sale.

Why don't early concessions work? After all, you would expect that giving concessions to the customer early in the sales process would get you in the door, establish goodwill and put you one step ahead of the competition. However, it's not a good strategy to begin with concessions because you are influencing the wrong half of the customer's value equation. As Figure 6.1 shows, in making any decision to purchase, customers must balance two opposing elements. One of these is the seriousness of the problems which your product would solve. The other is the cost of your solution, measured in terms of money, inconvenience or risk.

If the problem is so serious that the cost of solving it seems small in comparison, then the customer will probably buy. But sometimes it's the other way round. The problem may not seem significant enough to justify the price of your solution. In this case, the customer will probably continue to live with the problem or will look for a cheaper source of help. In selling, you generally try to build customers' perception of problems, but in negotiating you tend to concentrate on the other side of the value equation. By making concessions during negotiation, you attempt to reduce the side concerned with cost. If, for example, you offer a 5 per cent discount, what you are doing is making your product solution seem less expensive to the customer. If you've failed to build a

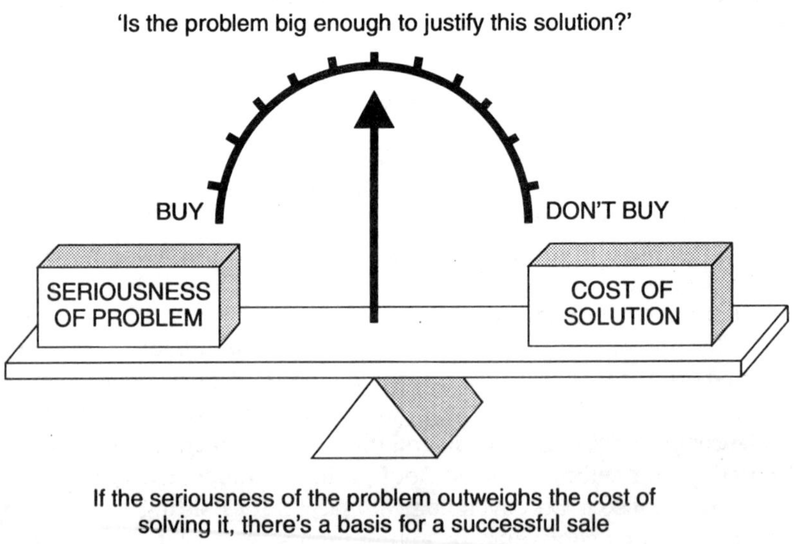

Figure 6.1 The customer's value equation

Which side of the value equation?

An overhead projector dealer authorized the salesforce to offer a 15 per cent discount to corporate clients buying two or more projectors. In other words, the salesforce was given the authority to negotiate price. One of the salespeople was John Connally. To gain interest from his prospects, he usually mentioned, in setting up the appointment, that he could give a discount. By doing this he was operating on the 'cost of solution' side of the customer's value equation, making his solution seem cheaper than expected. Predictably, his offer of a discount was a remarkably effective attention-getter allowing him to set up an increased number of meetings. However, because the projectors he was selling were expensive, even with a 15 per cent discount he had no real price advantage over most of his competitors. Although his order rate rose a little, it wasn't enough to compensate for the lost profit from a 15 per cent price reduction.

His lack of success convinced John that he should change strategy. So he shifted his attention to influencing the other side of the customer's value equation. Instead of initially promising a specific discount, he used terms like 'very competitive' to gain an interest without giving anything away. When customers asked about price or discount, he would reply, 'That would depend on things like quantity or which machine best meets your needs. Let me get an understanding of those needs and then I'll be able to give you a price.' Turning to the 'seriousness of problem' side of the equation, he uncovered dissatisfactions and built up their implications. In one case, for example, he found that the customer's present projectors would sometimes overheat. As a result, more than $2000-worth of damage had been done to one set of transparencies. Because he was able to show that his products were cooler in operation, he took an order on the spot for three new projectors without giving any discount. In the customer's mind, a problem which could cause thousands of dollars worth of damage was severe enough to make John's price differential seem insignificant. Increased attention to developing problems meant that John sold more effectively and therefore took more business. And, by selling better, there were fewer occasions when he was forced to negotiate discounts.

sufficient need before offering your price concession, then you've adopted a risky and potentially expensive strategy.

The case of John Connally is a simple one in a straightforward selling situation. But even in complex sales, the same principle applies. Give your primary attention to developing the 'seriousness of problem' side of the customer's value equation. It's better to get the business by building stronger needs than by trying to make your solution cheaper.

NEGOTIATION: AN EXPENSIVE WAY TO RESOLVE CONSEQUENCES

Using negotiation too early, so that it becomes a substitute for selling, is the most obvious mistake which sellers make. Giving away concessions early in the sales process is not the best way to gain customer interest. But there's another less obvious area where people make the mistake of negotiating when it would be far more effective to be selling instead. This danger point comes at the end of the cycle, just when negotiation would seem the most sensible strategy for getting the business.

Sometimes, as the final purchasing decision approaches, customers experience concerns or fears about the Consequences of buying from a particular vendor. These Consequence issues are rarely expressed openly by the customer but may nevertheless exist under the surface. Typical Consequence issues might be a customer's doubts about the stability of a vendor, concerns over the integrity of the seller, or worries about how the customer will convince key internal people that the decision is the right one. As we saw in the last chapter, customers may be reluctant to express some of these reservations directly and may therefore choose to raise them in the respectable form of price issues. We once carried out a follow-up study of fifty lost sales where the customer had turned down a vendor on the stated grounds of price. Interviews with these customers revealed that in 32 cases out of 50, price was only a secondary concern. The real grounds for rejecting the vendor were unresolved. Consequence issues.

In cases like these, where price isn't the real concern, how effective will it be to attempt to negotiate by making price concessions? Almost certainly negotiation isn't the best answer. It will be more effective to uncover and resolve the Consequence issue, as this next case study shows.

When price isn't the issue

Two small vendors were competing with a computer giant in selling a central electronic filing system. The customer was concerned that in the highly volatile state of the computer industry the small vendors might not survive. Naturally, given that the decision involved several hundred thousand dollars, the customer was afraid of buying an installation from someone who might go out of business and leave the system unsupported. This type of concern isn't easy to express. So the customer, as often happens, chose the easy way out and raised price as a reason for not wanting to go ahead. One vendor took these price concerns at face value and revised their proposal, shaving another 4 per cent off the cost of the system. The effect on the customer was opposite to the one intended. 'They must be desperate for business, it's a bad sign, we should steer clear of them' was the consensus among members of the customer's purchasing committee.

The second small vendor adopted a different approach. 'We're already cheaper than the big competitor', they reasoned, 'so price is a smokescreen for some other concern. We'd better find out what the real problem is.' By probing for the Consequence issues, they revealed the customer's concern about their stability. They then arranged series of actions designed to reassure the customer, including a meeting with the vendor's bankers, discussions with existing key accounts and a confidential inspection of the vendor's order books. Reassured, the customer went ahead and signed the contract at the originally proposed price. The first small vendor who, in reality, was every bit as financially viable as the second, lost the business by negotiating when there was still an important selling job to do.

Larger vendors must also contend with Consequence issues, although these may take a different form. For example, it's common for customers to have concerns such as, 'How do I explain this to my MD who prefers their competitor?' Negotiation about price, delivery or support won't make the fundamental fear go away. It's better to resolve the real issues, rather than to bargain your way through a smokescreen.

SHOWSTOPPERS

So far we've talked about when *not* to negotiate. We've said:

- Don't negotiate early in the selling cycle: negotiation should never be a substitute for selling.
- Don't try to negotiate your way out of Consequence issues or non-specific concerns.

In summary, the best strategic advice is negotiate late and negotiate little. But, however well you sell and however hard you try to avoid negotiation, there will be times when the customer will not do business unless you can change your product offering or your proposed terms. These are the showstoppers – barriers to moving forward which can't be overcome by selling skill alone. For example, a couple of weeks ago one of my customers called to ask whether we could bid on a consulting contract which involved designing and delivering a programme in French. The sale was clearly in Evaluation of Options phase. The customer had identified a need to provide a programme for French-speaking salespeople. By inviting bids from consulting firms like mine, the customer was beginning the process of choosing between vendors. Normally, we'd feel this would be much too soon in the selling cycle for us to begin negotiating. However, the reality was that we didn't have the capability to design a complex programme in the French language. We faced a showstopper. Either we would lose the sale or we'd have to negotiate an alternative such as designing a programme in English and getting the client to translate it into French. Selling skill alone couldn't solve the problem because it couldn't alter the fact that the customer had a need we were unable to meet. Unless we could find an acceptable alternative way to satisfy the customer's specification, we couldn't bid on the contract.

Most showstoppers arise because the customer has needs or requirements which you can't meet. But it's not only the customer who introduces showstoppers. Sometimes the seller's company can create them too. My organization, for example, has a policy that we won't provide sales training for companies selling tobacco products. More than once that's been a showstopper which has prevented us from doing business.

There are two pieces of strategic advice for dealing with showstoppers. First, be sure that the barrier is genuinely a showstopper. I've heard negotiators talk of showstoppers when a competitor has access to a decision maker and they don't, or when their price is marginally higher than competition. These are difficult selling situations but they are not showstoppers. The definition of a showstopper is that it's a barrier which is insurmountable using your present products or terms. You can't move forward unless you change your approach in some way, for example, by offering a different product, different terms or a creatively different approach. If you treat every competitive disadvantage as a showstopper it leads you into making too many concessions too early in the sale.

The second piece of advice is to deal with showstoppers relatively speedily. If you identify a potential showstopper, address it quickly, don't procrastinate. One of the common strategic mistakes I see in less experienced people is that they generally wait as long as possible before confronting any showstoppers. Their reasoning, I imagine, is that they want to build up a positive relationship with the customer first. They believe that the customer will be more likely to make concessions, or even give way entirely on the showstopper, if the tough issues are avoided until the last possible moment. But, plausible though this may sound, it's not what most experienced negotiators believe. If it's a real showstopper, then by definition it's likely to prevent the sale, so the sooner it's raised with the customer the better. If it's so serious that there's no way around it, if, in other words, it stops the show, then by raising it you've made sure that neither you nor the customer has wasted unnecessary time in a fruitless selling cycle. But if, as sometimes happens, there are creative ways to remove the showstopper, then the sooner you and the customer start problem solving the better. Remember that we're talking here about real showstoppers – where the customer won't move ahead unless you radically change something. In order to advance the sale you may have to consider major modifications to your selling strategy, such as

- offering a completely different product
- substantially varying your price or payment terms
- drastically modifying your proposed approach.

None of these options will be desirable and sometimes none will even be possible, hence the name 'showstoppers'. Although our general advice is to negotiate little and late, showstoppers are an exception. By their nature you must negotiate or you're out of the sale. Showstoppers are the only things you should negotiate during the Recognition of Needs or the Evaluation of Options phases of the sale.

THE RIGHT TIME FOR NEGOTIATION

If you've been fortunate enough to progress through a sales cycle without any showstoppers, you may find that you've successfully resolved Consequences and there are now some final points remaining which need to be hammered out before the final decision can be made. This is the point in the selling cycle where negotiation is an effective strategic tool.

The first question to ask yourself before any negotiation, is 'Do I have the power to vary the terms?'. Unless you have authority to change something, such as delivery, support or contract terms, then you're not able to negotiate and it's dangerous to give the customer the impression that you can.

Everybody negotiates

People tend to think of negotiation as a process which only takes place formally across a bargaining table. As a result they see negotiating as a very unusual, and very threatening activity. This narrow view of negotiation is dangerous. It leads people who have little experience of formal negotiation to feel insecure and ill-equipped. 'I'm not a negotiator,' they typically say, 'so I don't know anything about how to negotiate.' If that's how you see negotiation, you're missing a vital point. Everyone negotiates, and most people have developed their negotiating skills to a higher level than they may realize. In an average day you're likely to be involved in dozens of negotiations. You negotiate about priorities at work and at home, about budgets, targets and use of time. Whenever a resource is scarce and there are competing views about how to use it, you are likely to be negotiating. So don't think of yourself as knowing nothing about negotiation or as being totally inexperienced. You've probably developed negotiating skills which you haven't recognized.

Defining negotiation

Negotiation, as we've seen, is more than just a formal bargaining process. That's too narrow a way to look at it. It's an integral part of our everyday life. Some writers, taking account of this, have defined negotiation in very broad terms as, 'any conversation with a purpose'. But that's too broad. A more balanced definition of negotiation is that it's an attempt by two or more parties to reach an agreement where the following three conditions are present:

1 *Both parties can vary the terms*
That's the difference between negotiation and selling. If you can't vary the terms, you must sell, you can't negotiate.
2 *The resource is scarce*
When there's enough of something we generally don't bother to negotiate about it. In a meeting where there's enough coffee to go around we don't negotiate about who should get a cup. But if there are eight people in the meeting and only enough cups for five, then coffee may become a negotiable issue. We negotiate about money and time because they are such scarce resources.
3 *Agreement and conflict exist simultaneously*
Every negotiation can be seen as two overlapping circles. In one circle are the things you want, in the other the things that the customer wants (Figure 6.2).

In the overlapping area there are needs in common to both of you. For example, the customer wants to solve certain problems. You also want to solve those problems, by selling your product or service. Some of the customer's requirements may not be in your circle. It's probable, for example, that getting the lowest price is desirable for the customer but doesn't suit you. Or you might want something, such as the business the account is giving to your competitors, which the customer will be unwilling to provide.

It's not a negotiation if your circle and the customer's don't overlap at all. When that happens, you've a customer who doesn't want what you have to offer and isn't prepared to pay for it. Without common ground, neither party has anything to offer the other, so there's no basis for negotiation. If your circles overlap completely, then that's not a negotiation either. It means that you and the customer are in complete agreement. If that's so, why negotiate? There's nothing to negotiate about. Just take the business.

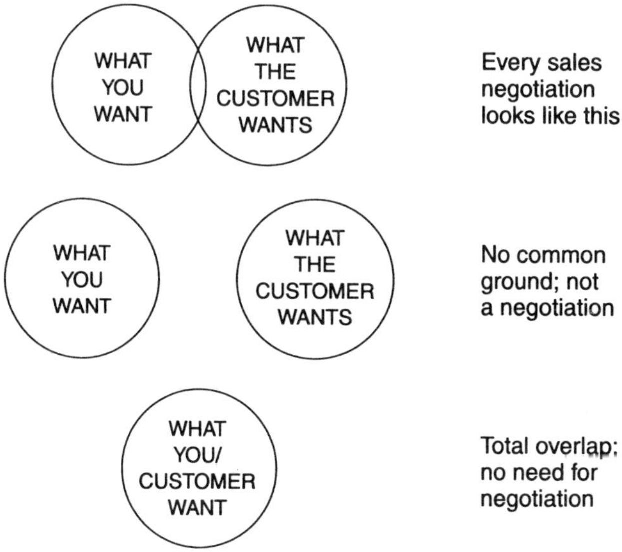

Figure 6.2 The overlapping circles of sales negotiation

The two circles diagram clearly shows one of the most important characteristics of negotiation. In every negotiation, potential agreement (the middle ground) exists side by side with potential conflict (the areas which don't overlap). One of the things which makes negotiation difficult is that you must deal with agreement and conflict in the same meeting. Negotiation simultaneously contains hopes and frustrations.

STUDIES OF EXPERT NEGOTIATORS

Some years ago, with the help of Bill Allen, I studied 51 expert negotiators during 107 negotiating sessions. By comparing the behaviour of these experts with results from a parallel study of average negotiators, we found that the experts showed marked differences in how they handled negotiations.

We defined an expert negotiator as one who:

- was rated as effective not only by the negotiator's own company but by the other party in the negotiation as well
- had a proven track record of negotiating complex deals successfully
- had a low incidence of implementation problems, so that once an agreement was negotiated it was carried through with a high level of customer satisfaction.

Short-term versus long-term

Many of the books you see on airport bookstands about how to negotiate are based on techniques for gaining a short-term advantage over a person you'll never see again. These books usually contain clever tricks and deceptions for pressuring the other party. Beware. In a complex selling environment there's no place for tricks and gimmicks. The lessons in these books only work in one-off negotiations where you don't expect to have further relationships with the customer. They are dangerously counterproductive if your objective is to build an effective long-term business relationship.

The skills and strategies which we investigated were those needed for developing a solid basis for future business. It's worth noting that the expert negotiators were chosen not just for their negotiating skill but also because the deals they negotiated were implemented successfully and therefore contributed to an effective long-term customer relationship.

The main purpose of our studies was to build behavioural profiles of skilled negotiators. We weren't specifically studying strategy. However, our contact with the expert negotiators gave us opportunities to talk with them about strategic issues. From our conversations, and from watching them during actual negotiations, we were able to draw some conclusions about common factors in their approach to negotiating strategy. We observed five ways in which the skilled negotiators seemed to execute strategy differently from their less skilled counterparts. These were:

- focusing on areas of maximum leverage
- establishing and narrowing ranges
- planning and using questions
- separating understanding from agreement
- rigorously testing for misunderstanding.

Let's look at these in turn and see how the points we observed in each area can help you implement an effective negotiating strategy.

Focusing on areas of maximum leverage

When less experienced negotiators meet to plan the negotiating strategy, price reduction tends to be the most discussed element. Inexperienced negotiators generally think of concessions largely or solely in terms of price. I've sat through dozens of meetings watching sales teams plan their negotiating strategy for key accounts. With depressing frequency the issue of price emerges, predominates and finally swamps all other items. I recall one such meeting was opened by the team leader with the words, 'Gentlemen, there are three items on the agenda. The first is price, the second is price and the third is price. Then, if we've any time left over, there are some price issues we should discuss.' Sometimes these strategy meetings don't even mention the customer. All their energy is taken up working out how to persuade their own senior sales management to offer a bigger discount. Less experienced negotiators act as if price is the only concession that will have an impact on the customer.

It's different watching very experienced sales negotiators discussing concession strategy during a planning session. Although price is sometimes the central topic of the strategy discussion, it's more likely that experienced negotiators will focus instead on other potential concession areas. The first question skilled negotiators ask themselves when they think about making a concession is, 'how important will the concession be to this customer?' It sounds such an obvious question that you might assume every negotiator asks it when thinking about concession strategy. Alas, that's not so. Most people don't ask themselves which concessions, of all the ones they might offer, will have the most impact on a specific buyer. I strongly suspect that the reason most people don't ask the question is that they couldn't come up with an answer. And the reason they haven't an answer is that they've not done a good job of uncovering decision criteria during the Evaluation of Options phase.

The better you understand a buyer's decision criteria, the easier it will be for you to decide which concessions will have maximum leverage during the negotiation. If, for example, you've discovered that early delivery is a crucial criterion to a customer and that price is only moderately important, then a concession which offers delivery a week early might have more impact than a sizeable price cut. Unfortunately for many salespeople, they haven't been trained to uncover decision criteria. As a result they never discover what's crucial and what's incidental to the buyer in making the decision; but their lack of knowledge doesn't entirely explain why they should assume that price is the only important decision criterion. Why do such people act as if a price reduction will outweigh all other concessions in its impact? There are several reasons. For example:

- *They don't see how decision criteria influence concession impact.* When you stop to think about it, it's obvious that if you can give a customer a concession in an area which is crucial, then you'll have much more impact than by giving a similar size concession in an area which is incidental. For example, assume you've a potential customer who is not particularly sensitive to price but whose most crucial decision criterion is that the equipment has good after sales service. This customer might be greatly impressed if you offered an extended warranty as a concession because your offer is in an area which is perceived as crucial. Offering the warranty would cost you much less than, say, a 5 per cent price reduction and would have, in this case, much more impact. In contrast, you might have another customer who hasn't even thought about after sales service and who would be totally unimpressed by the offer of an extended warranty. But obvious though this is, most people don't automatically think about how the impact of a concession depends on the importance of a decision criterion. Consequently, for most salespeople, a direct $5000 price concession feels as if it must be worth more to the customer than $4000 worth of concessions in terms of other commonly negotiable items like warranties, delivery or training support. But if, for example, it's training support which is crucial to the customer, then a $1000 of increased support may easily psychologically outweigh $5000 of price reduction.

- *They are misled by customer references to price.* We saw in Chapter 6 that customers tend to make more frequent references to price late in the selling cycle during the Resolution of Concerns phase. And, as we also saw, many of these references are a smokescreen for deeper Consequence concerns. Less experienced salespeople generally take price concerns at their face value. They will usually go back to their company and seek price concession authority from their sales management rather than try to uncover and resolve consequence issues.

Focusing on areas of maximum leverage

An example of how to maximize negotiating leverage was given us by a seller in the Computer Assisted Design business. He told us about a competitor, named Paul K., who was competing against him for a CAD contract. The customer was a high prestige engineering consultancy whose offices were located in a beautiful old mansion just outside Boston. Paul K's system was about 8 per cent more expensive than his rival's but, because the engineering firm was so well known, Paul's manager thought that this was an important enough account to justify negotiating additional price discounts if necessary. So he told Paul, 'Get this business at all costs. I'll let you cut our price by 10 per cent if you need to, so that we come in a little below the competition.'

Paul was a very skilled seller and he had uncovered a crucial decision criterion which he hoped would make a price cut unnecessary. He had noticed during the Evaluation of Options phase that the customer had questioned him closely about whether the equipment could be installed without damage to the building. 'We're asking all vendors about this,' the customer told him, 'because this is a fine historic building and we don't want you knocking holes in it when you install your communications cables.'

In the final selection process the customer was negotiating with Paul and his competitor. The competitor, equally anxious to get this high prestige business had made a significant price cut which made Paul's machines approximately 20 per cent more expensive. Paul knew that, even with the authority to make a 10 per cent price cut, he couldn't match the other vendor on price. So he played his trump card. 'You said that it was crucial to install this equipment without any damage to the building,' he reminded the customer. 'We believe we've found a way to do that. We propose to employ a skilled craftsman to install ductwork so that it will be invisible. The whole installation will be under the supervision of an expert in historic buildings. But unfortunately, because this will be costly work, I can't offer you any additional price concessions.' 'That's fine', replied the customer, 'if you're prepared to install the way you're describing, then that's far more important to me than a few thousand dollars' price reduction.'

Paul got the business. When all the costs of the expert installation were added up afterwards, they amounted to an equivalent of only a 1½ per cent price reduction. He succeeded because he realized that the value of concessions are measured by the customer more in terms of the importance of decision criteria, than in terms of dollars. His competitor (who told us this story) failed because he didn't understand that simple principle. He told us the story to illustrate the incomprehensible nature of customer behaviour. 'I was offering a discount which was ten times the value of their installation gimmick,' he complained, 'and I still lost the business. I can't understand why.'

Experienced negotiators have often told us how important it is to understand decision criteria in order to find which concession areas will offer maximum leverage. I recall that we trained some major account salespeople in the Health Sciences Market Division of Kodak in how to uncover decision criteria. Bill Irvine, who was at that time a Kodak negotiator deeply involved in major account negotiation, called me to say how much easier it was to negotiate after the salespeople had been trained. 'Since the training,' he told us, 'I'm getting a much more useful briefing from salespeople. Instead of just price, price, price, I'm hearing about a far wider range of negotiable issues which are important to the customer, like technical support or customer training.'

ESTABLISHING AND NARROWING RANGES

Some of our earlier work in negotiation showed that less skilled negotiators tend to set fixed point objectives, while skilled negotiators tend to set objectives in the form of ranges. Let me give you an example to show what this means. Assume that there's a negotiation pending where it's necessary to make a price reduction in order to get the business. A less skilled negotiator, planning a strategy for this negotiation, will tend to think of a *fixed point* when considering price reduction. So, typically, the negotiator might decide, 'I'll reduce the price by $5600' or 'I'll offer a 3 per cent reduction'. The figures in these examples – $5600 and 3 per cent – are examples of fixed points. In contrast, when skilled negotiators plan strategy, they usually think in terms of ranges. In an equivalent situation a skilled negotiator would be more likely to decide, 'I'll reduce the price by somewhere between $4000 and $5800' or 'I'll offer a reduction of between 2 per cent and 3½ per cent'. Put this way, it sounds as if the less skilled negotiators are precise and the more skilled negotiators are vague. The unskilled negotiators seem to know what they want, while the skilled negotiators sound as though they haven't really thought carefully about their objectives. But nothing could be further from the truth. The reason why skilled negotiators think in terms of ranges is to keep maximum flexibility during the negotiation. As the negotiation progresses, skilled negotiators will gradually narrow the range until, finally, they can agree a fixed point with the customer. So, in essence, less skilled negotiators tend to jump straight to a fixed point, while more skilled negotiators, although they end up at a fixed point, only arrive there after setting a range and progressively narrowing it.

This is one of those findings where, at first, it's hard to see how to use it to help your own negotiating strategy. When I've been teaching sales negotiation programmes, I've found that most people react with a polite yawn to the discovery that skilled negotiators set ranges and then progressively narrow them. I remember, during a coffee break in one such programme, overhearing one member of my class saying to another, 'The only reason why he made such a big deal about setting ranges is that he had fifteen minutes to spare before coffee and he didn't want to start on a serious topic'. 'Yes', agreed the other, 'after all, *everybody* knows how to set a range'. I wish that were true. The reality is that very few salespeople know how to set effective ranges and even fewer know how to narrow them progressively towards a point of agreement. Let's look in more detail at how to set and narrow ranges by considering a typical price negotiation.

Step 1 Set your upper and lower limits

At the start of most price negotiations all you usually know is that the customer is expecting some kind of price reduction and that, without it, you're likely to lose the business to your competition. It's at this stage, as we've seen, that the inexperienced or unskilled negotiator will often set an arbitrary fixed point, say a 10 per cent discount, and offer it to the customer. What's wrong with offering a fixed discount? Mostly that, at this early stage in the negotiation, you don't have enough information to know whether a 10 per cent discount is too high or too low. If, for example, it turns out that the customer will accept 5 per cent, then by offering a 10 per cent you've unnecessarily given away your margins. So, until you've had an opportunity to assess the customer's expectations more accurately, you should start by setting a broad range. The purpose of this first range is to help you establish your upper and lower limits. As we'll see later, you will have to narrow it before it can help you during the negotiation itself. The top of your initial range, as Figure 6.3 shows, is what you'd like best. In this case, you'd ideally like no discount at all, so you might set 0 per cent as the initial top of your range.

At the bottom of your range comes the highest discount you would be prepared to offer. Let's assume that, at an absolute maximum, and if you successfully convinced your management to treat this customer as a strategically important account, you could get the authority to offer a 20 per cent discount. Then the initial lower limit of your range would be 20 per cent and the top would be 0 per cent. You've now established your territory. You're negotiating a discount which will be somewhere between 0 per cent and 20 per cent. This is a very simple example where your upper limit offers no concession at all and your lower limit is the most that your management will allow you to give. In real life it's sometimes much less simple to establish limits, particularly at the lower end of the range, where you're trying to decide on the maximum concession which you would ever offer this customer. This is a fascinating and important area of negotiating strategy, but it's too detailed to discuss in a general work like this. If you'd like to read more, then try Ury and Fisher's book, *Getting to Yes* (Hutchinson, 1983). You'll find that their concept of a BATNA (the Best Alternative To Negotiated Agreement) gives useful advice on how to set the lower end of a negotiation range.

Step 2 Refine your upper limits

Your initial range will normally be too broad to serve as an effective negotiating tool. The upper point on your range, because it's what you'd like best, will almost certainly be an unrealistic expectation, like the 0 per cent discount in this example. So you must temper your upper limits by deciding what's the realistic best case. It's important to be realistic when you refine your upper limit because if you're too high in negotiating with the customer you face risks such as:

- The customer may walk away from the negotiation and decide not to negotiate further because, in the customer's eyes, your position is unrealistic. If you miscalculate your initial position in this way, there's

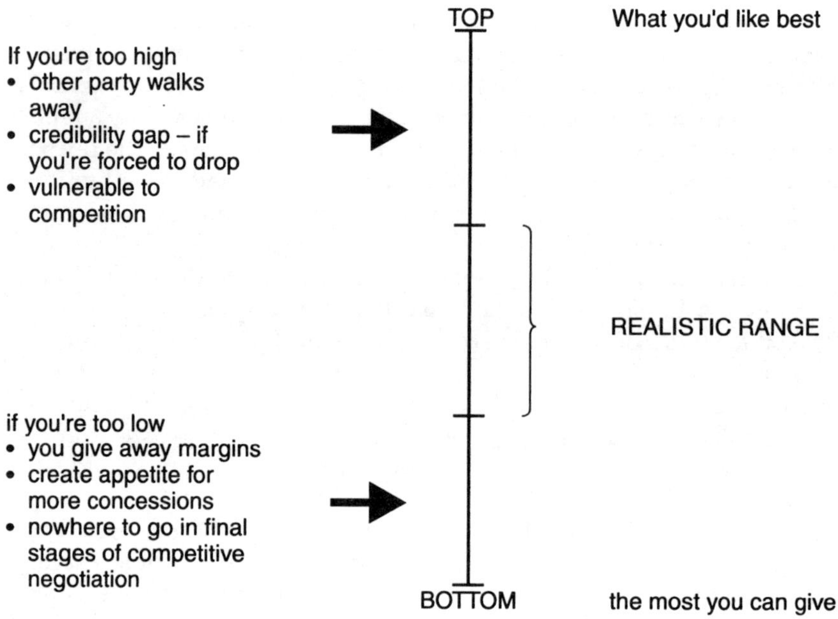

Figure 6.3 Using ranges

a good chance that you'll make the customer more entrenched and more demanding. There's some evidence that people who initially negotiate for an unrealistically high point on their range, will end up making greater final concessions than those whose initial offers are less at an extreme.

- You may create a credibility gap. Suppose, for example, you offer an initial 1 per cent concession, knowing that if the customer doesn't accept then you'll be quite ready to offer, shall we say, 8 per cent. Because your initial 1 per cent offer clearly wasn't a serious negotiating position, the customer will question whether your 8 per cent offer is just another negotiating ploy too. Remember that giving concessions often creates an appetite for further concessions. The higher on your range that you start, the more concessions you'll be forced to give, and the more concessions the customer may come to expect from you.
- If you initial point is too high, then you may become vulnerable to competition. I recall sitting in a negotiation where the negotiator I was watching started right at the top of his range and offered only very small initial concessions. His strategy was to return the following day with larger concessions which, he hoped, would impress the customer

> and lead to an agreement. 'Talk tough to start with,' he told me, 'and you can always soften up later.' Unfortunately, his unrealistic starting position was unsatisfactory and irritating to the customer. As soon as we left the meeting the buyer telephoned a competitor. The competitor was prepared to make a more realistic offer and, as a result, the meeting intended for the following day never took place. The sale was lost.

So your first step in narrowing the range is to set a realistic upper limit. It must be high enough to give you some negotiating latitude but low enough not to violate the customer's expectations. It must also take into account your competitive strength. In our example we had an initial range from 0 to 20 per cent. Refining the upper limit would mean that you must start from a more realistic point than 0 per cent. Suppose you're not quite sure what the customer will demand but you think it probable that the buyer will be expecting at least an 8 per cent discount and probably more. If you were the competitive front runner, you might set, shall we say, a starting point of 6 per cent as your upper limit. In doing so you've established a realistic starting point but you've kept a couple of percentage points of negotiating latitude in hand. But if you were competitively in a weak position, you might decide that even an 8 per cent cut would not be enough and you might set a realistic upper limit of, shall we say, 12 per cent. Of course, as we've said a number of times earlier in this chapter, you have to be very careful not to use price reduction as a substitute for effective selling and, as we saw in the last section, you shouldn't be making price concessions if you can achieve negotiating leverage more effectively in other areas.

Step 3 Refine your lower limits

Next, turn your attention to the other end of your scale: the maximum you're prepared to concede. This end must also be refined. If your lower limit is too low you run risks such as:

- Giving away margins. If the customer isn't expecting a 20 per cent discount, you shouldn't let 20 per cent enter into your thinking. The more you allow yourself to see 20 per cent as acceptable, the more likely you'll be to offer larger discounts than you need. So, irrespective of whether you have the authority to offer a 20 per cent discount, your range should never be greater than the customer's probable expectation. In our example, supposing the customer's probable expectation was 15 per cent, then that should become the bottom of your range rather than 20 per cent.
- If your lower limit is too low, you may create appetite for further concessions. In our example, suppose that you believe the customer is

expecting a discount of 10 per cent. The bottom of your range is 20 per cent, so you've a lot of latitude. When the customer asks you for a 10 per cent price cut, because it's so comfortably within the initial range you've set yourself, you're likely to agree. Unfortunately, if you agree too readily, it will be concluded that, because you gave in so easily, the buyer should have asked you for more. You may be pressed for additional price concessions, or concessions may be sought in other areas: such as delivery, add-on extras or after-sales support.

- If the bottom's too low, then you've nowhere to go. By negotiating near the bottom of your range, you've left yourself with very little latitude in the event of a competitive negotiation. If a competitor unexpectedly makes a further price cut you won't be able to match it if you're already at or near the bottom of your range.

Start too low and you've nowhere to go

Julian G was negotiating a consulting project with a bank. The bank had chosen three final potential consultants from an initial list of twenty. Julian's firm was one of the three. All three finalists were well equipped to do the job so, in preparing a negotiation strategy, Julian and his manager decided that price would be the key issue rather than other factors such as professional qualifications or experience. One of the three competing firms was very expensive and Julian wasn't worried about them. But the other competitor was almost exactly the same price. 'We should take the initiative here,' Julian suggested to his manager. 'We know we could afford a 10 per cent discount on fees. Let's get in first and offer the discount, so that we become the front runner.' Julian's manager agreed. The following day Julian met with the bank and offered the 10 per cent discount. As he'd expected, the bank was delighted. However, what he didn't expect was that the bank's negotiators immediately pressed him for further concessions in other areas: in particular they wanted the work to be carried out on site, which would add about 4 per cent to Julian's costs. 'I'm sorry', Julian told them, 'I've already given you everything I've got; there's no way I can add another 4 per cent to my costs.' Still, he wasn't unduly worried because he'd taken the initiative and his overall price was less than that of his competitors. He was especially pleased to hear during the meeting that his closest competitor had just offered a 5 per cent reduction, which meant that his own 10 per cent offer really looked the more favourable.

In the week which followed, the bank eliminated the most expensive competitor, leaving only Julian and his rival, who was now priced about 5 per cent higher than Julian. Then, early one morning, the bank phoned Julian. 'We're going to make the decision today,' they told him, 'We'd like you to think about whether you could include the extra on-site expenses in your price.' Julian and his manager spent all morning recalculating their figures. 'There's no way we can absorb that extra cost', his manager decided, 'we're on a very slim margin as it is'. 'But we've got to do something,' said Julian, 'because I sense that our competitor may be offering another reduction.' In the end, Julian's manager authorized him to absorb half the incremental on-site expenses: the equivalent of a further 2 per cent cut. Julian was delighted. He telephoned the bank with his offer and sat back to wait for their decision, confidently expecting that he'd won the business.

At the end of the day he received the awaited call from the bank. 'Sorry,' they told him, 'the business went to your competitor who was prepared to absorb all the incremental on-site expenses.' Julian was stunned. 'They only cut their price by an equivalent of 9 per cent,' he told his manager, 'while we cut ours by 12 per cent. I can't understand how they got the business.' Julian's mistake was that he started negotiating too near the bottom of his range. His strategy had the advantage that it made him an early front runner but, just before the decision when concessions really count, he ran out of negotiating latitude.

Step 4 Negotiate within your narrowed range

Once you've refined the top and bottom of your initial range, you've arrived at a realistic narrowed range which you can use for the actual negotiation. So, in our example, if we assume that you're in a strong competitive position and the customer isn't expecting a reduction greater than 15 per cent, your range might have narrowed from its initial field of 0 per cent to 20 per cent to a more realistic negotiating range of 6 per cent to 15 per cent. There are three useful rules for negotiating within your realistic range.

- *Start at, or near, the top of your range.* If you've narrowed your range realistically during your planning, then the customer shouldn't be surprised, or have any expectations violated, if you begin at the top of your range. Take our example of a 0 per cent to 20 per cent initial range which has now been narrowed to a 6 per cent to 15 per cent realistic negotiating range. If you started with the original top of your initial range and offered no concession at all, you'd almost certainly upset the customer's expectation and create a negative impact. But if you've set a realistic top of 6 per cent, then that would probably be your best opening position.
- *Make concessions in small increments.* Don't jump straight from a 6 per cent discount to, say, a 12 per cent or 13 per cent discount if you intend 15 per cent to be your bottom limit. Remember that the customer's negotiators are trying to judge how big a discount you're really

prepared to offer. If you make a large initial concession they are likely to judge that you've still got a long way to go. Moving from a 6 per cent concession straight to an offer of 12 per cent might unintentionally signal that you intend to give a lot more than 15 per cent and may cause them to pressure you for much more than you're able to give. On the other hand, if your initial concessions are relatively small, say an offer to increase from 6 per cent to 8 per cent or 9 per cent, then you signal that large extra concessions are less likely. Of course, you must also bear in mind that your concessions mustn't be too small. I once saw a multi-million dollar negotiation collapse because the negotiator, having been asked for a concession of about $85 000, infuriated the customer by coming back with an offer of less than $3000.

- *Signal the bottom by making smaller and smaller concessions.* Less experienced people generally give concessions until they reach the lower limit of their range and then they stop. But experienced negotiators don't just stop making concessions. They signal to the other side that they are approaching their limit by giving concessions more and more unwillingly and in smaller and smaller increments. They may also start making concessions reciprocal by saying, for example, 'If we give you extended maintenance, then you must give us an assurance that only trained and licensed operators will use the equipment'. So, if you feel that you've not much more you can give, make sure that your final concessions are small and are only offered under protest.

The ability to set and use negotiating ranges, which I've briefly described here, is an essential part of effective negotiation strategy. Whole books have been written on how to establish ranges. Many of these books, particularly the ones based on the mathematics of decision theory, are incomprehensibly complex. Even after three years of postgraduate study in statistics I can't understand some of them. Unfortunately this mathematical overkill has tended to give range-setting a bad name. That's a pity. Many practical negotiators have been frightened away from thinking about ranges because they are afraid they won't be able to understand how to use them. Like anything else, it's usually easy enough if you start simply. Follow the four steps I've discussed here:

- set your upper and lower limits
- refine your upper limit in terms of customer expectation and competitive strength
- refine your lower limit in the same way in order to arrive at a realistic range
- negotiate, starting at the top of your realistic range and making concessions in ever smaller increments until you reach agreement.

You'll find, if you follow these simple steps, that you can use the basic concept of ranges to improve the effectiveness of your negotiating strategy without getting into the complexities of decision theory models.

PLANNING AND USING QUESTIONS

The next general area of competence we observed in effective negotiators was in the way they used questions. In any form of persuasion, questions are central to success. People are persuaded much more effectively by questions than by statements. In selling, however well you describe your product, the questions you ask will have the greatest influence on whether you make the sale. Because negotiation is a form of persuasion, it's reasonable to expect that questions would be just as important to success in negotiation as they are in selling. Our research confirms this. Skilled negotiators ask lots of questions. People who don't use questions aren't likely to be effective negotiators.

Anyone who can sell successfully goes into negotiation with some useful questioning skills already established. And, although there are some differences in emphasis, there are also some differences in emphasis, there are also some clear parallels between the way questions work in selling and the way they can help you in negotiation. For example:

Questions reveal needs

In selling, a primary function of questions is to uncover and develop customer needs. Questions have a similar function in negotiation. Frequently customers put forward positions which you can't accept. For example, a customer might push you for immediate delivery when you can't supply for several weeks or months. The only way you can avoid deadlock is to ask questions to reveal the needs which underlie the position the customer is taking. So your questions might reveal that the underlying reason the customer wants immediate delivery is to allow payment from this year's budget rather than next. By finding ways to phase the payment, you may be able to alter the urgency of delivery dates.

The taking of fixed positions in negotiation often leads to a frustrating deadlock or stalemate where neither party is satisfied, and each becomes increasingly reluctant to shift. Vendors rarely win if the negotiation enters a stalemate. Using questions to break this kind of deadlock is one of the oldest and most useful of negotiating strategies. To understand how it works, it's important to be clear about the difference between a *position* and a *need*. When someone takes a position in a negotiation, they are adopting a narrow point of view based on just one possible solution to their underlying need. A need generally has several potential solutions, while a position is the single solution which the negotiator prefers. By getting behind the position and finding out what the need is which motivates it, you can often come up with acceptable alternative solutions.

The difference is easier to understand by taking a specific case. In this example, two negotiators take positions which could easily lead to failure:

Buyer: (*taking a Position*) We must have one of your technicians on hand 24 hours a day during the whole installation period.

Seller: (*responding with a Position*) I'm sorry, but my company's policy is not to provide resident technical support for an installation of this size.

What will happen now? Unless one side climbs down, there's unlikely to be progress. At best the two parties may bargain their way to an uneasy compromise which neither feels good about. How can you prevent this from happening in your negotiations? If the customer takes a fixed position, you can sometimes shift it by using questions to reveal underlying needs. For example:

Buyer: (*taking a Position*) We must have one of your technicians on hand 24 hours a day during the whole installation period.

Seller: Can I ask you a question: why would you need a resident technician?

Buyer: We must have that level of coverage.

Seller: Yes, but can you tell me why?

Buyer: Because we'll be putting some key work through the system and our whole business would suffer if there's a system failure.

Seller: Would you need to process this key work at night, or just during office hours?

Buyer: At this stage, while we're testing, the vital runs would be during office hours only. But we would be using the system round the clock for other work.

Seller: But the reason you want intensive technical support is for those important daytime runs?

Buyer: Yes.

Seller: Suppose the machine broke down, how quickly would you need it back in service so you don't suffer any serious business loss?

Buyer: Three hours would be the longest we could risk. Anything beyond that would be really serious: that's why I want one of your technicians on site.

Seller: Certainly a resident technician would be able to help you fix any minor system faults. But it sounds as if your real need is protection against systems failures that would take more than three hours to fix.

Even a resident technician can't guarantee you against the inevitable start-up problems of a new system.

Buyer: But that guarantee is what I need; three-hour maximum down time during office hours.

Seller: There may be an alternative way we could meet that need for you. For minor faults, our service people can guarantee you a one-hour response time during office hours. If something serious goes wrong, we can give you access to our own demonstration system as a back up. It's only twenty minutes away from here.

Questions expose problems

In both selling and negotiating, asking questions is a powerful way to uncover and develop problems. In selling, your objective is to uncover a problem your product can solve, to make that problem more significant and consequently more worth solving. Your objective in negotiating is usually a little different. Often, in a negotiation, you want to show that the position a customer is taking has problems or disadvantages. Rather than disagree directly with the customer's position, it can be more effective to reveal the difficulties by asking Problem and Implication Questions.

Asking about problems and their implications is particularly important as an acceptable means of exposing flaws and disadvantages in customers' proposals. This weakens customers' enthusiasm for their positions and makes them more receptive to any alternative solutions which you might introduce.

Questions reveal strategic information

In both selling and negotiating it's valuable to have as much information as possible about what the customer is thinking. In negotiation, this information is especially important. The more you know about the cards in the customer's hand, the easier it is to form an intelligent strategy for playing your own. Negotiation, as we've said earlier, involves an ability to make concessions: to vary the terms of the agreement. Unless you have an accurate picture of the customer's positions and the needs underlying them, it's hard to know which concessions you must make to get the business. The better the information you've uncovered, the better your strategy will be.

Questions control the discussion

In selling, the person asking the questions is controlling the discussion. The same is true in negotiation. But while it's generally accepted by both parties that the seller should ask most of the questions in a sales call, that acceptance is often challenged in negotiation. In negotiation, customers usually want to maintain control and may try to do so by asking most of the questions.

Many salespeople are surprised by this change in customer behaviour and respond to a sudden increase in customer questions by meekly answering each one. As a result, they leave negotiations having given customers a great deal of information and having found out very little in return. In short, they've lost control over the decision. Skilled negotiators don't let the other party use questions to control the negotiation. When two expert negotiators face each other, they even negotiate about who should be asking the questions. It's common to hear an effective negotiator say, 'I've answered one of your questions, now it's your turn to answer one of mine,' thus regaining control of the discussion.

Questions are an alternative to disagreement

Because negotiation always contains a possibility of conflict, the potential for disagreement is usually present. How do skilled negotiators handle situations where there's a potential conflict of views or positions? One of the most effective methods they use is to ask questions as an alternative to direct disagreement. For example, an unskilled negotiator might say, 'I disagree with your proposal because it would be unworkable.' A statement like this not only sets up a confrontational position, it also invites the other negotiator to ask the question, 'Why?'. The unskilled negotiator is now forced to defend the statement, giving the other negotiator opportunity to expose weaknesses in the reasons given.

In contrast, a skilled negotiator would be more likely to express any disagreement in the form of a question, such as, 'How would your proposal work in practice?' If a proposal really is unworkable, it will be hard to defend. So the negotiator who has asked the question is now in a strong position. And, by using questions instead of disagreeing, it will be easier for the other party to admit to difficulties without loss of face.

There's another bonus to putting disagreement in the form of a question. Suppose that the other side's proposal is workable. If you say, 'I disagree – it won't work', you commit yourself to an untenable position. You'll later be shown wrong and be forced to back down. But asking, 'How would it work in practice?' gives you a simple insurance policy. If their proposal does prove workable, you can gracefully accept it without losing face.

Questions give thinking time

We can only handle one complexity at a time. Whilst talking we can't simultaneously do a good job of thinking. If you are asked a question during negotiation, answering it will take most of your thought and attention. And while you are answering the question, with most of your attention focused on giving your answer, you can't adequately be thinking about your position or planning your next move. Many experienced negotiators use this to their advantage. When they are under pressure and need time to think, they will deliberately ask a question in an area where the answer will be time consuming but unimportant. While the other party is answering the question, they don't even listen to the answer. Instead, they use the time to plan their next move.

By asking questions you can take away some pressure and give yourself thinking time. Questions can also be used for the reverse purpose: to reduce thinking time for the other party and to exert pressure on them. One of the reasons why questions give control over the discussion is that the person answering questions is under pressure and unable to think, while the questioner gets a breathing space and can plan ahead.

Of all the tools and techniques which a negotiator has available, questions are probably the most important. A negotiator who doesn't ask questions is at a severe disadvantage. As Figure 7.4 illustrates, our research shows that skilled negotiators ask more than twice as many questions as average negotiators.

What is surprising about this research isn't the high level of questions used by skilled negotiators. After all, questions are clearly very powerful negotiating tools; any successful negotiator would be asking lots of them. What is unusual is the low level of questions which average negotiators

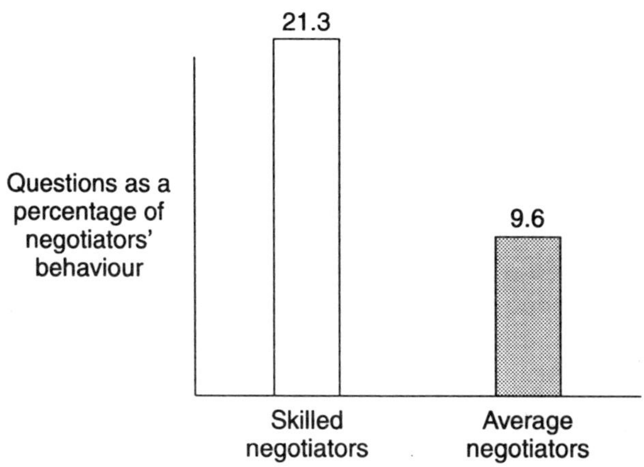

Figure 6.4 Asking questions

ask. Why is this so low? Even a totally inexperienced negotiator should realize that questions are important. But, strangely enough, many salespeople who are successful because of their ability to ask questions, suddenly stop asking them when they get into a negotiation. Unfortunately, people don't always apply their sales skills to negotiation. As a result, some experienced salespeople who would never dream of trying to sell by giving features, do almost the equivalent in negotiation. They try to persuade by giving reasons. The most important message we can offer to you as a negotiator is this: **reasons don't persuade**. Questions are just as crucial a part of successful persuasion in negotiation as they are in selling. The questioning skills which have helped you sell effectively will also help you negotiate.

Selling helps you negotiate

When we were looking for successful negotiators to include in our research study, Bill Allen introduced me to Tom T., one of the union negotiators in Esso. 'I'd judge Tom to be one of the half dozen best negotiators I've seen,' Bill told me. That was praise indeed: Bill had worked in high level negotiation all over the world and he knew what he was talking about.

We were able to watch Tom in several negotiations and, as Bill had promised, he was clearly very skilful. After one of these negotiations, in which Tom had successfully resolved a very difficult issue, I was talking to him over a cup of tea. 'Where did you get your training in negotiation?', I asked him. 'I've never been trained,' he told me, 'but I was in selling for eight years before I moved into labour relations. I've tried to treat negotiation as if I'm still selling. So I ask questions and I look for benefits for the other side. That sales approach has paid off for me: it's helped me handle some difficult negotiations.'

PLAN YOUR QUESTIONS IN ADVANCE

Average negotiators spend most of their planning time thinking about how they will explain their position to the other side. As a result they plan reasons, not questions. Good questions don't come any more automatically in negotiating than they do in selling. Planning the right questions is the foundation of a good sales call. It's equally important to plan them in negotiation. Before you go into any negotiation, produce a list of key questions which will elicit the following.

- *Uncover information* which will help you plan a better strategy. These are mostly factual questions and typical examples would be: 'How many units are we talking about?', 'Does it come into this year's budget?' or 'How has our competitor proposed to handle this issue?'.
- *Reveal underlying needs* which may be causing the customer to take a particular position. These questions typically ask, 'Why?'. Examples might be, 'Why do you want delivery so urgently', 'What's the reason for insisting on a six hour maintenance time?', or 'Is continuity of supply your real concern?'.
- *Expose problems* with the customer's position which may make it impractical or untenable. The purpose of these questions is to show disadvantages. They are similar to the Problem Questions you would use during a sales call. Examples might include, 'Could that cause a problem in this area?', 'Wouldn't that clause create difficulties with other suppliers?' or 'It sounds good in theory, but how would it work in your Denver laboratories?'.
- *Get agreement* from the customer to key points in your case. These questions get the customer to tell you the value of the points you wish to make. Typical questions might be, 'If we assigned a technical advisor to work with you throughout the implementation, what advantages would that have for you?', 'Why would it be useful to you to have the Q-unit installed first?' or 'It's clear that these payment terms would suit us, but wouldn't they have some value for you too?'.

By planning questions like these, and by asking them during the negotiation, you'll be more persuasive and therefore more effective. But remember that questions do need to be planned, they don't just happen. Effective negotiators, like effective salespeople, put time and effort into planning and preparation of their strategy.

SEPARATING UNDERSTANDING FROM AGREEMENT

A great deal of time is wasted in negotiation, and enormous frustration is generated, because each side commonly believes that the other isn't really listening and isn't interested in understanding another view. How does this happen? In most negotiations, people are reluctant to agree with points made by the other side because they are afraid that acceptance will weaken their case. As a result, when one side puts forward a point, the other side rarely shows any positive reaction to it. This is often interpreted as failure to listen or failure to understand. Consequently, the side putting forward the point will frequently repeat it several times at length, hoping that it will finally be communicated. This constant repetition slows the negotiation and creates unnecessary barriers between the parties. Skilled negotiators prevent this barrier from arising by continually expressing understanding of what the other side is saying, but doing so in a way which doesn't suggest agreement or acceptance. So they tend frequently to summarize their interpretation of what the other party has said. They use phrases like, 'If I'm understanding you correctly. . .' or 'What I think you're saying is . . .' By doing this they show that they are listening and, as a result, they reduce some of the time-wasting repetition which is such a common feature when inexperienced people negotiate.

RIGOROUSLY TESTING FOR MISUNDERSTANDING

The final difference we observed in how skilled negotiators implemented their negotiation strategies was that, throughout the negotiation, they continually probed and tested to ensure that both parties clearly understood the areas of agreement and, equally importantly, the potential areas of disagreement. What's the objective of a negotiation? The simple answer is that the purpose of negotiation is to achieve an agreement. But that's too simple. What's the use of an agreement if it can't be implemented successfully? Or if the customer later challenges important parts of it? The objective of a negotiation is not just to achieve an agreement, it's to achieve an agreement which works. A signature on a piece of paper is worth nothing if the whole contract collapses and results in recrimination and legal action.

WHY NEGOTIATIONS GO SOUR

Too many sales negotiations end up with a contract which later becomes a source of dispute between the parties. Why does this happen? Why do some implementations go sour? The most common reason can be traced back to the process by which the original agreement was negotiated. The average negotiator often thinks no further ahead than getting the signature on the contract. So, if there are potentially delicate areas where the customer might interpret the agreement differently – implementation schedules, warranty rights, penalty clauses or guarantees would be typical cases – the average negotiator may try to skate over them quickly, so they don't interfere with the all-important objective of getting the signature. So, unless the customer makes an issue of an area, the less skilled negotiator may try to rush ahead and get the agreement signed. But failure to establish a common understanding of a key point during negotiation can lead to expensive trouble afterwards. Worse, the longer a misunderstanding is allowed to go on, the harder it becomes to correct. We've said that the aim of a negotiation is to achieve not just an agreement but an agreement which works. And to survive all the tough and testing pressures of implementation, a successful agreement must be based on a common understanding between the parties. How do skilled negotiators ensure this common understanding? First, they recognize that it's important. They don't believe that leaving ambiguities alone will somehow make them go away. Bill Allen, who I regard as the best negotiator I've ever seen, had some simple maxims about negotiation which reflect the importance most skilled negotiators attach to making sure that each key point in an agreement is clearly understood by both sides. The advice he gave to other negotiators was:

- any point too delicate to stand up to rigorous discussion *during* the negotiation will never survive the strain of implementation after it
- ambiguities worsen like a cancer: an ambiguity during the negotiation grows into a misinterpretation afterwards. This, in turn, grows into the most fatal of all negotiating illnesses – mistrust
- you can't undo history: once mistrust exists, there's lasting damage. Misunderstandings which could have been cleared up earlier are magnified by mistrust into insurmountable barriers
- so when you're negotiating, *never* let misunderstandings or ambiguities go unchallenged.

It's good advice. Yet one of the most common strategic errors of inexperienced sales negotiators is to focus all their attention on getting the signature and, as a result, to skate quickly over potential areas of misunderstanding.

Misunderstandings come back to haunt you

Pam G had just succeeded in making the biggest sale of her career and one of the biggest in her company's history. She was meeting the customer to tie down some final details before the contract was signed. Only one point worried her. As a matter of policy, her company insisted on charging a standard $200 fee for on-site installation. This flat fee was not subject to any quantity discount and, because the revenue went to the service organization, the sales function had no authority to reduce or change it. In a smaller sale $200 wouldn't be an issue: the installation was complex and, for the work involved, it was a fair charge. However, Pam had sold 200 of the machines in this deal and she was afraid that the customer might protest at the thought of a total installation charge of $40 000.

During the meeting, Pam ran through the contract terms with her customer's lawyer and financial controller. When they reached the installation clause the contract read, 'There shall be a machine installation cost of $200.' 'You'd think we'd get that free,' grumbled the controller. 'It's not worth worrying about,' the lawyer reassured him, 'after all, $200 is only one dollar a machine.' Pam realized that the customers had misunderstood the installation charge. What should she do? If she corrected their misunderstanding, then it was clear that they would be unhappy about a $40 000 charge and it might stop them signing the contract. 'I'll pretend I didn't hear that comment,' she decided, 'then we'll sort it out after the sale.'

Two weeks later, when the customer found out what 'machine installation cost of $200' really meant, there was uproar. The customer cancelled the order and threatened legal action. The issue ultimately reached the President of Pam's company, who decided, in the interests of good customer relations, to give free installation. But, by this time, the customer had become so angry that this concession was no longer enough. In the end the customer reduced the order to 120 machines but retained the discount level for 200. Pam's company lost money on the deal.

Pam's mistake was to believe that significant misunderstandings during the negotiation can be overlooked and sorted out afterwards. She learned the hard way and so did her company that in negotiation it's dangerous to allow a misunderstanding to pass uncorrected.

A FINAL WORD ON NEGOTIATION

Before we leave negotiation, I'd like to summarize some of the ways in which you can apply the key ideas of this chapter to your own negotiations.

- *Differentiate between selling and negotiating.* Most people begin negotiating too early in the selling cycle. Remember, in dealing with your own customers, that you should never allow negotiation to become a substitute for selling. In particular, never fall into the trap of offering discounts, or other negotiable items, as a means of generating customer interest early in the selling cycle. Think of negotiation as something which will only be effective after you've done the best possible job of selling.
- *Don't try to negotiate Consequence issues.* As we saw in the last chapter, Consequence issues are resolved by discussion and confidence building, not by bargaining and negotiation. Negotiation is a very expensive, and not very successful, way to deal with Consequences. In your own accounts try to handle Consequence issues before you enter into final negotiation.
- *Focus on areas of maximum leverage.* Price concessions are often less important than you think. In this chapter we've seen how skilled negotiators use their understanding of customer decision criteria to focus on other areas where they have negotiating leverage. In your own negotiations, particularly if you're trying to handle price concessions in an area where you've very little latitude, look hard at

the decision criteria which are crucial to the customer. As we've seen during the chapter, a relatively small concession in an area which is crucial will often outweigh larger price concessions.

- *Establish and narrow your negotiating range.* We've seen that there are four steps involved in setting and using a negotiating range:
  - set your upper and lower limits
  - refine your upper limit in terms of customer expectation and competitive strength
  - refine your lower limit in the same way so that you arrive at a realistic negotiating range
  - start at or near the top of your range, making concessions in ever smaller increments until you reach agreement.
- *Plan and use questions.* Planning your questions is just as important to negotiation as it is to selling. Few of the inexperienced negotiators I've seen do an adequate job of planning questions. One cause of their neglect is that they become too concerned with putting across reasons and arguments. Remember that questions are generally more persuasive than reasons. In planning your own negotiation strategy, be sure you make a list of questions you intend to ask.
- *Separate understanding from agreement.* You may not be able to agree with the customer, but you can, and should, show that you *understand* the customer's position. When you hear something which you can't agree with – and if you don't want to challenge with a disagreement – it's important that you don't just ignore what the customer has said. Acknowledge that you've heard and understood, using phrases like, 'If I'm hearing you right, what you are saying is . . .'. This shows that you're listening and reduces the time-wasting repetitions of position that are so common in negotiation.
- *Never allow misunderstandings to persist.* In your own negotiations never be afraid to probe and explore areas where the customer may have misunderstood what you are offering. Remember that it's much easier to deal with a misunderstanding *before* the agreement than afterwards when an angry customer feels cheated.

Reading 7

Step into my parlour: a survey of strategies and techniques for effective negotiation

Terry Anderson

Reprinted from *Business Horizons*, May–June 1992, pp. 71–6, with permission. Published by The Foundation for the School of Business, Indiana University.

The idea of active negotiation is intimidating to most people. It conjures up images of smoke-filled rooms, raised voices, dirty tricks, and interminable haggling sessions encompassing a potential win-lose situation that could involve anything from personal relationships to nuclear warfare. Furthermore, most people are generally dubious of their own negotiating skills relative to those of other individuals. They consider encounters with blue-chip negotiators as perilous contests during which they stand a good chance of having the shirt talked right off their backs. Add to this the fact that the most significant negotiation activities are those associated with stressful, life-change events – the compensation package for a new job, custody rights in a divorce, the selling price of a new home – and it is no small wonder that most people have an instinctive aversion to the idea of negotiation. This fear of negotiation has made numerous lawyers, mediators, and professional arbitrators rich.

Like many things in life, negotiation is an aspect of reality that needs to be mastered rather than feared. In fact, skilled negotiators will only deliver a more thorough beating if they smell the fear of an opponent. As a result, it is important to learn effective negotiation techniques as a self-defense mechanism. Putting these techniques into practice and knowing when they are being used by others increase the probability of acquiring greater material rewards. Moreover, the likelihood of sustaining a productive relationship with others can be significantly improved. However, "despite its importance, the negotiation process is often misunderstood and badly carried out. Inferior agreements result, if not endless bickering, needless deadlock, or spiraling conflict" (Lax and Sebenius 1986).

Substantive and Relationship Outcomes

Of course, one of the primary incentives for negotiating is the pursuit of material, substantive outcomes: the raise, the promotion, or the rustproofing option on a new car. However, because a crucial context for any bargaining session is the negotiators' current and desired relationship with each other, the pursuit of these incentives is moderated by the pursuit of a positive relationship between the parties. Before rushing to secure the best possible substantive outcome, the negotiators must assess the impact of their respective negotiation strategies on the relationship that currently exists between them. Obviously, respective levels of power and conflict weigh heavily in this assessment.

The relative power of each negotiator is established by the extent of each party's dependence on the other. Individuals tend to assess the relative levels of power existing in a relationship and then choose whether to compete, accommodate, collaborate, or withdraw when negotiating with others. The level of conflict in a negotiation setting is established by how the negotiators perceive the effective dimension of their relationship – that is, its supportiveness or hostility. Indeed, the pursuit of a positive relationship between negotiating parties may be a primary motivation for continuing negotiation, even at the sacrifice of substantive outcomes, particularly if the relationship has deteriorated and is more highly valued than the issues on the table.

NEGOTIATION STRATEGIES

Only by appraising both their own and the other party's substantive and relationship priorities can negotiators effectively choose a negotiation strategy. To prevent reliance on intuition alone, researchers and academicians have developed formal models, such as simulation programs and decision trees, designed to train and assist individuals in selecting the most appropriate negotiation strategy. "Many people, due to their lack of awareness of any structured approach to the negotiating process, are forced to reuse self-taught methods that have merely appeared to work in the past – methods that were acquired, like diseases, from social contact. There is, however, an important and useful difference between merely knowing a few cunning homemade techniques and understanding the full cooperative human process of negotiation" (Nierenberg 1971).

Although formal approaches serve to add structure to the selection of negotiation strategies, they remain only barely perceptible outlines in a very foggy picture. For this reason, it is important not to be seduced into thinking that the process of negotiation is as simple as some of these models may imply, for the insight and intuition of the negotiator largely provide the musculature necessary to put these strategies into practice. With this in mind, it is useful to survey an entire spectrum of negotiation strategies in a structured yet realistic manner. Generally, negotiators and analysts tend to separate into two groups that are guided by conflicting conceptions of the bargaining process: symbiotic and predatory.

Symbiosis

This negotiation ideology is so named for its predisposition to create value by means of the bargaining process. Symbiotic negotiators tend to believe that mutual agreements are reached by being inventive, collaborative, and persistent in searching for substantial joint gains and the creation of value, relative to no-agreement possibilities. Stressing the importance of open communication and information sharing, symbiotic negotiators are sometimes apt to practice the immoderate strategy of open submission by conceding all but the barest substantive aspects of the negotiation in an attempt to build a productive relationship with the other party. The perception of relationship building as a positive outcome of such a negotiation yields the joint gains necessary for a symbiotic strategy. One side receives primarily substantive gains, while the other side receives the benefits of a strengthened relationship that could come to fruition in the form of future material rewards.

Another symbiotic bargaining strategy is often referred to as "win-win" negotiation, in which both sides win – or at least no one loses. Using this strategy, joint gains are achieved by avoiding actions that tend to worsen the relationship between the parties while increasing the substantive elements of the negotiation. This is accomplished through the bipartisan efforts of both parties to either make the value of the "pie" larger, or to find elements within it to satisfy both parties.

The Egyptian-Israeli peace treaty formulated at Camp David in 1978 illustrates the ideology behind this negotiation strategy:

> Israel had occupied the Egyptian Sinai Peninsula since the Six Day War of 1967. When Egypt and Israel sat down together in 1978 to negotiate a peace, their positions were incompatible. Israel insisted on keeping some of the Sinai. Egypt, on the other hand, insisted that every inch of the Sinai be returned to Egyptian sovereignty. People continuously drew maps showing possible boundary lines that would divide the Sinai between Egypt and Israel. Comprising in this way was wholly unacceptable to Egypt. To go back to the situation as it was in 1967 was equally unacceptable to Israel.
>
> Looking at their interests instead of their positions made it possible for Israel and Egypt to develop a solution. Israel's interest lay in security; they did not want Egyptian tanks poised on their border

ready to roll across at any time. Egypt's interest lay in sovereignty; the Sinai had been part of Egypt since the time of the Pharaohs. After centuries of domination by Greeks, Romans, Turks, French, and British, Egypt had only recently regained full sovereignty and was not about to cede territory to another foreign conqueror.

At Camp David, President Sadat of Egypt and Prime Minister Begin of Israel agreed to a plan that would return the Sinai to complete Egyptian sovereignty and, by demilitarizing large areas, would still assure Israeli security. The Egyptian flag would fly everywhere, but Egyptian tanks would be nowhere near Israel (Fisher and Ury 1981).

Creating Value via the Negotiation Process

In their highly publicized best-seller, *Getting to Yes* (1981), Roger Fisher and William Ury outline four points, each dealing with a basic element of negotiation. These comprise the foundation of a symbiotic negotiation strategy which they call "principled negotiation," or "negotiation on the merits." These four points are as follows:

Separate the people from the problem

The first step in reaching a mutually agreeable solution is to disentangle the substantive elements of the negotiation from the relationship between the parties and deal with each set of elements separately. Negotiators should perceive themselves as working side by side, attacking the problem instead of attacking each other.

Focus on interests, not positions

People's egos tend to become identified with their negotiating positions. Furthermore, focusing on positions often obscures what the participants really need or want. Rather than focusing on the positions taken by each negotiator, a much more effective strategy is to focus on the underlying human needs and interests that had caused them to adopt those positions.

Invent options for mutual gain

Designing optimal solutions under pressure in the presence of an adversary tends to narrow people's vision. Searching for the one right solution inhibits creativity, particularly when the stakes are high. These constraints can be offset by establishing a forum in which a variety of possibilities are generated before deciding which action to take.

Insist on using objective criteria

By discussing the conditions of the negotiation in terms of some fair standard such as market value, expert opinion, custom, or law, the discussion steers away from what the parties are willing or unwilling to do. By using objective criteria, neither party has to give in to the other, and both parties defer to a fair solution.

Symbiotic strategies tend to emphasize open channels of communication, separating the substantive aspects of the negotiation from the people involved in the discussion. By allowing negotiators to deal directly and empathetically with each other as human beings, these strategies increase the probability of reaching an amicable agreement. By focusing on the underlying human interests of each negotiator, they avoid the transactional costs associated with participants locking themselves into positions and then trying to dig their way out. Finally, by focusing on basic interests, mutually satisfying options, and objective standards, these strategies have the potential to produce an agreement that meets the legitimate interests of each side to the extent possible, resolves conflicting interests fairly, and takes into account the interests of associated third parties.

Predation

In direct contrast to their counterparts, predatory negotiators see the notion of a bargaining session characterized by openness, information sharing, clear communication, creativity, and an attitude of cultivating common interests as being naive and weak-minded. According to the predatory ideology, a pie of fixed size is being divided between negotiators, and each slice that each party receives must be taken away from the other. Hardball is the name of the game as each negotiator tries to claim as much of the value of the pie as possible by giving the other party as little as possible. At the extreme end of the spectrium, predatory negotiators try to devise Machiavellian ways to manipulate individuals in such a manner as to claim the entire pie.

Predation, as a negotiation ideology, is based on the view that negotiation is a hard, tough bargaining process in which neither participant cares about the needs of the other. In all cases, the relationship elements of the negotiation are perceived as subservient to the substantive gains achieved in an adversarial contest.

The object here is to persuade other parties that they want what you have to offer while you are only marginally interested in what they have to offer. Negotiation is a game to be won or lost. The outcome depends on each participant's ability to concede slowly, exaggerate the value of concessions, minimize the benefits of the other's concessions, conceal information, argue forcefully on behalf of principles that imply favorable settlements, wait out the other participant, and make commitments to accept only favorable settlements.

The toughest bargainers will make intransigent demands and threaten to walk away or retaliate aggressively if those demands are not met. Ridiculing, attacking, or intimidating adversaries is perceived simply as part of the game. For example, Lewis Glucksman, once the volatile head of trading activities at Lehman Brothers, utilized a very aggressive predatory strategy to seize control of Lehman from then-chairman Peter G. Peterson after being promoted to co-CEO status with Peterson. As co-CEO, Glucksman made a thinly veiled threat that unless he were granted full control of Lehman, he would provoke civil war within the firm and take the entire trading department elsewhere. When Peterson and others desperately sought less damaging accommodation, Glucksman refused to budge by indicating that "his feet were wet in cement," even at the cost of destroying the firm. Ultimately, Peterson left with a substantial money settlement and Glucksman presided briefly over the shaken firm until it was sold at a bargain price to American Express.

Claiming Value via the Negotiation Process

In his book *Negotiate Your Way to Financial Success* (1987), Ronald J. Posluns details his "Seven Golden Rules" of negotiating:

Negotiate tough

Negotiators are not necessarily popular individuals, but there is nothing wrong with getting the edge in any deal. However, do not confuse "tough" with arrogant, rude, bullheaded, or ruthless. "Tough" means sticking to your guns, letting the other side know that you mean business, and being unafraid to ask for extra concessions.

Scrutinize the details

The success of a negotiation strategy lies in the details of the final agreement. Go through each of them, point by point, and wherever an item is not settled, try to gain an advantage. Assume nothing, ask for everything, and consider no item insignificant. Negotiate hard on every specific item, especially the smaller ones, in an attempt to wear down your opponents' stamina and weaken their ability to negotiate for the major issues at stake.

Focus on the rewards

Maintain a myopic view of those things you want to take away from the bargaining table, and learn to counter your opponents' negotiating strategies. For example, emotional outbursts should be perceived as merely part of the game, not as personal attacks. The best thing to do when your opponents exhibit extreme emotion is to simply let them rant, rave, and pound on the table. Once they play their emotional card to no avail, you will have gained the advantage.

Avoid ultimatums

Give your opponents choices instead of ultimatums. Backing someone into a corner is similar to cornering a wild animal – predicting their reactions becomes impossible. When your opponents give you an ultimatum, the best thing to do is walk away from the deal. A good negotiator will not become committed to a deal that cannot survive another day of indecision.

Anything goes

Negotiation is not a game with established rules. You can stall for time, cloud the issues, or use facial expressions to indicate that the concessions your opponents desire are painful ones (whether or not they actually are). Another strategy is to purposely drop your briefcase, or make a mess with a fountain pen. As you lull your opponents into underestimating you, set them up for the kill.

Find your opponents' pressure points

If you discover that your opponents are facing a deadline, you can stall the negotiations by focusing on details until, as the final hour nears, your opponents are eager to agree on your main goals. Probe your opponents for vulnerabilities, then structure your negotiating stance to take full advantage of them.

Control the negotiation

Get your opponents to follow your game plan, not theirs. For instance, if there is a choice between "your place or mine," consider that you have a turf advantage at home, but when you are "away" you have the option of leaving the table in mock outrage. Another ploy is to let the other party prepare the working document under discussion. Mistakenly believing that this will give them an edge, the other party will happily draft a document that itemizes their substantive priorities and the numbers they attach to those items.

THE NEGOTIATOR'S DILEMMA

In reality, symbiotic negotiation strategies designed to create value through cooperation and collaboration directly conflict with predatory strategies intended to claim value. That is, no matter how creative and collaborative the negotiators are, and no matter how successful they are at creating value by means of the bargaining process, reality dictates that at some point each negotiator must claim part of the pie. Moreover, the use of tactics for claiming value necessarily impedes its creation, and the use of tactics for creating value is vulnerable to predatory negotiation strategies.

First, predatory negotiation strategies intended to claim value tend to impair efforts to satisfy the interests of both parties through symbiotic, value-creating strategies. Exaggerating the value of concessions and minimizing the benefit of others' concessions presents a distorted picture of each negotiator's relative preferences and thereby inhibits the communication process. Making threats or intransigent demands is not conducive to effective listening or understanding the interests of the other party. Concealing information will likely result in leaving joint gains on the table. In fact, excessively using predatory strategies may well sour the relationship between the parties to the point at which conflict escalates and the prospects for arriving at a settlement are virtually eliminated.

Second, openly sharing information required to discover and satisfy joint interests makes symbiotic negotiators more susceptible to being victimized by value-claiming strategies. Revealing information about one's relative preferences is risky, and the willingness to make a new, creative offer can often be taken as a sign that its proponent is able and willing to make further concessions. As a result, these offers, which may satisfy joint interests and provide each negotiator with benefits that could not be attained otherwise, typically remain undisclosed. Even purely shared interests can be held hostage in exchange for concession on other issues.

A Matrix of Outcomes

Although both negotiators may realize the importance of cooperatively creating value by means of the negotiation process in a symbiotic manner, they must also acknowledge the fact that each must eventually claim value through some degree of predation. The negotiator's dilemma lies in the fact that tactics to claim value tend to repel moves to create it. While an optimal solution normally results when both parties openly discuss the problem, respect each other's substantive and relationship needs, and creatively seek to satisfy each other's human interests, reality dictates that such behavior cannot always be expected to occur.

The legitimate attempts by one negotiator to employ symbiotic strategies will necessarily disclose information that makes that negotiator vulnerable to the predatory strategies of his opponent. As a result, the problem-solving atmosphere created by two symbionts is inevitably replaced by a competitive atmosphere of gamesmanship to the degree that at least one negotiator begins to utilize predatory strategies.

In a negotiation between a predator, who sees the bargaining process as competitive, and a symbiont, who sees the bargaining process as cooperative, the symbiont is highly vulnerable to the value-claiming strategies employed by the predator. For this reason, negotiators develop an inherent apprehension toward the use of symbiotic strategies to the degree that they expect their opponents to use predatory strategies. This mutual suspicion causes negotiators in many settings to leave joint gains on the table. Moreover, after being skewered in several encounters with experienced predators, the pull toward value-claiming tactics becomes insidious and symbionts often "learn" to become predators.

Finally, however, if both negotiators choose to employ predatory strategies, the probability of value being created through the negotiation process is virtually eliminated. This will likely result in both parties receiving only mediocre rewards, in terms of both substantive outcomes and building productive relationships with the other party. If the spectrum of negotiating strategies previously discussed is placed along vertical and horizontal axes, then for negotiating parties A and B, respectively, a matrix of possible outcomes emerging from the bargaining process can be developed to illustrate the negotiator's dilemma (see Figure 7.1).

Operational Implications

The negotiator's dilemma may enhance the productivity of the bargaining process by providing insight into the mental metabolism of the negotiators. However, regardless of each negotiator's strategy preference, several actions may be taken at the operational level to increase the probability of achieving favorable outcomes while taking the relationship between the parties into account. The basis for these actions are found in the "middle ground" of the strategic spectrum, borrowing concepts from both the predatory and the symbiotic ideologies.

Do your homework

Although it is the least glamorous aspect of the negotiating process, it is the most important. A good negotiator must realize the implications of

STRATEGY OF PARTY A		STRATEGY OF PARTY B: Symbiosis	STRATEGY OF PARTY B: Predation
	Predation	*Outcome:* Great for Party A Terrible for Party B	*Outcome:* Mediocre for Party A Mediocre for Party B
	Symbiosis	*Outcome:* Good for Party A Good for Party B	*Outcome:* Terrible for Party A Great for Party B

Figure 7.1 A Matrix of Negotiated Outcomes

each item on the table, the consequences associated with making various concessions, and what entails the "bottom line" of the negotiations.

Go to the top

Unless you talk directly with individuals who have the authority to make the changes you propose, your success will hinge on someone else's ability to communicate, in minutes, what was discussed over several hours. In addition, dealing with unauthorized subordinates lessens accountability and may hinder the proceedings.

Build relationships whenever possible

Even if you decide to employ a predatory strategy, remember that it is much easier to communicate with a friend than with a stranger, or even worse, an enemy. Relationship gains and losses are as much a part of the negotiated package as the substantive outcomes.

Avoid quick concessions

Making a concession without having fully considered the issues opens you up to the risk of giving up something unnecessarily and compromising your own needs. Use discretion when conceding from your stated position.

Accentuate the positive

By framing negative points in a positive way, you will be more likely to elicit a positive response. Couching controversial issues between positive points increases your chances of getting the other side to listen – and agree – to your demands.

Maintain your composure

In any negotiation, but particularly in protracted ones, emotions may flare up and people may lose their tempers. Under these conditions, it is imperative to maintain composure, sift through emotions, and try to discern the other party's needs and wants.

Don't give up

You may reach a point at which you do not like the proposed agreement, but still you do not see any alternatives. Remember that what seems like a dead end may actually be a corner. With a little perseverance, you can get around it.

At one extreme, the process of negotiation can be called a cooperative pursuit of joint gains and a collaborative effort to create value where none previously existed. At the other extreme, it can be described as a street fight. The negotiator's dilemma lies in determining where the cooperation ends and the street fight begins. Understanding this paradox more fully serves to reduce the anxiety associated with the process of negotiation by giving negotiators a structured approach to tailoring their strategies to both the substantive and relationship elements at stake.

Nevertheless, it is important not to be duped into believing that the bargaining process is as simple as any existing structured model may imply. The experience and intuition of the negotiator must inevitably provide the musculature necessary to put the structure into motion in a pragmatic and practicable manner. By taking a structured yet realistic approach to the negotiating process, and implementing established operational actions, the negotiator substantially increases the probability of acquiring substantive gains, as well as fostering a productive relationship with the other party.

Terry Anderson is a design engineer with General Electric Co., Louisville, Kentucky.

References

Deborah Asbrand, "Games B-School Never Taught You," *PC Computing*, April 1989, pp. 153+.

Ellen J. Belzer, "The Negotiator's Art: You Can Always Get What You Want," *Working Woman*, April 1990, pp. 98+.

Paul B. Brown and Michael S. Hopkins, "How To Negotiate Practically Anything," *Inc.*, February 1989, pp. 35+.

Roger Fisher and William Ury, *Getting To Yes* (Boston: Houghton Mifflin, 1981).

John M. Ivancevich and Michael T. Matteson, *Organizational Behavior and Management* (Homewood, Ill.: Irwin, 1990).

David A. Lax and James K. Sebenius, *The Manager As Negotiator* (New York: Free Press, 1986).

Cynthia Legette, "How To Improve Your Negotiation Skills," *Black Enterprise*, October 1989, pp. 106–110.

Gerard I. Nierenberg, *Creative Business, Negotiating* (New York: Hawthorn, 1971).

Ronald J. Posluns; *Negotiate Your Way to Financial Success* (New York: Putnam, 1987).

Michelle Willens, "The Manly Art of Win-Win Negotiating," *Money*, February 1987, pp. 119–202.

Reading 8

Gallery furniture and Dr Deming

Jim McIngvale

Reprinted from *British Deming Association, Sixth Annual Conference*, 13 May 1993.

Gallery Furniture is a 30,000 square foot retail furniture store servicing the medium to medium-high priced furniture market in Houston, Texas. From the beginning, Gallery Furniture differentiated itself from the competitors by offering same day delivery of furniture (up to 300+ deliveries in one day). Gallery Furniture had always been a sales driven organization, with high (according to industry standards) commission paid sales people. The emphasis was to make the sale by any method, as long as it was legal.

Gallery Furniture had the conventional management structure: CHAIN OF BLAME . . . WHO'S TO BLAME . . . or PLEASE THE BOSS. Business grew, because Gallery had great customers and great employees, in spite of managing by results, goal setting, incentive pay, and rating and ranking of employees. Top down management at its finest!

However, Top Management (me) became frustrated because the store's closing percentage (the number of visiting customers versus the resulting number of sales) seemed to never get above 45%, bearing in mind that the national closing percentage for a retail furniture store is only 24%. No matter how many extra incentives were offered, contests were started, or threats were made, things never drastically changed.

Then Top Management (me), came up with a brilliant idea. Keep the store open with only the best sales people (there were 80 at the time). We'd tabulate the results, and at the end of the month, top producers would be rewarded, being allowed to take as many customers as they pleased the next month.

Unfortunately, this didn't work either because I was using arbitrary goals which caused short-term thinking, misguided focus. All causing a great deal of conflict. The ten or so people who consistently won were embarrassed because of the differential treatment they were given. They were consistently going ahead of their friends, in the "Batting-Order Basis" in which customers were served. The other 70 salespeople felt like losers – failures. This, of course, caused salespeople to fudge their figures. It created increased fear of failure and unfortunately blinded the salespeople to the customer's needs and real concerns.

Adding further insult to injury, if salespeople sold less than 30% of their customers on a Saturday, they would have to "sit out the game" until all salespeople were busy. A reward for the so-called Producers, and a punishment for the "supposed" Under-Achievers.

There was a daily sales goal. And if the goal was reached, at the high point of the madness, the first place salesperson received $500, the second place winner would get $300, and third would get $200. The thinking was that people worked harder for a carrot. But the only thing that changed were the faces.

We consistently experienced a turnover of 10 to 15 salespeople every month. We were spending an ever-increasing amount of time and money on hiring, training and firing, in constant search for the super-achiever, always wondering why half the people were below average! The closing percentage never went up appreciably, and salespeople would do great one week, and poorly the next. It was a constant roller coaster of highs and lows. To say I was frustrated would be an understatement. There had to be a better way than the roller coaster ride we were on.

In October 1990, five Gallery Furniture associates and I attended Dr. Deming's four-day seminar in Houston. Most of the concepts made sense to me. But eliminate merit pay, incentive pay and commissions? Never! Those things built the business and took Gallery Furniture "From Crayons to Perfume", or so I thought at the time. But Dr. Deming's concepts intrigued me. I figured if his 14-Points were good enough for Toyota, Honda, Sony, General Motors and Ford, that maybe "parts of them" (and I would selectively "pick and choose" the ones I liked) might be good enough for Gallery Furniture. To make the selection process easier, I bought the Deming library tapes, and for the next several months I watched and listened to Dr. Deming, NBC's Lloyd Dobbins and Punk the Penguin.

I began to get a clear message . . . Gallery Furniture had been lucky and successful, in spite of my bad management practice, which crush people and their intrinsic motivation.

In December I took five other salespeople and attended another four-day seminar in Flint, Michigan, sponsored by Buick, Olds and Cadillac divisions of General Motors. I sat next to Carl Sewell, founder and owner of Sewell Village Cadillac, one of the most successful Cadillac dealerships in the country. Mr. Sewell built his Cadillac business in a similar manner to Gallery with high commissions, incentive pay and sales contests.

Carl and I discussed salary pay versus commission. I was beginning to think the unthinkable. We already had what *Teams Handbook* author Peter Scholtes describes as "Quality Commandos"; 4 or 5 salespeople who were ready to take the plunge to salary. But there were 85 other salespeople who remained skeptical. It was not quite time yet!

In January of 1991, my wife Linda and I took two of our converts, Don Ledford and Mark Gervich, and attended a four-day seminar. This time in Newport Beach, California. There we met Dr. Ed Baker who is a Deming master and was the head of quality for Ford Motor Company. He and Dr. Deming encouraged us to take a "Leap of Faith" and just do it!

You see, in January 1991, before this monumental change was made, salespeople had to produce a minimum of $7000 in weekly sales volume, plus $400 in "add-on" chemical sales (fabric, leather and wood care protection). When these quotas were met, a 10% commission would be paid, earning the salesperson approximately $700. However, if the quota was not met, no matter what the circumstances, the salesperson was paid only 5% commission, earning around $300 a week. Obviously, this prompted all types of games so that quotas could be met. Salespeople went to great lengths to cross that narrow line between a WINNER and a LOSER!

1 Some salespeople would work six or seven days a week to achieve their quotas. The more tired they got, the harder their quota became for them to achieve.
2 Our delivery department could expect to be overworked on Thursdays, the end of our pay period, when salespeople would force customers to take delivery of their furniture just so their quota could be met. "To heck with what the customer wants! I *have* to meet my quota!"
3 If the quota was met, customers would be convinced to take delivery the following Thursday so *that* week's quota and production dollars would be certain to be met.
4 Customers were not allowed to buy what they wanted, if it had little or no profit. Salespeople would actually turn down certain sales, and switch the customer to something else, causing customers to be agitated.
5 On Thursday evenings, it wasn't uncommon to see customers leaving with a dumb-founded expression on their face, their arms full with up to 30 bottles of furniture polish at one time.
6 Furniture would also be delivered to and stored in a salesperson's garage, before the Thursday night cut-off, to be later delivered to the customer at the salesperson's convenience.

The more I studied Deming the more I realized something must be done. But I wasn't ready for the 100% plunge! So, in January, 1991, we took *not a leap*, but a *hop* of faith, and removed all quotas. But still paid everyone commission. Amazingly enough, sales went up and attitude improved. Some fear was driven out, but not all.

Store closings were from 42% to 46% before removing quotas. After the quotas were removed, store closings climbed to, and consistently lingered around the 50% level.

During January, February and March, my wife Linda kept telling me to go all salary pay, but I didn't have the conviction to do it. However! In retrospect, those months of discussion of the "pros" and "cons" of going to all salary pay was good preparation for the change. In March of 1991, I had an opportunity to ask Dr. Deming if incentive pay, or commission, might be OK for salespeople! He scratched his then 90-year-old head, and in a somewhat frustrated manner, said, "Won't you ever learn?"

Dr. Baker told me that any change would bring with it a new set of problems, and I have to admit that I was sick and tired of the same old problems; i.e., battles over commission when more than one salesperson helped a customer-making payroll a real nightmare! Any new problems would be a welcome change. And things had to change!

So, in April of 1991, we decided to pay all salespeople a salary based on the same income they made in 1990. And, if the company profited, everyone would share equally in our profit sharing plan. Everyone felt this was a fair and equitable method, and it was a starting point.

We solicited the 20th century American expert Bart Simpson on the subject and he responded, "Radical move, Dude!"

The greatest reason why Deming converts and others hesitate to change to a salary program is the fear that salespeople will be lazy, having no incentive to do their share. We had the same fear in the beginning. Salespeople thought that they wouldn't make as much money, now not depending on their sales results for monetary reward. They also feared they would still be evaluated, rated, ranked and appraised in the same old criteria and measurements. Some thought Gallery Furniture was betting the company unnecessarily, on an all or nothing situation. And I had a few fears not worth mentioning.

But now all those initial fears are behind us. Almost immediately we made some amazing discoveries. People don't work less. They work more and are very eager to contribute and prove their worth. They jump in and get involved, and display talents we didn't know they have. Growth and success are measured in other ways, and management doesn't look at an individual's figures but the sum total of the whole system.

Now we view the organization as a system. How is the system doing? How can we constantly improve? What's important to our customers?

Associates have a vested interest in what they and their fellow associates do in contributing to the whole. They take more joy in their work. Finally, they are heard and effectively allowed to use their talents and abilities, and participate in the education of their fellow associates. They participate in merchandising and decorating. Now, a furniture buying team meets with representatives and travels to market, making decisions that were once made by overpaid buyers who had little or no contact with the buying public. This change alone has saved our company tens of thousands of dollars. As we continued to improve, more and more associates became players, further contributing to an ever-increasing whole and finding a place in the system where they can contribute, lending and blending their talents. It truly amazes me how much hidden talent has surfaced through all the changes. Here is one example, and there have been many:

Recently, we decided to do some major remodeling with two of our display areas. The commercial cost would have been in excess of $70,000 for what needed to be done. A team of our associates pooled their talents and built two of the most beautiful display galleries I have ever seen. The total combined cost did not exceed $7,000, with the savings going directly to the bottom line to be shared by all in the profit sharing program. In the past associates would be losing by doing something other than selling. Cross-training is now rampant. Before, we could not justify the time or the assumed revenue loss. Whereas, cross-training actually makes better use of the most valuable asset a business possesses . . . its employees. Performance appraisals have been completely eliminated, as people are simply asked to contribute in as many ways as they can, fully utilizing their knowledge, talents and abilities for the good of the whole. The older and senior sales associates now help the newer salespeople, seeing them as an asset, not as competition or a threat to their income. Sales turnover is down from the 10 to 15 salespeople who were fired or quit every month. The thousands of dollars we spent every week for sales ads in local newspapers ended entirely.

People are more secure and people crave security. Now for the first time, salespeople are able to budget their income without wild swings in a month's time. Salespeople work in every area of the business, including the warehouse, service calls and on deliveries. They now see the business as a system and the phrase "It's Not My Job" has completely disappeared. Everybody walks in everybody else's shoes, replacing criticism with compassion and judgement with understanding.

Customers' needs are taken into consideration and customers no longer feel pressured into buying something. Instead of focusing on making a living, sales associates focus on the customer's needs.

Downtime is now spent improving selling techniques and role-playing, and not pouring over computer printouts, calculating and worrying how close they will be in meeting their quota. Associates have learned that the customer is the business, and their business is the customer.

Payroll only takes an hour each week, and not the nine or ten hours it used to. Our lady in payroll no longer receives 300+ calls each week to answer inquiries about an associate's production. And how far they were away from, or over, their weekly quota. Or how much they had earned for the week.

Management is now spending time helping people, coaching and nurturing, not ranking, rating, firing or refereeing commission battles. A learning environment has been created and people love to learn and excel at their job for the sheer joy of just doing it. And what's wrong with enjoying your work? Like the members of a symphony orchestra, associates each play their part for the good of the whole.

The Mission of Gallery Furniture in May of 1993 is to:

1 Delightfully exceed customers' expectations with quality products and services
2 Help make all associates rich in mind, spirit and pocketbook
3 Benefit the community where we live, work and play
. . . MANAGE FOR THE LONG TERM.

The Aim of Gallery Furniture in 1993 is first, to please customers; second, to sell and deliver furniture; and third, to produce income. PLEASE CUSTOMERS. SELL AND DELIVER FURNITURE. PRODUCE INCOME. In that order. And shape the future by delivering high value products and services to customers at *low cost*. In other words, do more with less. Operate with low overhead and provide more value for the customer.

Southwest Airlines, based in Dallas, Texas, is one of the most profitable in the business. Unlike its floundering competitor Continental Airlines, Southwest has always maintained low overhead and a lean management structure. Southwest ground crews turn the planes in just 10 minutes. And CEO Herb Kelleher gets close to the customer by regularly serving as a flight attendent and by personally unloading passenger baggage.

Walmart founder Sam Walton has kept company overhead below 12% while Sears Roebuck overhead has stayed closer to 30%. In 1989, Sears had more management in its lawn and garden departments than in the entire Walmart company!

How do we make employees more productive? How do we do more with less? The answer is to increase the number of positive interactions between people and groups. To provide *more cooperation*. To manage the "white spaces" in the organization by increasing the number of positive interactions between people and between departments. Manage the "white spaces" so that the individual parts contribute to the Aim of the System. A system being a network of interdependent components that work together to accomplish the Aim of the System. The Aim of Gallery

Furniture is to 1) Please Customers, 2) Sell and Deliver Furniture, and 3) Produce Income.

In 1993, what does Gallery Furniture want and need? More positive interactions. For example, when the store is not busy, salespeople go to the distribution center and make deliveries. And on busy weekends, associates from the back office of the distribution center go to the store and type tickets.

In 1993, what does Gallery Furniture not want or need? Any negative interactions. Saying something nasty about another department or another person. At Gallery Furniture we've learned to bite our tongue rather than criticize.

A system must be managed. It will not manage itself. Left to itself, components become selfish, competitive. The secret is cooperation between components toward the Aim of Gallery Furniture. We can't afford the destructive effects of competition between people or departments.

There must be an optimization of the whole. Broken into its different parts and functions is the wrong way for a company to function. Where customer input only comes through the service department. And where sales and delivery and back office and data processing, all the departments, work independently and in competition with each other.

Optimization is the process of orchestrating the efforts of all components toward achievement of the stated Aim. Optimization is management's job. Everyone wins in optimization. Transformation starts with us. We must create a huge number of positive interactions between people and departments. Another example occurs at Gallery Furniture on Saturdays and Sundays when receiving crews work because our warehouse is small. Work on Saturday and Sunday rather than saying "That's not my job".

The Quality of a product is a result of how the parts fit together. The quality of a company is dependent upon how people *work together.* And by what method does Gallery Furniture help people work together? By creating more positive interactions. Instead of slog . . . slog . . . slogging along, making it difficult to learn and to cooperate. At Gallery Furniture we set up a system that forces people to cooperate because they do multiple jobs.

Gallery Furniture helps all associates with a system that supports positive interactions and prevents a return to the old ways. Supports associates with a system that prevents them from saying, "I could cooperate if it weren't for ________."

What business is, is dealing with people. Figuring out how to make lots and lots of positive interactions. Dealing with people is like sailing, working with winds. It is not powerboating – full throttle ahead, leaving people rocking in your wake.

The more people are involved in change, the less resistance. Let everybody win! Optimize the whole. Let people be both independent and interdependent.

People will work for reasons other than money. The volunteer sector in our country is its fastest growing. Gallery Furniture witnessed this in December of 1992 when it organized a Christmas for All at the Houston Astrodome and 5000 volunteers showed up on Christmas Day to serve the community!

Gallery Furniture constantly balances the sense of being an individual with the sense of being a *team member.* Organizations have a natural entropy, or the tendency to deteriorate into fragmented parts. (Look at the situation the world is suffering in Bosnia and Serbia.)

In his book *Leadership is an Art,* Max Depree, CEO of Hermann Miller, offers a list of the signals of organizational entropy:

- tension among employees
- leaders who seek to control rather than liberate
- people speaking of customers as impositions rather than opportunities to serve
- leaders who rely on structures instead of people
- problem-makers outnumbering problem-solvers, and
- a feeling that rewards and goals are the same thing.

Gallery Furniture works toward optimization. And to hold the historical gains, not the statistical. For example, if Mary "knows" that the day after July 4 is a bigger sales day for Gallery Furniture than July 4 itself, we prepare for the day after.

Gallery Furniture focuses on improving the system and helping everybody's performance. If each person did his or her best (best efforts), they could only improve 3–4%: 96% of improvement gains come from the system. Focus on systematic improvements. Gallery Furniture improved the system by putting associates on salary, forcing them to cooperate. We need to let go of our preoccupation with individual workers and work on the *system.*

Your responsibility and my responsibility is individual transformation. Transformation through Dr. Demings' four components: 1) system, 2) variation, 3) psychology, and 4) theory of knowledge.

A failure to understand variation is a central problem today. We must do detective work and work on the causes. Ask, "Why? Why? Why?" Look at the systems not the outputs. A psychological barrier was set up when Gallery Furniture required the weekly sale of $400 worth of chemicals in order to keep commissions from being cut in half. Now Gallery Furniture teaches *how* to sell and the sale of chemicals is more like $400 a day!

The future ain't what it used to be. Dramatic change is required.

Immediate delivery of furniture is now a minimum expectation. Peter Drucker says that, in order to start a turnaround, companies must rethink and re-examine their theory. Drucker cites as an example the attempt by IBM founder Thomas Watson, Sr. to keep the punch card alive by seeing it as an accessory to the then new computer. He gave strict instructions to his sales people to *never* push computers if doing so would endanger getting punch card orders. Fortunately for IBM, the Justice Department filed an anti-trust suit that forced IBM out of the punch card business or it would have persisted in going the way of the punch card.

Gallery Furniture today is in the *people delighting business*. How can we do it better?

- Please the internal and external customer
- Buy and sell quality products
- Solve *real* problems realistically
- Provide first-time buyer financing
- Give customers what they desire
- Care for non-buyers
- Be professional
- SURPRISE.

The significant problems that we face today cannot be solved with the present level of thinking. With the new trade opportunities with Mexico, if we can't speak Spanish, we can't communicate simply by shouting English!

Good solutions must be focused. At the Gallery Furniture store we focus on moving bed sales up. Leather sales up. Delivery fees up. Fabric protection sales up. Manager discounting up. At the distribution center we focus on improving deliveries. Improving safety. Improving the front dock. Improving the receiving process. And improving service. We focus on DELIGHTING THE CUSTOMER.

Today our sales, closing percentages and profit margins are way up. Customers are happy and more and more customers are coming to the store.

Store closings which started around 45% and moved to over 50% when sales commissions were removed, are now consistently exceeding 60%. Gallery Furniture year to year sales have gone up . . . up . . . up. Third quarter 1993 revenues are up 18% and net income up 23%. Revenue is up while the cost of goods and expenses have been held, providing value to the customer at *low cost*.

In 1993 Gallery Furniture is receiving a 14% return on sales. In the first quarter of 1993, Gallery Furniture made a profit sharing contribution of $91,500 – 5% of the first quarter profits. And an additional gain sharing contribution of $34,000 – 10% of the 1992 to 1993 increase in Gallery Furniture income.

Someone asked me recently, at one of the Deming downlinks, if I would go back to commission, if our sales were to slide. NO! ABSOLUTELY NOT! The biggest benefits of salary versus commission are unknown and unknowable. Employees are happier. Management is happier. And customers are treated better. The company makes more profit. And everyone wins. Is there really anything wrong if everyone wins?

We were sold down the river on competition. We think it's good. I win/you lose! I learned to compete at the University of Texas, 1969–1970. One of my best friends promotes competition in the field of sports. Bela Karolyi, coach of the U.S. Olympic gymnasts and such medal winners as Marylou Rettin and Nadia Cominiche. We must realize that the lessons we learn in sports and in school, do not apply to our business lives. Let everyone share in an ever-expanding piece of pie with innovations that expand the market.

In order for transformation to occur the biggest change has to take place with management's thinking. Here is an overview of Gallery before we eliminated commissions and how management has totally changed their view today:

BEFORE	*AFTER*
Individual events, firefighting, kicking butt & taking names	View company as a whole – not focus on individual events
Goodbye to below average staff	View employees as assets
No education, high turnover . . . spent on recruiting	R.O.I.: invest lots of $$$ in best asset . . . people!
Frustrated because people didn't "get the message"	Be less critical . . . appreciate diversity
Dwelled on problems . . . issued edicts	Job harder . . . fire prevention
Ignored the potential of competent, talented people	Found out that lots of people can contribute and want to!

The benefits are great and many. People are happier on the job. There is better morale. Attitudes are high. Associates view the business holistically and are eager to contribute their ideas, opinions and talents. It is now OK to take a chance, out on the edge where the rewards are found, rather than playing it safe in the middle of the road. No risk/no reward.

Associates improve through training and education. We now have fewer suppliers (150 down to less than 30). Management is listening. Associates are now transforming into system improvers.

There is now intense cooperation, where there was only competition. Everyone wins. It is a long and arduous task, but I am here to tell you that you can transform your business, and change the thinking that is putting us farther and farther behind in the world's economic trade picture.

At Gallery Furniture we had a choice to make. Continue focusing on the quick buck, or look down the road toward long term prosperity! We chose the Deming method. The chain it creates to:

Improve quality
Decrease costs
Improve productivity
Decrease prices
Increase market share
Stay in business
Provide jobs, and more jobs, and
Show a return on investment.
EVERYBODY WINS! THERE ARE NO LOSERS.

We must make continuous improvement. If you always do what you've always done, you'll always get what you always got. It means that groups must work together with intense cooperation.

Learning is not compulsory. Survival is not compulsory. In order to have transformation, there must be: 1) positive interactions, 2) better cooperation, and 3) better quality services and products. Positive interactions, better quality products/services, and more cooperation equal delighted customers.

The secret is cooperation between the components toward the aim of Gallery Furniture. The 1993 Action Plan for Gallery Furniture:

- Let go of person ego
- Work with other sales people
- Institute system of cross training
- Institute better training classes
- Achieve relationships outside of work
- Eliminate numbers
- Practice the GOLDEN RULE.

Transformation will only occur if we personally change. If we as individuals do not change, how can we expect others to? We need a transformation of thinking; a new paradigm. We need to change the way we interact with each other, in order to change the way people work together at Gallery Furniture.

The Gallery Furniture experiment continues, and we are just beginning to learn to cooperate. But the power of people, as seen with this cooperation, as they continue to cooperate and work together, has been the most amazing change I've encountered. Our costs are down significantly. Profits are up. People are happier. Everybody wins and that's what it is all about. Is there really anything wrong with everybody winning? With everybody going home with a blue ribbon?

And, by the way, I have learned that the American West was not won and settled by the lone wolf types, the Lone Rangers, working by themselves, but by the people working *together* to raise the barn. Raising the barn together for their neighbors in a spirit of cooperation.

Thank you, Dr. Deming. Thank you for teaching us how to cooperate and raise the barn together. You have truly changed our lives.

In order to have transformation we must ask ourselves three questions:

IF NOT NOW . . . *WHEN*?
IF NOT ME . . . *WHO*?
IF NOT TOGETHER . . . *HOW*?

IF IT IS TO BE, THEN IT IS UP TO ME.

The fifth century B.C. Chinese sage Lao Tzu best provides a prescription for 20th century leadership:

> As for the best leaders, the people do not notice their existence. The next best, the people honor and praise. The next, the people jeer; and the next the people hate . . . When the leader's work is done, the people say, 'We did it ourselves!'

Part 3

Database Marketing

INTRODUCTION

The readings in Part 1 gave a flavour of the changing nature of sales and customer relations. The rising costs of traditional field sales operations, reduction in the effectiveness of advertising, growing importance of key accounts, growth of direct marketing, and the impact of computing and communication technology were all discussed. Many of these changes are being driven by two forces. The first is the need to work closer with customers as reliance on major accounts increases and the competitive differentiation switches from products to customer service. The second is the possibilities which are now apparent due to developments in computing and communications technology.

One of the interesting aspects of database marketing is that the theme cuts across traditional functional areas. These are management of the field sales force, telemarketing, direct mail, dealers, order processing, customer service, and physical distribution. In addition to the database itself, there are the computerized communication systems which, linked together, form networks allowing remote access by mobile users. These developments are driving previously separate functions closer together forcing management to consider the issues of integration, organization culture and structure. Robert Shaw[1] argues that 'many people in general marketing and sales management are still failing dismally to capitalize on information technology. They just seem to ignore the vast wealth of base sales and marketing data available from retail scanners, direct marketing, order processing, financial services, enquiries, coupons, sales visits, trade directories and public databases.' According to Keith Fletcher[2], a survey in Direct Response, 1981

> found that while three-quarters of companies said they used database marketing, when questioned further two important facts emerged. Firstly, many respondents did not really know what the term

'database marketing' meant and secondly companies were not fully exploiting their existing database.

This part on database marketing examines some of the latest thinking in this 'new' industry. The readings range from practical case histories to papers which discuss the strategic implications. There are strong and obvious links with other sections in this book, particularly those on sales negotiation, customer service, and telesales. However, even the management of agents and distributors is influenced by these technological changes. For instance the reading from *The Economist* 'Lighting the way' (Reading 23, Part 5), is an excellent illustration of how the database and network communications have been used to knit the independent channel members together, in order to add value and improve service for the benefit of all. The network links together head office, product divisions, field warehousing, sales agents, distributors, specifiers, and contractors. Lead time has been reduced from nine days to under one day and sales have doubled in six years.

As a new discipline the experience of those researching and working in this field may be from a variety of areas such as direct marketing, sales management, customer service, telemarketing, marketing research, advertising, statistical services, systems or data management. Thus there are many differing perspectives on the subject and database marketing remains a little ill defined. Any particular reading is likely to be strongly influenced by the author's background and experience. According to Bob Hartley,[3] a more balanced view of the discipline is required. The following short explanation of the components of database marketing may be of use.

Database Marketing (DBM) is an interactive approach to customer contact management relying on the maintenance of accurate customer and prospect customer information, competitor information, and internal company information. The database is used to provide computer aided sales support, for direct response marketing, and to support customer information and service systems.

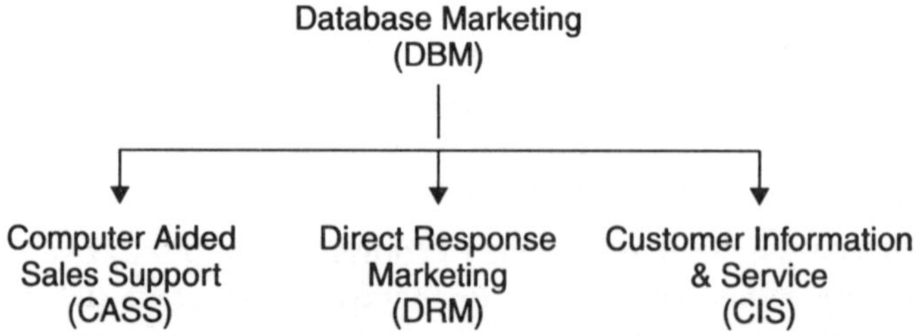

This attempts to embrace the potential applications and user groups of marketing databases. The three components of Database Marketing may be described thus:

- *Computer Aided Sales Support (CASS)* requires the field sales team, sales support team, and telemarketing team to have direct access to the database via PCs or notebook computers whether office based, mobile or located in outstations. In addition to access to records the system should support electronic communication and personal tools such as word processing, spreadsheet, and proposal generation.
- *Direct Response Marketing (DRM)* involves the use of the database for campaigns using addressable communications (such as direct mail, mail order, and telemarketing) targeted at existing or potential customers and for fulfilment of direct response advertising campaigns.
- *Customer Information and Service (CIS)* allows customers to contact the organization quickly and easily possibly using a toll free or a local number. The reasons for the contact may include bill query, warranty claim, technical problem, product/service information, or servicing required.

So one may take a very narrow view of database marketing and see it as supporting a particular application such as direct mail, or customer service, or field sales support. Alternatively, a broad strategic organizational and long-term view may be taken which sees database marketing as supporting a range of functions involving customer contact. The readings selected have been chosen to reflect these issues.

Database marketing should not be seen as being suitable only for large organizations. There are now many inexpensive off-the-shelf software packages available which are suitable for the PC. Reading 9, 'Database programs help build business' by chief executive George Platt, is a short case history which illustrates the use of database marketing in a small/medium-sized enterprise. Sales revenues were increased from $700,000 in 1982 to $15 million in 1995 with the aid of database marketing, and this was achieved in a 'fiercely competitive business' – printing. 'Database Marketing: building long term customer relationships for maximum profits', Reading 10, by Wendy Close looks at why database marketing is needed. She identifies the trends that are causing marketing executives to rethink their strategies. These are:

- Changing demographics and lifestyles
- Demands on personal time
- Overcrowded markets
- Weakening of the magic of television advertising
- Decline in brand loyalty
- Advertising clutter and overkill
- Feeding the discount promotion monster.

This is then followed with an explanation of database marketing, a useful note on the typical information collected for consumer products and for business-to-business products. Finally, there are tips on how to design and budget for your system.

Rowland Moriarty and Gordon Swartz in 'Automation to boost sales and marketing' (Reading 11) look at database marketing mainly from the perspective of supporting the field sales force and lead generation/tracking for business to business sales. The authors use the term marketing and sales productivity (MSP) systems rather than database marketing. According to their findings 'sales increases arising from advanced marketing and sales information technology have ranged from 10% to more than 30%, and investment returns have often exceeded 100%.' The authors discuss what the systems can do, how they aid productivity, how they help management, and the important issues to consider in the design and implementation of systems. Charts and maps of sample MSP systems are included. According to the authors 'Early adopters of MSP systems have gained superior competitive advantage. Compared with their "manual" competitors, they perform selling tasks with greater economy and impact.'

Reading 12 is from Terry Vavra, 'The database marketing imperative'. Once again the author chooses another notion, 'customer information files' (CIF), to describe the database systems. The benefits of database marketing are reviewed, and suggestions on how to construct a database are discussed. For example:

- Who is responsible for building the CIF?
- Who is to be included in the CIF?
- What information is to be collected?
- How will the CIF be organized?
- How will the CIF be used?

The costs of establishing a database are also identified as are the opportunities of enhancing the CIF with external information. The reading is written mainly from the perspective of consumer products but the author does cover issues affecting services, consumer durables, and packaged goods. If you are unsure of some of the terminology used in this field – flat or relational database, proprietary database, RFM, lifetime value, etc. – then this paper will help demystify the subject.

The title of the final reading in this section sums up the situation nicely, 'Strategic implementation of database marketing: problems and pitfalls'. Keith Fletcher, Colin Wheeler and Julia Wright argue for a strategic approach to database marketing (DBM) within an integrated marketing framework. They identify five factors affecting successful implementation:

- insufficient marketing and information orientation
- investment justification
- organizational barriers
- supply infrastructure
- legal constraints.

The authors suggest that some organizations have moved from direct marketing into more sophisticated database systems but have failed to appreciate the strategic opportunities of direct marketing. In short they are still using the more sophisticated database as a tactical direct marketing tool and not as a strategic weapon. They argue that DBM users should:

- build a customer rather than a market database
- see customer contacts as part of a long-term strategy to build loyalty, improve satisfaction and gain information
- calculate the life-time value of customers
- abandon the outmoded distinction between above- and below-the-line activities
- use measurability of direct marketing to assess the promotional effectiveness of campaigns
- be prepared for organizational disruption and the need for staff attitudes to change.

In conclusion the authors suggest that 'more and more firms will move towards a long-term, interactive view of their customer relationships'. Those firms with a fragmented approach to promotional activities and who lack detailed customer knowledge 'will be at a major strategic disadvantage'.

The readings in this part discuss the opportunities for improving customer contact management and building long-term customer relationships via the implementation of database systems and communication networks. As computing power increases and digital personal communications become the norm, the opportunities for organizations to knit themselves together into an information network may be realized. All staff involved in customer contact, whether they are a marketing manager, field sales executive, service engineer, telemarketing operative, direct mail planner, preparing quotations, prioritizing orders, scheduling shipments, or fielding customer queries, should have the information literally at their finger tips. In large organizations this will not come cheap, nor without organizational disruption or change in staff attitudes and culture. Small organizations will not be excluded from this revolution. The smallest of family businesses are able to hold customer records in an inexpensive software package which allows them to organize mail-outs, prepare quotations, process orders, and to handle incoming/outgoing calls/fax/e-mail. With personal communications and electronic notebooks no one will be out of touch, whether working in the office, from home, in the field, or in the plant. The limiting factor in the system will be the quality of the database. The main strategic issues remain with us, however. Competitive advantage gained by early adoption of these systems will be eroded over time as competitors catch up and the use of the technology becomes the norm. The technology should not be seen in isolation. The question is how should it best be used to improve customer satisfaction and help build long-term customer relations?

References

1 Shaw R. *Computer Aided Marketing and Selling*, Butterworth Heinemann, 1991.
2 Fletcher, K. *Marketing Management and Information Technology*, Prentice Hall, 1990.
3 Palmer, A. and Hartley, R.A. *The Business and Marketing Environment*, 2nd edn, McGraw-Hill, 1996.

Reading 9

Database programs help build business

George Platt

Reprinted from *Business Marketing*, November 1993, Vol. 78, pp. 60.

Database-driven marketing, targeted professional networking, customer service and quality control are vital, strategic tools in an integrated marketing campaign.

Database marketing might be the single most effective tool for capturing clients. Before databases, marketers could target a segment like a fishfinder spots fish. Display advertising, for example, is just fishing in a good trout stream. Now database marketers go right into the water after the keepers – it's like spear-fishing with scuba gear.

In July 1989, I sent a personalized letter to 463 small printers along the Northeastern seaboard announcing excess capacity on our full-color presses. A dollar bill was enclosed to draw attention to the price schedule. We received 42 requests for estimates, a 9% return, and six deals were closed. The total cost of the letter was $1,000; the immediate return was $118,000 in printing. In addition, four of the six small printers are current clients. We send out a similar letter annually, and have generated about $1.5 million in new revenue in a three-year period.

The mailings are followed by notes from our sales manager, enabling us to build and update our internal database, which was started in 1982 and currently comprises 1,043 clients and 2,831 prospects. The database is used monthly with highly personalized packages to targeted print buyers. In 1990, The Harty Press added 166 new clients to its database; in 1991, 202; and in 1992, 178.

Professional networking is another tactic for attracting new business. Three to five times a year, I speak at direct marketing seminars, and I also sit on panels at design seminars. Our primary prospects – business managers and creative professionals who buy print – attend these seminars and I usually find four or five new clients each time.

Strategies for attracting new clients, however, are only half the battle. There must be a program for retaining those customers. This is where service and quality control enter the picture.

Our approach to customer service could be called risk-reversal. We reverse the risk inherent to business transactions by guaranteeing our work with an on-time Guaranteed Delivery Program. If we miss a guaranteed delivery date, the client does not pay. On the front end of the business, we also offer a Pixel Perfect Guarantee, which ensures work prepped for printing meet clients' quality standards.

In August 1991, we acquired Pre-Press Graphics, a company that reported revenue of $471,000 through June. In January 1992, we began promoting Pre-Press with an expert newsletter dealing with desktop imaging, pre-press and printing. We made three drops of 10,000 with issue No. 1, then mailed the second and third issues to new subscribers and names in our in-house database. As a result, at midyear 1992, revenue at Pre-Press Graphics was up 75% to $826,000. Much of that new work entailed printing, so we had to ensure that we keep those customers through quality work and unmatched service.

We also use a programmed implementation of traditional marketing practices. This is a fiercely competitive business. So, while we're adept at managing the product and price elements of the marketing mix, the competition is as well. We have to excel in promotion and channel management. We advertise, hold special seminars, sponsor a design competition, conduct strategic PR – the works. We manage sales very aggressively, and when we get clients, we break our backs to keep them.

Our company's revenue has grown to more than $12 million in 1992, from $700,000 in 1982. We expect to reach $15 million in revenue by 1995, and $30 million by 2000.

George Platt is president and CEO of The Harty Press in New Haven, Connecticut.

Reading 10

Database marketing: building long-term customer relationships for maximum profits

Wendy S. Close

Reprinted from *Telemarketing*, November 1991, Vol. 10, No. 5, pp. 50–6. Published by Technology Marketing Corporation, One Technology Plaza, Norwalk, CT 06854 USA.

What can database marketing do? According to Skip Andrew, executive director of the National Center For Database Marketing, "Database marketing enables us to profile, clone, nurture and cross-sell our customers – all for the purpose of establishing a long-term relationship of trust and repeat business that enables us to garner and guard market share."

THE IMPORTANCE OF DATABASE MARKETING

At a time when many businesses are facing cutbacks, why is database marketing so important? First, database marketing provides a way to find the most responsive market segments and market directly to those individuals. Second, database marketing provides a way to cut marketing and promotion expenses by fine-tuning marketing programs. With database marketing, you will no longer be wasting time and money sending broad advertising messages to disinterested audiences. We have seen increased saturation and diminishing returns in most mass-media channels of promotion. Mass media has become too cluttered with information, and customers are learning to tune-out most advertising messages. "The real gift in uncertain times is that they teach, even force, us all to get extremely smart about how, when and who we mail, call or contact," said Andrew. Third, the effectiveness and reality of rising paper, printing, promotion, publishing, press, programming and postage costs are concerns. Last, with database marketing, you can quickly implement many cost-effective, large-response marketing programs on a small budget.

In order to survive in this increasingly competitive environment, you need to design and implement a system that enables you to compete with maximum efficiency, continued growth and long-term profitability. "Database marketing utilizes specially designed software to build, augment and parlay customer and prospect data into a systematic, ultra-profitable, promotional program personalized to the needs and interests of individual addressees," according to Andrew. "By gathering specific information about a customer – e.g., job function, size of company, product interests – we can narrow our media so that we target only to those most likely to respond favorably. On our end, it saves enormous amounts of money by eliminating mass, blanketed promotions. On the customer's end, it creates the impression that we send no junk, but only messages he or she wants to receive," said Andrew.

Due to the condition of today's marketplace, individualized database marketing offers the personal touch most customers are seeking. In addition, it increases your response rate per marketing dollar spent, lowers your cost per order, builds business and increases profits.

MARKETING TRENDS SHOW NEED FOR DATABASE MARKETING

Stan Rapp and Tom Collins, authors of *The Great Marketing Turnaround, The Age of the Individual and How to Profit From it,* define seven root causes, outlined below, for turning away from marketing practices of the past and rethinking the basics of marketing strategy in the '90s.

1) *Changing demographics and lifestyles* – The constant changing demographic mix of society means that yesterday's target markets are often simply not there today.

2) *Demands on personal time* – "Advertisers must almost literally run down the street to catch up with and buttonhole the hurrying customers."

3) *Overcrowding by too many new products, services and stores* – "The overcrowding of the marketplace is a fact of life that absolutely must be taken into account in the strategic planning of all marketing today."

4) *Weakening of the magic in network television advertising* – "Network television advertising rates (per ratings point) have continued to go up, up, up. And American households are bombarded by more, more, more commercials, which keep getting shorter and shorter."

5) *Decline in brand loyalty* "The ability of manufacturers to copy one another's most successful products, and the brand-hopping encouraged by tempting discounts, may be seriously weakening the grip of brand loyalty in many categories."

6) *Advertising clutter, overkill and waste* – "Studies show that a typical consumer is bombarded by 5,000 advertising messages a day, and the

number of ads is expected to increase steadily. That trend has many executives in the industry worried about the cost of breaking through the growing advertising clutter."

7) *Feeding the discount promotion monster* – "The A.C. Nielsen Co. did a study of 862 packaged goods promotions and came up with some startling results. More than 50 percent of the events had no impact on sales, and only one promotion in 10 generated a volume gain of 10 percent or more."

Rapp and Collins noted, "If you work in an annual marketing budget that is only in the five-figure or six-figure range instead of tens of millions of dollars, you may wonder what many of the outlined trends have to do with you and your problems. What they have discovered is that this crisis in mass advertising effectiveness is beginning to cause many large advertisers to make a complete turnaround in their thinking about marketing. And the directions they will pursue are directions you, too, can pursue. Furthermore, you may be able to move quicker and get there sooner because you're not burdened with corporate bureaucracy or constantly changing management."

HOW DATABASE MARKETING WORKS

Let's elaborate on the definition of database marketing. According to Skip Andrew, "Database marketing consists of managing a computerized relational database system, in real-time, of comprehensive, up-to-date relevant data on customers, inquiries, prospects and suspects, to identify our most responsive customers for the purpose of developing a high-quality, long-standing relationship of repeat business by developing predictive models which enable us to send desired messages at the right time in the right form to the right people – all with the result of pleasing our customers, increasing our response rate per marketing dollar, lowering our cost per order, building our business, and increasing our profits." We will break this down into steps to build a database and implement database marketing.

First, you need a sophisticated system for managing data in real-time. Ideally, the database marketing software should be designed for and written in the highest-level computer language available (i.e., a fourth generation language or 5GL) as well as be centered around a powerful, true relational database with industry-standard interface capabilities (i.e., Structured Query Language or SQL).

A 4GL is more advanced, flexible and portable than the older 3GL languages such as Basic, Cobol or "C." Depending upon the 4GL, it may operate on many different types of hardware in either a centralized, decentralized or remote environment, which is important if you wish to provide complete mainframe to lap-top capability. The 4GL also provides greater customization capability. Therefore, as business needs evolve, the system can be quickly modified to meet changing needs.

The relational database will provide you with unlimited capabilities in managing and reporting the data. Instantaneous retrieval, tabulation or reporting of information will provide you with a powerful tool to help in marketing or customer service decisions. The power of industry-standard interface capabilities becomes more evident when the need to integrate other corporate databases with the marketing system exists, as well as integration with corporate telephone systems, mainframes, LANs, etc.

Figure 10.1 shows a sample budget for installing a sales, marketing, telemarketing, customer service and database marketing system for 50 users (assuming hardware is not currently in place).

Next, data is built for customers, inquiries, prospects and suspects so that telemarketing programs and other promotional campaigns can be designed to meet the needs of specific market segments. Rapp and Collins stress that you must start with the end result you want to accomplish – which is the individual relationship you want to cultivate with prospects and customers. This sets the criteria for building your database. Here are some typical questions you need to ask yourself. These questions have been outlined by Harry S. Dent, Jr., author and consultant in business forecasting, in a recent article published in Small Business Reports titled, "Individualized Marketing, Using Databases to Build One-on-One Customer Relationships.'

- What do we need to know about our customers?
- What key attributes differentiate the needs and qualities of our customers?
- What do customers need to know about us and our products?
- What are the best media by which to communicate with our customers? Which media allow for more personalized communications?
- How personal should the relationship be, given cost constraints?

• 50-user software license fee	$75,000
• Hardware	$75,000
• Annual software support & update	$12,000
• Software enhancement, modification and integration	$10,000
• Consultation service	$10,000
• Installation and training	$7,500
• Database preparation	$7,500
Total	$197,000

Figure 10.1 Sample budget for installing a database marketing system

- What type of image do we want our customers to have of our company?
- How often is it appropriate or beneficial to communicate with the customer?
- What frequency or types of communication could be received negatively or perceived as an annoyance by the customer?
- What are the means by which the customer can communicate his or her needs and problems to us?

Even more subjective information should be collected and recorded when relevant to future sales and service efforts, such as:

- What are the customer's specific needs?
- What specific products and services is he or she interested in?
- How quickly does the customer need delivery?
- How quality-sensitive or price-sensitive is the customer?
- Who has to approve the purchasing decision?

Figure 10.2 summarizes some of the types of information that are typically collected in databases by consumer and business-to-business marketers.

You can collect this information directly from customers and prospects, or you can tap commercial, consumer and business databases. Ways to obtain information include:

- Telemarketing campaigns,
- 800-number customers,
- Coupons with print ads, reader service cards, free samples,
- Direct-response inquiry advertising,
- Send out questionnaires with incentives,
- Collect and record information at the point of sale,
- Warranty cards,
- Tradeshows and trade journals,
- Offer benefits for frequent purchases, like clubs,
- Have salespeople tactfully solicit information on sales calls,
- Collect information from incoming orders, complaints or inquiries,
- On-line database services such as DIALOG's Business Connection, EasyNet, Delphi Information Systems, Dow Jones News/Retrieval, NEWSNET, Orbit, etc.,
- Directory databases such as the D&B Electronic Yellow Pages, and Marquis Who's Who,
- Numeric databases for statistical data through the federal government's Bureau of the Census and the Bureau of Labor Statistics,
- Overlay information onto the individual prospect or customer files in your own database by working with companies like Infobase Services, or May & Speh Direct,

Consumer	**Business-to-Business**
Name	Name of key contact
Address	Title
Age, gender	Company name and address
Income	Other company divisions and offices
Family members	Gender
Job or profession	SIC code/industry
Product/service interest	Status of account (prospect, customer
Lifestyle	Past purchase by product
Special interest	Average purchase
Past purchase by product	Frequency of purchase
Average purchase	Delivery requirements
Frequency of purchase	Special product specification
Media preferences (magazines, TV)	Approvals required
Past problems/complaints	Other key decision makers
Credit cards/credit limits	Credit limits and payment status
Delivery (Fed. Ex, etc.)	Past complaints/problems
Other product interest	Other product interests
Propensity to try new products	Propensity to try new products
	Type of account (dealer, consultant)
	Source of account
	Number of employees
	Annual sales
	Equipment used (hardware, software)
	Call/marketing history
	Quotes
	Remarks

Figure 10.2 Typical information collected in databases

- Share customer lists with a company that offers related products and services, such as the hotels, airlines and rental-car industries have done.

In summary, everything in your marketing efforts is a means of collecting information from your customers, developing personalized relationships and building your marketing database. As Dent points out, "Each piece of information increases your ability to customize marketing efforts at a lower cost."

Now, it's time to identify your most responsive customers, targeting these specific niches with specific offers. You can divide your customers and prospects into groups that share common traits. Meaningful advertising programs, telemarketing campaigns, direct mail and promotions can be tailored to each group's demographics, product interests, business size, etc. The system can then produce incremental sales by a process called cloning – noting the characteristics of a group within the database on whom a promotion works best, and then finding more people or businesses that have that group's characteristics and promoting to them as well. "You can change the message and change the media to reach the market niche for your special product or service. Or you can take the next step and reshape the product or service itself to suit the special needs of an important niche in your market," according to Rapp and Collins. Database marketing increases the probability that your customers, and potential customers, perceive your mail and phone calls as wanted, valuable information. The more they perceive you as meeting their specific needs, the more enduring the relationship, encouraging repeat business and referrals.

"You can also develop predictive models using sophisticated mathematical techniques of multi-variate analysis, allowing you to determine which telemarketing and segmentation strategies are most likely to work in a particular situation," said Skip Andrew.

Fine-tuning individualized messages to identified, profiled prospects and customers has replaced the steamrollering marketing of the past. Tom Peters, noted co-author of *In Search of Excellence*, agrees with a nationally syndicated column headlined, "Mass Marketing Is Out, Databases Are In."

When used correctly, your database marketing system will build loyal customers, increase your response rate per marketing dollar, lower your cost per order and build your business. This works because your customers will like what you are sending them, you are promoting less and only to those most likely to respond, with greater promotional efficiencies, concentrating resources on those areas where your business can grow optimally. Equally as important, your database marketing system is a corporate asset that makes it more difficult for competitors to penetrate your market share or lure your customers away.

Wendy Close is with Data Systems Support which is a 10-year-old firm specializing in sales and marketing automation software. Data Systems Support developed and markets Sales Information Response System (SIRS ™), a multi-user telemarketing, database marketing, marketing, sales and customer service productivity system for the UNIX/XENIX/AIX, OS/2, Novell and many other operating systems

Reading 11

Automation to boost sales and marketing

Productivity gets a lift from information technology

Rowland T. Moriarty and Gordon S. Swartz

Reprinted from *Harvard Business Review*, January–February 1989, pp. 100–8, with permission of Harvard Business Review.

By automating the sales and marketing functions, companies have increased sales anywhere from 10% to more than 30%.

In the rush to automate, the marketing and sales function is the next frontier. As everybody knows, over the past decade information systems have been making great inroads in engineering and manufacturing. Automation has cut direct labor to a small fraction of production costs – an average of 8% to 12% in manufacturing companies. Therefore, wringing yet more cost reductions from production labor is increasingly difficult. In such technically advanced industries as computers, semiconductors, airframes, metalworking, and autos, incremental investments are now garnering diminishing returns.

On the other hand, investments in marketing and sales automation systems hold tremendous potential for productivity improvements. Marketing and sales costs average 15% to 35% of total corporate costs (not just production costs). So a focus on marketing and sales provides a welcome lever for boosting productivity. Moreover, the importance of marketing and sales services is growing. According to the U.S. trade representative and the National Association of Accountants, manufacturers' service activities account for 75% to 85% of all value added.[1] This means that the price a product can command is less a reflection of raw materials and labor than of marketing-related services like selecting appropriate product features, determining the product mix, and ensuring product availability and delivery.

In cases we have reviewed, sales increases arising from advanced marketing and sales information technology have ranged from 10% to more than 30%, and investment returns have often exceeded 100%. These returns may sound like the proverbial free lunch, but they are real.

Because of the complexity of their marketing organizations, large companies are good prospects for what we call marketing and sales productivity (MSP) systems. Tangles of national account management, direct sales, telemarketing, direct mail, literature fulfillment, advertising, customer service, dealers, and distributors all offer opportunities for efficiency improvements. But even small companies that adopt MSP systems can expect impressive results.

Marketing automation investments by a $7 billion electronics manufacturer and an £8 million custom printing company each produced a first-year return of more than 100%. The electronics concern installed a sales support system for more than 500 salespeople. Sales rose 33%, sales force productivity rose 31%, and sales force attrition dropped 40%. The reduced attrition alone produced savings in recruiting and training costs that paid for the company's $2.5 million investment in less than 12 months. At the custom printer, an $80,000 investment in a minicomputer and telemarketing software returned a 25% increase in sales and attained payback in less than 6 months.

Increasing marketing productivity even a small amount can have a great impact on the bottom line. MSP systems have a double punch because they can reduce fixed costs and variable costs. Lower fixed costs mean lower breakeven points. So a given percentage increase in sales produces a correspondingly larger increase in operating profits, as the chart on the next page shows (Figure 11.1). Meanwhile, lower variable costs mean that every sale contributes more to the bottom line. Indeed, because lower variable costs make the slope of the new contribution curve steeper, the absolute size of the financial advantage continues to grow as sales rise.

Despite the proven worth of this technology, few companies have automated any part of their marketing and sales functions. Even fewer appear to understand the significant strategic benefits that can accrue from marketing and sales automation; most early adopters have automated as a matter of faith rather than as part of a strategy for gaining competitive advantage. A better approach begins with an understanding of what marketing and sales automation can do, how it works, and how it can be implemented.

WHAT THE SYSTEMS DO

Distinct from general office automation systems, MSP networks are of course specific to marketing and sales. They support more intense product or service differentiation, improved customer service, reduced operating costs, and more streamlined operations. Here are some MSP systems and the tasks for which they are customarily used:

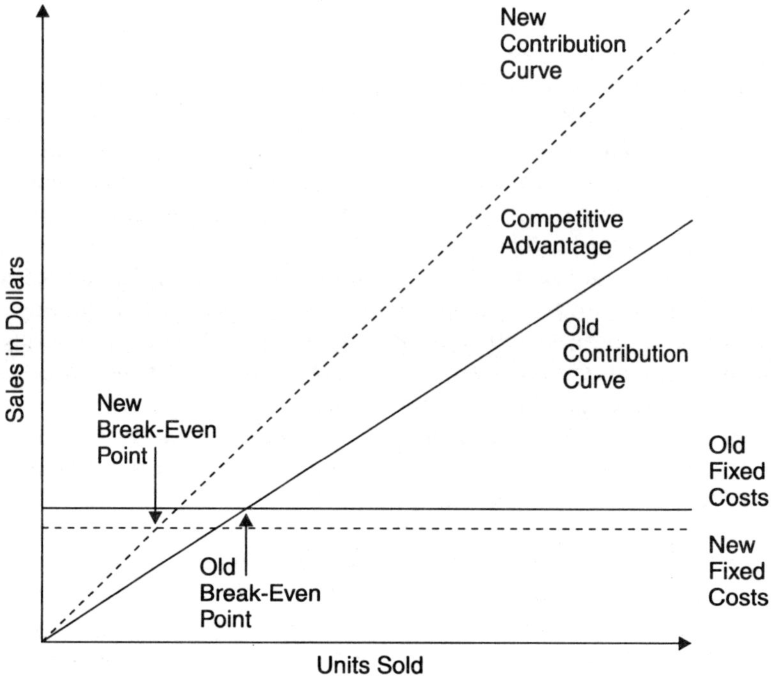

Figure 11.1 An MSP System creates a financial advantage

Salesperson productivity tools – Planning and reporting of sales calls, reporting of expenses, entering orders, checking inventory and order status, managing distributors, tracking leads, and managing accounts.

Direct mail and fulfillment – Merging, cleaning, and maintaining mailing lists; subsetting lists (or markets); tracking and forwarding leads; customizing letters, envelopes, and labels; generating "picking lists" for literature packages, and managing literature inventory.

Telemarketing – Merging, cleaning, and maintaining calling lists, subsetting lists (or markets); tracking and forwarding leads; ranking prospects; and prompting scripts (sales, customer service, and support).

Sales and marketing management – Providing automated sales management reports (sales forecasts, sales activity, forecasts versus actuals, and so on); designing and managing sales territories; and analyzing marketing and sales programs by such criteria as market, territory, product, customer type, price, and channel.

MSP systems can automate the work of a single salesperson, a single marketing activity like direct mail, or a company's entire marketing and sales operation. MSP systems also cut across every type of information technology from single-user PCs to networks of PCs, minicomputers, and mainframes serving thousands of users.

A simple system meets the needs of one fast-growing $25 million producer of data communications equipment that sells its products through 65 distributors. To cut down on paperwork in handling sales leads, the company adopted a PC-based MSP system. (See Figure 11.2 showing its operation.) Compare this with the networks supporting the more than 5,000 direct salespeople of a major office automation vendor. (See Figure 11.3 showing its operation.) This vendor's system combines direct selling, distributor relationships, telemarketing, and direct mail to: generate, qualify, rank-order, distribute, and track sales leads; fill prospects' requests for product and price information; update customer and prospect files; provide sales and technical product support by telephone; and automate order entry and sales reporting.

While the scales of these two networks are obviously vastly different, both of them collect, organize, and update information about every lead

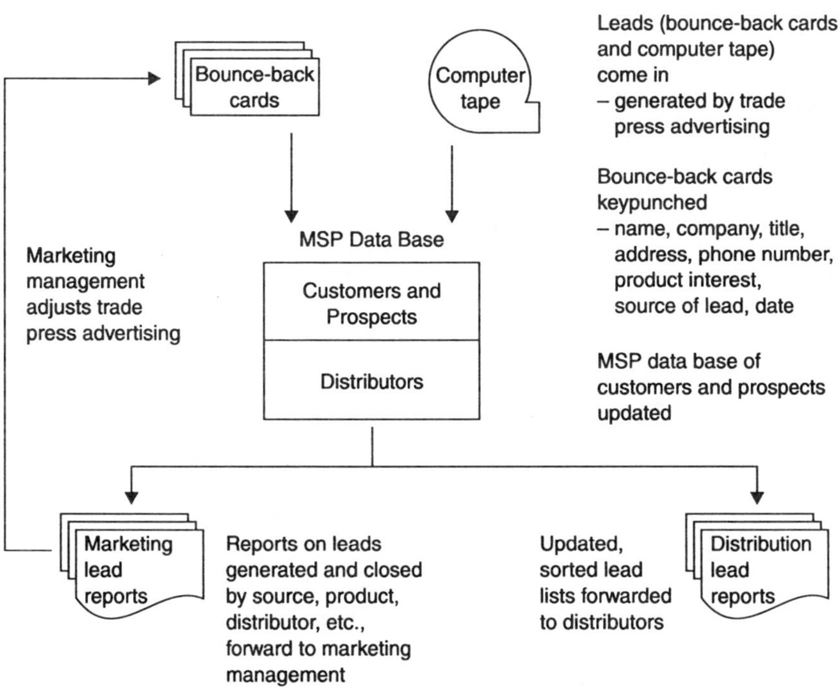

Figure 11.2 A simple MSP flow chart for handling leads

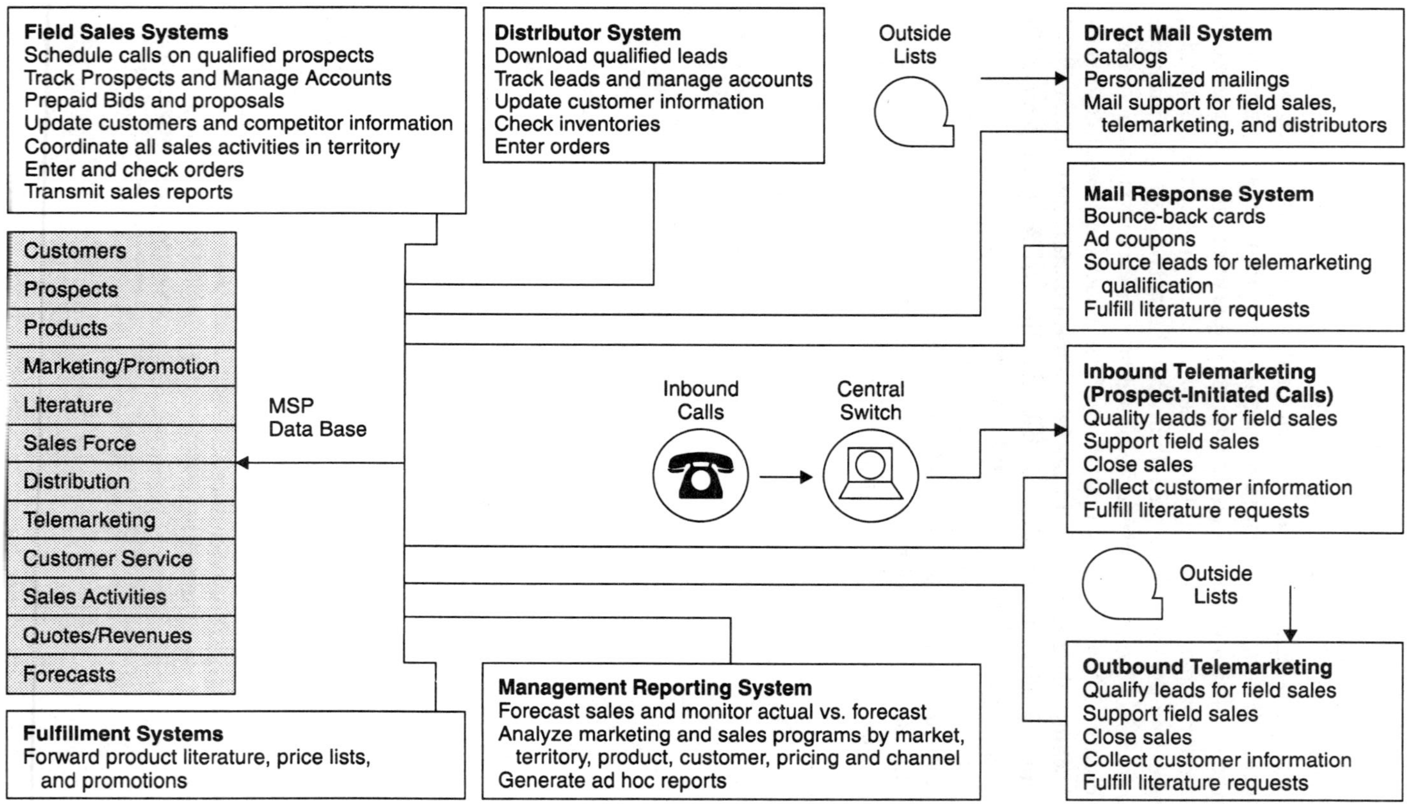

Figure 11.3 Map of an integrated MSP System for a major office automation company

generated, every sales task performed, and every customer or prospect closed or terminated. What is less obvious, but no less important, is the basis both systems provide for improving marketing and sales executives' decision making.

Most MSP data bases contain essential information on customers, prospects, products, marketing programs, and marketing channels. Some systems supplement the essentials with industry data (growth rates, entries, exits, and regulatory trends) and data on competitors (products, pricing, sales trends, and market shares). For most businesses, the information incorporates a subtle but important shift from other data bases. Rather than focusing on products (What was the cost to produce each unit? How many units were made, sold, and shipped?), the MSP data base is customer driven.

Whenever marketing or sales activities are performed, the data base captures information that answers questions about customers and their needs. Who were the prospects? What were their interests? How were these interests generated? Which sales or marketing personnel performed which tasks? When were the tasks performed? Which follow-up tasks are required and when? Did any sales result? Gradually the data base becomes a rich source of marketing and sales information, enabling management to track marketing activities and measure the results of marketing programs.

HOW THEY AID PRODUCTIVITY

MSP systems improve productivity in two ways. First, automation of selling and direct marketing support tasks boosts the efficiency of the sales and marketing staff. Second, automating the collection and analysis of marketing information improves the timeliness and quality of marketing and sales executives' decision making.

These networks make direct sales and direct marketing more efficient by automating highly repetitive support tasks, like answering requests for product literature and writing letters, and by reducing the time salespeople spend on nonselling tasks, like scheduling sales calls, compiling sales reports, generating proposals and bids, and entering orders. In 1985, Xerox installed an internally developed MSP system in its southern region. Xerox credits the system with a 10% to 20% gain in sales force productivity and with trimming $3 million off the company's 1987 marketing support and overhead budget. By automating sales administration and support tasks, Xerox has given its salespeople more time to sell.[2]

MSP systems for direct marketing also hone the efficiency of customer contracts. For example, a system for the telemarketing function can schedule and dial calls based on the prospect's priority, prompt the telemarketer with a sales script, and automatically update customer files. At Aratex Services, a $500 million uniform supply company based in Encino, California, telemarketers using the company's old manual system each made 35 to 40 calls per day and about one sale per month. Working with an automated system, each telemarketer now makes 50 or 60 calls daily and lands three or four sales per month.[3]

Automated networks also elevate the impact of each sales communication. Access to the central data base gives salespeople and direct marketers information to improve the quality of the contract, whether it is by mail, by telephone, or in person. A large financial services concern uses a telemarketing system to handle account inquiries. While responding to a customer's request or query, the telemarketer is prompted by the system to update the customer's profile information and to cross-sell other financial products.

At a division of Vanity Fair that makes women's and children's apparel, salespeople use laptop PCs to access the corporate data base for up-to-date inventory and order status information on 2,000 stock-keeping units. This step has trimmed the company's order cycle from more than two weeks to just three days. It also has made ordering more accurate, resulting in greater customer satisfaction, reduced order cancellations, and a 10% increase in sales.

In companies with many channels, MSP systems upgrade efficiency by using the central data base to track and coordinate all marketing activity. Without this cooperation, independent marketing groups often unwittingly pursue conflicting goals. At one multibillion-dollar office automation company, a direct salesperson had just nailed down a big order by giving a key account the "maximum" price discount. Before the deal was signed, however, the telemarketing group reached this customer and undercut the salesperson's price by 10%. Aside from the damage to its reputation, this vendor lost much of its expected margin on the sale.

This company is now installing an MSP system that will collect and organize information on all marketing programs and activities, including: (1) all customer contacts, whether by mail, phone, direct salesperson, or national account manager; (2) the status of all sales efforts; (3) the origins of all leads; (4) all leads that are being qualified internally and by whom, and all leads that have been forwarded to distributors; (5) all customers who decided to buy; (6) what and when they purchased; and (7) any incentives or promotions that helped close the deal. Coordination of information through this system is expected to prevent further embarrassments.

A MANAGEMENT TOOL

Creation of an MSP data base is an investment in astute management. The data base chronicles every one of a company's marketing and sales activities, from advertising that generates leads to direct mail and telephone qualification of the leads to closing the first sale – all the way through the life of each account. It enables marketing and sales management to relate marketing actions with marketplace results.

At the $25 million data communications company whose lead-handling system we diagrammed, marketing managers use the system to evaluate media placements on the basis of sales closed. Before this procedure was in place, the company had no way to link information on leads to sales and evaluated media placements solely on the number of leads generated, not closed.

MSP systems also reduce marketing inertia because they streamline the implementation of marketing programs. For example, after designing an in-house system to organize and manage its customer/prospect files, one $2.5 million industrial manufacturer let 70 manufacturer's agents go and replaced them with in-house direct mail and telemarketing functions. The results? The company raised its accounts by 50% and cut marketing costs from 18% of sales to 13%.

Systems for sales force automation also drive the rapid implementation of less drastic changes in marketing programs. By using telecommunications software and laptop PCs, Du Pont's Remington Arms division has trimmed the time requirement for a national rollout of pricing and promotional programs from two weeks to less than two days.

As marketing managers become accustomed to these systems, they find new uses for them, like analyzing and modeling the buying behavior of prospects and customers. The data base at Excelan, a $39 million marketer of circuit boards and software in San Jose, California, was essential in identifying a shift in customers' buying behavior from a very technical product focus to an office automation orientation. This discovery has influenced the marketing and sales managers' decisions about hiring and training employees as well as about selecting and developing new target markets.

Account histories also improve management's ability to devise and implement account management policies based on profits. By linking orders, services delivered, and prices paid with the actual costs of lead generation, preselling, closing, distribution, and postsale support, MSP systems furnish the tools for analyzing and adjusting the marketing mix. Grede Foundries, a Milwaukee producer of castings for original equipment manufacturers, has used the MSP system to develop a "perceived quality index" that yields a more complete and more accurate measure of customers' reactions than simply tracking returned goods. The system also provides pricing support. By tracking quoted prices and final selling prices, the system gives management a better idea of the price that will win a particular job.[4]

Economies of Scale?

Small businesses may gain an initial competitive edge from MSP systems because they often can adopt these systems much faster than their big counterparts. With fewer levels of management, small companies are faster on their feet in making decisions. They also tend to have simpler marketing organizations, usually relying on a single-method, single-channel selling system like a small direct sales force.

Large companies face two imposing barriers. First, they generally have both multiple layers of administration and cross-functional decision-making groups. When analyzing, evaluating, and adopting MSP systems, large companies draw in not only marketing and sales but also the accounting, finance, and MIS functions. Second – as a glance at the flow chart and map shows – their marketing organizations customarily rely on complex arrangements of communications methods and selling channels. Accordingly, their MSP systems require great sophistication and customization.

In large companies, marketing and sales automation is a high-stakes decision needing the support of many parties. In a major telecommunications company, the evaluation and selection of an MSP system called for: (1) initial screening presentations by three software vendors; (2) detailed presentations to 15 senior executives; (3) a visit by eight managers to a company with an operating MSP system; and (4) at least nine internal follow-up meetings, including presentations to the vice presidents of marketing and sales, the general managers of the ten operating companies, the directors of the MIS and MIS-procurement groups, several financial analysts, and several senior salespeople. More than 40 people had a hand in the decision. All this work occurred in a period of more than nine months after the corporate decision to automate marketing and sales.

But the story doesn't end there. Once the company had selected a $200,000 off-the-shelf system, it spent 18 months and $250,000 more installing and customizing the software. During the next two years, functional additions to the system and training of the end users added more than $1 million to the cost.

Moreover, automated networks coordinate and direct sales resources – including salespeople, distributors and agents, direct mailers, telemarketers, and manufacturers' representatives – toward the highest priority prospects and customers. Hewlett-Packard's Qualified Lead Tracking System (QUILTS) electronically transmits inquiries to a telemarketing center, which qualifies and ranks them and electronically returns them to H-P headquarters. The company has trimmed the turnaround time for leads from as much as 14 weeks to as little as 48 hours. "Hot" leads are handled even faster; they are telephoned to the field sales force from the telemarketing center.[5] Similarly, field salespeople in Chevron Chemical's fertilizer division in San Francisco use laptop PCs to access rank-ordered prospect lists in the company's mainframe. At any time, the salespeople have access to leads that are only 24 hours old. Before automation, new prospect lists were printed at headquarters and mailed to the field reps, which took one to two weeks.

Finally, the MSP data base is a management tool for making better use of marketing resources – that is, ensuring that they are employed to further corporate goals rather than the goals of individual marketing or sales groups. While this may sound like something management does without effort, our research shows that optimizing marketing resources is much more easily said than done. In several companies we've looked at salespeople routinely discard hundreds or even thousands of sales leads, making little or no effort to evaluate or review them. In essence, they are dissipating the resources that generated these leads – budgets for advertising, trade shows, public relations, and other communications media.

In their defense, the salespeople complain that pursuing raw leads is a waste of time. And they are generally right. In one of these companies, salespeople who followed up the raw leads averaged only one or two sales per month, while those who followed their "instincts" averaged more than three. The cost of pursuing the raw leads was at least one lost sale per salesperson per month. To the salespeople, ignoring the leads was common sense. On the other hand, the advertising group, which was evaluated on the number of leads generated, was increasing its budgets to generate more and more leads. One company has solved this problem by implementing an MSP system that will use telemarketing to qualify leads before sending them to the salespeople. The system will also close the loop, allowing management to evaluate both the company's advertising placements and its sales efforts on the basis of their contributions to revenues and earnings.

Efficiencies gained through task automation and improved marketing management are interdependent and reinforcing. Task automation drives the collection of more complete customer and marketplace information, and more informed decision making targets marketing and sales activities where they are most effective. In this way, marketers get a bigger payoff from low-cost, low-impact selling methods, like direct mail and catalogs, as data bases customize the timing and content of mass-marketing campaigns. At the same time, high-cost, high-impact selling methods, like personal selling and national account management, become more efficient as MSP systems perform routine sales support tasks, reduce nonselling time, and synchronize the use of these resources.

When you combine low-cost, low-impact methods with high-cost, high-impact approaches to gain just the right amount of stimulus at just the right time, you can obtain hefty impact at minimum cost. Hewlett-

Packard, for one, has taken advantage of this synergy and has discovered the savings made possible by orchestrating direct mail, telemarketing, and personal selling.

HOW TO GET FROM HERE TO THERE

The cases we have reviewed show that companies implementing MSP systems encounter many of the same barriers they would confront adopting any new technology.[6] From our observation, the process can be streamlined by following six guiding principles.

1. *Clarify the scale of the project as well as potential additions.* An audit of the marketing and sales tasks will yield these categories: those that must be automated now, those that will or may be automated later, and those that will not be automated. This simple exercise will identify marketing and sales activities that must be coordinated and focus the automation effort on getting measurable results without sacrificing flexibility.

It is important to view the project not from the perspective of the marketing groups but from a corporate perspective. With a corporate view, the company can build a "battleship" – a system that takes advantage of information-sharing and task-coordination synergies. Without this strategic perspective, independent marketing groups are more likely to invest in a number of incompatible and wasteful "rowboats." And even a rowboat can cause problems. At a big high-tech manufacturer, eight salespeople had their own PC-based sales force automation system installed. By raising issues of compatibility, data entry, and "file structure definitions," they delayed the start-up of a companywide, 300-salesperson MSP system for more than a year.

2. *Concentrate on tasks that can add value for the customer.* As in other corporate activities, marketers can get competitive advantage in two ways: by lowering costs and by enhancing the differentiation of the product or service offering. At the custom printer we referred to, streamlined job-costing and order-entry processes enable customers to price and place orders with one phone call. The "real-time" order-entry and order-tracking capabilities of the Vanity Fair unit's salespeople have upgraded its customer service. In both cases, customers benefit from better service, and sellers benefit from lower costs.

Other companies add value by using automation to improve the exchange of information during sales calls. The 22 salespeople in Hercules's Fragrance and Food Ingredient Group use their laptop PCs and a computer program called Flavor Briefs to consult with prospects on applications. Otherwise, Hercules salespeople would be unable to provide such detailed advice on their product line's many applications. The system saves the customer and the salesperson time and also furnishes a valuable service.

3. *In the budget process, account for hidden costs and intangible benefits.* Budgeting for an MSP system entails overcoming three principal obstacles: high perceived financial risk, poorly understood benefits, and biased capital budgeting systems.

First, automating marketing and sales is costly. A typical hardware and software outlay per salesperson ranges from $4,000 to $7,000 – so automating the tasks of 100 field salespeople can cost between $400,000 and $700,000. In addition, if the MSP system must communicate with other corporate information systems, it is likely to require the development of specialized minicomputer, mainframe, or communications networking software.

Department-level telemarketing or direct mail systems range in price from $30,000 to more than $100,000. Sales or marketing management software may up the price another $30,000 to $100,000. Of course, the cost of tying all these pieces together depends on how many pieces there are, where they are located, and how they communicate. It would not be unusual for a company with 500 salespeople as well as telemarketing, fulfillment, and direct mail operations to spend between $3 million and $5 million on integrated MSP hardware and software.

But the budget process must anticipate and account for hidden costs too. In a number of cases we studied, in-house information was so scattered and communications equipment so incompatible that simply preparing a customer list required a major effort. Other hidden costs include system customization, expert consulting, and end-user training. Depending on the circumstances, these services can double or even triple the overall cost.

Because malfunctioning of an automated marketing system can threaten a business's revenue stream, it's advisable to budget for the cost of two systems – automated and manual – until the network has proved out. Naturally, all these expenses ratchet up the perceived financial risk of MSP automation.

On the other side of the equation, estimating the full financial benefit of an MSP system is extremely difficult. Tangible productivity gains, like increases in selling time and cost reductions on telephone campaigns, can be gauged fairly accurately. But intangible productivity gains, like better marketing decision making, more responsive customer service, and deeper understanding of customers, are much more difficult to track.

Still, it would be a mistake to ignore them, especially since capital budgeting processes are often biased against intangible productivity investments. Furthermore, few marketing managers and even fewer sales managers know much about their companies' capital budgeting processes – especially when huge investments in information technology are at stake. Senior executives have to take care that the process remains flexible enough to give MSP automation a reasonable evaluation.

An MSP system is a strategic investment for the whole corporation. But unlike other assets that are consumed over time, the more it is used, the more valuable it becomes. So it should be viewed as a long-term asset, not as the expense of a functional group. And, needless to say, senior management must match the scale of the company's investment to the scale of the project. Otherwise, fragmented marketing budgets will foster fragmented automation. The result, as noted above, may be many MSP rowboats with little or no coordination or compatibility.

4. *Make any tests realistic.* Because launching a full-scale network can be tremendously risky, most companies hedge their bets first by piloting automation on small portions of their marketing operations. A single function, like telemarketing or personal selling, is usually the test site. If this pilot is successful, the company adds more functions.

This ramp-up strategy, however, has serious drawbacks. It permits no insight into the complexity of coordinating multiple marketing and sales activities. Though single-function solutions may yield gratifying returns, evidence of their true worth may also stay hidden until they are combined into a system that demonstrates synergy. Consequently, estimates of financial returns based on single-function pilots may be negatively biased.

Finally, critical performance limitations may remain hidden unless the complexity and scale of the test parallel the system's actual use. One big manufacturer's telemarketing pilot ran flawlessly, providing the telemarketers with a steady stream of calls and instant access to customer profiles and scripts. But eventual integration of telemarketing with other MSP networks seriously degraded the performance of the overall system. Every time the telemarketers asked for new information during a call, they were confronted by blank computer screens for more than 40 seconds. As the business manager put it, "That's a long time to talk about baseball."

A company with a multichannel, multimethod marketing system is better off with a pilot plan that automates a multifunctional subset of the marketing organization. In this type of pilot, an integrated system, encompassing all marketing and sales functions, is installed for a single division, region, product line, or customer group. This experience is likely to be more realistic than the single-function approach.

5. *Pinpoint the roles and responsibilities of those selecting, designing, and operating the system.* Even standard MSP systems, though they may be touted as off-the-shelf products, require extensive customization. This necessity complicates the selection or design process in a number of ways.

- The process requires expertise in technology (computers, data communications, and software) as well as in marketing and sales.
- Naturally, a company's existing MIS systems are likely to constrain the choice (or development) of an MSP system.

• Marketing professionals and MIS professionals rarely speak a common language, and they often approach marketing automation projects with different perspectives. While marketing thinks about functionality (e.g., Will the system help perform marketing and sales tasks?), MIS people often focus on technical considerations (e.g., Will the system interact with other corporate information systems? Who is responsible for ensuring the integrity of corporate data bases?).

It's senior management's job to make sure that the MIS and marketing professionals talk to each other and work together. It's not easy. An MIS group may automate its conception of marketing and sales only to discover later that the automated system does not actually work. Everybody knows of cases in which the MIS department loads the sales force down with reams of report forms to complete and return to headquarters. Of course, much of the requested information is irrelevant from the salespeople's standpoint, and the report forms end up in the same round file as the old lead cards.

During the long, complex process of designing and implementing a major MSP system, responsibilities sometimes become diffuse and project accountability gets blurred. In one case we know of, poorly defined responsibilities for MIS and marketing have caused big headaches. Bickering over cost allocations and data-base controls has made the company's $1 million MSP system useless. The MIS group will not allow marketing to access the corporation's data bases. But the marketing group's computer budget is too low to keep the marketing data base up-to-date. (Not surprisingly, headquarters viewed the entire MSP development process as a marketing expense instead of a corporate investment.)

6. *Modify the technology and the organization to support the system.* As in every instance in which management implements new technology, it must pay close attention to the attitudes of people in the organization. In successful MSP implementations that we have seen, both the organization and the MSP system have gone through an interactive process of change – altering the technology to fit the marketing and sales environment, then altering the environment to fit the technology.

To be useful, for example, the MSP data base obviously must contain accurate, up-to-date information. Because obtaining this information requires salespeople to use the system and to support the information collection process, they have to become adept at using the new technology. Problems can result, however, if the end-users lack computer skills or if they are uninterested in using the system.

Training can overcome skill problems (if enough money is budgeted and enough time set aside), but lack of interest is harder to deal with. Experience suggests that the best way to sell the sales staff on the network is to demonstrate that it can give every user something back.

That is, by helping salespeople or telemarketers work more productively, MSP systems can boost not only the company's sales but also *their* sales and *their* compensation.

For many companies, postponement of automation of the marketing function may seem to be a good way of skirting a difficult decision, but this do-nothing posture condemns the organization to being a marketing laggard. It may also be a costly mistake. Early adopters of MSP systems have gained superior competitive advantage. Compared with their "manual" competitors, they perform selling tasks with greater economy and impact. They know their customers better and can tailor their sales communications to supply just the right amount of sales stimulus at just the right time. Overall, they craft and control their marketing programs more intelligently. In the long run, the competitive barriers they establish may change the nature of marketing in their industries.

In view of this impressive record, some marketers about to embark on automation may embrace unrealistically high expectations. But MSP systems cannot work miracles. They will not offset a poorly conceived or poorly executed marketing strategy. They will not compensate for an inferior sales force, and they will not sell inferior products. Complex MSP systems are difficult to implement, and the associated returns, like any other lasting accomplishment, have to be earned.

Rowland T. Moriarty is an associate professor of business administration at the Harvard Business School, where he currently conducts a course on creative marketing strategy. Before entering teaching, he held sales management and marketing positions at Xerox and IBM. Gordon S. Swartz is a research associate at the Harvard Business School and was formerly research director at the Competitive Assessment Center, a computer industry research company.

Authors' note: We thank Professor Thomas V. Bonoma of the Harvard Business School and Charles A. Khuen, president of Adelie Corporation, for helpful comments on early drafts of this article.

References

1 James Brian Quinn, Jordan J. Baruch and Penny Cushman Paquette, "Technology in Services," *Scientific American*, December 1987, p 50.
2 Thayer C. Taylor, "Xerox: Who Says You Can't be Big and Fast?," *Sales and Marketing Management*, November 1987, p. 63.
3 Kate Bertrand, "Converting Leads with Computerized Telemarketing," *Business Marketing*, May 1988, p. 58.
4 Louis A. Wallis, *Computers and the Sales Effort* (New York Conference Board, 1986).
5 Karen Blue, "Closing the Loop: Hewlett-Packard's New Lead Management System," *Business Marketing*, October 1987, p. 74.
6 Dorothy Leonard-Barton and William A. Kraus, "Implementing New Technology," HBR November–December 1985, p. 102.

Reading 12

The database marketing imperative

A good customer information file can get managers back to the future

Terry G. Vavra

Reprinted from *Marketing Management*, 1993, Vol. 2, No. 1, pp. 47–57. Published by the American Marketing Association.

Executive briefing:
The market of the 1980s was characterized by vast amounts of information at the aggregate market level. The '90s "decade of the database" is being characterized by information at the individual customer level. By using the data in interactive customer files, marketing managers have an opportunity to establish the type of "personal" relationships salespeople once had with their customers. Instead of single-mindedly pursuing new customers, managers will be able to focus on "aftermarketing" activities to retain current customers. The challenge is to learn as much as possible about database marketing and then rapidly apply this knowledge to marketing practice.

Prior to the 1960s, marketing was implemented primarily through salespeople establishing relationships with customers. They took pride in knowing customers personally and in building special and lasting relationships with them. Such relationships, they found, kept customers returning.

But during the '60s, '70s, and '80s, as marketing was acknowledged and given a distinct corporate role, its predominant focus shifted to achieving greater distribution. Dealer networks, retail chains, and other intermediaries proliferated, inviting some marketers to abdicate their responsibilities of customer contact. Separation from customers put them out of mind.

At the same time, consumers started expecting greater variety in the products and services they were buying. In response, marketers vastly expanded their product and service offerings, but the complexity of the market combined with marketers' isolation from their end-use customers made focusing on customer needs difficult.

Marketers attempted to cope by collecting and studying volumes of information about "typical category consumers." Attitude and usage studies became marketers' primary view of their customers, and relationships with individual customers were replaced by relationships with "average customers." Marketers also became dependent on the mass media as the primary channel of communication with their customers. However, as media costs and clutter increased, marketers began to doubt the efficiency of this approach.

During the same three decades, computer technology underwent significant improvements in storage capacity, storage costs, and processing speed; a similarly impressive increase in the availability of data accompanied these developments. All of these factors combined to form the essential marketing tool in the 1990s: the database.

Marketers who implement marketing strategies with well-designed databases, or CIF's (customer information files), will be able to interact with their customers in as personal a way as their sales counterparts did in the '40s and '50s.

KNOWING YOUR CUSTOMERS

Treating customers as individuals has long been the perspective of direct marketers, who observe purchase behavior and keep detailed records at the individual level. This perspective has made direct marketing accountable for its programs: sales results easily can be attributed to specific tactics, strategies, or products.

Mainstream marketing, in contrast, has operated with little information at the individual customer level. Rather, the mainstream marketer's understanding of the "typical customer" has come from mathematical averages or inferred profiles. (The advent of UPC scanner panels has recently made more precise information available, but only in limited marketing areas among consumers willing to participate.)

Direct marketers also have had a different orientation toward their customers. Using updated databases of individual customers, they have invested in forming long-term relationships with customers. They record each purchase a customer makes, track the customer's "lifetime" purchases, and calculate the customer's value.

Four basic direct marketing capabilities are missing from traditional marketing:

- Addressability – being able to identify every customer and reach each one on an individual basis.
- Measurability – knowing whether or not the customer purchased; exactly what was purchased; how, where, and when it was purchased; and the purchase history.

Preparing for Doomsday?

Philip Morris' database activities show how aggressive some marketers can be in relating to their customers. The entry form for the company's recent Penske RM1 Corvette Sweepstakes is more of a questionnaire than an entry form. Those wishing to enter are asked to provide (1) their signature guaranteeing the respondent is 21 years of age, a licensed driver, and a cigarette smoker; (2) their regular brand of cigarettes; (3) the type of cigarette their regular brand is considered; (4) the length of time they have smoked their regular brand; (5) the quantity in which the regular brand is purchased and (6) their gender, birthdate, and telephone number.

Philip Morris adds the entrants' names to its database and periodically sends each new member relevant communications and product samples.

It has been suggested that Philip Morris' communicating with customers is more than just an "occasional project" for the company. Industry rumor has it that the tobacco giant is creatively seeking solutions for a "doomsday marketing scenario" in which over-the-counter sale of cigarettes in many retail establishments may be prohibited by law. If that should happen, direct-mail sales would be the company's only viable distribution channel.

Speculation is that Philip Morris and its chief competitor, R.J. Reynolds Tobacco Co., are seizing every customer identification opportunity and constructing the most accurate and complete customer lists possible to prepare for this scenario. These lists would serve as a platform for the direct distribution of tobacco products in the future.

- Flexibility – having the opportunity to appeal to different customers in different ways, at different times.
- Accountability – having quantitative data on the gross profitability of any marketing event and qualitative data showing the type of customers who participated in each particular event.

All marketing professionals can benefit by using the tools and technical skills of direct marketing to create marketing programs that reach customers at the individual level. Although these capabilities do not come free, the ultimate payoff generally exceeds the initial development costs. Marketers who invest in developing a CIF will surpass their competitors in marketing to and servicing their customers.

WHO SHOULD USE A CIF?

CIFs are a natural component of most financial services. When applying for a loan, consumers can hardly refuse to answer a bank's questions about number of children, ages of children, and older dependents, for example. By answering this short series of questions, consumers provide the financial services marketer with a wealth of information with which to properly target them for future campaigns. But the availability of information on customers will vary by the nature of the industry and by category.

Services Marketers

Many services marketers are in the enviable position of being able to collect information from their customers as a normal part of doing business. This advantage is a consequence of an application procedure or the customer-marketer interaction that characterizes the delivery of most services.

Interestingly, the information collected doesn't always have to be volunteered through applications or questionnaires completed by the customer. ChemLawn, the lawn maintenance company, reportedly plans to develop several additional door-to-door services from analyzing its lawncare CIF. Similar business development opportunities await most services marketers who have the ability to observe the needs, behaviors, and purchases of their customers.

Durables Marketers

Durables marketers – especially those whose products are represented and sold by middlemen – are not convinced, as a group, that databases are a useful tool. Many would still claim that customer relationships are the responsibility of their channel representatives. The problem is that the typical dealer or agent handles products or services from more than one marketer and thinks nothing at all about diverting customers from one marketer's products to another's. Forgetting that their business depends on the manufacturer's reputation, these dealers jealously guard the identities of customers they consider their "own".

In light of this resistance, durables marketers have been forced to employ various tactics to learn the identities of consumers using their products. One such tactic is owner identification and warranty-registration cards that are packed with or accompany the products. The returned cards enable marketers to interact directly with their end-use customers, without having to rely on the cooperation of dealers or retailers.

To gain the cooperation of middlemen in collecting customer information, manufacturers must either provide a sufficient incentive or convince them of the joint value of the information. The astute marketer will create a program that makes the middleman the immediate benefactor – such as merchandise coupons redeemable only at one retail chain.

Consumer Packaged-Goods Marketers

For the most part, packaged-goods manufacturers have prejudged customer databases as being too costly and offering too little return on investment, but there are notable exceptions. The two largest U.S. tobacco companies have invested hundreds of millions of dollars in constructing customer databases. Kraft General Foods has experimented in several of its divisions with the opportunities afforded by databases, and Quaker Oats has established a file of 18 million households. At the 1992 Direct Marketing Association conference, 275 packaged-goods companies said they were building customer databases.

Kimberly Clark, Kraft General Foods, and Pepsi-Cola were early packaged-goods entrants into database exploration. Huggies disposable diapers used a database of expectant mothers to sell Huggies and cross-sell other Kimberly Clark products. Kraft General Foods has experimented with customer files for its Crystal Light and Kool-Aid beverage mixes and Gevalia gourmet coffee. And Pepsi has introduced a multisponsor database project centered on a plastic ID card. Anticipating competitive actions, all of these marketers are reluctant to discuss the actual results of these efforts.

Packaged-goods marketers who ignore the potential of databases most likely are focusing on short-term results. Ten million dollars spent in advertising or promotion will almost surely spike sales in the short-term, relaxing pressure from upper management and satisfying stock-holders.

The same $10 million invested in database construction or maintenance will not generate a similar sales spike. Database construction and maintenance is, by definition, a long-term venture. The results from investing in database construction may not be realized for several years, possibly exceeding the tenure of the marketing manager who made the original commitment to database marketing.

A parochial, brand-centered organizational view and qualms about whether the payback justifies the expense further impede the ready adoption of databases by packaged-goods marketers. But databases are in the future of virtually all packaged-goods marketers, for several reasons:

- Sales promotion effectiveness is being eroded by the inefficiency of mass-distributed coupons and the general "promotion overload" visited on every U.S. household. More than 276 billion coupons are distributed each year. That's 3,000+ coupons per household!
- Continuity programs are gaining favor over coupon programs because the former promise to build customer loyalty. Conveniently, they also happen to provide input for database construction.
- UPC scanners at retailers' cash registers are collecting data and creating databases at the local level.

- National marketers will need to "combat" local retailers' increased database sophistication.
- Retailers are becoming increasingly greedy regarding the fees they exact from marketers for placing products on their shelves.

The general reticence displayed by packaged-goods marketers will ultimately be overcome, some experts believe, by technological advances that decrease database costs as well as the costs of reaching customers.

THE BENEFITS OF A CIF

The purpose of the CIF is to form an electronic link with the customer. A well-designed database can help to implement "aftermarketing," or customer retention activities, in several ways:

- Marketing efforts become more efficient and effective by virtue of the marketer being able to identify her most important customers and present them with the right offer, product, or service at the right time.
- Computer technology allows marketers to interact with customers in a truly personalized manner.
- Marketers can maintain a "dialogue" with consumers to supplement the representation offered (or not offered) by intermediaries.
- Changes in purchase patterns can alert the marketer to the possibility of a defecting customer, creating a real-time continuity program.
- Marketers can establish and reinforce brand loyalty by acknowledging and rewarding repeat purchases.
- New product development is facilitated by knowing who has purchased a product, how satisfied they are, and if any performance improvements would enhance their satisfaction.

The CIF can bond customers to marketers as never before. And marketers can cement this bond with two tactics: appreciation and relevance.

Appreciation

Marketers must actively acknowledge the value of customers by knowing and recognizing their particular needs and desires. Marketers in the microcomputer software industry learned how important this knowledge can be when end-users, perceiving that software marketers were indifferent to their needs and interests, formed their own user groups. Requests from these groups carried far more weight than a letter from any single user ever could have.

Another more common reason that users form groups – the sharing of information and networking – suggests a further failure on the marketer's part to support such customer needs fully.

Marketers can express appreciation by constantly inviting customers' opinions and asking them to review new product development plans or prototypes. For example, many marketers circulate magazines or newsletters to all registered customers, celebrating their "customership" and providing useful information to ensure long-term satisfaction. Stories in such publications can feature or identify other customers and, by doing so, may further reinforce individual customers' selection of the product or company.

Relevance

Database marketing enables the marketer to customize at the individual customer level. A CIF is capable of bringing the special relationships of niche-marketing to mainstream marketers. The result of this customization is consistent with Peter Drucker's 1973 description of customer-oriented marketing: "The aim of marketing is to know and to understand the customer so well that the product or service fits him and sells itself."

HOW TO CONSTRUCT A CIF

From direct marketers' experiences with creating customer databases, I have devised four maxims for effectively building a customer database:

1 Anticipate as many customer facts and responses as you'll require in the foreseeable future.
2 Plan the components of the database carefully, but expect changes in the future.
3 Don't delay building the database while trying to specify the ultimate structure. It's better to construct a smaller, less grandiose database and use it sooner to gain experience and assess its value.
4 Involve as many departments and individuals in the construction as possible.

The key to successful database marketing is having customer information drive the firm. Make the database available to all relevant departments. The file will get more use and will be improved by the input from many different sources. As the data added to the CIF becomes more diverse, the CIF serves the indirect purpose of helping to integrate the many customer-contact activities and departments of the organization.

For example, the following activities could be captured within or linked to the CIF: field sales reports; customer financial reports; product development opportunities from customer comments and complaints; customer transaction reports including service requests, promotion participation, and literature requests/fulfillment; processing of customers' orders; and information from questionnaires and surveys.

The successful CIF will capture virtually *all* interactions between customers and the organization. It also should be dynamic and expandable. If the CIF is constructed using a "relational structure," the components of the database can always be modified in content and changed in number.

Who Will Build the CIF?

Propriety is an issue when considering who will build the file. Generally, if a CIF is constructed internally, it will be a proprietary database. Several different combinations of origination and access are possible.

In the case of a proprietary database built by an external service bureau, the database could ultimately be brought in-house for day-in, day-out upkeep and maintenance.

"Shared" databases also are becoming popular. Two or more noncompetitive marketers (whose products are likely purchased by the same consumers) join together to co-fund the formation of a database that each can use. Although sharing is a financially attractive alternative, it may be difficult to find the right partners for such a collaboration. And, one marketer will need to expend the extra effort to organize the venture. An external vendor would likely construct and maintain a shared database.

Deciding whether to construct the database internally or externally is a difficult decision. Few managers wish to advocate spending money on "the outside" for resources that are available internally. However, many experts warn of problems that may arise when relying on a corporate MIS department to construct and maintain the customer information file.

- Generally, an MIS department will not be equipped with either the right machinery or talents to construct the database.
- Placing the database in-house may lead to a "tug-of-war" over computer storage space and talk of downscaling the database to make it fit into the surplus space currently available.
- In-house production priorities will generally work against the CIF. A marketing project is likely to receive a lower run-time priority than inventory, payroll, accounts receivable, or manufacturing jobs.
- The MIS "culture" is often at odds with the dynamic nature of a CIF, which will require constant testing, updating, and on-line access.
- On-line operations require a special know-how and a real-time system. The need to access a CIF on a continual basis will not easily coexist with the arbitrary shutdowns of many MIS systems.

The decision comes down to control. Marketing rarely, if ever, manages the MIS function. Therefore, the marketing department may have little, if any, clout within the MIS department. The speed with

A New Twist for Sales

Launching a new product is an anxiety-producing experience for any manufacturer. How best to promote the product? Who will buy it, and why? What product features will influence the decision to buy most? Will sales have "legs," or will the product bomb like a bad movie?

The Skil Corp. faced those questions when it introduced its cordless power screwdriver, The Twist. Skil conducts an extensive owner registration program by including a detailed questionnaire with each product it sells. The company analyzes these cards closely when it introduces new products, and those returned for The Twist provided some very useful positioning information. Skil product development people then conducted follow-up interviews with purchasers, said Ron Techter, manager of worldwide product development for Skil, who explained what happened next.

"The research proved quickly that the screwdriver was not a fad, which had been one of our fears, but a viable power tool," he said. "That database enabled us to launch a multimillion dollar ad campaign," because responses from the registration cards confirmed the product.

The Skil product registration cards and the follow-up interviews also yielded a surprising fact. Although the do-it-yourself aspect was a chief product benefit, "We hadn't realized the arthritis implications," said Techter. "The Skil cards and our follow-up uncovered something we hadn't thought of." In response Skil began advertising in publications geared to older Americans.

Source: "A New Twist for Sales," *Focus*, National Demographics & Lifestyles, Spring 1988.

which changes can be made to the CIF will depend on MIS programmers' availability. In contrast, an external database supplier is willing to meet requests in a timely fashion and has the appropriate database construction expertise. External suppliers build the database on their own system and then either maintain it there or move it to the client's marketing department system.

The issue of access is equally complicated. A syndicated supplier will manage the collection of a marketer's customer information or will transfer existing records into its own preformatted files for a reasonably small per-record fee. Although this process may ease the financial burden of establishing the customer information file, it does place the file somewhat at "arm's length." Requests for custom reports and analyses must be made to the supplier and will likely incur charges and time delays. In deciding who will build the CIF, the marketer must balance access, control, and cost.

Who Will Be Included in the CIF?

Although you may want to consider many groups for specific applications, four general constituencies ought to be included in every CIF:

- Current customers, marked by frequency of purchase, average order volume, lifetime value, and recency of last purchase.
- Prospective customers, identified by their similarity with existing customers or from purchased files of category users. Some may be committed to competitors, but knowing their identities may lead to an investigation of why they buy from the competitor, answering the question, "What's the competitor's advantage?"
- Lapsed or lost customers, even though beyond the immediate goal of retention, should be retained in the file and sent correspondence. (Ongoing studies conducted among "lost customers" repeatedly show many can be won back. Eliminating them from the database removes them from access.)
- The stores, dealers, or merchandise customers use derived from their purchases. Information such as the preference for different departments, stores, branches, or dealerships or the attractiveness of merchandise lines can be deducted from the purchase records of customers.

Flexibility and imagination should prevail in the selection of each component group.

What Information Will Be Collected?

The information to be included in the customer information file will necessarily be customized to the marketer's specific needs, but traditionally the three most important components of a customer database have been:

1 Recency: When was the customer's last purchase made?
2 Frequency: How often does the customer purchase?
3 Monetary value: How much money has the customer spent over a specific period of time?

These components collectively have been referred to as "RFM." The availability of each component may vary with the marketer's category.

Because computer database storage costs have fallen dramatically, marketers are becoming more ambitious about the range of information they'd like included in a CIF.

How Will the CIF Be Organized?

The storage structure you select has a profound effect not only on how adaptable and easily updated the file will be, but also on how easily the structure is understood and how quickly it can be built. Two types of structure for the CIF are:

Flat (or sequential): In a flat file, the customer records are all the same length because they are composed of the same number and type of fields (whether each field is relevant to each customer or not). All the records reside in one database.

Relational: In relational files, an infinite number of physically separate database files can be linked together. When you want to incorporate new information into the CIF, a new file is established and related (indexed) to the existing main database.

The computer hardware itself is the second concern. Although many people assume that a large-scale CIF requires storage and access through a mainframe, powerful personal computers are now a feasible alternative for all but the very largest of applications.

Controlling software is another concern. "Off-the-shelf" programs are able to handle standard applications. But for highly customized applications, marketers may need a more sophisticated software package or custom programming.

How Will the CIF Be Used?

In addition to its primary role in customer retention, the CIF can be used for a variety of practical marketing activities, including:

- Segmenting the customer base according to purchase frequency, volume-use occasions, and purchase preferences.
- Tailoring marketing programs to fit the individual needs of customers to make the marketing mix more relevant.
- Generating a profile of customer types to guide current marketing procedures and stimulate the development of new, complementary products.
- Enhancing the potential of the file further with surveys and lifestyle databases that increase the degree of intimacy with which the customers are "known."
- Supporting customer service operations better by making information in the CIF available to customer service reps as they interact with customers.
- Identifying additional, high-likelihood purchasers on the basis of their profile similarity with current customers or their known use of the category.

SPECIFIC BENEFITS OF A CIF

The CIF lets the marketer assess the value of individual customers in ways never before possible. Three of the most important measures are determining the lifetime value of a customer, identifying the costs of acquiring a new customer, and facilitating customer "scoring" and "affinity modeling."

Lifetime Customer Value

One of the most useful constructs of a CIF is the ability to calculate the lifetime value of a customer. Procedures for calculating lifetime value range from the pragmatic to the sophisticated. Some modeling procedures provide a level of precision that goes far beyond what is typically known about today's packaged-goods segments, i.e., females 25–34.

Pragmatic methods of calculating lifetime customer value can be based on the total customer base or more precisely calculated within customer cohorts on the basis of some event such as date of first purchase, type of offer originally redeemed, and so forth.

Once the customer group is selected, the next step is to define which customers are to be considered active. Customers have a distinct life within an organization – from their first purchase to their last. The problem is, while a first purchase is easily identified, the last is not as evident.

Defining who may be considered an active customer depends on the purchase cycle of the category or industry. A customer missing a specified number of purchase cycles should probably be considered lost. Even though it's human nature to try to deny the loss of a customer, it serves no purpose to delude oneself by optimistically extending the definition of an active customer beyond a certain number of missed purchase cycles.

Once the definition of an active customer is established, the marketer can use it to identify all the customers who meet this criterion. An aggregate estimate of lifetime customer value can be made by determining the total lifetime purchases of all active customers and then dividing by the total number of active customers:

$$\text{lifetime value} = \frac{\text{total purchases of all active customers}}{\text{total number of active customers}}$$

Average lifetime value is then defined as the average dollars of purchases made by the typical customer during his or her "lifetime" as a customer.

If the marketer selects a cohort analysis, the estimates of lifetime customer value will be more precise. First, determine the average lifetime

Enhancing a CIF With External Information

The two major sources for appendable information that can be added to a company's own customer information file are proprietary databases and external databases.

Proprietary Databases

These lists belong to another marketer operating in a noncompetitive category. Well-known companies that may rent their lists include Sharper Image, Bloomingdale's By Mail, and Hertz Rent-A-Car Gold Club.

External Databases

Several national suppliers offer major database files that can be combined with internal customer files to enhance them. Major types of lists include: mass-compiled, financial-based, questionnaire-generated, and combinations of these (known in the industry as "multisourced enhancement files"). These databases will include information on consumption behavior, financial interests and status, automobile ownership, and so forth.

The following descriptions identify the most important suppliers of each of four basic types of external data.

Mass-Compiled Databases

R.L. Polk & Co. Polk originated its principal mass-compiled database, X-1, in 1973. By 1990, it contained data on more than 87 million U.S. households (well over 96% of all households). The X-1 is produced by cross-referencing data from 22 different data sources and updating the file six times a year.

The most important source files are: current auto registrations; truck registrations; households contacted by Polk's door-to-door interviewers: residential telephone listings; new car buyers; records of births, high school and college enrollments, and graduations; direct mail respondents; home owners; credit card users; questionnaires; and members of the National Demographics and Lifestyles database.

Donnelley Marketing. Donnelley's master file; the Donnelley Quality Index^2 Peoplebank, is a "super" database of 124 million consumers and their home addresses. The database has been culled from 4,700 telephone directories, automobile registrations, drivers license data, voter registrations, birth records, Donnelley's Carol Wright coupon distribution program, direct mail donors, and mail order buyers.

DQI^2 can be accessed at any level of geography from the smallest (block group) to the largest (national) and offers five subsets: The Automobile File, The Seniors List, New Movers List, The Creditworthy Enhancement, and The Affluence Model.

Metromail. This division of R.R. Donnelley maintains its National Consumer Database of 83 million households and 185 million individual names and addresses that includes information from new home owners, new movers, families with births, and households with high school or college students. The database is updated 65 times a year.

The National Consumer Database can be tied directly into R.R. Donnelley's Selectronic printing and binding technology offering the possibility of totally customized mailings to members of the database.

Financial Databases

TRW, a long-time credit checking service, recently entered the consumer information services field by upgrading the contents of its database. It offers the Performance Data System, a database of 143 million individuals with credit and demographic information. TRW draws its information from three sources: public records, financial institutions, and retailer accounts. The database contains more than 300 demographic characteristics and 400 financial variables, but excludes credit-related information.

Questionnaire Generated Data

Computers for Marketing Technology. CMT offers BehaviorBank, a questionnaire generated and maintained database of 25 million consumers. CMT is very active in mailings to its database members, regularly offering sample packs and updating questionnaires.

National Demographics & Lifestyles. NDL pioneered the field of questionnaire-generated databases with its 1978 introduction of Lifestyle Selector. By 1990, the database contained 27 million names, with demographic and lifestyle information. NDL gathers information from more than 15 million new questionnaires a year and uses it to expand and refresh the Lifestyle Selector. The questionnaires are included with consumer goods (mainly durables such as cameras, electronic equipment, appliances, and sporting goods) from more than 80 major manufacturers. The information also is used to build a database of proprietary information for each participating manufacturer.

Lifestyle Selector data elements consist of 10 key demographics: gender, exact age, marital status, occupation, home ownership, family income, number and ages of children, credit card usage, and description of individual participation in more than 50 lifestyle activities and interest areas (such as tennis, foreign travel, gourmet foods, and so forth).

Donnelley Marketing. Donnelley maintains its Shareforce database, a file of 17 million individuals, by demographic, geographic, and lifestyle characteristics. The file is updated from responses to a questionnaire inserted in Donnelley's Carol Wright co-op direct mail program. The questionnaire includes occupation, presence of children, hobbies and interests, and some financial information. Shareforce clients (which are primarily in the packaged-goods industry) also include some proprietary questions.

Multi-Sourced Data

Infobase Services. Infobase Premier is that company's enhancement file. Because of its size (200 million American consumers with 170 different data elements), the file is able to offer an enhancement match rate of 60%–80% (the common match rate in enhancing an internal database is usually only about 45%–60%).

Information from these sources is either rented from the vendor or obtained through program participation and then "overlaid" with the marketer's CIF on the basis of a particular "key." The key can be Zip code or some other element the external resource and the internal database have in common.

The cost of such external information can vary immensely, from annual licensing fees of thousands of dollars to single-use fees assessed by the individual characteristic required.

In general, information drawn from the external databases to enhance the CIF, will be one of four basic types:

- Demographic Data: Demographics, the barebones of consumer descriptors, are provided most accurately by the U.S. Census Bureau, which collects 73 different variables.
- Geodemographic Data: Geodemographics is based on the notion that "birds of a feather flock together." Geographic clusters, determined either by Zip code, Zip plus 4, or census tract data, provide thumbnail psychographic sketches of people residing in various areas.

Generally, marketers find a disproportionately high concentration of their customers is located in a small set of certain Zip clusters. Knowing the psyche of these clusters helps the marketer better understand and, therefore, better communicate with the customer. Vendors supplying such databases include: CACI Inc. (ACORN), Claritas (PRIZM), Donnelley Marketing (Cluster Plus), and Equifax (Microvision).

- Psychographic Data: So-called "lifestyle" segmentation of customers has been carried out on an ad hoc basis during the past 20–30 years. Only with the advent of SRI International's VALS (Values and Lifestyle Segmentation) approach, however, was psychographic segmentation formalized with a theoretical underpinning.

Psychographics is based on the reasoning that marketers can better anticipate purchase and behavioral actions of consumers by knowing their similarities in attitudes, interests, and opinions, rather than relying on demographics alone. VALS 2, the latest formulation from SRI, offers a truly "tested" schema for psychographic segmentation.

- Behavioral Data: Many marketers are beginning to view data that records actual behavioral transactions as being the most relevant. UPC scanners and transaction-oriented data systems will make this kind of information more readily available in the near future.

of customers within each cohort and estimate their average lifetime value. Then calculate overall lifetime value as a weighted average using the number of customers in each cohort as the weights.

The magnitude of the lifetime value is totally dependent on the time definition given to an active customer. Extend the time frame of the definition and lifetime value will necessarily increase. Contract the time frame of the definition and lifetime value also decreases.

Once lifetime sales are calculated, a marketer can easily determine the net profit associated with each active customer. Using a marketer's average percentage for net profit before taxes, the average lifetime value can be easily transformed into the average lifetime net profit before taxes, appropriately discounted to present value.

The simple message of lifetime value is: the longer a customer stays with a firm, the greater the customer's value. As simple as this principle is, some marketers operate as if they are totally unaware of its existence. Also, several studies and authors have previously pointed out that it's easier to keep a current customer satisfied than to win a new one.

Costs of Acquiring a Customer

Calculating lifetime value may encourage the marketer to calculate another per-customer figure: the average cost of acquiring a customer. Even though costs for acquiring new customers may be less certain in mainstream marketing than in direct marketing, the marketer can make estimates on the basis of typical conquest rates. (In any campaign or promotion in which results can be traced, this figure will be much more easily obtained.)

It should be immediately apparent that the cost of acquisition should be less than the lifetime net profit before taxes in order to survive and profit. Likewise, the difference between the lifetime value of a customer and that value less the cost of acquisition certainly quantifies the value of keeping current customers and extending each customer's lifetime beyond the average.

Customer Scoring Models

Another concept supported by the CIF is scoring. This means rating each customer's likelihood of purchasing on the basis of a typical offer. Direct marketers use scoring models to (1) present new products, services, or offers only to those customers who evidence the greatest likelihood of buying and (2) treat prospects differently according to their (scored) likelihood of purchasing.

Affinity Modeling

A fully functioning CIF also supports affinity modeling, or making guesses about how likely customers are to purchase other products or services (hence "affinity"). Affinity scores can be very useful in ranking customers by their likelihood of responding to cross-selling efforts.

COSTS OF ESTABLISHING A CIF

Establishing a customer database incurs both monetary and time costs. The monetary cost seemingly can be negotiated with greater ease than the time required to construct the consumer file. Because no one wants to advocate constructing an inferior database, managers may overcompensate by setting their sights on one of such quality that its construction will take an inordinately long time.

Industry experts agree it's better to start experiencing the value of an imperfect database, than to aspire to a perfect, yet unattainable, one. If construction takes longer than 12–18 months, the planned database is probably unrealistically complex, and the project should be abandoned. Here's why:

- Organizations resist change; the longer it takes to get a CIF into active use, the more likely it will be canceled without ever being used.
- While waiting for construction, the company is incurring opportunity costs.
- By waiting longer than a year, competitors have the chance to surpass the company.
- Database marketing is a process, not a goal. The sooner the CIF is established, the sooner the learning experience can begin.

Because of the generally fluid structure and composition of most CIFs, the database will never contain everything every potential user wants. Consequently, it will always, by definition, be outdated or inadequate. As is the case in learning to use any new tool, usage will prompt ideas for more applications. And new applications will suggest the need for additional data and improvements.

The three distinct costs incurred in setting up a CIF are the data (basic and enhancement), the processing, and the output.

Data Costs

Acquisition of the information and its enhancement make up the data costs. If the names are generated by the marketer, he or she will pay no list purchase fees. However, the costs of conducting a well-designed "registration program" will be expensive. The most significant component will be the communication costs (postage or telephone).

If names for the CIF are purchased from an outside list broker, the fees may range from $40 per thousand for one-time use to more than $120 per thousand for unlimited use for one year.

Fees for the use of enhancement files will vary by the amount of information needed and the list owner. Charges tend to run $4–$15 per thousand per data item for one year's use; a flat fee of $30–$40 per thousand will provide access to all of the list's information fields.

Typical costs for establishing a CIF will run from $200,000–$10 million. A good rule of thumb is to plan on $2–$3 per household or customer. (The trade press reports that R.J. Reynolds has invested over $100 million in its work to establish a database of all Americans who smoke cigarettes.)

Processing Costs

The second major cost, processing, depends on how much must be done to the CIF as it is established and periodically updated. Generally a new file is "cleaned" to ensure that individuals' titles, addresses, and Zip codes are correct.

Processing costs are usually the sum of two components: computer time and data storage. (Data storage may not be charged unless the database is maintained on-line.) Usually processing charges are a function of the size (number of records) of the database. Annual charges will depend on the cost of transactions required and the number of records processed.

The frequency of updating can influence processing charges substantially. Different information components of the CIF can be updated in different periods. For example, the marketer may decide to add new customers weekly, add purchases monthly, and update addresses biannually.

Output (Reporting) Costs

Service bureaus customarily provide rate schedules for each type of "report" (output option) desired. Each charge will be record-based, except in the case of smaller jobs, which will incur some form of minimum setup fee.

For internal maintenance, the major expenses will be the capital acquisition of the hardware and software and the labor costs of dedicated or part-time operators. The marketer will not pay for incremental charges by the type of operation performed.

Enhancing the CIF

Once the marketer establishes the basic CIF, its value can be enhanced by adding information to it (see page 54 for sources of information to append to a customer database). Information contained in a database falls into four categories:

- Declared information: facts the database members have voluntarily supplied about themselves.
- Implied information: assumptions the marketer makes about database members based on generally accepted correlations (e.g., high-income customers living in the suburbs will probably own two or more automobiles).
- Overlaid information: information added to the database – using a key variable or address-matching techniques – from external sources.
- Appended information: additional information gleaned from matching two or more different CIFs.

A vast number of other characteristics can be added to a customer file, all from external sources. The cost of external information can vary immensely, from annual licensing fees of thousands of dollars, to single-use fees assessed by the individual characteristic required.

THE CHALLENGE OF CIFS

The battle lines are drawn. Competitors are quickly amassing as much information about their customers as they can, hoping to seal customer relationships in their categories and pre-empt their competitors. Understanding and using the tools of their direct marketing will be critical to survival in tomorrow's marketplace.

Mainstream marketing practitioners must adopt the technical skills and capabilities that enable them to create aftermarketing programs and reach customers individually. Such individual access will allow marketers to:

- Become more accountable for their activities and programs; customer lifetime value will be used as the key assessment criterion.
- Reestablish relationships with their end-use customers, relationships which have previously been abdicated to dealers, representatives, franchisees, and retailers.

- Develop new products and services faster because of the satisfaction feedback made available through the CIF.
- Target customers and match marketing programs to customers' particular needs, allowing even small niche markets to be profitably addressed.

The critical importance of the CIF will begin to be felt by most American companies before the mid-'90s, and those marketers who have developed genuine relationships with their customers will survive "the decade of the database."

Terry G. Vavra has over 20 years experience as both a teacher and practitioner. He teaches marketing strategy and services marketing in the MBA program of Pace University in White Plains, N.Y. This article has been adapted from his 1992 book, *Aftermarketing: How to Keep Customers for Life Through Relationship Marketing,* ***published by Business One Irwin, Homewood, Ill. He is also president of Marketing Metrics, a marketing consulting and customer retention firm that designs and conducts national and international customer relationship programs for clients such as Cellular One, Ferrari, Motorola, Rolls-Royce, and Seiko Instruments. He received his bachelor's and master's degrees from UCLA and his PhD from the University of Illinois.***

Reading 13

Strategic implementation of database marketing: problems and pitfalls

Keith Fletcher, Colin Wheeler and Julia Wright

Reprinted from *Long Range Planning*, 1994, Vol. 27, No. 1, pp. 133–41. Published by Elsevier Science Ltd, Oxford, England.

Database marketing is a new approach using customer databases to communicate briefly with customers and monitor the building of customer relationships and sales. In many industries the implementation of database marketing systems has become a priority but success is not guaranteed and this paper discusses a number of problems and constraints based on research findings. These can be classified as insufficient marketing and information orientation, the difficulties of investment justification, organizational barriers, supply infrastructure inadequacies and legal constraints.

In recent years a new term has invaded the marketing literature, database marketing. To many direct marketing practitioners database marketing is another term for mailing list management. To others it is customer knowledge as part of a marketing information system, to be used for business development and strategic planning.

While the heart of database marketing (DBM) is the mailing list, developments in computer technology have made it possible to enlarge and enhance the list. This increased sophistication allows direct marketing to be used in a way which was not possible or affordable in the past. For some firms database marketing is an evolution rather than revolution in techniques[1] but in marketing terms a fundamental change is taking place. Companies are centring their business around their customers rather than their products, and the customer database allows companies to communicate directly with clearly defined target segments in an interactive cost-effective manner. Database marketing is thus a new approach to marketing, being a new way of doing business and requiring a redefinition of the relationship between a company and its customers.

Database marketing is therefore more than a new way of communicating to customers, or 'direct marketing done properly'. It uses its data to identify and communicate with precisely targeted customers and prospects, within a planned framework, while exploiting long term customer relationships. Its immediate aim may be tactical but the ultimate aim is to maximize life-time customer value.

In the past direct marketing has been criticized for its lack of integration into the marketing mix, and its short term tactical focus. This often led to an overemphasis on sales as an immediate objective without regard to longer term implications. Its specialized needs also resulted in many above-the-line agencies shunning the technique, or using it badly.

Despite this, direct marketing has grown rapidly in recent years, with a recent report suggesting that it has accounted for over 50 per cent of the advertising spend for a sample of major companies.[2] Even slow-down in growth over the past 2 years has not been as severe as the decline in traditional media advertising, as companies recognized the advantage of personalized targeting over blanket coverage through whatever media.[3] Direct marketing is therefore frequently the main impetus behind the development of a customer/marketing database. British Telecom and the Automobile Association are examples of UK companies, with large, sophisticated database marketing systems, who initiated database developments to improve direct communications but have moved beyond this to a more strategic, long term approach.

The financial services sector has shown substantial interest in the strategic use of direct marketing, backed by computerized customer information files, and the success of Direct Line, the Royal Bank of Scotland's general insurance subsidiary, underlines the scale of the threat to less innovative competitors.

When the company began direct telephone sales of motor insurance policies in 1985 the experiment was dismissed by many in the industry as unworkable. After 7 years Direct Line has a 4.5 per cent share of the £4bn plus a year motor insurance market and is making in-roads into the home insurance market, resulting in 1992 pre-tax profits of £15.1m and a 48 per cent increase in asset value. This performance won its founder, Peter Wood, a £6m bonus.

Direct Line's approach was to change the basis of competition within the industry by short-circuiting the traditional chain of distribution through brokers and agents and going direct to the customer. By investing in sophisticated software immediate underwriting decisions were possible, saving costs of skilled underwriters and managers. The cost base was reduced even further by the computerized system allowing greater productivity per clerk than traditional insurers.

The data base is also used to fine tune the premiums charged and to be more selective in risks accepted, while giving improved levels of service.

This has resulted in an 85 per cent retention rate of customers, much higher than competitors.

This success has attracted imitators such as Churchill and The Insurance Service and in 1991 direct writers had 13 per cent of the motor insurance market and are increasingly threatening the composite insurers, resulting in a fundamental rethink by the industry as to how to proceed in the 1990s.[4]

To initiate such success and to fulfil the promise identified by many authors[5,6] direct marketing needs to 'come of age' and by using computerized customer data within an integrated marketing framework develop a similar strategic orientation. The remainder of this article therefore considers the factors which may inhibit the successful strategic use of direct and database marketing, based on a study of the literature and an exploratory survey of expert opinion.

FACTORS AFFECTING SUCCESSFUL IMPLEMENTATION

In general terms the uses made of a company's database and direct marketing will be determined by a combination of strategic priorities – and operational necessities. However, there are many problems and constraints affecting the developments of DBM by companies, which will reduce its successful implementation. These can be classified as:

- insufficient marketing and information orientation:
- investment justification;
- organizational barriers;
- supply infrastructure;
- legal constraints.

MARKETING AND INFORMATION ORIENTATION

Although no universal definition of DBM exists, there seems to be a general agreement among experts that database marketing is an interactive, customer-orientated approach to marketing; and that its special strength lies in the techniques it uses to harness the capabilities of computer technology for a range of applications.

It therefore follows that, if the marketing concept is not well established in a company's management, philosophy and operating methods, then the adoption and successful use of database marketing is unlikely. A marketing orientation is needed at the pre-planning stage since a company's decision to adopt DBM will be determined by the way in which it perceives its market(s). If the marketing department does not play an 'integrating' role within the company and if other departments do not perceive the need for the database, DBM's *full* potential (in terms of research, new product development, customer servicing – as well as direct marketing) will remain unexploited. Database marketing yields the greatest long-term benefits when it is planned and implemented at a strategic level and when it is perceived by various departments as a *corporate* asset.

The sophistication of database marketing usage is therefore likely to be related to the degree of marketing sophistication of the firm. A firm which has a sales orientation is likely to exploit the tactical elements of DBM, albeit in a sophisticated manner. A marketing orientated firm will make greater use of the strategic capabilities of DBM.

Database marketing enables a company to stay close to its customers 'by recording and keeping an electronic database memory of customers, prospects and all communication and commercial contacts to help improve all future contacts'.[7] The basic tool of DBM, then, is a customer *database*, in which such data is stored as an organized set of files. The value which a company places on information, and its attitude towards data collection will therefore promote or inhibit its use of database marketing.

The fragmentary nature of most marketing information systems, identified in a number of recent surveys[8–11] is no doubt an indication of low levels of commitment to information. Once again, this may provide a partial explanation of the relatively low number of sophisticated DBM users in the UK.

To some experts, the marketing database should be seen principally as a research tool; and, secondly, as a medium of communication. In this way, DBM will also benefit such areas as new product development and pricing. This implies that the research function within a company should be well developed. Certainly, organizations which have successfully moved into DBM (such as the Automobile Association and, although at an earlier stage of development, the Scottish Widows) have large market research sections which both promote database development, and benefit from the database themselves.

However, in many companies the research function is *not* fully developed. In the words of one respondent 'quite often the market research person is a "lap-dog" and treated as a junior with some disrespect'. Companies therefore lose both potentially invaluable support for the use of DBM; and the crucial skills (in terms of computer and marketing knowledge) which market researchers possess.

In the opinion of one DBM supplier, attitudes towards data collection act as one of the main constraints to DBM adoption and successful use. In *all* companies he had encountered, the attitude had been *entirely* product/fulfilment driven – for example if a company needs to know five things about a person in order to sell them an insurance policy, it will ask those five questions. If a company needs to know nothing about a customer (because he is a depositor) other than his name and address then it will only know the names and addresses of customers because booking is done through agents. 'We work as a country on the basis of *minimum data collection* to fulfil orders. Company databases tend to be developed, parasitically, on the back of that data', said the respondent. The standard of data in many companies is therefore a major obstacle to successful database marketing.

In the long term, the strategic use of DBM requires the reshaping of the way in which the organization collects its data. Firms with existing information systems designed to capture and collect market intelligence and customer data are therefore more likely to implement DBM, and have less difficulty in doing so.

INVESTMENT JUSTIFICATION

The cost of implementing and maintaining database marketing is high and, as such, may act as a disincentive to potential adopters. Justifying the investment to senior management is commonly cited as a major problem, since many of the benefits of database marketing are only apparent in the long term.

Cost of Database Marketing

Although the cost of computer technology has declined in recent years, DBM can still represent a substantial investment in hardware and software, and processing stations. The exact cost incurred will vary according to:

- the size of the company;
- the uses to which the database will be put;
- the extent of computer technology (especially hardware) within the firm: many companies will run DBM functions on their existing mainframe while others may need to invest from scratch. However, even the costs of amalgamating three or four existing databases can be phenomenal.

Several major 'hidden' costs are also inevitable. Investment in staff training, and in new personnel (such as statisticians and analysts) can be expensive. Moreover, 'successful applications breed ideas for additional applications'[12] which lead to more investment. The Automobile Association experienced particular cost problems when it built its current corporate database externally, with the cost estimates being way adrift of the actuals, both in terms of building the system and, more fundamentally, running it. The previous system was of low sophistication, being out of date with limited data, and no costing of data services was possible. The AA therefore entered a period where, for 3½ years, there was constant investigation of the true costs of running such a different system. Costs were eventually stabilized just before the system was brought in-house. However, the database is always in a growth situation, since divisions will always want to input more data. The marketing research division has consequently taken steps to *limit* the data stored – by removing records and data each year that is not used on a regular basis.

Senior Management Support

Given the potential costs associated with database marketing, users and suppliers alike agree that obtaining and maintaining senior management support is vital for successful use. If managers understand from the beginning the *potential* applications of DBM then they will. *1.* be more willing to commit sufficient funds for development and 2. be better positioned to implement and manage the organizational changes which inevitably follow. However, lack of top management support will lead to new systems and activities working below their potential which continues to be a problem in some companies. Although the *marketing* director may be convinced of the benefits, he may find it difficult to justify the investment 'up the line'. One supplier cited the case of a Building Society which has tremendous potential to develop DBM (since around one-third of British households had an account), but had not realized it. Reportedly, there was not sufficient management commitment – in terms of money, resources and people. According to another supplier, however, the situation is gradually changing as the growing role of IT in business, as well as the increasing demand for the accountability of marketing communications expenditure, creates a commitment for change at senior levels within companies.

Perception of the Benefits of DBM

If the marketing database is seen as a corporate asset, then in the opinion of one supplier, 'you cannot say that it should be paid back over a certain time. Companies should be bold enough to say: we invest in our customer database. It is the way we control our market, it is essential to the survival of the company'.

Certainly, some of the most valuable benefits which database marketing can offer, such as improved customer relations, cannot realistically be priced. Building customer loyalty is a long-term process, encouraging firms to calculate a 'customer life-time value'. Traditionally, however, investment in information systems has been justified on the basis of reducing costs and increasing the efficiency of operations. The very 'intangible' qualities which make DBM such a valuable long-term investment, often result in its being given a low priority.

Investment justification should also involve looking at the benefits of DBM to each of the company's *internal* customers – notably system efficiency; particularly in areas such as product development and market research. Ultimately, however, most would agree that there must be a simple bottom-line pay-off. This may partially explain why fast moving consumer goods companies have been slow to adopt DBM: the product needs to be sufficiently valuable to absorb the immediate, short term cost. According to one supplier, 'most business managers have terrible pressures to produce profit *now*: this is terribly pervasive in British business'. Andersen Consulting have noted that many marketing and sales managers are solely interested in short-term success, because the objectives against which they are measured are geared to short term. Fewer companies have therefore been able to recognize ways in which the costs of investment in strategic database marketing can be offset by the long-term strategic advantage to be gained. Recent surveys[9,10] agree that this has led to investment in fragmented solutions which bring tactical, cost cutting benefits.

There are, nevertheless, ways in which the investment barrier can be overcome. Indeed, for a large company like BT the cost of investment may not be a problem. To many, the agency has the responsibility to reduce the initial risk; and there are many ways to set up pilot schemes, which can keep costs extremely low. The general consensus among experts appears to be it is more practical to start with a limited system – perhaps used only for some direct marketing purposes. Once the system has proved its worth, expansion will be easier to justify. Overall, the problem points to the need for client education. Managers need to understand the *long-term* value of DBM. It has, for example, been suggested that one of the educational aims should be to specifically train medium-sized companies so that they can benefit from DBM without it being necessary to afford a huge expenditure. Since systems development and testing can be a lengthy process, the real problem is to get companies of whatever size to be sufficiently *long-term orientated* to make the investment stay with the company over the long term.

The firm which takes a realistic long-term view of both costs and benefits, even when these are intangible or not directly incurred by the system, is therefore more likely to recognize the company wide implications of DBM. This will ensure the need for senior management support if the project is to proceed. Without this commitment DBM will stay at a low level of development.

ORGANIZATIONAL BARRIERS

The introduction of database marketing to an organization can have potentially wide-ranging effects on its existing structures and procedures. Organizational barriers to such change may take the form of reaction or resistance to change. Such barriers can become the main problem facing successful DBM adoption – particularly in large companies. Much is made of the 'techno-fear' of managers and staff; however, 'it is often more the *implementation* of the database through the organization that people are fearful of', according to one respondent.

Marketing Management

As companies move into direct and database marketing, the increased accountability (often the justification for database investment) which results often exposes the general lack of management discipline in their database operations. Typical examples include:

- late, incomplete briefing by 'internal clients', resulting in hurried campaign development cycles and badly handled campaigns;
- over-aggressive objectives relating to database coverage, leading to high volumes of low quality customer data being brought onto the database;
- lack of analysis of past results, leading particularly to poor targeting and wrong media choice;
- lack of communication with, for example, field sales staff and branch workers, leading to the development of systems which do not meet their requirements.

Many marketing managers are unwilling to have their methods criticized; again, education may be the way to overcome the problem. Those companies that do recognize the need for change are reported to be investing in improved marketing organization structure, better planning and management skills, and improved information and communication systems.

However, the organizational impact of database marketing reaches further than the marketing department. One organizational problem identified is the conflict between the marketing and information systems departments. Different backgrounds and objectives often result in poor communications and problems of priority.

The Information Systems departments have insufficient time to devote to DBM development, and most mainframes exist for other than marketing purposes. It is frequently the case that marketers therefore cannot get access to relevant data, or have to run their programs at inconvenient times when other work has been completed. This had led many DBM systems to be designed as separate entities from the mainframe/IS department, being based around networked PCs.

One supplier identified certain general roles within the organization which need to be developed in order to make DBM survive, namely: an administrative/management role; a decision support role; and the campaign/marketing role. Except in companies such as American Express, Reader's Digest and traditional mail order firms, these roles are, by and large, not fully defined – i.e. the structures of many companies do not support DBM usage.

The problems posed by organizational structure will vary from industry to industry. It could, for example, be said that a major reason for the slow adoption of DBM by FMCG companies is that they are organized on brand management lines. DBM is therefore a major departure from their business practice. The introduction of techniques such as multiple branding and house holding may meet with resistance from brand managers who have their own brand loyalties, budgets and rules.

Smaller companies which should have tight control often face fewer organizational barriers than large organizations which often have immense organizational and logistical barriers. British Telecom, for example, found that the majority of opposition to the marketing database came from their operating districts. Prior to privatization, the decision had been taken to decentralize; this led to the creation of local marketing departments in total control of their districts. The database development was consequently seen as 'the ultimate in centralization'. BT have therefore had to actively demonstrate the system's benefits to the districts in order to regain confidence.

Organizational barriers, such as structure, process and skills, are therefore likely to be related to the type of DBM usage and its successful implementation.

THE SUPPLY INFRASTRUCTURE

The quality of services offered by suppliers is a key variable in the adoption of database marketing, since they will inevitably influence the success and reputation of the user company. However, most experts agree that, despite an improving situation, there is still a serious quality problem in the supply infrastructure.

The suppliers of DBM technology may be the manufacturers themselves; or computer bureaux and consultancies who develop their own proprietary software. The problem that these suppliers face is to match the *service* which their technology offers to the needs and capabilities of the user. According to one user, however, many suppliers try to persuade companies of the need for all-singing, all-dancing databases when they are often not needed and when economies of scale make very detailed segmentation non-viable. Many clients frequently experience problems with post-installation support and service, which can mean the difference between long-term success and failure of database marketing within a company.

More fundamentally, there appears to be a shortage of good suppliers of databases and software, the statistical packages being a particular problem. As one supplier has remarked, a large corporation buying a database development will be used to high quality documentation and delivery of services; and will therefore certainly be disappointed by the quality of *most* of the database developers. One user argued that although bureaux offer much cheaper services than the large consultancies, they often also provide bad documentation, functional shortcomings, and are bad at inspiring any level of confidence in the buyer.

It could be said that there is almost an oversupply of direct marketing agencies. In 1990 the BDMA distributed a list of about 70 specialist agencies, virtually all of which had appeared in the last 10 years. It is perhaps the relative newness of the agencies which is the root cause of numerous complaints about the quality of their services: principal complaints levelled include high charges, poor service and below-par creative work.

However, increased agency sophistication has not been universal. A 1988 survey (*Direct Response,* June 1988) showed that while almost 50 per cent of companies now use one or more specialist direct marketing agencies, most still used them on a project-only basis, a finding confirmed by respondents in our study. This again highlights the need for client as well as agency education. Many clients still do not understand DM's role in overall strategy; and frequently are unaware of the requirements and work method (in terms of finance and briefing, etc.) of the agencies.

The same argument can be extended to problems with other suppliers, such as list brokers, mailing houses, etc. Although poor levels of expertise are often the root cause, one respondent pointed out that 'clients are demanding . . . a higher level of competence from mailing house personnel, but they're not prepared to pay for it'. As a result, investment (and improved efficiencies) become more difficult. Suppliers are also accused of not having a 'service mentality'.

Although the situation has improved over the last few years, it is, in the eyes of one expert, prevalent in the major supplier companies eroding confidence and leading to problems in campaign work.

With the implementation of the Single Market, pan-European database driven marketing strategies are becoming more evident in spite of the difficulties of operating with the supply infrastructure and market conditions in Europe. A North American airline has run a pan-European campaign targeted at business travellers in all the European countries from which the airline flies to North America. Campaign copy and enquiries were handled in the local language wherever possible. The company has built a European database to drive its marketing strategy in spite of the difficulties of operating across national boundaries. For example the laws governing mailing and holding data vary country by country. Switzerland, unlike other countries, does not allow a firm to mail outside the country and collect responses within the country. Both mailing and responses had to take place in Switzerland. The development of list broking is uneven across Europe and the airline depended on the knowledge of its agency staff for list selection. Accurate handling of names and addresses needed care because of the different name, address, salutation format and rules for each country. The differing speeds of development within countries must therefore be monitored and responded to.

LEGAL CONSTRAINTS

The Data Protection Act of 1984 aims to protect the consumer through tight regulations of personal data. As such, it could be seen as in the interests of direct marketing, since it aims to improve customer attitudes towards direct mail and the senders of direct mail. Indeed, most experts and users agree that Data Protection registrar (notably Guidance Note 19 and its replacement, Guideline 4) have led to a further tightening of the laws. The laws will have a positive effect from a *qualitative* point of view, however, the laws are likely to reduce the amount of direct mail sent. The European Commission is also stimulating debate with its draft direction aimed at determining how information about individuals should be used, and what protection should apply. There are also proposals for the harmonization of legal protection of electronic databases, with serious implications for copyright protection.[13,14]

However, many users and suppliers believe that Data Protection laws will mainly affect the part of the market which relies on 'cold lists', i.e. the transfer of data between companies; and that companies building their own customer database should not be greatly hindered. Indeed many companies – especially in financial services – find that their direct marketing efforts are more deeply affected by legislation in their own industry sectors.

CONCLUSION

It appears that underlying many of the problems facing database marketing is a widespread lack of understanding of the concepts. Indeed, many believe that the current skills shortage – on both the client and supplier sides – is the single greatest problem facing the industry. The situation can no doubt be partly explained by the recent and rapid growth of DM/DBM: many within the industry have different experiences and different levels of comprehension of the strategic uses of DBM.

Many companies invest in database marketing after using direct marketing successfully. However, many clients (and agencies) still fail to understand the potential strategic impact of direct communication and therefore still use direct marketing tactically. Moreover, on the semantic level, direct marketing often means different things to different people: direct mail, door drops, etc.

On the database side, database marketing is not well understood for several reasons: people still confuse DBM with the technical definition of the word 'database': secondly, people who have not been exposed to the industry find it very hard to understand the core concept of DBM, i.e. building up sufficient information or data on individual people so that you can carry out complex communications programmes with them. The solution to these problems must lie in education, through in-house training programmes as well as industry-wide initiatives.

It would appear that the two most significant constraints on the successful adoption of database marketing relate to the insufficient marketing and information orientation of potential users, and the general skills shortage of DBM specialists.

These two constraints underlie many of the other problems identified and, while it is important not to over-generalize, in most cases the solution to the problem can be found by tackling these root causes. The problems faced by firms will vary by type of industry and size but the issues identified are barriers to the successful exploitation or development of direct marketing at a strategic level.

The British Direct Marketing Association (BDMA), now amalgamated into the broader based DMA, recognized the problem of the skill shortage and need for education provision. Through links with the Direct Marketing Centre in England, and the Scottish Direct Marketing Forum in Scotland, it is actively publicizing the field of direct marketing. The DMA diploma is a useful starting point for potential users, and numerous conferences and seminars are now being offered for the wider audience.

In America, the Direct Marketing Educational Foundation (itself founded about 25 years ago) launched in 1987 the *Journal of Direct Marketing*, reflecting the greater study of direct marketing where over 500 professors deal with direct marketing either as full credit courses, or as part of other courses. However, until direct/data-base marketing has the same knowledge background as advertising and marketing, it will continue to be seen as the poor relation. Without an understanding of how database marketing techniques should operate, and why they are successful, users will have to rely on chance and experience, which can be costly.

As marketing becomes understood and adopted by more companies, encouraged by the Chartered Institute of Marketing and the many Business Schools offering marketing qualifications, the firms themselves will begin to demand integration of direct marketing into their activities. The pressures will therefore be twofold, from users and suppliers alike, that the problems and pitfalls are understood and avoided.

For users the implications seem to be as follows:

1 Existing information flows need to be analysed to assess their potential relevance and use in building a customer, rather than market, database.
2 All customer contacts should be treated as part of a long term strategy to build loyalty, improve customer satisfaction, and gain customer information.
3 To encourage this long term view the life-time value of customers should be calculated, and the role of direct marketing in improving this value considered.
4 The increasingly out-moded distinction between above and below-the-line activities should be abandoned and direct marketing considered during the development of market strategy and planning.
5 Use the measurability of direct marketing, and the modelling capabilities of the computer, to test and refine campaigns and measure promotional effectiveness in a way previously not possible.
6 Be prepared for the organizational disruption created by the new flows of information and direct customer focus. An attitudinal shift may be needed by many staff.

For suppliers the implications are that:

1 They must decide whether to be reactive to changing client needs, or whether to be proactive and promote the new approach, educating the client if necessary.
2 The measurability of direct marketing will encourage much clearer advertising and communication objectives, and the rigorous post-testing of campaign effectiveness. This may come as a shock to some above-the-line advertising executives.
3 The advertising and promotional budget will increasingly be seen as an investment for the future, rather than simply an immediate cost, and be integrated into the achievement of wider business objectives than usual.
4 The possibilities and the precise targeting will require a sophistication and set of skills absent in some agencies. Similarly some agencies may not have the experience in dealing with the wide variety of suppliers of services and skills necessary to successfully run a database marketing campaign.

While this paper has identified various constraints on the strategic implementation of database marketing there is little doubt that as the marketing and computing sophistication of firms grow, and competitive pressures increase, more and more firms will move towards a long term, interactive view of their customer relationships. Those firms who insist on fragmenting their promotional activities and do not have the facilities and procedures to gain detailed knowledge of their customers' needs and behaviour will be at a major strategic disadvantage.

This reading is based upon preliminary research funded by a research grant from the University of Strathclyde. It involved a review of existing literature in the field and an exploratory survey of expert opinion from both supplier and users of direct/database marketing in the UK. Semi-structured interviews were conducted with senior personnel following an interview guide developed to cover the areas of interest. The respondents were purposely selected to represent a range of suppliers (i.e. full service agencies, specialist and direct marketing agencies and consultants) and users (financial, service, industrial and consumer). A total of 30 interviews were conducted.

Keith Fletcher was Professor Business Administration at Strathclyde Graduate Business School where he lectured on marketing and database marketing. He is now Dean of Management at the University of East Anglia. He has published numerous articles on information systems in marketing and is the author of *Marketing Management and Information Technology* ***published by Prentice-Hall.***

Colin Wheeler is senior lecturer in Marketing at the University of Strathclyde and is a member of Strathclyde International Business Unit.

Julia Wright was a research student at Strathclyde before joining Arthur Anderson as an IT consultant.

References

1 Jenkinson, Is it database marketing or mailing list management, *Direct Response*, May, 49–54 (1987).
2 Dunn Humby, *Computers In Marketing Survey Reports*, Dunn Humby Associates, London (1990).
3 *Precision Marketing*, 7 September (1992).
4 R. Lapper, Direct Line rings the changes, *Financial Times*, 4 December, 23 (1992).
5 K. Fletcher, C. Wheeler and J. Wright, The Role and Status of UK Database Marketing, *Quarterly Review of Marketing*, **16** (1), 7–13 (1990).
6 S. Sapp and T. Collins, *Maxi Marketing*, McGraw-Hill, New York (1987).
7 R. Shaw and M. Stone, *Database Marketing*, Gower, New York (1988).
8 K. Fletcher, Information systems in British Industry, *Management Decision*, **21** (2), 25–36 (1983).
9 Martech, *Martech Survey into Marketing Information*, London (1989).
10 Oasis, *A Report on the Management of Information*, Organization and System Innovations Ltd, London. In Association with the Institute of Marketing (1989).

11 D. Reid, Data Access and Issue Analysis in Strategic Planning, *Marketing Intelligence & Planning*, **7** (1), 14–18 (1989).
12 M. Roberts and P. Berger, *Direct Marketing Management*, Prentice-Hall, Englewood Cliffs (1989).
13 M. Wilson, Laws of Duplication, *Precision Marketing*, 10 August, 15–16 (1992).
14 T. Coad, Direct Mail and Data Protection, *Marketing without Frontiers*, The RMI Guide to International Direct Marketing (1991).

Part 4

Customer Service and Relationship Marketing

INTRODUCTION

Customer service means different things to different people. To some it may be the department in the organization that deals with after-sales enquiries, or the one that handles customer complaints. Christopher, Payne and Ballantyne[1] cite a number of definitions such as, 'Timely and accurate delivery of products ordered by customers with accurate follow up and enquiry response including timely delivery of invoice.' However, their view is that customer service is much broader and is 'concerned with building bonds with customers and other groups to ensure long term relationships of mutual advantage'. Customer service is, therefore, really more of a business philosophy.

Many products are now so similar that it is often hard to distinguish one from another. Providing outstanding customer service offers the opportunity to differentiate oneself from the competitors. Furthermore, there are sound economic reasons for this. Customer service guru Ron Zemke[2] believes those organizations that focus on customer service grow twice as fast as their counterparts, increase their market share three to four times more, and can also charge a premium price.

Many customer care programmes fail to live up to their expectations or just run out of steam. The first reading in this section by David Clutterbuck (Reading 14) is called 'Why customer care programmes don't work'. The paper describes the result of a survey of UK companies. Some of the findings were:

- 20 per cent of companies set no measurable objectives for their training programmes
- most training was relatively superficial – two days or less in two-thirds of companies
- only 43 per cent gave employees the authority to deal with problems
- only 21 per cent of programmes have fully met objectives – 40 per cent have mostly done so

The main reasons for failure seemed to be due to:

1 failure to set measurable objectives
2 failure to achieve ownership
3 attacking the problem at the wrong point
4 underestimating the effort involved
5 driven from the top only.

Michael Quinn and John Humble in Reading 15, 'Using service to gain a competitive edge – the PROMPT approach', argue that while the 1980s was the decade of product quality the 1990s will be the decade of service quality. Poor customer service, however, is still widespread. Only a few companies provide excellent service. Although customer service is seen as important it will become increasingly so as customers' expectations rise. The PROMPT approach has been devised as memory aid for managers to provide a basis for action. It contains the following elements:

- **P**rioritizing customer needs
- **R**eliability is critical
- **O**rganizing for customers
- **M**easuring customer satisfaction
- **P**ersonal training and
- **T**echnology focusing

To achieve service excellence managers need to:

- identify their current position (as perceived by the customer)
- clarify their service vision (desired state)
- develop an action plan.

Reading 16 in this section on relationship marketing is by J. Davis Illingworth, called 'Relationship Marketing: Pursuing the Perfect Person-to-Person-Relationship'. In it he describes Toyota's (Lexus) definition of relationship marketing as putting the customer first. Successful relationship marketing in the automobile industry rests at the dealer level. To the customer the dealer is the company. It is worth reflecting on a comment from a satisfied customer, 'it is unusual today to find a salesperson who is willing to put the customer first. J. M. Lexus salesperson Helen Fajardo certainly made us feel special by her unpressured manner of selling'.

For years businesses have paid much attention to gaining new customers. Salespeople applying for a new job would expect to be asked at an interview how they would go about developing and winning new prospects for the business. The subject of looking after and retaining existing customers would have been unlikely to have been raised. Following the publication of a paper in 1990[3] from research by Bain & Co. attention has now been refocussed not so much on gaining new customers, but more on retaining existing ones. Defecting customers reduce profitability. The research found that if the defection rate can be cut by 5 per cent then profits by 25–85 per cent (depending on the industry). In some industries, such as credit cards, it may take a year or two to recoup the cost of acquiring a customer. Over time customers may become more profitable. To maintain customer loyalty a company must provide superior value. Loyalty[4] has three effects:

- revenue grows as a result of repeat purchases and referrals
- costs decline as a result of lower acquisition expenses and efficiencies of serving experienced customers
- employee retention increases because job pride and satisfaction increase, in turn creating a loop that reinforces customer loyalty and further reducing costs as hiring and training costs shrink and productivity rises.

Philip Kotler[4] believes the key to customer retention is customer satisfaction. This is because a satisfied customer:

- buys again
- talks favourably to others about the company
- pays less attention to competing brands
- buys other products from the same company.

According to Frederick Reichheld[5] of Bain & Co. satisfying customers is not a surrogate for customer retention, as between 65 per cent and 85 per cent of customers who defect say they were satisfied or very satisfied with their previous supplier. The automobile industry (USA) has satisfaction ratings of 85–95 per cent, however, the repurchase rate is only 40 per cent. Satisfaction ratings do not tell what percentage of customers stay loyal and for how long.

The reason for such a high attrition rate is put forward in the final reading in this part by Thomas Jones and Earl Sasser, 'Why satisfied customers defect' (Reading 17). They examine the link between satisfaction and loyalty. They refer to two types of loyalty, i.e. *genuine long-term loyalty* and *false loyalty*. The latter can be due to government regulations restricting competition, high switching costs, proprietary technology and loyalty promotion programmes such as frequent flier programmes.

The link between satisfaction and loyalty discovered in the Xerox study discussed in Reading 17 was examined in other markets – automobiles, hospitals, airlines, and local telephone services. In only local telephone services (near monopoly) did the relationship between satisfaction and loyalty turn out as expected. Removal of any of the artificial restrictions detaining customers and only the completely satisfied customers may remain loyal. When satisfaction increases so does loyalty, but the relationship is neither linear nor simple. Most managers underestimate the difference complete satisfaction makes to customer loyalty as opposed to those who are merely satisfied. In markets such as automobiles (referred to above) there is a huge difference between the loyalty of satisfied and completely satisfied customers. Loyalty can also change very rapidly due for example to deregulation (airlines, telecommunciations), loss of patent protection (pharmaceuticals), entrance of new competitors (electronics, US automobile industry) and new technology (computers). The authors argue that customer satisfaction information can show how well an organization is serving its customers and also what it needs to do to increase satisfaction levels until the majority of customers are completely satisfied. A three-stage process for achieving this is outlined.

The American Customer Satisfaction Index (ASCI)[6] is a new economic indicator that was set up in October 1994 to measure customer satisfaction across a wide range of goods and services. While it is important to track customer satisfaction, one-off or annual surveys of customer satisfaction are just not enough. Frequent measurements need to be recorded and studied over time.[7] Managers in world class companies such as Lucent Technologies (formerly A, T & T Power Systems), 3M and Toyota are using Statistical Process Control (SPC) to learn how business processes behave and improve them. However, we

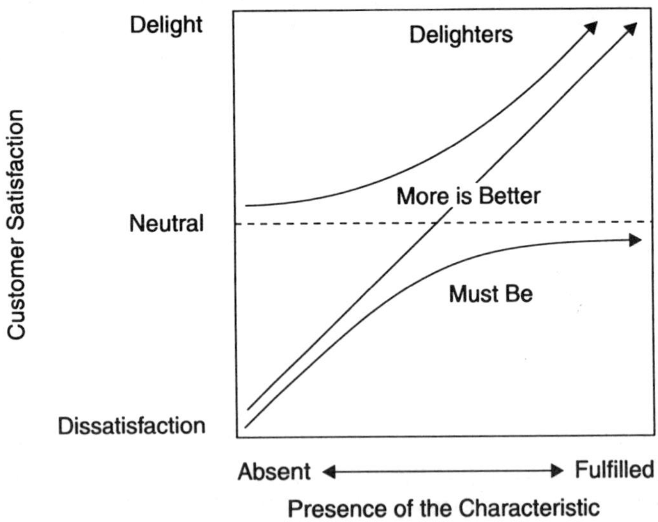

Figure P4.1 Kano's model of customer perceptions

Source: Fourth generation management by Brian L. Joiner. Reproduced with the permission of Joiner Associates Inc. (McGraw-Hill Inc., 1994)

know from the readings included in this section that satisfaction per se is simply not good enough in order to retain customers. Similarly, many quality systems that define quality as conformance to specifications or fitness for use also miss the point. In 1986 Dr W. Edwards Deming[8] warned,

> it will not suffice to have customers that are merely satisfied. A unhappy customer will switch. Unfortunately a satisfied customer may also switch, on the theory that he could not lose much and might gain. Profit in business comes from repeat customers, customers that boast about your product and service, and that bring friends with them.

According to quality guru Brian Joiner[9] customer satisfaction (including complete satisfaction) is not enough. It is necessary to *delight* the customer. This he explains with reference to Professor Noriaki Kano's model of customer perception, which helps to separate characteristics that cause dissatisfaction, satisfaction and delight. There are three characteristics of customer perceptions (see Figure P4.1) namely:

- 'Must be'
- 'More is better'
- 'Delighter'.

The 'Must be' are those characteristics that we expect to be present and take for granted. For example, in a hotel you expect there to be hot water and clean linen. The absence of any of these characteristics will cause annoyance, but presence will do no more than bring dissatisfaction up to a neutral level. For 'More is better' the response may range from disappointment if an enquiry takes a long time to be answered, through neutral or even delight if say we are surprised by the speed with which an enquiry was handled. 'Delighters' are the unexpected characteristics that surprise the customer. If they are absent there is no negative effect, however, their presence does have a positive effect. 'Delighters' may become in time 'Must be'. For instance Joiner says that TV remote controls, which initially were 'Delighters', are now taken for granted.

Trying to please the customer can have its problems. Things can go badly wrong and, worse still, the company might not even know about it. A colleague recalled a recent experience of a widening gap between 'expectation' and 'actual perception of quality'. He was staying in a hotel for four weeks in the Far East while delivering a module of our MBA programme. Week 1 the hotel gave him a basket of fruit. Week 2 he got a base ball cap. He eagerly awaited week 3 only to find he received nothing. Consequently, he was disappointed. In this case the provision of 'gifts' cannot be classified as a 'delighter' as the absence was not neutral, but caused dissatisfaction. Clearly the way an organization manages the process of customer satisfaction and delighting customers must be carefully thought through for each customer or market segment. We should not be surprised about difficulties in meeting customer's expectations. Dr Deming recounts[10]. 'There is much talk about customer's expectations. [You should] meet the customer's expectations. The fact is that the customer expects only what you and your competitor have led him to expect. He is a rapid learner.'

The above account of a colleague's hotel experience elicited the following anecdote from Professor Kano[11] on how to ensure the customer is always delighted,

> The story which you describe reminded me of a joke related to the market release of word processors. A customer purchased a new machine which was cheaper and had more functions than the previous one. He became disappointed when two weeks later another new machine came out with higher specification and at a cheaper price. Then we discussed *when* he should purchase a machine so as not to be dissatisfied. The answer was to purchase just a few days before death.

Professor Kano believes:

> That the widening gap between expectation and perception should be a motivator for the product or service provider to find another way of delighting the customer. This has been the history of product development in Japan. Some new products may delight customers longer than others. The difference may come from whether a new product reflects the essential needs and wants of customers or not. For example I fitted a navigator to my car 4 years ago and I am still delighted with this.

To retain customers or markets organizations must strive to find ways to continue to delight them. Professor Kano[12] has proved that this can be done even in mature markets such as cameras and industrial sewing machines. This means working closely with customers or others in the supply chain to see how products are actually used. For instance Konica, who make cameras, visited a film processing laboratory. A Pareto analysis showed that there was a high failure rate due to under exposure, out of focus and blank film. The solution was to build in a flash, auto focus, and auto winder. The Juki Corporation, the leading manufacturer of industrial sewing machines, visited a garment manufacturer. They found that there were a few defects in garments caused by machines, however, the biggest problem was due to lack of training for new machine operators. Professor Kano's perseverance persuaded the company to treat this as 'a machine problem' and not 'a training problem'. In 1981, using microprocessors they redesigned the sewing machine so that even untrained operators could use it without making mistakes. The result was the biggest selling machine of its type, which was exported to over 160 countries. To succeed and create a quality product or service requires a thorough understanding of the three characteristics of customer perception namely 'Must be' (expected quality), 'More is better' (unitary quality) and 'Delighter' (attractive quality) (Professor Kano's terms are in brackets).

Product quality cannot be determined in isolation. To help ensure that we have a quality product and delighted customers we need to consider the interaction between the product, the user and the supplier (see Figure P4.2). Each of the interactions is a separate process and needs careful consideration and management. The computer software industry is renowned for putting onto the market products that fail to live fully up to expectation when first released. These interactions in computer software[13] might involve the following:

User-supplier

- information about products in sales promotion, training courses, manuals, help lines
- information about user needs, difficulties, and opportunities.

Product-user

- listen to what your customers say
- never believe that they know what they want
- study the way they actually use the product.

Supplier-product interaction

- reliability
- ease of use
- conformance to specification is no longer adequate
- leap ahead of user's expectations.

Salespeople have a vital role to perform. They are the 'eyes' and the 'ears' of the organization. The information they provide can have a key

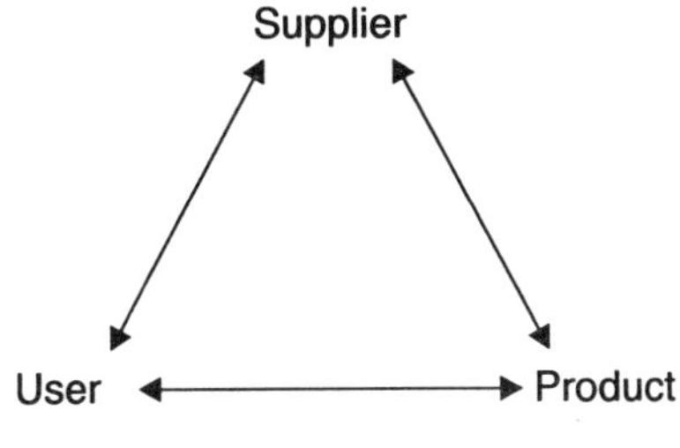

Figure P4.2 The three corners of quality

Source: 'Out of the Crisis' by W. Edwards Deming – adapted by D.F. Kerridge

influence in determining the delivery of a quality 'product' or 'service'. This in turn will help towards ensuring that customers are no longer merely satisfied, but delighted. Responsibility for quality is top management's alone, it cannot be delegated.

References

1 Christopher, M., Payne, A. and Balantyne, D. *Relationship Marketing*, Butterworth Heinemann, 1991.
2 Managing Customer Service, BBC Training Video.
3 Reichheld, F.F. and Sasser, W.E. 'Zero Defections: Quality Comes to Services', *Harvard Business Review*, September 1990.
4 Kotler, P. *Marketing Management*, 7th edn, Prentice-Hall, 1991.
5 Reichheld, F.F. 'Loyalty-Based Management', *Harvard Business Review*, March 1993.
6 American Society for Quality Control – Internet home page, URL http://www.asqc.org.
7 Starkey, M.W. 'Using Statistical Process Control to Improve Marketing Performance', *Journal of Targeting Measurement and Analysis for Marketing*, 1995, Vol. 4, No. 2.
8 Deming, W.E. *Out of the Crisis*, Massachusetts Institute of Technology Center for Advanced Engineering Study, 1986.
9 Joiner, B.L. *Fourth Generation Management*, McGraw-Hill, 1994.
10 Deming, W.E. *The New Economics for Industry, Government and Education*, Massachusetts Institute of Technology Center for Advanced Engineering Study, 1993.
11 E-mail correspondence with Professor Noriaki Kano, Science University of Tokyo.
12 Kano, N. 'Upsizing the Organisation by Attractive Quality Creation', in *Total Quality Management, Proceedings of the First World Congress*, edited by G.K. Kanji, Chapman and Hall, 1995, pp. 60–72.
13 From information supplied by Professor D.F. Kerridge, Assistant Director of Research, British Deming Association.

Reading 14

Why customer care programmes don't work

David Clutterbuck

Reprinted from *Managing Service Quality*, March 1991, pp. 125–6.

The pathway to service excellence is paved with programmes that didn't deliver their promises, or ran out of steam before they achieved lasting change. Why is it so difficult? And, how can you prevent your customer care programme going the same way?

A while ago, we set out to create a book of case studies to illustrate best practice in customer care programmes. We approached companies which had publicly expounded on their programmes at conferences; consultants who had been employed to help devise and implement programmes at various levels; and a variety of other interested observers – all of whom could direct us towards examples of successful schemes.

The project rapidly began to resemble a game of musical chairs. At every stage, one or two of our cases dropped out, because the programmes had run into difficulties. Frequently, we found that the person responsible for a company's service excellence activities had resigned in frustration at not being able to drive through the changes he or she regarded as essential if the organisation was to progress beyond initial enthusiasm and hype.

A survey we conducted during this period served to emphasise the point. Sent to over 1,000 personnel managers, it elicited a response from 75 companies, most of whom clearly regarded their programmes as representing best practice. In many ways it made depressing reading:

- 20% of the companies did not set measurable objectives for their programmes, and slightly more failed to set objectives for the training element of their programmes.
- Training was relative superficial in most cases, amounting to two days or less in two-thirds of the companies (and less than half in 18%).

- Just over two-thirds of the companies applied quantifiable measurements to test the effectiveness of their training.
- Only two-fifths of programmes involved training in customer-oriented leadership.
- Only 27% trained top management.
- Only 43% gave employees authority to deal with customer care problems, although 49% did so 'sometimes'.
- 45% of the companies reported that their employees saw the programme as flavour of the month; 36% viewed it with suspicion. However, 42% said employees perceived it as a genuine and welcomed change of orientation.
- Only 21% of programmes have fully met their objectives; 40% have mostly done so.

TRACKING THE CASES

The survey provided a number of clues as to why so many programmes didn't deliver. Other causes were established through visits to companies with ailing programmes and through several audits of programmes. The primary causes appear to be:

Failure to set and use measurable objectives. This is common. In one case, top management and the training department agreed viable objectives, but then commissioned an off-the-shelf training package, which did not address these issues and did not allow for any form of measuring the results.

By contrast, one of the most successful programmes – by Kwikfit – is based almost entirely on measurement and reward against very high standards. Another, the capsules division of Eli Lily, achieved major improvements because it first established what the ideal customer service would look like, then the level of service that was actually being delivered, and finally gave managers throughout the organisation six months to halve the gap. Knowing what would be measured and why, and given both the freedom to achieve results in their own way and support from above if they needed it, these managers delivered.

Failure to achieve ownership. The only 'packaged' solutions that worked were those where the programme was driven by the company's own training managers – preferably with active involvement and consultation of line managers at peer level – and where the materials were heavily customised. Bringing outsiders in to inject customer care often leads to rapid rejection of the message by the internal customer.

Attacking the problem at the wrong point. There was in many companies an assumption that the objective of a customer care programme was to improve the attitudes and behaviours of people at the front-line. In reality, however, these people will only think and behave differently if the organisation itself changes to support the new behaviours. There has to be a whole new style of management and sometimes radical changes in the structures, systems and standards.

Underestimating the effort involved. The training manager of an airline complained: 'I had £100,000 last year to launch customer care. When I put in my budget this year, they crossed out the customer care expenditure on the grounds that we'd done that last year'. Many programmes are seen as just that – programmes, with a finite and usually short life. We now advise companies to talk in terms of processes, which need years to evolve, require constant maintenance and improvement, yet can still deliver significant initial results if handled well.

Driven from the top only. The most effective programmes appear to be those where people are able to change the organisation as it attempts to change them.

THE NEED FOR A FOCUSED APPROACH

Relatively few companies we examined had managed to get far beyond initial awareness – indeed, relatively few had really tried. But, the experience of those who had, suggests that making service excellence an integral part of 'the way we do things here' involves a lot more than a generalised 'throw some training at them and hope it will stick' approach.

Instead, the emphasis must be on a focused, strategic approach with the flexibility for different expression at different levels of the organisation. Having research data that pinpoints real need for change is a major help here, because it allows people to convince themselves that 'something must be done'.

The focused approach combines two centres of interest:

- Those improvements in service quality which will have maximum beneficial impact on the customer's experience of doing business with the organisation.
- Those improvements in service quality which will have a significant impact upon internal customer relationships and thus lead to productivity savings. (Although many pundits say that it is wrong to emphasise productivity as a reason for quality initiatives, in practice people generally do respond well to it as a secondary or supporting goal.)

The focused approach recognises that it is not possible to change the entire organisation at one time; improvements must be planned, sequential and mutually supportive; and the primary source of effort for making change happen rests with management, not with the people in the front-line.

Indeed, it is both myopic and arrogant for any company to assume that people at the primary customer interface, who are usually at or near the bottom of the organisational hierarchy, have more than a marginal opportunity or authority to initiate substantial changes in service quality. As US consultant Roland Dumas expresses it:

> Front-line workers don't create service quality, they just deliver it. Expecting training alone to deliver service quality is like making a loading docks worker responsible for the quality of products.

The value of a friendly smile should not be underestimated, of course. Nor should it be overestimated. The stewardess may apologise magnificently for the poor condition of the toilets on board a long flight, or for the loss of a passenger's luggage. But, if the same passenger experiences similar problems on a second occasion, there has been little gain. There usually isn't a third occasion – by this time the passenger has switched to another carrier and will only come back by necessity or if convinced by experience elsewhere that all carriers are equally incompetent.

The only way to gain true commitment throughout the organisation is for top management to start the process of change itself. Before it asks other people to change their behaviour, top management must change its own.

Demonstrating commitment by visiting the training courses attended by lower grades is one thing – but this is at best a veneer unless executives are also seen to be managing in a different, more customer-responsive way. (The chairman of a major chemical company who told me he did not see that visiting customers was part of his job had clearly not got the point – perhaps the subsequent deterioration in share price and profit levels will enlighten that organisation.)

At the same time as changing themselves, top managers must also change the structures, systems and standards that constrain customer-responsive behaviour. It is here that the issue of focus comes into its own, in selecting and targeting those areas which will contribute most to delivering the customer promise.

David Clutterbuck is chairman of The ITEM Group plc, a business communications company based in Burnham, UK, and author of several books on excellence themes, including The Winning Streak. He is European editor of Tom Peters' newsletter *On Achieving Excellence.* ***His new book,*** *Making Customers Count,* ***a study of practical experience in implementing service excellence, was published by Mercury Books in 1991.***

Reading 15

Using service to gain a competitive edge – The PROMPT approach

Michael Quinn and John Humble

Reprinted from *Long Range Planning*, 1993, Vol. 26, No. 2, pp. 31–40. Published by Elsevier Science Ltd, Oxford, England.

Customers are vital to business success. Customer service is a business priority today and is 'key to future growth and success'. Everybody is in service, including manufacturers. Unfortunately, exceptional service is the exception. Poor service is rife and customer expectations continue to increase. Also, while the service literature continues to grow it has been aimed mainly at other academics, not the business community. The PROMPT acronym contains six essential service practices: Prioritizing customer needs, Reliable service delivery, Organizing for customers, Measuring customer satisfaction, Personnel training, and Technology focusing. These are the hallmarks of providing service excellence. The PROMPT acronym is a guide for managers in delivering excellent service. Finally, three broad steps are identified to help managers begin their search for a service advantage.

SERVICE – THE NEW COMPETITIVE EDGE

Service is more important than you might imagine. Why? Customers are 'five times more likely to switch vendors because of perceived service problems than for price concerns or product quality issues', according to recent research (Whiteley). Product quality is important for recruiting customers, but service quality is key to retaining customers. Both product and service quality are important. The 1980s was the decade of product quality and the 1990s will be the service quality decade. So to obtain a competitive edge, service may be more potent than managers think. In the battle to recruit and retain customers, service – superior service that is – may provide you with a distinct and lasting competitive advantage. A recent international survey by John Humble and Management Centre Europe (see Figure 15.1) attests to the critical and growing importance of service in the 1990s. 'Service is a key to future growth and success', writes Humble. 'Service is the new competitive edge.'

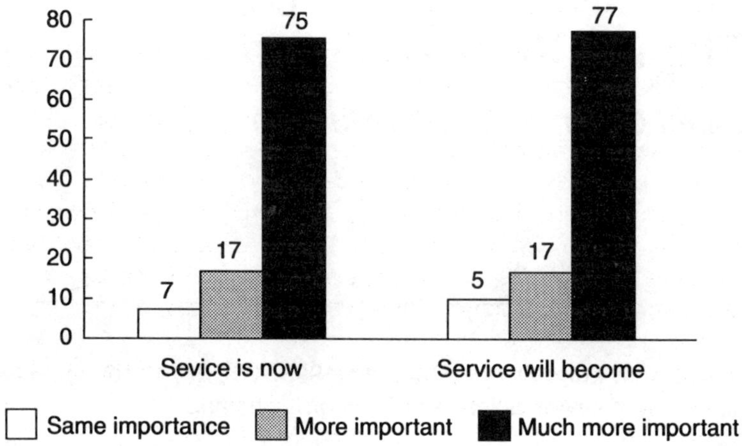

Figure 15.1 Service is a business priority

Source: Irish Service Survey, Michael Quinn, for Digital Equipment Corporation and Market Institute of Ireland

But although service is important, only a few companies provide excellent service. Poor service is everywhere. Some authors believe that there is a *service crisis looming*. 'A customer service crisis is building throughout the business world and most managers don't know it' (Davidrow and Uttal). This creates an opportunity for companies to outperform their competitors. 'The spoils will go to those few companies that both perceive the crisis and learn how to out-service their competitors.'

There is 'considerable customer dissatisfaction with service quality', according to Professor Evert Gummesson at the Service Research Centre, Sweden. But, rather than complain, customers just switch their business to another company. In a recent Irish study only half the companies surveyed produced regular reports on customer satisfaction or had service performance standards in place. Humble's global service survey found that customers are becoming more demanding, and managers worldwide acknowledge that customer expectations are increasing.

More worrying still, the Japanese 'are bringing to service the same intensity they brought to product quality', according to Humble. Gummesson also issues a warning about the Japanese intent 'to dominate' service. He believes we have to 'prepare for more intense competition' – in service quality – in the future. Berry and Parasuraman, from their service research, issue a call to arms to businesses to respond to the dismal state of service in America. They suggest a revolution to 'raise service aspirations' and make 'continuous improvement a habit'.

THE IRISH SERVICE SURVEY

A survey sponsored by Digital Equipment Corporation, and carried out by Digital and the Marketing Institute of Ireland, repeated John Humble's survey. Some 1000 questionnaires were sent to senior managers of leading companies in Ireland – completed questionnaires were received from 424 managers. Seventy-five per cent of the managers who responded indicated that keeping the customer satisfied is now a *critical priority* and will become much more important over the next 3 years. They view service as a major source of differentiation. Intense competition and increasingly demanding customers are the two major forces driving service.

The academic community has been alert to the importance of service for many years (see Figure 15.2). Levitt raised the call for business to focus on the intangibles as well as the tangibles. He even went so far as to say that 'there are no such things as service industries, only industries whose service components are greater or less than those of other industries. This means that we are all in service. Manufacturing companies should think of themselves as also being in service. The total customer experience is part product and part service'. Gronroos further refines service into two dimensions; technical quality – the *what* and functional quality – the *how*. The *what* is associated with product characteristics. The *how* typifies the service dimension, how the customer experiences the process of obtaining the product. Today there is a substantial library of academic literature devoted to Service and it is expanding rapidly.

Some businessmen have advocated the need to devise new strategies for today's customer-driven economy (Carlzon) and to 'crown the customer' (Feargal Quinn). These leaders provide the proof that good service pays. Carlzon has been credited with providing the inspiration for British Airways' turnaround.

EXPECTATIONS ARE INCREASING

The rules for success are changing. Customer expectations do not stand still. Philip Kotler believes that, 'Service excellence will be a major competitive platform for the 90s, primarily because Service, by and large, is *poor* in most countries and in most industries'. A few companies achieve Breakthrough service (Heskett). They have been able to change the rules in their industries by consistently meeting or exceeding customers expectations. But these are in the minority.

While the academic literature has become more abundant in recent years, it has not been aimed specifically at managers but at other academics. On the whole, it is not 'management friendly'. A bridge is

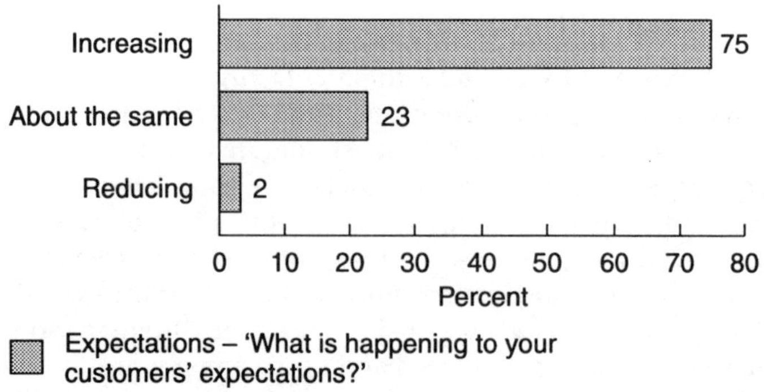

Figure 15.2 Customer expectations

Source: Irish Service Survey

required to bring the academic literature to management audiences and in business language rather than academic language. The academics must market their insights on service to the business community, in a language which businessmen can understand.

This article tries to bridge the gap between the academic findings on service and business practice. My purpose is to provide a model that bridges the academic findings on service with the needs of the business community. My basic assumptions are that managers require a summary of the key literature findings, in a way which is easy to remember and with an action orientation.

PROVIDE PROMPT SERVICE

After repeating the Humble survey on Service in Ireland and reviewing the literature findings I have devised the PROMPT approach to assist in this task (see Figure 15.3). I am using PROMPT here as memory aid to identify the critical findings on service and to provide a basis for action by managers. Managers can use PROMPT to assist their companies in achieving a service advantage. It can also be used as a diagnostic of their company's and their competitor's service practices. It may be useful in identifying gaps in achieving service excellence or to benchmark and learn from the best.

The PROMPT Service approach contains six elements:

- Prioritizing customer needs,
- Reliability is critical,
- Organizing for customers,
- Measuring customer satisfaction,

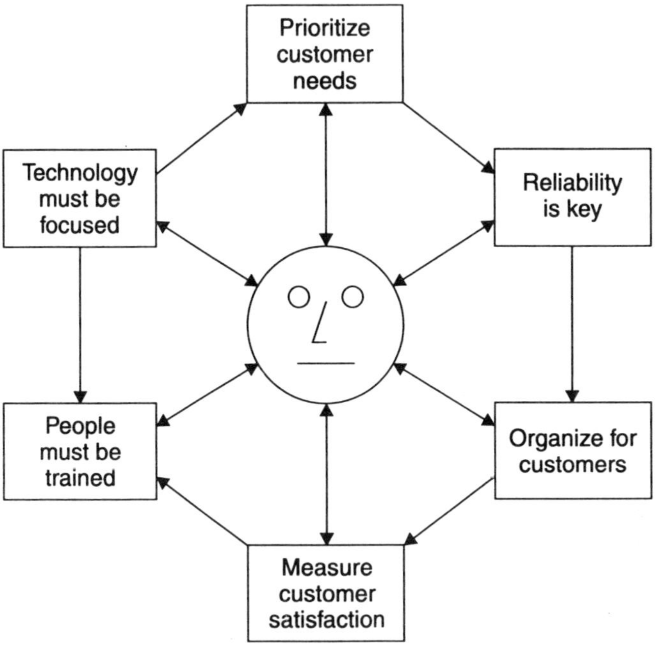

Figure 15.3 The PROMPT service approach

- Personnel training, and
- Technology focusing.

PRIORITIZING CUSTOMER NEEDS

Customers determine what is important. Understanding customers' needs must be the starting point. Those factors that are important in influencing customers to buy must determine the business agenda. This is what recruiting and retaining customers is all about. Strategy is not about beating the competition according to Kenichi Ohmae but in 'serving customers better than the competition'. Selecting which customers to serve is the starting point of business strategy according to Derek Abell. Matching company capabilities to customer needs is the essence of good strategy.

Recent research from the Strategic Planning Institute by Clayton underpins the need to 'specialize to get good returns'. He found those service companies who had a narrower range of products or services than their competitors earned returns of over 50 per cent on capital employed. So for 'service businesses offering a narrower range to customers is an important element of success'. This '*Focus*' strategy is one of Porter's three strategy types. He identifies three generic strategies to obtain a competitive advantage in an industry. The other two strategies are *Low Cost* – being the low cost producer in an industry – and *Differentiation* – providing unique value for customers and therefore obtaining a price premium. However, trying to serve too many customer groups with conflicting needs can cause a situation where no customers are served well. Porter calls this 'stuck in the middle' a situation where a business has no competitive advantage.

Identify the key factors which drive customer buying decisions. These will help you understand what determines the customer's decision to buy. The key buying factors identified by managers in the Irish service survey were (in order of priority):

Quality – fitness for use as perceived by the customer,
Reliability – meeting customers' expectations as promised,
Speed of delivery – being responsive to customer needs,
Courtesy – respect for the customer as an individual.

But customer priorities often differ *significantly* from what managers think they are. Karl Albrecht, a leading author and management consultant believes that 'the longer a business has been in existence, the more likely it has lost sight of what is important to customers'.

An example of this mismatch in priorities comes from the Strategic Planning Institute's PIMS programme. The institute has a formal process called 'quality profiling' that helps uncover the needs of customers and compare them to the view of management. In one example, an Austrian shirt manufacturer discovered that their customer priorities were indeed different. The company thought that fashion, filling a contract, flexibility and meeting the specification were the most important factors for customers. They were surprised to find a different order of priorities. Fashion, finish, delivery and image were perceived important by customers; this formed the basis for management action (see Figure 15.4).

A survey of Irish Hotels by Dr Aidian Daly revealed that 'hotels are failing to detect the needs of customers'. He pointed out that 'there is a tremendous eagerness to satisfy customers but I was astounded by the lack of market research'. 'For instance on the question of interior design, decision makers might canvass the opinions of staff but the customer is rarely consulted.' He stressed that managing the 'encounter points' with the customer is crucial for the success of any service business. Jan Carlzon of SAS calls these 'moments of truth' and believes that SAS has 50 million of these moments of truth to manage each year in their business. These moments will 'ultimately determine whether SAS will fail or succeed'.

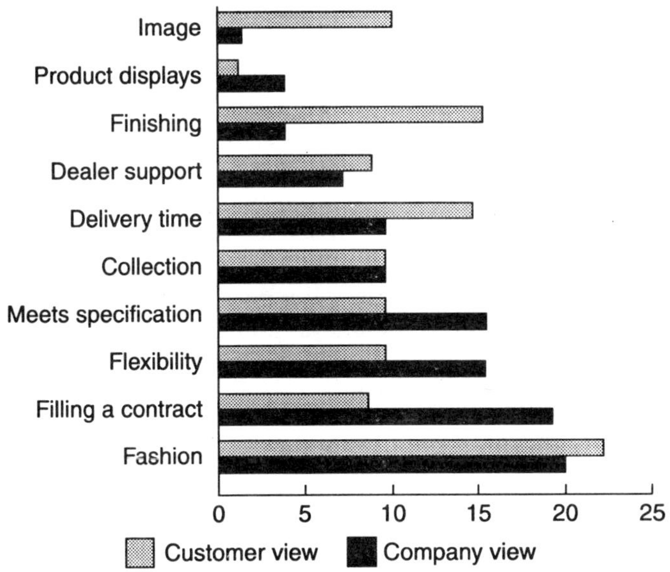

Figure 15.4 Customer priorities often differ from the Company's view

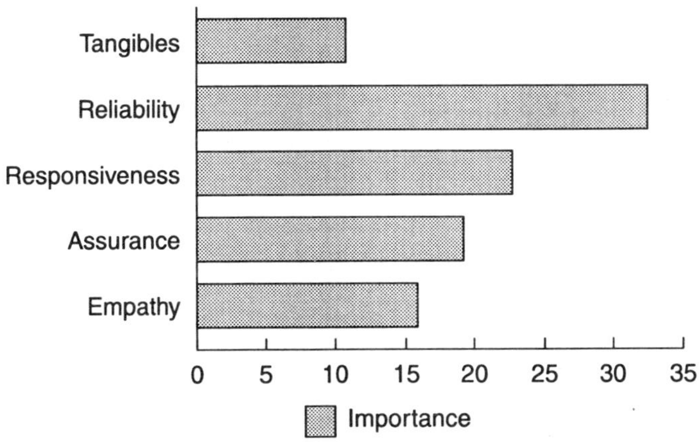

Figure 15.5 Reliability – the most important factor in service. Source: Berry et al.

Identify Customer Needs

The Irish survey on Service probed the methods that were being used by management to explore customer needs. The approaches most frequently used and considered effective are regular contacts between customers and senior management (89 per cent) and regular discussion with sales personnel (90 per cent). Seventy-one per cent use market research on potential customers but only 47 per cent find the research effective. This contrasts with the experience of Japanese managers who find market research very effective (83 per cent). Questionnaires, customer 'clinics', and comment cards are widely used but not considered very effective by Irish managers. However, Japanese managers are using all these approaches to discover and anticipate customer needs, and give a high rate of effectiveness to all of them.

RELIABILITY IS CRITICAL

Service reliability – meeting the customer's expectations as promised – is a vital element in providing service excellence. Reliability is the most important factor in service as perceived by customers, but is not perceived as important by managers (see Figure 15.5). Leonard Berry who is a leading academic and author on service believes that 'service reliability is the heart of service market excellence'. His research has identified the main elements which service businesses must manage. These are:

Reliability – the ability to perform the service as promised dependably and accurately. (32 per cent)
Tangibles – the appearance of physical facilities, equipment, personnel and communications materials. (11 per cent)
Responsiveness – the willingness to help customers and to provide *prompt* service. (22 per cent)
Assurance – the knowledge and courtesy of employees and their ability to convey trust and confidence. (19 per cent)
Empathy – the provision of caring, individualized attention to customers. (16 per cent).

Reliability regularly comes out on top as the most important factor in service. Federal Express, for example has made this promise of reliability explicit in its advertising by stating 'when it absolutely positively has to be there overnight'. They have focused on the most critical dimension in their business of parcel delivery, and they use this to differentiate themselves from their competition. Domino's pizza has also set a standard for reliable delivery of a pizza (30 minutes) and will pay the customer if this promise is not kept.

The Irish survey on service identified reliability as the second most important buying factor after quality. However, the Japanese had a different ranking of the buying factors showing reliability first followed by quality. Perhaps the Japanese view reliability as the future battleground, having already mastered quality. Their lower positioning of quality does not indicate its importance but rather that, having achieved world-class quality, they are moving on to reliability as the next hurdle to overcome. Quality is necessary to win customers, reliability is the key to keeping them. To succeed, businesses must provide both quality products and reliable service.

ORGANIZING FOR CUSTOMERS

The customer, not the organization, is the business. Yet many of today's organization structures do not reflect this, especially in their dealings with customers. The legacy of functional organization structures is still with many of these companies. The Motorola experience is that it 'takes a horizontal organization to serve a customer' according to George Fisher, President and CEO. One of Motorola's key initiatives in rediscovering the customer is 'to work more participatively within the organization and more co-operatively across organizations and functions'. Marketing, Design and Manufacturing people form teams to develop products that meet customer needs and can be produced quickly.

Xerox, the office equipment manufacturer has been focusing on making customer satisfaction its top business priority. This has led to organizational changes in its U.K. operation aimed at serving customers better. They have divided the U.K. into five regions and brought sales, service and administration together. This has devolved the power to act into the regions' in order to become truly responsive to customers'.

The Irish service survey probed the degree to which red tape is eliminated in organizations. Over 53 per cent of managers indicated that when bureaucracy gets in the way of serving customers it is not (but should be) quickly eliminated. The organizational work that needs to be done is enormous. Managers should guide the organizational discussions around what the customers need and not get drawn into corporate politics. The risk of losing valuable customers is too great compared with the cost of keeping inappropriate structures.

MEASURING CUSTOMER SATISFACTION

The majority (81 per cent) of managers in Ireland feel that improving quality and service to customers is the key to competitive success. But less than half of the Irish respondents (48 per cent) measured customer satisfaction on a regular basis. This was one of the major critical service

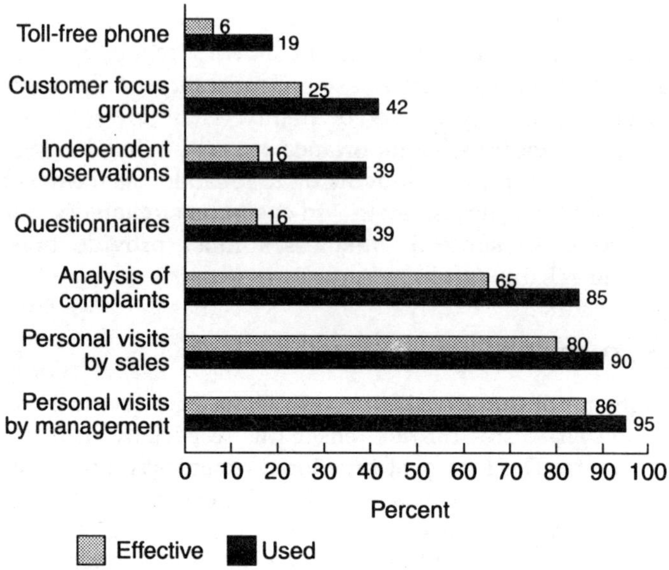

Figure 15.6 Measuring customer satisfaction – Personal contact is best

Source: Irish Service Survey

gaps found in the survey. Those respondents who did measure customer satisfaction used many methods. Failure to measure customer satisfaction is a recipe for eventual disaster.

Personal contacts by management, visits by salespeople and the analysis of complaints were the most frequently used methods. Customer complaints were used by most of the Irish respondents (85 per cent), but seen as effective by only 65 per cent. Contrast this with the Japanese who found this device to be the most effective (96 per cent). Focus groups were used by only 40 per cent and found effective in only 25 per cent of the cases (see Figure 15.6).

Customer 'voice' or 'feedback' is critical in determining the level of satisfaction or dissatisfaction. In 1970, Albert O. Hirschman in a famous economic book called *Exit, Voice and Loyality* – written about the recuperating role which voice can play – as a response to decline in firms. As an economist he was interested in 'repairable lapses' as a result of a deterioration of economic performance. Management, he indicated, can find out about its 'lapses' in two ways, *Exit* – when customers stop buying – and *Voice* – when they express their dissatisfaction directly.

Xerox U.K. believes that in 1990 customers discontinued using 5500 machines. This alone would be worth an extra over $8.5m in profits in

1990, or about $30m over a 3 year period, according to Rob Walker, U.K. quality director. This is the *exit* option in action. 'The financial impact of dissatisfied customers is large', states Walker. The company believes that they have a 7 per cent rate of customer dissatisfaction and aims to reduce this to zero by 1993.

To achieve this 'recuperation' Xerox U.K. are exercising the *Voice* option. Each year they send out, through an independent agency, two types of questionnaire to measure customer satisfaction. One is an annual survey to gauge satisfaction. They then spend much time analysing the comments, seeking to identify and eliminate root causes. They focus on unhappy customers as these give important clues as to the main problem areas requiring action. A second questionnaire is sent out after the installation of a new machine. From this a list of 'vulnerable' or dissatisfied customer complaints are identified for further analysis.

It is not enough to measure customer satisfaction, you must *fix the processes* that cause dissatisfaction. Just measuring customer satisfaction – without fixing the processes – may cause further customer dissatisfaction. This is especially true if customers see no progress as a result of voicing their concerns.

Zero customer defections can be very profitable, as indicated by a recent study by Bain consultants and published in the *Harvard Business Review*. The authors Frederick Reichheld and Earl Sasser show how just reducing the defection rate by 5 per cent can generate profit by 25 per cent in credit insurance and 85 per cent in bank branch deposits. The message is clear – the lifetime value of a customer is significant and *companies should aim for zero customer defections*. Make sure your customers keep coming back.

One major pitfall to avoid in measuring customer satisfaction is to focus only on the dissatisfiers. Sullivan observes that Japanese companies *focus more on what the customer likes* – the satisfiers – while U.S. manufacturers pay more attention to fixing what the customer do not like - the dissatisfiers. Focus on motivators but make sure you also take care of the 'hygiene' factors. Focusing on the 'hygiene' factors alone is insufficient.

Asking the right questions is also important and may be the key to determining customer satisfaction and repurchase intentions. John Goodman of the TARP consulting company finds that the best measure to improve customer satisfaction is to ask the following question: '*Would you buy these or other products made by this company, or recommend our products to a friend or business associate?*'

PERSONNEL TRAINING

Service excellence requires investment in training to satisfy customers on what is important to them. Claus Moller of TMI believes that '*the key to successful change is training and education*'. Becoming customer-driven

Figure 15.7 More managers are trained in customer service but few other employees are

Source: Irish Service Survey

requires focused investment on training employees how to respond to customers. Motorola, for example, is investing $40m a year on training and 'we consider it an essential investment', says George Fisher.

The Irish Service survey highlights the lack of training, especially of front line employees, as a specific problem. While many companies have provided training for their managers (44 per cent) little customer orientated training has been provided for people who serve customers (25 per cent). This means that twice as many managers are trained in customer service than service providers (see Figure 15.7). The Japanese, however, train both managerial and non-managerial employees in customer service almost equally.

Many employees may be willing to serve customers and meet their specific needs but are unable to do so because they are not trained. Leonard Berry has constructed a four-box matrix to highlight this issue where a service performance gap can arise. He has identified specific factors affecting employee willingness and ability to perform the service tasks that include 'role conflict', and 'role ambiguity'. *Role ambiguity* occurs when employees do not have sufficient information or training to understand and perform their jobs. *Role conflict* is when customer needs, for speedy service in a bank teller line, are at odds with management's needs for cross selling bank products.

Training in customer service is not a standard product to be bought off the shelf. It must be customized, that is based on what the customer wants, focused on specific customer needs. Training should be viewed as continuous, and on the job, not just a one off 'dump' of information on employees. To be meaningful to employees training must be relevant to the role employees are doing, add a new skill, and assist employees in their career development.

British Airways began by asking customers what they wanted. Surveys showed that *'friendly staff' who 'treated me as an individual'* was twice as important as operational factors such as food service. They then invested in a training programme called 'putting people first' and its task was to convince and show their 35,000 employees how to treat their customers as individuals. This illustrates the correct use of *customer-focused training.*

TECHNOLOGY FOCUSING

We are living in the Information Age, the 'third' industrial revolution. Information technology is fundamentally changing the nature of work. It is providing new opportunities to serve customers even better. The management in the 1990s programme was undertaken by Massachusetts Institute of Technology to understand the impact of information technology on the corporations of the 1990s. Its findings suggest that information technology will be a major force in the search for competitive advantage. 'With new information technology, well-managed companies tend to get better, poorly managed companies tend to get worse.' However, there is a caveat: 'Investment in leading-edge information technology does not guarantee success'. The investments must have a business focus, and what better focus than in helping serve customers, better than the competition?

When asked to identify the various external pressures driving companies to give more attention to customer service, the Japanese placed significantly more emphasis on developments in advanced information technology. Humble's global service study suggests that the Japanese seem to understand better the significance of IT in the new global economy. They see the development of advanced information technology as being more significant (4.2 on 5 point scale) than the Americans (3.3) or Europeans (3.2). They seem to understand the increasing significance that technology will play in the 1990s.

In the Irish service survey many companies indicated that they were using and benefiting from information technology to build electronic links with suppliers and customers. IT has also helped improve customer service by helping companies reorganize and through improved delegation. Some 75 per cent of Irish companies surveyed have reorganized in the last 3 years to improve service.

A serious problem remains. There is a weak link between IT strategy and customer service. Only 31 per cent of Irish respondents have an IT strategy statement that refers to customer service. Forty-nine per cent of British companies have one. It is not surprising therefore that many companies have failed to exploit technology as a competitive weapon. Many companies claim that they are not getting value from IT, but few focus the tool on the service task. Understandably, human and organizational factors are also involved in this complex business problem.

Mass manufacturing is giving way to mass customization – the ability to tailor a product uniquely to the individual customer's needs. Consider the bicycle, which has always come in standard frame sizes and product styles. Thanks to information technology this has changed dramatically at the National Bicycle Company of Japan. They now have the capability to 'tailor' a bicycle to the specific needs of an individual. In the company showroom customers get 'fitted' for the bike they want; this profile is then faxed to the factory and the specifications are fed into a Digital computer. Production delivers a 'one-of-a-kind' bike from a possible 11 million variations of 18 models, 199 colour patterns, and in about as many sizes as there are people. Everybody is happy, the customer has a unique bike, and with premium prices business margins are healthy.

Companies must leverage information technology because it is the means to an end. It must help the business to be better at serving customers. *Computer application that help serve customers better are 'strategic', particularly for service companies.* In many businesses today information is a key ingredient and is part of the product or service. But, appropriate technology can be deployed only once the service or the business problem is understood. The 'acid test' for management is whether the customer is better served after the implementation. Only the customer can answer that question. The customer should perceive a significant change on an important service dimension.

The Royal Automobile Club (U.K.) has used *appropriate technology* to help it serve its customers better. Its aim according to Arthur Large, its Chief Executive was 'to answer the phone quickly, to get to the motorist quickly and to remobilize him' in the event of a breakdown. This objective caused the RAC to rethink how information technologies could help. They invested £30m in a 'Computer Assisted Rescue System' (CARS). This is a central computer-based 'command and control' centre which supports 17 regional centres with direct two-way communication to the patrolmen via mobile data terminals. This has brought the RAC significant advantages. Membership has expanded two and a half times to 5.2 million customers, the RAC market share has increased. Profits

SERVICE PROBLEM	TECHNOLOGY: Appropriate	TECHNOLOGY: Inappropriate
Well Specified	Payoff Assured	Low Payoff
Poorly Specified	Pot Luck	No Hope

Figure 15.8

were nearly twice the market leaders (the AA) in 1990 and the organization has become more streamlined, with two layers less than the market leader.

CONCLUSIONS

Service is a vital ingredient in retaining and keeping customers. This is also true for manufacturing companies. I have tried to blend my findings from the Irish Humble survey with the literature and link it to management practice. The result, the PROMPT approach intended to provide a bridge between the literature and the urgency for prompt management action in service.

So where should management begin in the search for a service advantage? To achieve service excellence three broad steps or phases are needed. First, identify your service position as perceived by your customers – the current state. Second, clarify your service vision – your desired future state. Third, develop an action plan to get you from where you are to where you want to be – the desired state (see Figures 15.8 and 15.9).

DETERMINE YOUR SERVICE POSITION

The company's competitive position will determine the nature, scope and urgency of the service task ahead. The PROMPT model suggests that management should start with the customer. That is identify their current service position, as perceived by their customers.

1. Determine your service position
2. Clarify your service vision
3. Develop an action plan

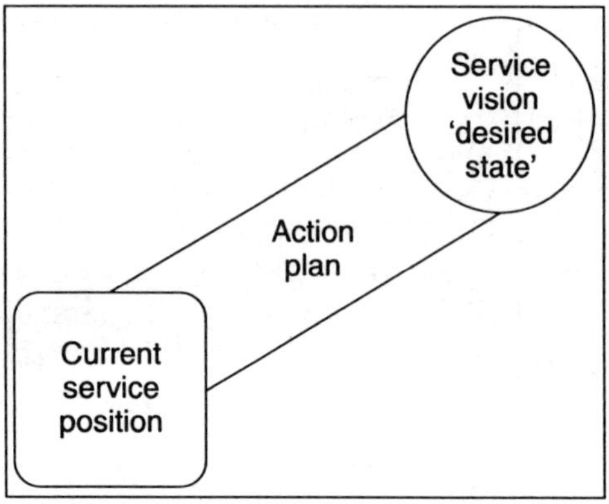

Figure 15.9 Getting started

The purpose of a service audit is to identify how good the company is at retaining and recruiting customers. So management should focus their attention on these two critical business activities. Managers should not delegate this but get involved personally. It puts them in touch with what is happening 'out there' and provides live data to act on. Two groups of customers will provide valuable data quickly. New customers will say why the company won their business and lost customers will tell them why they won't buy again.

Order-winning factors represent the company's unique competences in recruiting customers against the competition. To determine what these factors are requires a customer's perspective. Management should focus their attention on new or recent customers to determine their reasons for choosing the company. These are the company's strengths as perceived by new customers.

Order-losing factors are those which annoy the customer to such an extent that they take their business elsewhere. This is the Exit Option in action and is usually done silently. These factors represent the company's major weaknesses at keeping customers. They must be understood, and then repaired, promptly. Management should focus their attention on some customers who recently placed their business elsewhere. This provides a dual learning insight. First it identifies the company's major business weaknesses; furthermore it provides insight into why they choose the competition.

Competitors do not stand still, they move on. What are their unique service advantages and what new competences are they adding? What moves are they making to serve the customer better? Why do they win or lose orders? What actions does the company need to take to out-service their competitors? Benchmark the best! Look outside the industry to identify service excellence and learn from their 'best practices'.

The service audit will determine the company's service position and objectives. Some companies have already achieved a service advantage, so their objective is to stay ahead. Others have achieved service parity with their competitors and their goal is to out-service their competitors by performing better in areas which customers value more. A third group of companies may find themselves at a competitive disadvantage, with no competitive differentiators and no compelling reasons for customers to continue buying from them. Their task is service turn-around or transformation and the objective is to regain service parity.

CLARIFY YOUR SERVICE VISION

A *service strategy* should define the purpose or mission of a company with respect to serving customers. This answers the age old strategy question: 'what business are we in?' The strategy identifies: (a) the group(s) of customers that the company intends to serve and (b) the customers needs which the company intends to fulfill, stated in terms of results to be produced for customers. The service strategy says specifically what it takes to retain and recruit customers. These factors will be identified during the service audit.

A *service 'vision'* is a statement of intent about the future. It describes how the company would like to have its products and services perceived by customers. Whiteley describes a vision as 'a vivid picture of an ambitious, desirable future state that is connected to the customer and better in some important way than the current state'. British Airways for example wants to be perceived by customers as 'the world's most friendly airline'.

To be effective, communicate the vision to all employees. *Employee communication* is a pre-requisite to making the vision a reality. After all, it is employees, front-line employees, that make strategy happen every day for the customers. Therefore it makes sense to communicate the company's strategic direction to them. This ensures that all employees' efforts are deployed in the same direction, rather than pulling in different directions.

The Japanese win because they focus on providing value to the customer. Focus instead on serving the customer better. This is the central message. We can learn from the Japanese, but to get preoccupied with the competition is a recipe for staying behind. *You only get ahead by meeting customers' needs better than the competition.*

DEVELOP AN ACTION PLAN

Once the vision is set, the gap between the current reality and the vision becomes more apparent. Good vision alone is not sufficient. Management must chart a route between the current reality and the desired future state. Develop detailed action plans and assign resources to these tasks. To get started management should focus their energy where it will have the most impact.

First look at improvements in areas that are important for customers and in which the company is doing poorly. Close these gaps as a matter of priority. Closing the gaps means that customers will perceive the improvements. It is of little use to make internal improvements that are not perceived by customers. Better still if these improvements are in areas where the company has an advantage over the competition. However, some gaps will be easier to close than others.

Select early moves which are both important for the customer and easy to implement. This ensures two points: first, that the customer perceives the company is serious about improving service and second, improvements are seen internally as being successful and this will inspire further improvement efforts.

Processes, not people cause the most customer offence. Identify critical customer serving processes that are causing the most aggravation for customers and re-engineer them from the customers point of view. For example the customers may find it difficult to contact the company in an emergency, so management should focus on making this process easier for customers to access.

People who lead the change efforts and display outstanding performance improvements should be recognized and rewarded for their efforts. Recognition creates *'service champions'* and spurs on the efforts of other individuals or teams. They show the way for others and give examples of new required behaviours in how to serve the customer better.

Acknowledgement

I wish to thank John Humble for allowing me to use his survey in Ireland; John Corrigan, Colin McCrea and Jane Reid of the Marketing Institute in Ireland for their help with the Irish Survey; Bill Egan of Digital Equipment Ireland for his support; Wilf Regan of Digitals European Software Business (ESSB) for producing the survey; Professor Dominique Turpin of IMD and Dr. Aidan Daly of UCG for their encouragement; and also Nick Winkfield of ICRADA for compiling the statistical data base.

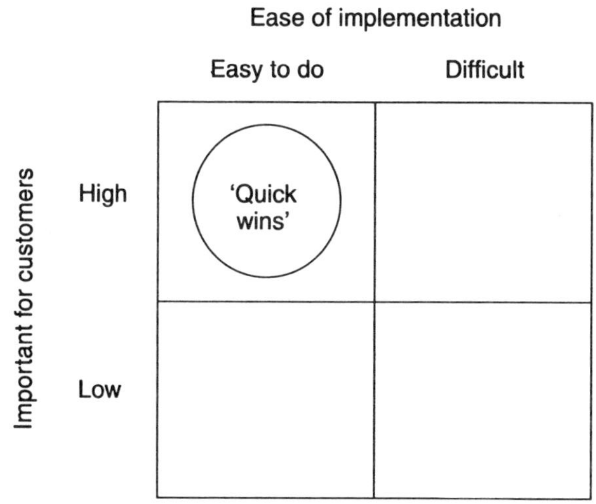

Figure 15.10 Quick wins

Michael Quinn is the strategic planning manager for Digital Equipments European Software Supply Business (ESSB) based in Galway, Ireland. John Humble is an international management consultant and is corporate advisor on service to Digital UK. He is a Director of the Minit Corporation and Dun and Bradstreet Ltd.

Bibliography

John Humble and Management Centre Europe, *Service: the new competitive edge.*

Michael Quinn and John Humble, *Service: the new competitive edge, a survey of executive opinion of senior managers in Ireland;* Sponsored by Digital Equipment and carried out by Digital and the Marketing Institute.

Evert Gummesson, Nine Lessons on service quality, the *TQM magazine*, **1** (2), Feb (1989).

Leonard Berry and A. Parasuraman, Prescriptions for a service quality revolution in America, *Organizational Dynamics*, Spring (1992).

Ted Levitt, *The Marketing Imagination*, Free Press (1986).

A. Parasuraman, V. A. Zeithaml and Leonard Berry, A Conceptual model of service quality and its implications for future research, *Journal of Marketing*, **49**, 4150, Fall (1985).

Christian Gronroos, Designing a long range marketing strategy for services, *Long Range Planning*, **13**, (1980).

Christopher Lovelock, Classifying services to gain strategic marketing insights, *Journal of marketing*, Summer (1983).

Jan Carlzon, *Moments of Truth*, Ballinger (1988).

Feargal Quinn, *Crowning the customer*, O'Brien (1990).

William H. Davidow and Bro Uttal, *Total Customer Satisfaction*, Harper and Row (1989).

Philip Kotler, Strategies for marketing service excellence, *The Global Service Conference*, London, March (1991).
James L. Heskett, W. Earl Sasser, Jr and Christopher Hart, *Service Breakthroughs*, Free Press (1990).
J. H. Davidson, *Offensive Marketing*, Cassel (1972).
Kenichi Ohmae, *The Borderless World*, Free Press, Collins (1970).
Karl Albrecht, *At America's Service*, Dow Jones-Irwin (1988).
PIMS, European conference proceedings (1988).
Robert D. Buzzell, Bradley Gale, *The PIMS Principles*, Free Press (1987).
Aidian Daly, The marketing of services, Ph.D. thesis, U.C.G. (1990).
V. A. Zeithmal, A. Parasuraman and Leonard Berry, *Delivering Quality Service*, Free Press (1990).
Professor Christopher Lovelock, Federal Express, Quality Improvement Program – case study I.M.D.
George Fisher, Our time has come: a manufacturing renaissance, Executive speech, October (1988).
Simon Holberton, In pursuit of repeat business, *The Financial Times*, 13 May (1991).
Alberty O. Hirschman, *Exit, Voice and Loyalty*, Harvard University Press (1970).
Frederick R. Reichheld and W. Earl Sasser, Jr. Zero defections: Quality comes to services, *'Harvard Business Review'*, September/October (1990).
Lawrence P. Sullivan, Quality function deployment, *Quality Progress*, **19** (6), June (1986).
John A. Goodman, Measuring and quantifying the market impact of customer problems and setting rational quality improvement priorities, First Global Service Conference, MCE, March (1991).
Claus Moller, Sustaining service excellence through effective training and development, First Global Service Conference, MCE, March (1991).
Leonard Berry, David R. Bennett and Carter W. Brown *Service Quality – A Profit Strategy for Financial Institutions*, Dow Jones-Irwin (1989).
Mike Bruce, An extract from learning in BA: A case of putting people first.
Susan Moffat, Japan's new personalised production, *Fortune* (1990).
John, Humble and Geoff Shingles, Service – the new competitive edge, the role of I.T. (1991).
D. F. Abell, *Defining the Business: The Starting Point of Strategic Planning*, Prentice Hall, Englewood Cliffs, N.J. (1980).
Richard C. Whiteley, *The Customer-Driven Company*, Addison-Wesley, (1991).

Reading 16

Relationship marketing: pursuing the perfect person-to-person relationship

J. Davis Illingworth

Reprinted from *The Journal of Services Marketing*, Fall 1991, Vol. 5, No. 4, pp. 49–52.

When the Lexus was conceived, Toyota clearly understood that one of the keys to this division's success would be how effectively it could separate itself from other luxury car manufacturers. To help it do this it established a theme, "The Relentless Pursuit of Perfection." The "Pursuit of Perfection" is more than an advertising theme, it's the cornerstone of all Lexus activities.

THE IMPORTANCE OF PERSON-TO-PERSON RELATIONSHIPS

Several years ago, a local bank in Cincinnati established, a branch made up completely of automated tellers. It was felt that this would help enable busy commuters to bank, at their convenience, within the community. It failed miserably. People wanted the opportunity to deal with another person more than they wanted to save time.

Obviously, you can't improve on a person-to-person relationship. You can, however, improve the *quality* of the relationship. The goal at Lexus was to perfect these person-to-person relationships, or at least to come to as close to perfect as possible.

Lexus target buyers, are affluent and sophisticated. Typical LS 400 buyers are 47 years old and college-educated, 75 percent have been to graduate school. They have a median income of $160,000, and nearly 30 percent of them earn more than $250,000. Twenty percent list their job title as president or CEO. Sixty-five percent pay cash for their vehicles. These customers not only expect, but demand to be treated in a highly professional manner in all their business dealings, including buying a car. If they do not receive the type of professional treatment they expect, they don't complain, they simply walk away and never return. But if you work hard to build a solid relationship, they will not only return, they will recommend your operation to others.

Here is an example of the importance of relationship marketing. My secretary recently left me a message from potential customer on the East Coast asking that I call back the next day at precisely 1:00 o'clock. As it happened, I was able to call back at that time. The person said he was a BMW owner but was considering a Lexus and just wanted to see if I would call back. I sold him a car.

The Lexus division defines relationship marketing simply as putting the customer first. This philosophy was established more than 50 years ago by Toyota's founder, Sakichi Toyota, whose creed was customer first, dealer second, Toyota third. This creed still governs everything the company does, and at Lexus it is taken a step further. More than two years prior to the division's launch, it was decided to write a covenant that would combine the pursuit of perfection theme and Toyota founder's customer-first directive. In short, the covenant says: "We will treat each customer as we would a guest in our home . . . and we will do that by having the finest dealer body in the industry." A covenant puts a lot of pressure on management and the dealers to be the best in the business.

THE IMPORTANCE OF THE DEALER

In the auto industry, the key to successful relationship marketing rests at the dealer level. As far as the customer is concerned the dealer is the face of the company. How the dealer performs – either good or bad – is how the company will be viewed. As a customer in Houston recently summed it up: "My image and opinion of Lexus comes through the local dealer and his dedicated people."

It is for this reason that Lexus is so selective in choosing its dealers and so determined to develop programs to support them. Lexus looks for dealers with a proven track record in customer satisfaction, broad management experience, sound capitalization, and the willingness to build new facilities or retrofit their existing facility to exacting standards. Most important the dealers must be committed to building long-lasting relationships with their customers.

More than 1,500 candidates have applied. About 650 of them went into considerable time and effort to submit complete proposals for review. Those who were non-Toyota dealers were flown to California to make their presentations. Initially, less than 100 earned a Lexus dealer franchise. By the end of the year there will be about 120 in operation.

The selected dealers have made substantial investment of between $3 and $5 million. More than 80 percent built new facilities. The dealership design is very important because the right setting is essential for one who wants to establish a longterm relationship with luxury buyers. These buyers are highly selective and will reject not only product, but environments that don't meet their expectations.

Lexus management wanted the dealership to deliver the same image as the product: an image of solid engineering and innovative design on the outside, warmth on the inside, with an overall feeling of quality and prestige. Every facet of the dealership, from landscaping to wall decor, was carefully researched before it was incorporated into the facility. CALTY, Toyota's California-based design studio, participated in the design of the dealership, the first time a studio participated in the design of both a car and the dealership it would be sold in.

When a customer walks into a Lexus dealership, he or she is greeted by a receptionist behind a marble desk. Gone are the salesmen wearing plaid jackets and white shoes swooping down on customers like vultures. Only upon request will a receptionist call a sales representative to assist the customer. There is no high-pressure, because when you're trying to build a relationship, first impressions are important. If a customer just wants to browse, he or she can learn more about Lexus from a media wall consisting of videos and still prints with information about Lexus and its products.

A customer who does request assistance will be dealing with a highly trained professional. Months before the first dealership opened its door, there were intensive sales training programs, dubbed "boot camps" by the participants. And even though the model line up has only minor changes for 1991, these training sessions are continuing, because the marketplace and competitors are continually changing. The Lexus sales force must be prepared to respond to those changes.

Lexus sales people report that they spend an average of 90 minutes presenting a vehicle to a customer. That's a staggering amount of time in the auto industry. It must be worth it, because consumers have been quick to make known that they appreciate Lexus salespeople. Here are excerpts from two letters sent by customers:

> I was especially impressed by your Stevens Creek Dealership (in California). Salesman Alexander Gloner did an excellent job of explaining the features of a superb car . . .
>
> It is unusual today to find a salesperson who is willing to put the customer first. J.M. Lexus salesperson Helen Fajardo certainly made us feel special by her unpressured manner of selling.

That kind of praise for a car salesperson is not too common, but it's exactly what Lexus expects to hear.

THE IMPORTANCE OF SERVICE

Service is another area of critical importance to the success of relationship marketing. The contact often takes place under challenging conditions, but research continually shows that consumers appreciate automotive service performed correctly.

Right from the start Lexus did some things differently in the area of service. The number one complaint car owners have with automotive service is having to bring the car back because the problem wasn't fixed properly the first time. Further, Lexus research indicated that customers felt their problems were never adequately explained to the person actually doing the service work. As a result, cars were not repaired correctly and return trips were necessary for any owner, but especially busy luxury car owners, return visits are an unaffordable waste of time and the kiss of death of a long-term relationship.

To address this problem, each Lexus dealership is equipped with a special diagnostic quality control center, where an owner talks directly with the diagnostic specialist. The owner also can watch the diagnostic process and be assured that the car's problems are correctly understood before the repair process begins.

Lexus's pursuit of perfection was put to a severe test last year when it decided to recall its flagship LS 400 model. It had received one customer contact on two separate product problems but were concerned that other customer's cars could be affected. It immediately decided that all cars must be recalled in order to ensure the quality owners expected.

Dealer reaction to the recall was outstanding. They did not wait for notification letters to reach a person's home or for the owner to read about it in the newspaper. Rather, most buyers were contacted directly by dealership personnel the day the recall was announced. When owners picked up their cars at dealerships after the work was completed, the cars were washed and the gas tanks were filled. If the owners lived more than 100 miles from the dealership and it was inconvenient to bring the car in for the service, a technician was dispatched to the owner's home. In one case, a technician even flew from Los Angeles to Anchorage to service a car that had originally been bought in Portland.

The result was that one publication called the "Perfect Recall." Many owners praised the way the recall was handled. One wrote a glowing letter to the *Wall Street Journal* and several others wrote to automotive publications. Thus, a potentially embarrassing and disastrous event was turned into a positive because Lexus and its dealers were committed to developing and ongoing relationship with others.

With dealers willing to go the extra mile in this way, it's important for the company to protect their investments. If dealers are not making money, they are less likely to provide the type of person-to-person satisfaction needed for a long-term relationship.

Realizing that Lexus dealerships would be located near luxury buyers, where land is more expensive, the company established realistic land and facility requirements, smaller than those for most dealerships.

In a move to increase personal contact opportunities while at the same time generating business for the service department. Lexus set 1,000 and 7,500 mile free-to-the-owner maintenance checkups, even though the engineers said it was not really necessary.

Also, dealers were not asked to stock large – and costly – inventories. Instead, each dealer is linked to Lexus headquarters in Southern California by satellite. Not only does this link permit next day parts, delivery, it also tracks the service history of every Lexus vehicle, recording every part replaced and every service performed. Customers can go to any Lexus dealer in the country and that dealer will have immediate access to the complete vehicle service history.

Dealers are also encouraged to be proactive. They have the authority to resolve customer concerns on the spot, no matter what has to be done, and their decisions will be backed-up to 100 percent.

Telephone follow-ups is another important area stressed with dealers. Salespeople are encouraged to contact buyers shortly after delivery to answer any questions or hear any concerns a new owner may have. In addition, telephone follow-up is stressed after each service visit to make sure the owner is happy with the results.

The same thing is done at Lexus headquarters. Every employee, from the newest secretary to the vice-president, calls one owner a week, just to touch base and see if there's anything the company can do for them.

So far these efforts seem to be working. For example, *Car and Driver Magazine* has been conducting an annual buyers study since the mid-1970s and this year the LS 400 recorded the highest score ever, 9.7 on a scale of one to 10.

Popular Mechanics Magazine has been doing a similar study dating back nearly 40 years and again the LS 400 received the best grades ever from owners. And the J.D. Power organization's Initial Quality Survey, the one quoted in all the advertising, named Lexus the top nameplate for 1990. This is even more impressive when you consider that the survey was done last December, at the time of the recall.

Lexus management believes it can do even better in the years ahead, because it has the best dealer body in the auto industry and the commitment to do its best to support those dealers.

J. Davis Illingworth (Dave) is group vice president and general manager of Lexus and an officer of Toyota Motor Sales, U.S.A., Inc. Since joining Toyota in 1980, he has held such positions as assistant to the national sales manager, national

customer relations manager, national market representation manager, Denver Region general manager, and Cincinnati Region manager. He has been with the Lexus Division since its inception in January, 1987. During that time, he served as vice president and general manager and corporate manager overseeing sales, service, and marketing operations.

Prior to this time, Dave had a ten year career with Chrysler Corporation.

A native of Youngstown, Ohio, Illingworth attended Ohio University, where he received a B.A. in sociology.

This article was developed from a speech at Annual Marketing Conference, The Conference Board.

Reading 17

Why satisfied customers defect

The gulf between satisfied customers and completely satisfied customers can swallow a business

Thomas O. Jones and W. Earl Sasser, Jr.

Reprinted from *Harvard Business Review*, November–December 1995, pp. 88–99, with permission of Harvard Business Review.

The scene is familiar: the monthly management meeting attended by a company's senior officers and the general managers of its operating divisions. The company's eight divisions operate in diverse markets, including light manufacturing, wholesale distribution, and consumer services. All are feeling pressure from strong competitors, and the corporation has created a customer-satisfaction survey as one method of measuring the impact of its quality-improvement process.

After dispensing with several items on the agenda, the group turns to the third-quarter customer-satisfaction indices, and a transparency is placed on the overhead projector (see Figure 17.1). The CEO proudly points out that 82% of the customers surveyed responded with an overall satisfaction rating of either 4 (satisfied) or 5 (completely satisfied). Everyone in the meeting agrees that the company must be doing pretty well because only 18% of its customers were less than satisfied.

There are three divisions with average ratings of 4.5 or higher. There is general consensus that they have reached the point of diminishing returns and that further investing to increase customer satisfaction will not make good financial sense.

The group next examines the results of the division with the lowest average rating, a 2.7. This business unit manufactures bulk lubricants and sells to companies that repackage the product for sale to the retail channel. It is a highly competitive, commodity-type business and operates with very tight margins. The group concludes that the lubricant division's market is difficult and that its price-sensitive customers will never be satisfied. Moreover, the division's rating is equal to or above those of most competitors. There is a general consensus that its

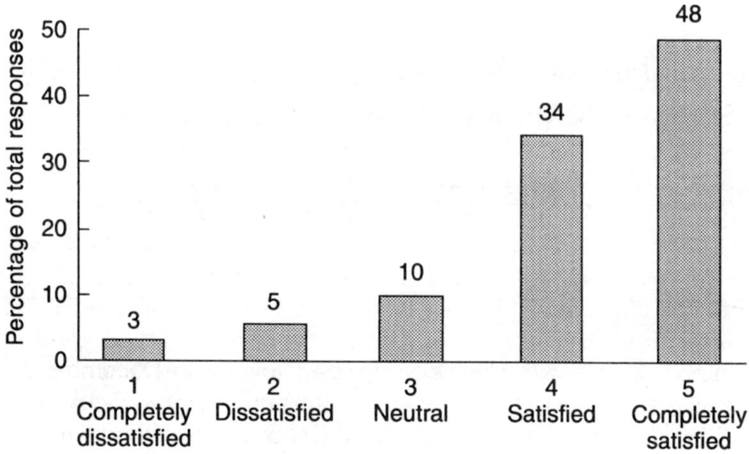

Figure 17.1 Third quarter satisfaction index

customers are a lost cause and that it does not pay to make additional investments to try to satisfy them.

Finally, the discussion turns to four business units whose customers generally are neutral or pleased but certainly not delighted. Two divisions manufacture large industrial machinery. Two other divisions provide after-market service for the products of both the company and its competitors. Each division has an average rating between 3.5 and 4.5, meaning that, although the majority of their customers are not dissatisfied or neutral, a significant number are. "Our battle plan is to find out what's making the least-satisfied customers mad and fix it!" the head of one industrial-machinery division says. The others nod in agreement.

Implicit in this discussion are a number of beliefs widely held by managers of the dozens of manufacturing and service companies we have studied. First, it is sufficient to satisfy a customer; as long as a customer responds with at least a satisfied rating (a 4), the company-customer relationship is strong. In other words, a level of satisfaction below complete or total satisfaction is acceptable. After all, this is the real world, where products and services are rarely perfect and people are hard to please. Second, the investment required to change customers from satisfied to completely satisfied will not provide an attractive financial return and therefore probably is not a wise use of resources. Indeed, there may even be instances – most notably, when competing in a cutthroat commodity market – where it doesn't pay to try to satisfy any customers. Finally, each division with a relatively high average rating (3.5 to 4.5) should focus on the customers in its lowest-satisfaction categories (1 to 2). Striving to understand the causes of their dissatisfaction and concentrating efforts on addressing them is the best use of resources.

The extensive research that we conducted on the relationship between customer satisfaction and customer loyalty, however, shows that these assumptions are deeply flawed. They either ignore or do not accord enough importance to the following aspects of the relationship:

- *Except in a few rare instances, complete customer satisfaction is the key to securing customer loyalty and generating superior long-term financial performance.* Most managers realize that the more competitive the market, the more important the level of customer satisfaction. What most do not realize, however, is just how important the level of customer satisfaction is in markets where competition is intense, such as hard and soft durables, business equipment, financial services, and retailing. In markets like these, there is a tremendous difference between the loyalty of merely satisfied and completely satisfied customers (see Figure 17.2). As the steep curve for the automobile industry shows, completely satisfied customers are – to a surprising degree – much more loyal than satisfied customers. To put it another way, any drop from total satisfaction results in a major drop in loyalty. The same applies to commodity businesses with thin profit margins, the potential returns on initiatives to increase satisfaction in such businesses can be as high as the return on initiatives in more profitable businesses. In fact, attempts to

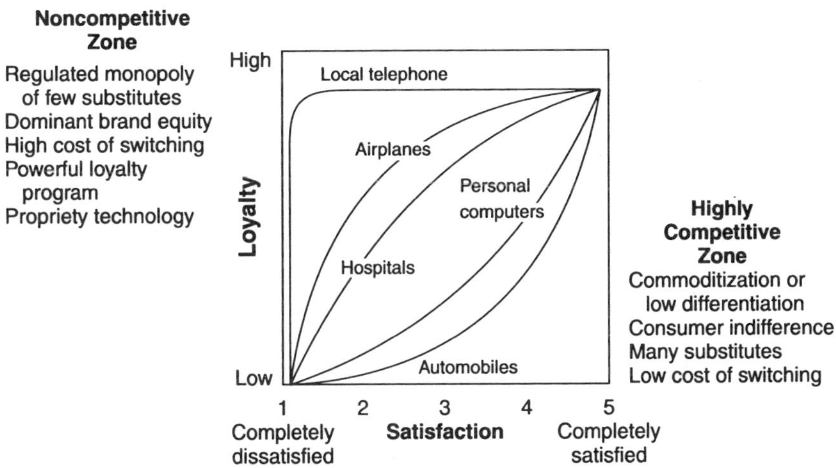

Figure 17.2 How the competitive environment affects the satisfaction-loyalty relationship

create complete customer satisfaction in commodity industries will often raise the product or service out of the commodity category. In most instances, totally satisfying the members of the targeted customer group should be a top priority.

- *Even in markets with relatively little competition, providing customers with outstanding value may be the only reliable way to achieve sustained customer satisfaction and loyalty.* There are two types of loyalty: true long-term loyalty and what we call false loyalty. A variety of factors can generate false loyalty or make customers seem deeply loyal when they are not. They include: government regulations that limit competition; high switching costs such as the cost of changing hospitals in the middle of treatment; proprietary technology that limits alternatives; and strong loyalty-promotion programs such as frequent-flier plans. But we made a startling discovery about customers in such markets. Whenever these customers have choices and feel free to make a choice they act like customers in markets with intense competition. They will only remain rock-solid loyal if they are completely satisfied. That is why seemingly loyal customers defect when they exhaust their frequent-flier miles, when they complete a course of treatment at a hospital, when a regulated market is deregulated, and when alternative technologies are offered. In such markets, it is the companies, rather than their customers, who ultimately have no choice. They must strive to provide their prized customers – those they can serve most profitably – with outstanding value. The message is clear: It is absolutely critical for a company to excel in both defining its target customers and delivering a product or service that completely meets their needs.
- *Very poor service or products are not the only cause – and may not even be the main cause – of high dissatisfaction. Often the company has attracted the wrong customers or has an inadequate process for turning around the right customers when they have a bad experience.* Customers typically fall into one of two categories: the right customers, or target group, whom the company should be able to serve well and profitably, and the wrong customers, whose needs it cannot profitably serve. Having the wrong customers is the result of a flawed process for attracting or obtaining customers. The company that retains difficult-to-serve, chronically unhappy customers is making an expensive long-term mistake. Such customers will continually utilize a disproportionate amount of the company's resources, will hurt the morale of frontline employees, and will disparage the company to other potential customers. Managers should actively discourage such people or organizations from remaining customers and should do their best not to attract others like them. On the other hand, managers of companies that are generally delivering high-quality services or products obviously want to keep their targeted customers and should strive to make amends when, inevitably, some-

thing goes wrong. Marked unhappiness among targeted customers often means a problem was not resolved to their satisfaction.

- *Different satisfaction levels reflect different issues and, therefore, require different actions.* The levels of satisfaction among targeted customers are a good indicator of the level of quality of the products or services that they are receiving. But the way to raise the level of customer satisfaction from neutral to satisfied or from satisfied to completely satisfied is not just a matter of doing a better job of delivering the same value or experience that the company is currently delivering. There are four elements that affect customer satisfaction: the basic elements of the product or service that customers expect all competitors to deliver; basic support services such as customer assistance or order tracking that make the product or service incrementally more effective and easier to use; a recovery process for counteracting bad experiences; and extraordinary services that so excel in meeting customers' personal preferences, in appealing to their values, or in solving their particular problems that they make the product or service seem customized. As we will discuss later, the satisfaction or dissatisfaction level of the majority of a company's customers helps determine which of these elements the company should focus on delivering.
- *Even though the results of customer-satisfaction surveys are an important indicator of the health of the business, relying solely on them can be fatal.* Customer-satisfaction surveys can generate valuable information that enables a company to compare the performance of one business unit or several business units in different time periods and locations. They can provide leading indicators of market shifts and can provide a clear sense of the product or service attributes that individual customers most desire. However, customer-satisfaction surveys cannot supply the breadth and depth of information about customers needed to guide the company's strategy and product-innovation process. Satisfaction surveys alone will not enable a company to fend off new competitors or to keep products and services attuned to customers changing needs. For this reason, companies must also utilize a variety of other methods to listen to existing, potential, and former customers (see the insert "How to Listen to Customers", p. 273).

THE SATISFACTION-LOYALTY LINK

Executives at Xerox Corporation, which had conducted in-depth satisfaction studies of its office-products customers, played a major role in helping us define our research project. Xerox's intense interest in measuring customer satisfaction sprang from a set of beliefs that we share. High-quality products and associated services designed to meet customer needs will create high levels of customer satisfaction. This high level of satisfaction will lead to greatly increased customer loyalty. And increased customer loyalty is the single most important driver of long-term financial performance. Separate research has validated these beliefs (see Zero Defections: Quality Comes to Services, by Frederick F. Reichheld and W. Earl Sasser, Jr., HBR September–October 1990).

Although these assumptions might seem relatively simple, one discovery by Xerox shattered conventional wisdom: its totally satisfied customers were six times more likely to repurchase Xerox products over the next 18 months than its satisfied customers. The implications were profound: merely satisfying customers who have the freedom to make choices is not enough to keep them loyal. The only truly loyal customers are totally satisfied customers.

The Research

Xerox's discovery intrigued us. Was this relationship between satisfaction and loyalty unique to Xerox? To investigate, we scrutinized more than 30 individual companies and analyzed data from five markets with different competitive environments and different types of customer relationships. The five markets were automobiles, personal computers purchased by businesses, hospitals, airlines, and local telephone services. To measure customer loyalty, we decided to rely mostly on customers' stated intent to repurchase products or services (see the insert "Measures of Loyalty", p. 273). We selected the five markets for particular reasons.

- *Automobiles*. We chose automobiles to test whether Xerox's discovery – that its completely satisfied customers were significantly more likely to repurchase its products than its simply satisfied customers – was a fluke or the norm in highly competitive markets. By highly competitive markets we mean those in which there are many alternative products or services offered, the cost of switching is low, or the product is not important to the buyer (that is, where a valid substitute is no purchase at all). Our data on the buyers of 32 automobile models were provided by Robert Lunn of J.D. Power and Associates, the market-research company based in Agoura Hills, California. J.D. Power surveyed these individuals one year after they had purchased their vehicles. The 32 nameplates included both foreign and domestic models with high, medium, and low prices.
- *Personal Computers for Businesses*. We studied this industry to explore the satisfaction-loyalty relationship in a market where the user is not the actual purchaser. Although the personal-computer market is highly competitive, considerable barriers prevent individual business users from switching to another manufacturer's personal computer: for example, centralized purchasing and corporate standards. On the other hand, central purchasing departments do periodically reconsider their suppliers. And in the last ten years, corporate purchasing departments

have placed a greater focus on pleasing their customers: the actual users of the equipment they buy. To test how satisfaction affected the loyalty of the end users, we analyzed data from J.D. Power's 1994 survey of more than 2,000 business users of personal computers.

- *Hospitals*. We chose the hospital market because of two interesting characteristics: Although it is shifting from a market dominated by semi-monopolies to one characterized by intense competition, there still remain significant barriers that impede end users (patients) from switching. Several factors affect the choice of a particular hospital. The patient's physician, health maintenance organization, or insurer often determines where he or she goes for treatment; after beginning treatment in a hospital, a patient tends to complete treatment there; and finally, in many parts of the country, there is only one hospital within a convenient distance. Nonetheless, there are moments when the barriers drop and patients can and do switch. To test how these kinds of barriers affect the satisfaction-loyalty relationship, we relied on data taken from 10,000 surveys of patients treated at nearly 82 hospitals in a range of locations in the United States. David Furse, president of NCG Research – a company based in Nashville, Tennessee, that measures service quality and customer satisfaction in the health care industry – provided us with the data.
- *Airlines*. This market interested us because it is one in which the varying level of competition on routes and strong loyalty-promotion programs affect purchasing decisions. Since airlines are relatively efficient in responding to competitors' price changes, most people flying on a particular route heavily base their purchasing decisions on two other factors: time of departure and frequent-flier programs. Although some routes are highly competitive, the fact of the matter is that people who have to go to a certain place at a certain time often have few if any alternatives: the route is a virtual monopoly. To explore the impact all these factors on the satisfaction-loyalty relationship, we analyzed data from a survey that J.D. Power conducted in the first quarter of 1994. The survey questioned approximately 20,000 passengers who used the eight largest domestic airlines and flew on 72 routes.
- *Local Telephone Services*. We analyzed data provided by a Bell operating company to explore the nature of the relationship in actual or virtual monopolies, in which satisfaction seems to have little impact on loyalty. More specifically, we wanted to understand better how the satisfaction-loyalty relationship might change if the competitive environment suddenly changed – a critical issue for monopolies facing deregulation, global competition, and technological change. By actual or virtual monopolies, we mean companies that operate in markets where, thanks to government regulations, proprietary technology, or very strong brand equity, there is little or no competition. Others in this category include: electrical utilities with special rights of way; companies with brand

identities that are so strong that the customers perceive there to be no other choice, and companies in competitive industries where the barriers that prevent customers from switching to another supplier are high (a restaurant at the top of a ski lift, for example).

The Indications

Of the five markets, local telephone service, with nearly complete control over customers, was the only one for which the relationship between satisfaction and loyalty turned out exactly as one would expect. Customers remained loyal no matter how dissatisfied they were. But our study of other actual or virtual monopolies did yield one vitally important discovery: when the source of a monopoly's hold on customers suddenly disappears – whether the cause is deregulation, the emergence of an alternative technology, or the arrival of new competitors – the curve can snap into the shape of a highly competitive market in an astonishingly short period of time.

According to conventional wisdom, the link between satisfaction and loyalty in markets where customers have choices is a simple, linear relationship: as satisfaction goes up, so does loyalty. But we discovered that the relationship was neither linear nor simple. To a much greater extent than most managers think, completely satisfied customers are more loyal than merely satisfied customers.

In markets where competition is intense, we found a tremendous difference between the loyalty of satisfied and completely satisfied customers. In the automobile industry, even a slight drop from complete satisfaction created an enormous drop in loyalty. This dramatic phenomenon is not limited to markets for manufactured products: it also occurs in services. In his study of the loyalty of retail-banking depositors, John Larson, a vice president of Opinion Research Corporation in Princeton, New Jersey, found that completely satisfied customers were nearly 42% more likely to be loyal than merely satisfied customers.

How about the curves for hospitals, airlines, and personal computers sold to businesses – industries whose holds on customers fall somewhere between automobiles and local telephone services? They also held surprises. We discovered that customer satisfaction in those industries, too, can affect customer loyalty much more than managers generally assume. Equally if not more important, we discovered that at certain times or under certain circumstances, satisfaction has a much bigger impact on loyalty. In these cases, the curve can snap into the shape of a curve of a more competitive – even a highly competitive – market.

Of the three midrange markets, the steepest drop in the loyalty of end users relative to satisfaction was in the business-PC market. Why should manufacturers of personal computers care? Why should manufacturers care? Because, when the time comes for IT or purchasing departments to replace the current generation of PCs, end-user satisfaction may suddenly have a big impact on customer loyalty. The curve snaps.

The next steepest drop in loyalty occurred in the hospital market – and it promises to become steeper as competition in the industry intensifies. Nonetheless, most hospitals are still operating as if they had little effective competition. They continue to place little emphasis on patient satisfaction. One can speculate about the reasons. Perhaps their managers think that the centralization of purchasing power makes health maintenance organizations and insurers, rather than individuals, the ones to please. Perhaps they think this centralization will only raise the barriers that block dissatisfied patients from switching. If so, they may be in for a shock. After all, many HMOs and insurers provide their subscribers with a menu of hospitals from which to choose. Moreover, individuals often can switch health plans if they don't like the hospitals on the menu – a fact not lost on HMOs. Although a patient may not be free to change hospitals at any time, there will be a time when the patient or HMO or insurer can. The curve snaps.

In mixed markets such as airlines, achieving a high level of customer satisfaction matters for several reasons. Although a combination of limited choice and artificial restraints such as frequent-flier programs often cause even completely dissatisfied airline customers to remain fairly loyal, the relationship between satisfaction and loyalty does resemble a competitive market on routes where several carriers offer flights at around the same time. This fact means that complete customer satisfaction is very important on both competitive routes and monopoly routes. Why is it important on monopoly routes? Because, as several larger airlines have learned, customers who have suffered years of mediocre or poor service on such routes can still take their revenge. When traveling on other routes where there is competition, they can choose another airlines. And if a new, lower-priced competitor suddenly challenges the monopoly, even a frequent-flier program will not be enough to retain them.

Take heed. Although customers sometimes defect en masse, their departure may also occur in harder-to-spot dribs and drabs or spurts. Patients typically defect only after completing a course of treatment. An advertising agency client may defect only when it is time to undertake a new marketing campaign. A major corporate customer may defect from a bank only when an account executive with whom the customer had a personal relationship leaves. In these cases, the business is suddenly operating in a more competitive environment. The curve snaps. It is a time of maximum vulnerability for the company. And if it takes a while to lose such customers, it takes just as long to recapture them once they have moved to another supplier.

Table 17.1 They suffered the consequences

Industries or Companies That Experienced a Rapid Change in Customer Loyalty	*Reason for Shift in Customer Loyalty*
Telecommunications, airlines, electrical power, savings and loan associations	Deregulation
Xerox, Roche (Valium)	Loss of patent protection
Electronics, U.S. auto industry	Entrance of new competitors
American Express, IBM	Reduction in brand dominance
IBM, Digital Equipment Corporation	Advent of new technologies

Table 17.2 Interpreting Levels of Satisfaction

Response	*Description*	*Loyalty*
5	completely satisfied	very loyal
3–4	satisfied	easily switched to a competitor
1–2	dissatisfied	very disloyal

What is the overarching lesson? Customers are reasonable, but they want to be completely satisfied; if they are not and have a choice, they can be lured away easily (see Table 17.1). In today's turbulent world, measuring customers' outward loyalty does not suffice. Nor does knowing whether the satisfaction-loyalty relationship a company enjoys with the majority of its customers is the norm for its market. It is essential to understand what portion of customers' seeming loyalty is true loyalty based on a company's delivery of superior value and what part is artificial. Measuring customer satisfaction is one of the safest ways to obtain this information. If there is a solid likelihood that the level of competition in a market is going to increase, it is obviously better to seek to increase customer satisfaction before the curve snaps than after. The safest approach is to seek total customer satisfaction.

Consequently, most managers should be concerned rather than heartened if the majority of their customers fall into the satisfied category. Those customers have reasons for not being completely satisfied. Some element (or elements) of their experience with the company was not acceptable, and that shortfall in performance is sufficient for them to consider alternatives. Some might ask, then why did these customers say they were satisfied in the first place? The answer is: regardless of how they feel, customers of companies with reasonably good product or service quality tend to find it difficult to respond negatively to customer-satisfaction surveys. As a result, their satisfaction responses typically fall in the upper end of the scale – a 4 or 5 on a scale of 1 to 5. Rather than thinking of customers as loyal or disloyal, managers would be better off treating them as three separate groups (see Table 17.2).

Like the managers of the company described at the beginning of this article, most managers probably would be happy to learn that 82% of their customers fell into category 4 or 5. The more appropriate reaction would be, "We have a problem. Only 48% of our customers are completely satisfied, and 52% are up for grabs."

USING CUSTOMER-SATISFACTION INFORMATION

Customer-satisfaction information can be a critical barometer of how well a company is serving its customers. This information also can show a company what it needs to do to increase its customer satisfaction level by level until the majority of its customers are totally satisfied. The key is understanding what customers are saying when they provide various responses.

The first step is to make the measurement of customer satisfaction and loyalty a priority and to ensure that the process is unbiased, consistent, broadly applied, and able to capture and store information on individual customers. The process should be unbiased because typically there are forces within the company that will attempt to distort it for their own purposes. It should be consistent so that period-to-period changes have meaning. It should be broadly applied so that products, locations, and business units can be compared in order to help managers decide how to use the company's limited resources most effectively. Last but not least, the measurement process should capture information on individual customers so that the company can tailor its satisfaction-improvement programs to its individual customers' situations.

The second step is to create a curve by plotting individual customer responses. In addition to assessing how satisfied or dissatisfied customers are, managers should compare their company's curve with those shown in the industries we surveyed and consider the factors that shaped their own company's curve. Is the company retaining its customers through false-loyalty mechanisms, or is their loyalty the result of the value that the company provides through its product or services?

The third step is to determine the most appropriate strategies for raising customer satisfaction (see Table 17.3).

A dissatisfied customer is probably having problems with the core value of the company's product or service – the basic elements that customer expect everyone in the industry to be able to provide. Although it may seem obvious that the basic product desired by customers often shifts as competitors improve, new competitors arrive, and new technologies redefine the game, it is even more obvious from business

Table 17.3 How to decide what actions to take

	Bulk of Responses	Strategic Response
Stage 1	2–3 (dissatisfied)	Deliver the basic product or service elements as expected of anyone in the industry
Stage 2	3–4 (neutral)	Provide an appropriate range of supporting services
		Develop proactive service recovery to make amends when something goes wrong
Stage 3	4–5 (satisfied)	Understand and achieve results in customers' terms

history that keeping up with such shifts is one of management's most difficult challenges. The match between the basic product or service and the customers it is designed to serve must be reviewed continually to ensure that there is still a good fit.

A neutral customer is probably happy with the basic product or service but would like to be offered a consistent set of support services. And to ensure that neutral and satisfied customers do not slip back into the realm of the dissatisfied if bad luck happens to strike, companies also need highly responsive recovery processes. Well-designed support services – and they almost always are *services* – make the basic product or service easier to use or more effective. And recovery processes help the customer get back on track if problems occur.

The vast majority of companies that excel in satisfying customers rank the ability to react when something goes wrong as one of the most important factors in satisfying customers. That ability greatly influences whether customers heap scorn or praise on the company when talking to others (see the insert "Apostles and Terrorists: A Company's Best Friends and Worst Enemies"). Strong recovery processes are especially vital in industries such as airlines, automobiles, production equipment, and mail-order retailing – businesses in which the product or service is complex or some delivery and servicing processes lie outside the company's control.

A completely satisfied customer typically believes that the company

---

* Not all customers are saying the same thing. Opinion Research Corporation's John Larson has performed several studies comparing the satisfaction drivers for customers at different levels of satisfaction. In a study for a large information-services company, he found that dissatisfied customers were interested in core product attributes such as accuracy of data. Neutral customers were interested in account management issues such as the account manager's ability to relay account status quickly and accurately. And satisfied customers were interested in the degree to which the company's services supported the customer's strategic business objectives.

excels in understanding and addressing his or her personal preferences, values, needs, or problems. To figure out how to satisfy customers in this fashion, a company has to excel at listening to customers and interpreting what they are saying.*

Consider the experience of having a car repaired. A customer's basic goal is to have it fixed properly. To obtain a relatively neutral customer, a dealership or service station must repair the customer's vehicle competently. In the last decade, a large number of dealerships have expanded their services to include overnight and express drop-off, loaner vehicles, and free washing and waxing. Some also have instituted the practice of checking back with customers within 24 hours to make sure the problem was properly fixed, and a handful of really great dealerships check again after two weeks. If there is still a problem, fixing it becomes the top priority. These value-added support and recovery services are crucial for moving customers from neutral to satisfied. In recent years, dealerships that sell Japanese cars – most notably, Lexus dealerships – have reexamined the car-servicing experience from the customer's perspective. They found that what most customers want is to have their car repaired with minimum inconvenience and that *their* definition of the car-servicing experience includes taking the car to the dealership, arranging for transportation while it is in the shop, and picking it up once it is fixed. These dealers *completely satisfy* customers by picking up their cars at their homes or offices, leaving loaner vehicles, competently repairing, cleaning, and waxing the cars, returning them later in the day, picking up the loaners – and, of course, checking later to make sure that the cars were properly repaired.

An independent multiplex movie theater that we came across in the Southwest last year is another example of a business that excels in figuring out what its customers really want and giving it to them. Its managers discovered that customers' actual movie-going experience started about two blocks from the theater, where the typical customer, especially one who is running a bit late, enters the traffic approaching the parking lot and starts to become anxious about parking and purchasing a ticket. To address such concerns, the theater's managers placed attendants two blocks from the theater to sell tickets and help people enter the parking lot. The managers discovered that customers also resented having to leave the viewing area and then stand in line in the lobby to buy food. In response, the theater began to serve food throughout the facility; it even served seated customers until the main features began. Finally, the managers learned that customers detested dirty bathrooms. In response, the theater began cleaning its bathrooms four times an hour. The end result: a large number of highly satisfied, highly loyal customers.

The three-phase approach to increasing customer satisfaction has important implications. First, different actions are required to raise the satisfaction of customers of a family of products or services whose level of satisfaction differs. Second, it is absolutely critical to accomplish the three stages in order. It is possible to make a quantum leap – to move customers from neutral to completely satisfied, for instance – by completely redesigning the product or service, by introducing new technology, or by reengineering the underlying delivery process. But we have found that not many companies succeed at that. Such leaps often fall short because the company overlooked the support services that had evolved informally over the years and did not redesign them, too.

In the final analysis, the company that will survive and flourish over the long term is the one that continually works to understand the relationship between satisfaction and loyalty for each of its customers, for each of its business units, and for each of the industries in which it competes. Horst Schulze, president and COO of the Ritz-Carlton Hotel Company, the 1992 winner of the Malcolm Baldridge National Quality Award, put it the best. "Unless you have 100% customer satisfaction – and I don't mean that they are just satisfied, I mean that they are excited about what you are doing – you have to improve," he said. "And if you have 100% customer satisfaction, you have to make sure that you listen just in case they change . . . so you can change with them."

How to Listen to Customers

At the heart of any successful strategy to manage satisfaction is the ability to listen to the customer. There are five major categories of approaches that companies can use to listen to their customers. Most highly successful companies employ several, if not all. Many average or poor performers either use very few or, if they use many, do a poor job of incorporating the results into their strategies. The five categories are:

Customer-Satisfaction Indices. Surveying customers about their level of satisfaction and plotting the results can help managers understand just how satisfied or dissatisfied customers are with both their dealings with the company in general and with various elements of the company's product or service in particular. The fact that such indices are quantitative makes them a useful tool for comparing results from different time periods, locations, and business units.

Feedback. Customers' comments, complaints, and questions fall into this category. A company cannot implement a recovery strategy – a plan for making amends when something has gone wrong – if it does not know who has had a problem. Therefore, it is important to review the company's approach to soliciting feedback – especially complaints – on product and service quality.

Market Research. Although companies traditionally invest significantly in this area, they often overlook two critical listening points. Customers should be interviewed both at the time of arrival (when they become customers) and at the time of departure (when they defect) about the reasons for their behavior. New customers should not only be asked, "How did you hear about us?" but also, "What major experiences influenced your decision to try our product or service?" The answers to the first question will provide data about the effectiveness of the company's awareness advertising, and the answers to the second will supply information about specific factors that actually sparked the decision to try the product or service. It also is absolutely critical to understand why a customer defected. Gleaning that information requires a high degree of sensitivity and skill because most customers will blame the price or some other relatively basic product attribute in order to avoid discussing the real issue. Carefully questioning departing customers is important for two reasons: to isolate those attributes of the company's product or service that are causing customers to leave and to make a last-ditch attempt to keep the customer. One company we studied found that it recaptured a full 35% of its defectors just by contacting them and listening to them earnestly.

Frontline Personnel. Employees who have direct contact with the customer provide a superb means of listening. To take full advantage of frontline employee's interactions with customers, however, a company must train them to listen effectively and to make the first attempts at amends when customers have bad experiences. They also must have processes in place to capture the information and pass it along to the rest of the company. Many companies that excel in satisfying customers have institutionalized one other practice: All employees – not just those with frontline jobs – spend a significant amount of time interacting in depth with customers.

Strategic Activities. Some companies go to extremes to involve the customer in every level of their business. MTV, the cable music channel geared to 18- to 24-year-olds, insists that most of its employees must belong to the demographic target group. Southwest Airlines actually invites frequent fliers to its first round of group interviews with prospective flight attendants and considers these customers' opinions in decisions to invite certain candidates back for individual interviews. Intuit, the financial-software company, regularly brings in customers to participate in product-development sessions.

Measures of Loyalty

Broadly speaking, customer loyalty is the feeling of attachment to or affection for a company's people, products, or services. These feelings manifest themselves in many forms of customer behavior. The ultimate measure of loyalty, of course, is share of purchases in the category. In the automobile business, it is share of garage. In the clothing industry, it is share of closet. And in the restaurant business, as Taco Bell president and CEO John Martin says, it is "share of stomach."

Unfortunately, such information is rarely available at the individual customer level. But there are alternative measurements, which we have grouped into three major categories.

Intent to Repurchase. At any time in the customer relationship, it is possible to ask customers about their future intentions to repurchase a given product or service. Although their responses are simply indications of future behavior and are not assurances, they have very important benefits. First, companies can capture this information when they measure satisfaction, making it relatively easy to link intentions and satisfaction for analytical purposes. The fact that intent to repurchase can be measured at any time in the customer relationship makes it especially valuable in industries with a long repurchase cycle. Finally, intent to repurchase actually is a very strong indicator of future behavior. Although this measure will generally overstate the probability of repurchase, the degree of exaggeration usually is fairly consistent, meaning that the future results can be predicted fairly accurately. For example, an average of 60% to 80% of automobile customers queried 90 days after buying a car say they intend to repurchase the same brand, and 35% and 40% actually do so three to four years later.

Primary Behavior. Depending on the industry, companies often have access to information on various transactions at the customer level and can measure five categories that show actual repurchasing behavior: recency, frequency, amount, retention, and longevity. Although they are important measures of actual behavior, they only provide a glimpse of overall share and are most useful as an indication of changes over time. Moreover, sometimes they can send the wrong message. For example, the credit-card industry traditionally measured the willingness of the consumer to pay the annual fee as its prime measure of retention. During the late 1980s and early 1990s, those same companies saw that willingness rise while actual "share of wallet" – the degree to which customers used their particular card for making purchases when they had the option of using a credit card – decreased. The consumer was willing to pay the fee to have the credit card available but often did not use it. Therefore, recency, frequency, and amount of purchase were significantly better measures of loyalty.

Secondary Behavior. Customer referrals, endorsements, and spreading the word are extremely important forms of consumer behavior for a company. In most product and service categories, word of mouth is one of the most important factors in acquiring new customers. Frequently, it is easier for a customer to respond honestly to a question about whether he or she would recommend the product or service to others than to a question about whether he or she intended to repurchase the product or service. Such indications of loyalty, obtained through customer surveys, are frequently ignored because they are *soft* measures of behavior that are difficult to link to eventual purchasing behavior. However, since secondary behavior significantly leverages the positive experiences of a single customer, it is very important to understand what types of experiences create such behavior.

Apostles and Terrorists: A Company's Best Friends and Worst Enemies

Although it is important and valuable to track and understand the satisfaction and loyalty of customers as a group, it is equally critical to understand the attitudes and behavior of individual customers. Depending on their unique behavioral attributes (prior individual biases), intensity of satisfaction or dissatisfaction (attitude), and ability to act on their satisfaction or dissatisfaction

Table 17.4 Individual customer satisfaction, loyalty, and behavior

	Satisfaction	Loyalty	Behavior
Loyalist/Apostle	high	high	staying and supportive
Defector/Terrorist	low to medium	low to medium	leaving or having left and unhappy
Mercenary	high	low to medium	coming and going; low commitment
Hostage	low to medium	high	unable to switch; trapped

(competitive market dynamics), customers behave in one of four basic ways: as loyalists, as defectors, as mercenaries, or as hostages. Turning as many customers as possible into the most valuable type of loyalist, the apostle, and eliminating the most dangerous type of defector or hostage, the terrorist, should be every company's ultimate objective (see Table 17.4).

The Loyalist and the Apostle

In most cases, the loyalist is a customer who is completely satisfied and keeps returning to the company. The loyalist is a company's bedrock. This customer's needs and the company's product or service offerings fit exceptionally well, which, not surprisingly, is why loyalists often are the easiest customers to serve. Occasionally, the match is so good that even a 5 on a 1-to-5 satisfaction scale doesn't fully capture the strength of the relationship.

Within the loyalist camp are individuals who are so satisfied, whose experience so far exceeds their expectations, that they share their strong feelings with others. They are apostles.

One company that excels in creating apostles is Intuit, maker of Quicken, the phenomenally successful financial-management software. Although Intuit has fewer than ten sales employees, it has hundreds of thousands of salespeople: its highly satisfied customers, who found the company's product and its customer-service staff so responsive to their unique needs that they had to tell someone else. "When you treat a customer so well that he or she goes out and tells five friends how great it is to own your product – that's when you're doing it right," says Scott Cook, Intuit's cofounder and chairman of the board.

Treating customers exceptionally well does not mean merely treating them well when everything basically is going right. It also means treating them exceptionally well when something goes terribly wrong. Highly dissatisfied customers typically include people who were highly satisfied until they purchased a single shoddy product or suffered a service failure or a sequence of unrelated failures. If a company excels in making amends – that is, in recovering – when such failures occur, customers' faith in the company is not just restored, it is deepened; and they become apostles, spreading the good word about the company to potential customers.

Of course, a company can only turn such customers into apostles if they come forward. For this reason alone, it more than pays to provide customers with numerous opportunities to express their dissatisfaction. Companies with world-class recovery organizations frequently ask customers if they are satisfied, provide toll-free customer comment numbers, fully involve frontline employees in the crusade to identify and help customers frustrated by service or product failures, and regularly review their approaches to dealing with customer problems.

The Defector and the Terrorist

Defectors' ranks include those who are more than dissatisfied, quite dissatisfied, and neutral. The merely satisfied – many more than most managers realize – defect, too. And as we've said, so do once highly satisfied customers who have encountered failures. Letting those customers defect is perhaps the biggest mistake managers can make. When a company has strong processes in place to understand such customers' needs better and to shower attention on them if isolated problems strike, most of them can be converted or turned once again into highly satisfied customers.

Not all defectors should be retained, however. The unreasonable demands of unhappy customers whose needs do not fit with the company's capabilities can devour excessive resources and wreak havoc on employee morale. For just this reason, such outstanding service organizations as Nordstrom department stores, Sewell Village Cadillac Company in Dallas, and Southwest Airlines regularly "fire" customers they cannot properly serve. They recognize counter-productive efforts when they see them.

The most dangerous defectors are the terrorists. These are the customers who have had a bad experience and can't wait to tell others about their anger and frustration. They are the airline passengers who because of bad weather were stranded at an alternative airport and were not given appropriate assistance. They are the retail customers who found that the product they just bought did not work and encountered an inept or uncaring service employee when they tried to get help or compensation. They are the new car owners who had to return countless times to try to get the same problem fixed. With each telling, their stories grow in intensity and the actual facts become increasingly distorted.

Unfortunately, terrorists generally are far more committed and hence more effective at telling their stories than apostles. Like many apostles, they had bad experiences. But in their case, no one listened, no one responded, no one corrected the problem.

The Mercenary

Another customer who can make a company's life miserable is the mercenary. This individual defies the satisfaction-loyalty rule: he may be completely satisfied but exhibit almost no loyalty. These customers are often expensive to acquire and quick to depart. They chase low prices, buy on impulse, pursue fashion trends, or seek change for the sake of change. Although it often takes as much effort to please them as to please long-term loyal customers, they do not remain long enough for the relationship to turn a profit.

The Hostage

Hostages are stuck. These individuals experience the worst the company has to offer and must accept it. Many companies operating in a monopolistic environment see little reason to respond to the plight of hostages. After all, these customers can't go anywhere. So why bother to correct the problems?

There are two important reasons why companies should bother. First, if the competitive environment suddenly shifts, these companies will then pay the price. Their customers will defect quickly and many will become terrorists. Second, hostages are very difficult and expensive to serve. They may be trapped, but they still take every opportunity to complain and to ask for special service. Hostages can devastate company morale, and their negative impact on per unit costs is astounding.

Thomas O. Jones is president of Elm Square Technologies, a company in Andover, Massachusetts, that is developing advanced customer-service software. He formerly was a senior lecturer in the Harvard Business School's service management interest group. W. Earl Sasser, Jr., is the UPS Professor of Service Management and senior associate dean responsible for executive education at the Harvard Business School in Boston, Massachusetts.

Part 5

Managing Agents and Distributors

INTRODUCTION

The use of sales agents (sometimes referred to as manufacturers' representatives) and distributors is not confined to small firms selling simple products. Many medium-sized and large organizations selling complex products and services rely on sales agents. This is particularly so when an organization moves outside its home region or country or to cover thin territories. The decision to use agents/distributors may be taken in order to complement or substitute the field sales force. Surprisingly, then, few of the many books written on sales management address this topic in any detail. In a recent review by Bob Hartley[1] of eight textbooks on sales management, none had a full chapter on the management of sales agents and distributors and only two had a part chapter devoted to the topic[2,3]. In short, nearly all marketing and sales textbooks when discussing organization of the sales force and territory planning assume that all salespeople and managers are employees of the firm.

The usual distinction between the terms 'agent' and 'distributor' is that sales agents do not take title to the goods, whereas a distributor takes title to the goods and sells on his own account. An agent acts on behalf of the principal to search out buyers, but the contract of sale is between the supplier and the buyer, not the agent. Many agents do not stock nor handle the product in any way. Having arranged the deal, they earn their living by working on a commission basis, usually a percentage of the selling price. However, there are many types of agency and some may hold stock and manage physical distribution such as consignment agents. Title still rests with the manufacture until the goods are sold to the customer. The consignment agent would expect a higher commission than a sales agent to cover the costs of handling and storage. Likewise a sales agency which looked after the marketing of the products and sold the products via its own sales network, would work on a higher commission with possibly a flat fee element included in the arrangements to cover marketing expenses. The terms used to describe sales agencies vary and tend to be industry and country specific. A distributor usually buys on their own account and takes full title to the goods. The distributor stocks and handles the goods and income is the difference between the 'buying in' price and 'selling out' price. The manufacturer, then, has reduced access to customers and less control over final selling prices when using a distributor.

As the costs of employing a direct sales force rise and the professionalism of sales agents improves then more firms are likely to review their approach to the organization of the sales function. This may be particularly so in those organizations which have experience in outsourcing other professional and managerial services, and feel comfortable with the reduced level of direct control.

The use of sales agents raises a number of issues which are also discussed elsewhere in this book, notably section four on 'Customer Service'. The nature and level of customer service is an important issue, but now it needs to be addressed at two levels. The first level is the services provided to the agent and/or distributors by the principal, and the second level is the services provided to the customer or end user by the agent or distributor. Whether the supplying organization sees the provision of services as simply an operational and logistical function or whether it sees itself building long-term relationships to enhance customer value, will be critical. The use of information systems, database, and telemarketing can all help to knit the supply chain together into a partnership under the control of the manufacturer (see Reading 23 'Lighting the way'); but the most important factor is attitude. The relationship between the organization and agent should be built on trust.

'Why use agents?', Reading 18 in this part, discusses the advantages of using agents such as reduced direct staffing costs, reduced staff turnover on the territory, higher territory knowledge, the level of sales and marketing expertise, and higher motivation. The problems of control, product knowledge, and the difficulty of implementing promotional programmes are acknowledged.

Reading 19, 'Agents report on the services they perform', is based on a survey conducted by the Manufacturers' Agents National Association, (USA). In addition to selling the following services are performed:

- market research
- preparation of sales forecasts
- manning trade shows
- training distributor sales people
- servicing products sold
- product installation, service and maintenance.

Although the list may seem predictable to the experienced reader the survey does note changes over time, and also discusses to what extent these are paid for directly or indirectly by the principal. Concerns are also noted particularly regarding the pressure applied by retailers on 'agents and the factories who serve them'.

'Selecting a manufacturer's representative', Reading 20, is based on interviews with a number of experienced executives. Is the process of selecting an agent different from that for selecting a representative for the direct field sales team? If so how? To what extent is the process of selecting an agent governed by objectively assessing the functions and services they claim to be able to provide? And to what extent is this process governed by the softer human issues surrounding the chemistry of the people involved? This paper has some of the answers.

Erin Anderson and Barton Weitz in Reading 21, 'Forging a strategic distribution alliance', take the theme of selection further and delve into the development of long-term indepth partnerships. They ask such questions as: Are there any benefits to developing strategic alliances between the supplier and distributor? What factors influence commitment? Are there any differences between partnerships involving physical products and those involving services such as insurance? The paper examines commitment from the distributor and from the supplier and gets beyond the rhetoric of the endless pleas to build relationships. It discusses the practical aspects of how to go about 'making a distributor commit to you'. The authors suggest that the supplying organization usually needs to demonstrate commitment to the distributor first before they will reciprocate. They also suggest that to build confidence the investment by the manufacturer should be in the distributor. Such things as using the distributor's name in the manufacturer's advertising, dedicating personnel to the distributor, training the distributor's people, and paying for business development programmes, are all important.

Agents and distributors are often chosen as the preferred method of entry into export markets due to the need to hold down costs on small volume sales and the requirements for local knowledge and service. Reading 22 'Finding the right distributor [. . . in Europe]' by Barbara Berkman, highlights some of the pitfalls of using distributors in export markets. The differing business cultures, characteristics of local markets, and national legislation do mean that there is a need for caution. Many an experienced European organization has made the mistake of assuming the USA can be treated as one market; failing to appreciate the shear size and diversity of the country and the power of state legislators. Also many US companies assume that now most of Europe is governed by the European Union, a single marketing and sales strategy will do. While much European legislation has been harmonized there are still many aspects of business and consumer law which are covered by national legislation. Add to this the different languages, currencies, business practices and cultures then the complexity of selling in export markets becomes apparent. What type of agent or distributor is appropriate for Europe? Is it possible to have one agent to cover Europe or is it best to have an agent for each country? What legal protection against contract termination does an agent in the Europe Union have? These are some of the questions discussed.

Finally, Reading 23, 'Lighting the way', is a fascinating case history which illustrates how one lighting equipment manufacturer modified its relations with the trade. In the company, there is a complex network of relationships between the head office, product divisions, field warehousing, sales agent, distributors, specifiers, and contractors. The business links in the network were reviewed, relationships examined and computer systems modified. Agents are at the hub of the system which now includes computer-aided design, automated flexible manufacturing, on-line inventory status and ordering systems. Lead times have been cut from nine days to under one day. Specifiers, distributors and agents all benefit. The company doubled sales in six years and more than doubled profits.

As mentioned earlier, few marketing or sales books discuss in any detail the management of independent sales agents and distributors. Yet it remains an important means of serving customers for many companies manufacturing products and providing services. Any organization which is interested in developing long-term relationships, building customer loyalty, and improving its service to customers will need to review its use of agents and distributors.

References

1 Hartley, R.A. *Sales Management or Management of Sales, Marketing Education Group (UK), Conference Proceedings, June 1994, pp. 467–76.*
2 Dalrymple, D.J. and Cron, W.L. *Sales Management: Concepts and Cases*, Wiley, 1992.
3 Comer, J.M. *Sales Management*, Allyn and Bacon, 1991.

Reading 18

Why use agents?

MANA manufacturer members have many reasons

Anon

Reprinted from *Agency Sales Magazine*, July 1992, Vol. 22, No. 7, pp. 13–14. Published by the Manufacturers' Agents National Association.*

Recently, we asked MANA* member manufacturers to tell us why they had decided to go the agent route. We expected most to tell us that economies played a key role, and we weren't disappointed. However, we were extremely pleased to hear from many that they were satisfied with the economic part of the equation, but that their decisions were based on other factors that they felt were as important, or even more important.

"Agents give you instant coverage in a territory," one manufacturer told us. "When you sell through agents, you have access to the customer base that they (the agents) have spent years in developing. They know who is buying what, and how much. Factory direct people have to first find their way around the territory, then get to know the buyers before they can be effective. When we set up our agent sales force (11 years ago), we looked at the long-term picture. Our strength is in manufacturing (fabricated metal parts), and not in marketing. So we decided that we wanted to have partners in agents whose strength was marketing. It's worked out very well for us.

"Of course, some of the first agents we appointed were not really right for us. But we have learned over the years and have built a team that loves us. And we love them."

Another manufacturer explained that his initial intent was to get his business going with agents and then to switch to a salaried sales force. "I figured that we could use agents to get us going, and then switch to

* Manufacturers' Agents National Association, PO Box 3467, Laguna Hills, CA 92654–3467, USA. (714) 859–4040, Fax (714) 855–2973.

factory people when we could afford them. Well, our initial approach may have been to save money, but when we learned what agents were all about, we discovered that direct cost was only a minor consideration. We learned that agents – good agents – are much more effective than factory people in many ways. Sure, we have less direct control over them, but that is far less important to us than the bottom line. We found that agents are far more motivated than the typical factory salesperson. They have to be. Working on commission alone is one strong motivator."

Here are a few other comments that members passed along:

"We decided to sell through agents mainly because they are going to be in their territories a lot longer than most salaried salespeople. Factory people tend to want to move out of the territory into management, or they move on to take jobs with other companies. Agents are fixtures in their territories."

"We sell through agents because they are professional marketing people. We're not."

"Agents don't bug me about raises. They just go out and sell more so their commissions are higher."

"Sure, agents go where they want to go when they want to go. But when you back them up from the factory, they take you places a factory person might never know existed."

"Frankly, I'd like more direct control over my agents. But I'd rather have motivated independent agents, and less control, than employees who need constant direction."

We'd like to conclude this report with comments from Mark Barton, who is national sales manager of BUG-O Systems, Inc., Pittsburgh, Pennsylvania.

"The BUG-O division of Weld Tooling Corporation still maintains one direct sales manager while using agents throughout the balance of the country. This was not always the case. At one time, the entire country was covered on a direct basis. The decision to replace all but one of the direct salespersons was made on the 'cost of sales.' We were paying a high percentage of sales income to keep direct salespeople. Where this was not the case, we retained our direct person. We were caught in a catch-22 type situation. We needed to have large territories to justify a person, but because the territories were large, our distributors and customers did not see much of our salesperson – out of sight, out of mind. Using agents has given BUG-O a greater presence with our distributors and customers. Plus, it doesn't hurt that we know what our cost of sales is – a fixed percentage.

"There are some negative aspects to using agents. Initially, we received some complaints from our distributors and customers that our agents did not know the product line. While we had a training program in place, we have an extensive product line. The problem was that there does not seem to be an overabundance of agents in the welding industry. At least the majority of equipment manufacturers have direct sales. That complaint is not as prevalent today. We have not had a great turnover in our agency organization, and our agents have come to learn the line much better.

"The other area of concern is that you have more control over a direct sales force. Implementing programs seems to be easier with a direct group of salespeople. They're quicker to respond to requests from the 'home' office. Manufacturers' agents tend to, and rightly so, look at a given situation as how will this program affect their company. What might be in the best interest of an agency might not be in BUG-O's best interest. Example – an agent's largest distributor for one product line might not be the best distributor for ours. It may be very difficult and costly for the agent to remedy the situation.

"While I realize that the above negatives represent good business practices for them, there are concerns for their principals. These have not been major concerns, but when switching from a direct sales force to one comprised of agents, they are things that perhaps are not initially thought about.

"Having managed both a direct sales force and one almost comprised totally of agents. I can honestly say that my opinion of agents has greatly improved. I had my concerns and doubts in the beginning. Maybe they do it for my benefit, but after a week on the road with an agent, I need to come home to rest."

Marks' comments are well taken. Essentially, he is saying that there are trade-offs, whichever way you go. And that when you know in advance what they are, there will be no surprises. However, as you've seen from some of the comments, agents do have a lot of advantages going for them.

Reading 19

MANA* survey report

Agents report on the services they perform for their principals . . . in addition to selling

Anon

Reprinted from *Agency Sales Magazine*, December 1990, Vol. 20, No. 12, pp. 27–30. Published by the Manufacturers' Agents Association.*

Time was that agents did nothing more than sell the products made by their principals. This, of course, was a really big step from selling direct for many manufacturers. But times change. Agents change, and so does the business climate. Today, the typical manufacturers' agency is much more than just a selling machine. It's a company which undertakes many of the marketing responsibilities in addition to selling.

In many ways, the agencies of today are really working partners of their principals. There are even some agencies whose gross exceeds that of some of their individual principals. Yes, the single-person agency is still an important factor, and even that solo practitioner is doing a lot more than just carrying the products to the field.

The agents who responded to our survey told us that their agencies were structured as follows: Corporations, 55%; Small corporations, 17%; sole proprietorships, 24%; and partnerships, 4%.

The last time we conducted this survey was in 1988. There have been some significant changes in the two years since the last survey. But before we get into the actual survey results, let's look at a picture of the markets sold to by the agencies that responded to our survey (see Table 19.1).

We have attempted to refine the picture of the agencies that responded to our survey this time. Our next report will compare the data using the new categories.

---

* Manufacturers' Agents National Association, PO Box 3467, Laguna Hills, CA92654-3467, USA. (714) 859-4040, Fax (714) 855 2973.

Table 19.1

	1988	*1990*
End users	37%	—
OEM	58%	59%
Retail chain/mass merchandisers	—	12%
Wholesale/distributors	50%	55%
Capital goods in primary industries	—	19%
Contractors/architects	—	21%
Government/municipalities/institutes	—	20%
Capital goods in manufacturing	—	25%

Table 19.2

	1988	*1990*
Market research	52%	56%
Preparation of sales forecasts	73%	66%
Manning trade show booths	80%	88%
Training distributor salespeople	37%	51%
Servicing products sold	52%	47%
Product installation, service and maintenance	—	22%
Other	11%	22%

Now, let's begin to look at the main elements of this survey. The next question we asked was: *What services do you provide, in addition to selling?* Since most agencies provide more than one additional service, the percentages will sum to more than 100%. [What our respondents told us is shown in Table 19.2.]

There have been changes in both directions. Some come as no surprise; others do surprise us. For example, we never would have thought that there would be a drop in the use of agencies to help prepare sales forecasts. Most manufacturers consider direct field information indispensable in their forecasting. We can only hope that the manufacturers who do not seek input from their agencies are getting direct field information from other sources. It's critical for good planning and budgeting.

We did anticipate that more agents would be helping to train distributor salespeople, but we never thought there would be such a jump in the activity. There is a stronger interest in selling to distributors, we have noticed. We feel that this interest lies mainly in the fact that distributors often buy in considerable depth, representing much larger single orders than the manufacturer would ordinarily get from any single direct customer. Of course, selling to a distributor involves discounts. But the discounted price is usually offset by the larger orders. And, of course, the manufacturer can build stronger customer relations with a local source, when the products warrant it.

It's for this reason, we feel, that there has been such a big increase in distributor sales training activity.

There was a doubling of the "other" category. It's interesting to note that many of the agents who took the time to fill in specific answers to this were working in the retail field. Many of the jobs they were being asked to do included direct merchandising efforts, such as helping with in-store displays and promotional programs.

One MANA member included a letter which tells a story. This member asked to remain anonymous, for obvious reasons. Here's what he told us:

"I feel a strong need to tell you that major retail chains are making unconscionable demands on both the agents and the factories who serve them. From month to month the pressure on us mounts to provide labor and other services, the value of which begins to exceed the amount of the commissions earned on the accounts.

"In my opinion, this has reached proportions so alarming that a national exposure of the situation is past due." Since a number of the comments in this category did come from our members serving the retail trade, we feel that there must be something to the complaint. We will try to get a handle on it in the future.

Some of the "other" things mentioned by members are:

- Handling spare parts,
- Dealing with the U.S. Customs on importation of foreign products,
- Writing architectural specifications,
- Writing product promotional material,
- Engineering and development of new designs,
- Seminars for computer usage,

Table 19.3

	1990
Negotiated fee prior to specified work	10%
Commissions increased for a set period of time	3%
Share costs for services performed	9%
Not compensated	83%
Other	13%

- Advice on principal's corporate strategies, and
- Inventory control.

The next question we asked was: *How are you compensated for these services?* We do not have comparable data from 1988. Here are the numbers:

On the surface, it looks like agents do a lot of work other than selling for which they are not compensated. However, you must remember that because agencies have taken it on themselves to provide additional services to be competitive, many of these services will not be paid for directly by principals. In a way, offering more services has made many manufacturers more dependent on agents. Many agents are doing work that might have been done by salaried employees of the manufacturer in the past.

However, the economies of scale and the use of automated equipment, such as a computer, has made it a lot easier for most agents to perform services previously handled by their principals.

This doesn't mean, however, that there are not inequities. When a manufacturer demands that an agent do something that is not going to relate directly to the bottom line of the agent, it is out of line. Time is the currency of the sales agency. Improper demands by manufacturers have been responsible for more than a few resigning accounts.

Thirteen percent of our respondents checked the "other" box. Here's what they told us:

- Built into the price of the equipment we sell,
- Part of the profit margin,
- Compensated by extra warehouse fees,
- Commission on tooling and prototypes,
- Paid by the hour for service performed by our technicians,
- Value added to the retail price,
- It goes with the territory!
- Part of an agent's job! and
- Efforts produce greater sales for all of us.

It's worth looking closely at some of these comments. Of particular interest are those which refer to the price of extra service built into the price of the product. This, of course, translates to a higher total dollar income to the agent. Therefore, the 83% who indicated that they did not receive any direct extra commissions does include those who did indeed make more money because the cost of the service was covered by increased cost to the customer.

Quite a few said something similar to the agent who said, "It goes with the territory." This is the comment we made earlier, and it relates to the last comment we listed, "Efforts produce greater sales for all of us."

Now, let's fully qualify the question of noncompensation for additional work. The next question we asked our members to answer was: *If you checked "not compensated" do you feel that non-sales work is simply part of the normal selling routine?*

Yes – 78%
No – 8%
No reply – 14%

Here, again, looking at the write-in comments will help put this thorny question into clearer perspective. Our members told us:

- It's just part of customer service,
- Benefits agents and manufacturers to produce sales,
- These efforts produce sales,
- Creates new markets for us and for our principals,
- No choice if we want to keep the lines,
- Takes away valuable selling time,
- Much non-sales work leads to additional business,
- Some things. Budget and survey work should be paid for. We do this for good principals, and
- Pressure on agent because of account size.

Apparently some feel that the additional work they perform for their principals is part of the job. In some ways, this is accurate. As sales agencies evolve from the pure selling machines they were right after World War II to larger and more complex marketing organizations, some of this work does, indeed, come with the territory. This is not to say that when a principal has a project which falls out of the bounds of the usual marketing tasks that their agents shouldn't be paid for their efforts.

Perhaps this example will clear the picture some. One agent we talked with had been a market research consultant for more than 10 years before starting his agency. In other words, this man was a real research pro. He was capable of doing some major research projects – and his principals knew it. When one of his principals asked him to do more than the routine gathering of information in the course of making sales calls, he told him he'd be happy to do it, and quoted the professional fee he had charged when this had been his occupation. At first, the manufacturer balked, but the agent held his ground. Then the agent explained what he would do without charge. Seeing the difference between the two levels of research, the manufacturer agreed to the fee, and everyone was happy.

In this case, the work expected was extraordinary and should have been paid for. But when an agent is asked to ask one or two questions of his customers during calls and to report the results to his or her principals, it should "come with the territory."

The definition, it seems to us, should be anything that takes away from direct selling in any measurable way should be compensated for. Otherwise, it "comes with the territory."

The last question we asked was: *Do your principals pay the expense for trade shows outside your territory?*

Nearly half told us that their trade show expenses are fully paid when the show is outside the territory. Although we didn't ask the question, it does seem that most manufacturers will pick up at least some of the costs when the show is outside an agent's territory.

We did ask if manufacturers paid for expenses of regional shows. Sixty-six percent told us that their principals paid for all or some of the expenses.

These responses are in line with what we would have expected. It's impressive to note that 12% actually pay all the agent's expenses when the show is in the agent's territory. These are, indeed, enlightened manufacturers.

THE BIG PICTURE

In general, we're pleased with the way non-selling services are compensated for by manufacturers. Of course, there's room for improvement. But, in general, the trend is in the right direction.

Again, we want to stress that although 83% said they were not compensated directly for their non-sales activity, the write-in answers indicated that many are compensated *indirectly* through increased cost of the product. Of course, a percentage of x + y is better than just a percentage of x.

As agencies continue to evolve and become more marketing-oriented, they will take on more and more of the non-sales tasks. In some cases, manufacturers will take advantage of this. In others they will see the real benefit to all and will make whatever they can to see that the agencies are given their due.

Reading 20

Selecting a manufacturer's representative

Manufacturers describe the characteristics most important to them in selecting manufacturers' representatives

Anon

Reprinted from *Agency Sales Magazine* January 1990, Vol. 20, No. 1, pp. 17–21. Published by the Manufacturers' Agents National Association.

Even the most sophisticated personnel specialist will admit that after he had gone through the range of tested and validated techniques to screen a job applicant, he still has certain criteria which could accurately be called gut reactions. The gut reaction alone is a pretty shaky way to go – and so is depending totally on the numbers. It's no different with manufacturers who are faced with deciding to appoint one agent and reject another. Each has his or her own set of criteria which relate to the industry and the market. But it then becomes a very subjective task.

To see if we could develop any patterns, we asked some MANA* member manufacturers for their thoughts on the most effective techniques for making the final selection. We had a surprisingly rewarding response in terms of quantity and quality. We wish we could include all of the responses, but we just can't. However, we do want to acknowledge the effort of everyone who kindly responded to our questions. The responses we selected for this report mirror the feelings of most of the manufacturers we contacted. Thanks go to all.

We open the forum with an unusually well thought-out and keenly perceptive response from Bruce Broxterman of Richards Industries, Cincinnati, Ohio. For the Richards firm, selecting sales agencies is far from a hit-or-miss activity. They look at sales agencies as an integral part of their organization and treat the selection process with the same respect as they would the process of recruiting a senior executive for their firm. Richards Industries manufactures regulator and control valves, sheet metal fabrication, general machining and other related products and services. Here are Bruce's ideas on the selection of agents.

---

* Manufacturer's Agents National Association, PO Box 3467, Laguna Hills, CA92654-3467, USA. (714) 859-4040, Fax (714) 855-2973.

At Richards Industries, we feel that selecting the proper sales agency is the most important thing that our sales management team does. In order to reach corporate goals of growth and increased profitability, we feel strongly that we must have the right agent with the ability and motivation to consistently work our lines and to produce increased sales.

Over the years we have developed a complete recruiting process that we hope will give us the best agent for each territory. A properly executed recruiting campaign takes a lot of work, much time, and a substantial investment. However, it will pay off several times over if the right match is found.

Once the initial mechanics of the information gathering process is completed, there are several key areas to be investigated with each potential agent that helps narrow down the final selection. Here are several of these important areas that we look at:

- Is their customer base compatible with ours? Are they calling on the industries and the decision makers within those industries where our products are used?
- Are their other products compatible with ours? We can't be successful with an agency that carries a product that is competitive with ours. Likewise, it is important that their lines are sold to similar industries and customers. It's difficult to get an agent to make special, separate calls on your line alone.
- We're looking for agencies that are aggressive in their growth plans. The agency that is satisfied with their current level of performance is not compatible with our growth philosophy.
- Are they willing and able to give the sales time necessary to promote our product lines to mutually acceptable levels? Is it better to have a one-man organization working hard on a few lines than a larger organization with a few key lines and several that are neglected?
- Does the agent have the technical and sales competence to sell our products? The successful agent must have both of these abilities.
- In considering territory size, sales volume, and products handled, does the agency have enough manpower to get the job done? Inside sales support must be considered in addition to field sales levels.
- Do we have the potential to become one of their two or three major lines? If not, the match is not right.
- Are they financially stable? Have they been consistently profitable? Are they reputable and professional? The local perception of our company will depend heavily on the local perception of our rep agency and their sales force. Is it the right match?
- Is this a relationship we will enjoy? Are these the kinds of people that we'll want to spend time working together with in the field?

- Are their salespeople conscientious, reliable, honest? Do they have integrity?
- Is the agent aware of the territory involved and is it compatible with his typical calling pattern? We never want to give an agent a big territory and then have him appoint subagents. We want to keep our territories as concise as possible to get the best coverage.
- Can the sales manager and/or principal owner hire and motivate others? Is there continuity in their organization? Are arrangements made as to who would take over if the owner would suddenly die, or if the key salesman were to leave?'

For some manufacturers, special sets of marketing conditions guide their selection of manufacturers' agencies. D. Fred Lowe of LTV Steel Tubular Products Company has a set of first-hurdles which an agency must overcome, and that is extensive experience in selling to electrical distributors. As anyone knows who has sold to distributors, there are special skills involved that may not be as important for a product which is sold to the OEM or to end users. The agent must be able to further motivate sales through the distributors. LTV manufactures electrical conduit. Here is how Mr. Lowe looks at his agency selection task.

In our circumstance we utilize manufacturers' representatives only on electrical conduit products which are sold through electrical distributors. The factors which influence agency selection are colored by that fact.

- Market acceptability – buying influencers have a desire to do business with the agency and a track record is established.
- Continuity – the agency has people in the wings who will carry on the agency after the principals retire.
- Distributor oriented – the agency calls on distributors most of the time but also has a program for calling on specifiers and contractors.
- Well-balanced line card, i.e., lines that are contractor oriented and well-balanced. We prefer to see no more than eight to ten.
- Recommendations – other manufacturers, customers and other agencies.

John Cummings of Ceilcote/Air Pollution Control, Berea, Ohio, is not alone when he puts heavy emphasis on the chemistry of the relationship. He also makes an excellent point when he discusses the profit potential of the line in terms of the agency's overall growth plans. In short, John's views are that of a solid partnership. He wants to make sure that the product line is going to contribute significantly to the agency's total profit. And, John makes good points when he discusses the real value of a technical understanding of his company's product line. Ceilcote/Air Pollution Control manufactures engineered scrubber systems, fiberglass reinforced plastic centrifugal and axial fans and other products for use in environmental control situations. These are John's comments.

> The four factors which we have found to be extremely important in making the manufacturers' agent selection process successful for both of us are as follows:
>
> 1 Our product line must be compatible with other lines handled by the agency. Agents will not normally search out and call on customers who buy only one of their lines. Where lines are compatible we can expect much more selling time for our products.
> 2 In order to achieve a strong, mutually beneficial relationship with an agency, the long term commission income potential from our line must be at least 20–25 percent of the agency's total income. The intensity of the relationship will be directly proportional to the income potential.
> 3 Agent comfort with the technology that drives our products is critical to a successful relationship. Whether this comfort level is acquired through previous experience, formal or informal training or self-help is unimportant. The crucial issue is whether the agent knows enough or can learn enough to be comfortable with our technology in front of a customer. Very few people, salesmen included, will knowingly expose themselves to a situation where they may appear ignorant. Without this comfort level, sales calls don't get made. In other words, we all tend to aggressively sell the thing with which we are most comfortable. In the case of something about which we know very little, we hope to 'take orders.'
> 4 Finally, we are left with that elusive commodity called 'chemistry.' The best analogy I can think of is finding Mr. or Miss Right. You can't define it but you know when you have or don't have it. Good chemistry is not something of which you can be absolutely sure at the start of a relationship but, if it doesn't feel right at the start, it probably won't get better. Ultimately, 'chemistry' boils down to a relationship characterized by mutual respect, a willingness to work out problems, and the wherewithal to stick together through good times and bad.

Gary Sausman, Cattron, Inc., Sharpsville, Pennsylvania, looks for technical competence, but he is more concerned with the comfort level he has for the individual or the agency under consideration. He's not alone in the evaluation. Many manufacturers, especially those who consider their agents as an integral part of the organization, feel that the chemistry factor is especially important. Interestingly, those who pay less attention to personal chemistry end up with a succession of agents, rather than building a strong loyal team. Cattron manufactures portable remote controls and RF data links. Gary's comments follow.

> Of the several factors involved with selection of a prospective sales agency, my number one concern is the blend of my product to the agent's existing line. We want to create an opportunity for the agent to increase his value to his customer base with the addition of our customer base. We place a strong emphasis on searching for other agencies through referral from our existing network. We have found that these firms are the best fit to our needs. Another source I like to use is the sales manager, or equivalent, from the top firms our agents are representing.
>
> When narrowing down the selection, I have several criteria which come into play. One of the most important factors for my decisions is the 'comfort level' I have with the individual, or the key person, in the organization. First impressions are very important to me. I have found that the level of experience of the agent, either in our technical field or in the agency business, is not always as important as the ability to communicate and work well together. Two of my top five producers fall into this category. One has been an agent less than seven years and was previously in the retail grocery business, now selling high-tech, high-price electronic controls! I have found that these agents, with the high level of good personal chemistry, like working with us for the same reason and therefore put forth a fine effort for our product and our company.
>
> As for the territory arrangement, we have our territories aligned by zip code. We can be fairly flexible this way and try to accommodate the agents' desires as much as possible rather than making the agency fit our territory exactly.

Dan Jobe of Norris/O'Bannon, Tulsa, Oklahoma, looks at agency selection from a direct and very pragmatic perspective. His major concerns are compatible lines and geographic coverage. However, despite this direct and practical view, personal chemistry looms quite large in the schemes of things for Dan. Norris/O'Bannon manufactures butterfly valves, sleeve couplings, repair clamps and fittings. Dan explained his approach to agency selection this way.

> The most important factors we look at are compatible lines and geographic coverage. If those two parameters are met, we then have an in-person interview at the rep's business. We are then inquiring about how he sells his product, i.e., distributors or direct, and how our personality meshes with his. We feel that we must have the same type of chemistry as our potential reps.

Other smaller factors come into play such as manpower, personal recommendations, calls to other manufacturers that he represents and experience.

The two key factors are compatible lines and personal chemistry.

James Compton of Evanite Permaglas, Inc., Corvallis, Oregon, has set criteria which relate specifically to his industry, roofing products. This is what Jim said:

Most important to us are:

1 Agent concentrates on products in our area of business only (roofing in our case).
2 Agent handles *no* conflicting product lines.
3 Agent considers our product line as the *prime* product to be represented and gives it majority of time expended.
4 Agent is experienced in our type of products, systems and technology.
5 We prefer single-person agencies.
6 We prefer 'mature' agents.
7 We prefer agents that can develop high penetration in reasonably small geographic zones.
8 We prefer agents that have previously been salaried sales reps for major roofing manufacturing companies.

Quite apart from the expected considerations – compatible lines, product experience, territory coverage, etc. – most manufacturers told us that personal chemistry was a critical variable. This is especially interesting in terms of the way manufacturers today relate to their agents. It seems to indicate that agents are sharing the same personal status as would employees of the company. They are considered as an integral part of the team – not just those agents in the field.

This analysis is borne out by one other factor mentioned often – continuity. Today, most manufacturers are looking to their agencies to play long term roles in their growth. They see their agencies growing with them and surviving past the life of the founder.

It's more than reassuring to read the comments of those who have allowed us to quote them for this report. Their reasons for selecting agencies represent a solid balance of the practical with a healthy share of personal considerations. Most said that personal chemistry is critical. This is really refreshing when all we have heard for the past 10 years or so is the bottom line mentality. Sure, profit is the ultimate goal. But there are many ways to get there. And you might as well get there with compatible people than not!

Reading 21

Forging a strategic distribution alliance

Erin Anderson and Barton Weitz

Reprinted from Chief Executive, November 1991, No. 72, pp. 70–73.

More than a marriage of convenience, a strategic alliance with your distributor can be a match made in heaven, but only if that relationship is based on real commitment and (gasp!) trust.

"Strategic alliance" has entered the terminology of business with a vengeance, serving as a catchall phrase for a variety of working arrangements – formal and informal – between organizations. In its true sense, a strategic alliance is a close, open-ended (no set termination date) relationship linking distinct organizations. Such alliances are usually designed to fill a specific purpose, such as developing a new product, exploring a new technology, manufacturing more effectively, or exploiting a market opportunity. Sometimes strategic alliances are embodied in a new organization, such as a joint venture. More frequently, they are embodied in contracts or business understandings, embellished, adapted, and cemented as working relationships grow.

Executives often think of forging strategic alliances in connection with their suppliers, firms making complementary products, customers – or even their competitors. This article concerns a more prosaic (but perhaps more important) candidate to be your strategic partner – your distributor.

A strategic alliance with a distributor? Isn't a distributor just somebody who removes your pallets from the factory loading dock and sends you a check from time to time? Many an executive sees distributors merely in these terms. But most managers recognize that your distributor is your marketer and is therefore in a position to make or break your product. What better ally than the organization that connects you to your customers (and can disconnect you as well)?

It is one thing to decide that a strategic alliance (or a marketing partnership, as some prefer to call it) with a distributor is in order. It is quite another to build such a relationship. Merely announcing to distributors that they have been selected for "partnership" is unlikely to produce results, distributors have heard such corporate propaganda before and will not be impressed. But if words won't create commitment, what will?

To answer this question, we mounted a three-year study of 378 relationships between manufacturers of industrial products and the distributors who take these products to market.* In parallel, we also studied 246 relationships between insurance companies (who provide an intangible, a service rather than a physical product) and their "distributors," i.e., independent insurance agents. By contrasting industrial hard goods and an intangible consumer service, we wanted to isolate how much the dynamics of alliances with resellers depend on what is being sold to whom. The answer we found is this: surprisingly little.

Below, we sketch the profile of a committed reseller that emerged from the boxes of information we collected on these hundreds of pairs of manufacturers and their resellers. (We will concentrate on distributors and merely note where insurance agents differ.) Our information is unique: we asked both the manufacturer and the reseller to describe their relationships. Then we compared the two images to search for the features that distinguished committed manufacturers from indifferent ones, as well as the committed from the indifferent resellers.

WHAT IS COMMITMENT?

From extensive interviews and reading, we determined that a committed distributor has all of these features:

- Expects to continue selling this brand indefinitely;
- Intends to invest in its relationship with the manufacturer;
- Will make sacrifices (within reason) to maintain and grow the relationship;
- Feels an emotional attachment to the manufacturer.

Of course, a committed manufacturer is one that feels the same way about the distributor. A committed distributor exhibits several visible symptoms of its allegiance to you, the manufacturer. Do the following conditions describe your distributor?

- Is happy to see your people (rather than closing the blinds when they drive up);
- Is willing to take the time needed with your people to get business matters settled thoroughly;
- Is patient with your mistakes;
- Offers constructive criticism and recommends new ways to improve efficiency;
- Will help you out with a favor from time to time (for example, sharing a price cut with a big customer);
- Accepts your suggestions if given good arguments;
- Takes the attitude that things will even out in the long term;
- Is willing to do the odd "extra job" (such as market research);
- Turns down other lines that offer slightly better terms;
- Is eager to grow with you.

If the answer is yes, chances are this distributor feels strongly committed to you. And if you find yourself behaving the same way, chances are you feel committed to them.

The business advantages of such a relationship are obvious. At the extreme, such a relationship is so tight that economists call it "quasivertical integration" (two organizations function like one).

MAKING A DISTRIBUTOR COMMIT TO YOU

One question executives ask is whether commitment can be one-sided (for example, can a manufacturer be indifferent, yet enjoy commitment from its distributor)? While we found a few such relationships, they were unusual. On the whole, it appears that it is hard to fool the other side – and difficult to get commitment without giving it. The data strongly indicate that a distributor will not commit unless it believes the manufacturer is also committed. In other words, the distributor won't "get married" if it believes you only want to date. Further, distributors have a reasonable (though not completely accurate) picture of how committed a manufacturer really is, firm propaganda aside.

Indeed, a distributor must believe you are committed before it will reciprocate. We have mentioned that the truth about the manufacturer plays into the distributor's picture. Intentionally or not, the manufacturer's personnel and policies signal how serious the manufacturer really is to the distributor. But other signals operate as well.

In particular, distributors place their confidence in manufacturers whom they see investing in them. Further, not just any investment will do. The investments that reassure distributors and inspire their confidence are investments in them that cannot be used later to benefit their replacements! Such "idiosyncratic investments" (idiosyncratic to the relationship between supplier and distributor) include:

- Putting the distributor's name in your advertisements;
- Going to considerable lengths to link your name with the distributor's;
- Dedicating personnel to this distributor;
- Going to extra lengths to learn the distributor's idiosyncrasies and forge working relationships with its personnel;
- Sponsoring (this means paying for) business development programs for the distributor;
- Training the distributor's people (at your expense).

What these efforts have in common is that they are not easy to redeploy should your relationship with this distributor end. The knowledge, relationships, mental associations, and capabilities built up in this way become obsolete if termination occurs. Some idiosyncratic investments (such as linking brand name and distributor name) may even hinder the transition to a replacement distributor. Effectively, these investments constitute a penalty or fine to be forfeited if the relationship ends (economists call them "exit barriers" because they glue manufacturers into their relationships). Distributors who see these investments being made greatly increase their confidence in the manufacturer and their willingness to enter a strategic alliance with their supplier.

A key word here is "see." In some cases, we observed manufacturers who did make these investments, yet tried to disguise them or downplay them to the distributor. Why? These manufacturers were afraid that the distributor would think the manufacturer was dependent on them, hence vulnerable. Herein lies the rub. If manufacturers must commit to inspire commitment, and if they have to prove it by publicly erecting barriers to their own exit, then they are vulnerable! This is a reality of strategic alliances of any kind. Strong alliances bring substantial benefits but at substantial costs. One of these costs is the flexibility to change your mind and exit the relationship painlessly. Manufacturers who try to downplay their investments in order to disguise their vulnerability throw away the benefit of a public investment. It inspires the partner's confidence and invites reciprocal commitment from the partner. Otherwise put: pretend you don't need your spouse, then discover that your spouse loves you less.

The implication is obvious: don't get married to just anybody. Manufacturers that have carefully selected their distributors (rather than selling to anyone willing to write a check) will find themselves far more able to manage the vulnerability that a strategic alliance demands.

We find the marriage analogy fits well in describing many features of committed relationships. One of them is history. Just as couples who have always fought find it difficult to trust each other, so distributors who have had a stormy past with a manufacturer find it difficult to believe the manufacturer really is committed to them. A contentious history in a business relationship appears to be very difficult to live down, while a harmonious past constitutes an asset.

Another feature is selectivity of representation. A distributor's confidence in its supplier's commitment increases the more the supplier limits its representation in the distributor's market. Distributing intensively (blanketing a market with outlets), while it does increase product availability, reduces the distributor's confidence in the manufacturer, thereby lessening the distributor's willingness to commit to a strategic alliance.

Interestingly, we found that the terms of the contract (if any) between manufacturers and distributors had no discernible impact on the strength of their relationships. Indeed, many of our respondents had trouble telling us what their contracts said! The implication is that contracts interest lawyers more than the participants to a business relationship. The relationship evolves into a working understanding that supplants contract clauses in shaping what each party expects from their arrangement.

THE DISTRIBUTOR'S ACTIONS AND IMPRESSIONS

While it is important for a distributor to believe in its supplier's commitment before it will reciprocate, distributors also take actions that operate to align them more tightly to the supplier; these actions serve as an impetus to the distributor to increases its loyalty to the supplier by making the relationship more important and less readily replaceable.

One of these actions is to limit brand name representation in the supplier's product category. Doing so goes against the nature of a distribution business, which appeals to customers partly by offering one-stop shopping (stocking a panoply of brands in a category). Yet some distributors narrow their brand offering, reducing the degree of competition to the supplier's brand on their shelves. At the extreme, they offer the supplier brand exclusivity. (They carry no competitors in the category.) Our data strongly indicate that the more the distributor concentrates on one brand, to the exclusion of competitors, the more it feels committed to the supplier. In other words, exclusive suppliers are not merely responding to manufacturer pressure or to consumer pull: They are cementing their ties to the manufacturer.

Which comes first, the commitment or the exclusivity of representation? Undoubtedly, they operate in an escalating cycle. Creeping commitment makes the distributor more amenable to limiting its stock of competing brands. But that voluntary restraint, in turn, fuels the distributor's interest in, allegiance to, and dependence on the supplier, thereby contributing to further limitation of stock, and so forth. Over time, the cumulative effect is a strategic alliance with the supplier.

Distributors respond to a manufacturer's efforts to communicate with them. Communicating with distributors should be distinguished from communicating to them. It is exchanges of communication that enhance the distributor's commitment. This means listening, adapting, and acting on the distributor's impressions. It also means respecting and soliciting distributor opinion and using it. Indeed, one feature of committed relationships is that the manufacturer respects the distributor as a business (a corresponding feature of less close-knit relationships is that the supplier believes, and may even declare, that its distributors don't know how to run their businesses well). Respect enhances two-way communication, which in turn strongly increases the distributor's allegiance.

Distributors monitor how a supplier treats its other distributors. If a manufacturer acquires a reputation (rightly or wrongly) for mistreating its resellers, it pays a price. Distributors, even those who do not themselves feel mistreated, withhold commitment from these suppliers. Hence, a reputation for fairness in distributor dealings is an asset in cultivating strategic alliances.

Here we come to the major point of difference between our industrial distributors of hard goods and our insurance agents (sellers of unstockable intangibles to consumers). Distributors assessed the overall quality of the manufacturer's personnel, yet appeared not to factor these assessments into their commitment levels. Insurance agents, in contrast, conditioned their commitment very heavily on their evaluations of the worth of the insurer's personnel. Strikingly, the same is true for supplier commitment to resellers. Industrial suppliers' commitment to distributors was little influenced by their evaluations of distributor personnel. Yet, insurers were much more committed when they perceived their agents were competent, effective businesspeople.

Why this divergence? The answer is based on the nature of what is being sold. For industrial distributors, the product is paramount. It can be seen, held, measured, and assessed; it is constant and it is real. It can embody the supplier. But for an intangible such as insurance, the "product" is more ephemeral. Therefore, the insurer's people (who make judgments about how a policy may be adapted to a client and how a claim will be handled) come to embody the product – and the supplier. The old saw that a company is its people seems to be far more appropriate for a service (especially an intangible one) than for a physical, stockable good.

THE CEO'S CONTRIBUTION

Many an executive is attracted by the lure of strategic alliances, and the logic of such relationships is especially compelling when the proposed partner is one's own reseller, the link between a company and its market. But such alliances do not come free, or even cheap. Corporate pronouncements will not do. To convince a distributor to become a genuine marketing partner, a manufacturer must put its resources – and its own commitment – behind its pronouncements. Distributors will demand your commitments – your reciprocity – before they will extend theirs.

Ultimately, strategic alliances are based on mutual need. Mutual need, in turn, creates tension and conflict. (Ask any marriage counselor). But if managed well, such relationships are the basis for a formidable marketing advantage.

Erin Anderson is an associate professor of marketing at the Wharton School of the University of Pennsylvania.

Barton Weitz is a professor of marketing and the J.C. Penney Eminent Scholar at the University of Florida.

Reading 22

Finding the right distributor

There are plenty of mistakes that can be made in Europe. Here is a guide to distribution dos and don'ts

Barbara N. Berkman

Reprinted from *Electronic Business*, December 1990, Vol. 16, No. 23, pp. 154–5.

Last March, Rich Maxwell arrived in Paris to set up a European distribution network for Stallion Technologies Inc., an Australian marker of add-on cards for Unix-based personal computers. The problem, he says, was that Stallion's existing distributors "had not been managed very well from Australia."

But since then, Stallion's fortunes haven't improved much. "Germany is a problem for us because we are late to the market. The distributors are already filled with competitors' lines, and it is difficult to get them to change," reports Maxwell. The situation in Italy isn't much better, he says. "I have been talking to one company for over a year. It is very frustrating."

Stallion is not alone. Small companies that have plunged into Europe without the financial muscle to establish direct-sales offices find setting up a distribution network hard work. The distributor's location, size, and ability to handle technical products can spell distribution success or failure. In addition to that, "Europe is a long way away, and you are doing business in different languages," says Gary Kibblewhite of Europartner Consultants in London.

But by following the advice of those familiar with the European market, U.S. companies can avoid many common pitfalls.

Unlike a U.S. distributor, a distributor in Europe is a local company that stocks the product and handles design-in, marketing, advertising, trade shows, after-sales support, customer service, and order taking. They serve small markets, which makes them self-supporting and better equipped for technical support. The most common partner for a small to midsize U.S. manufacturer is a distributor who imports as well. "That implies familiarity with the physical passing of goods through

Table 22.1 Comparing European distributors (averages for each country's electronics distribution industry, 1989)

	U.K.	*France*	*Germany*	*Italy*	*U.S.*
Expenses (as % of sales)	20	22	19	8	17
Salaries (as % of total costs)	45	70	60	8	60
Sales per employee ($ thousands)	270	275	300	360	350
Receivables (days)	70	110	30	140	50
Vacation days per employee	27	25	30	31	10–15

Source: Europartner Consultants

customs and with international methods of payment and currency fluctuation," notes Charlie Thayer of European Marketing in Chevenoz, France.

An agent is basically the equivalent of a sales representative and is the unique source of product for all of Europe. The agent has a network of distributors and serves the OEMs directly.

A European representative is an organization that works only with distributors and agents and has no direct customers. The rep works on a commission basis and arranges contracts directly with the manufacturer.

U.S. companies traditionally lower export costs by shipping to their own facility in Europe or by appointing an agent to distribute the shipment. That can shave about 25% off the cost of transporting products to individual distributors.

Satellite distribution hubs have their drawbacks, as Osicom Technologies (U.K.) Ltd. discovered when its French hub failed. "We didn't have enough local expertise. A strong local distributor works much better," advises Michael Connolly, marketing manager of the Cardiff, Wales, subsidiary of the U.S. computer-systems maker.

An alternative to distributors and agents is a company that arranges for the physical movement of goods from manufacturer to customer. Among them is Van Ommeren-Intexo of The Netherlands, which specializes in electronics for companies such as diskdrive maker Quantum Corp. The company invoices customers on the manufacturer's stationery, uses EDI, and provides office space for the manufacturer and a multilingual staff to take sales orders.

Such companies are an intermediate step to testing European waters, which can be pretty choppy. Some distributors, for example, will accept your product line just to keep it off the market. "It is a delay tactic. They know a U.S. company will give them at least a year in Europe because the design-in cycle is so long," warns David Sherwood, managing director of

Applied Materials & Technology, a European marketing and management service in Bristol, England.

A U.S. company will send someone over to Europe to visit key OEMs only to return to Europe three months later to find their lead is eaten away by a local. "Americans will do a whistle-stop tour of Europe with a suitcase full of faxes they have received from European distributors, and they will interview them in the hotel lobby," says AMT's Sherwood. "They could have had the same conversation on the telephone."

Instead you should be looking at their financial resources, making sure they have the technical experience, visiting their customers, and looking to see if the product manager's role is well-defined, because the product manager is the one that sells the product to the sales force.

Some experts say an even better plan is to hire a local or an American with European experience to do the job. "If they are really serious about setting up in Europe, my advice is to send someone over from the States who is experienced in European marketing and who can appreciate the customs here. It is very, very difficult to find those people, which is why companies use consultants who know Europe but don't know your product," says Fred Henley, managing director of Transtel Communications Ltd., the European sales and support arm of holding company J.W.P. Inc. in New York.

To be sure, many smaller U.S. companies are scurrying to Europe themselves to attempt to wed their products with the perfect distributor. But they soon realize that the ideal mate isn't easy to find.

U.S. companies must understand that regional and national differences exist among European distributors. In Italy, for example, receivables run to 140 days, compared with 30 days in Germany. And Italian chip customers – unlike the British customer – tend to shop around.

What to ask a distributor

1 Do you sell a complementary product line with the same applications?
2 Do you have at least 10 employees?
3 Do you have good bank and trade references?
4 Does the U.S. commercial office have information on you?
5 What do the country's customers think are the most important features and benefits of your products?

Some experts argue the need for two regional distributors, particularly in the north and south of Italy and Germany. Others say regional distribution is generally disappearing.

"Business in Italy is much too concentrated to warrant a north-south divide," according to Silvio Barconchelli, chairman of Italy's National Association of Electronic Distribution. He estimates that the area south of Rome accounts for less than 10% of the total market; that the Milan region accounts for 40%; and that the corridor of Turin, Venice, and Bolgna accounts for another 35%.

U.S. companies also can choose among the pan-European networks cropping up all over Europe. Many of the major suppliers prefer to be with pan-European distributors, particularly when their reason for handing the business over to distributors is to cut their cost of sales, points out Gary Ranallo, managing director of Arrow Electronics (UK) Ltd.

Opponents of pan-European sourcing say fluctuations in exchange rates make it too risky. "Don't allow yourself to be dragged into cross-border franchises. You have got to look at each franchise as a separate company," advises Sherwood.

U.S. companies also underestimate the amount of support European distributors need – especially since European customers won't wait patiently until the start of the U.S. business day for the answer to a question.

Europe's last distributors have good technical support capability but often won't bother with new products that take a long time to design in. "You have so many start-ups that come here. Their products are so new, people are not eager to talk to them," says Giorgio Ghezzi, president of Italy's largest chip distributor, Silverstar SpA.

But smaller distributors often lack the financial and technical muscle necessary to market highly technical U.S. electronics products in Europe. Mips Computer Systems Inc. has worked hard to educate the European market about Unix products, explains Stratton Scalvos, acting general manager for Europe. "There are not a lot of good distribution channels for Unix and larger systems."

The problem is a common one. Iomega Corp. is the European subsidiary of the U.S. maker of a removable, crashless disk-storage device. "Our product is not a commodity product. In penetrating European markets it is a continual exercise to educate the customer, dedicated dealers, and our distributors," says Mason Herzog, director of European sales of Iomega's European subsidiary in Brussels.

Daniel Roberts was stymied when he tried to find distributors in France and Germany for the $130,000 laser-printer subsystems manufactured by Advanced Technologies Inc. of Milpitas, Calif. There were a number of small aggressive companies in Germany but none that could handle that complex a product. "We instead went to marketing agents, and we will support them directly," says Roberts, president of Opportunity Europe Ltd. in London. France, too, was a problem. "The smaller companies don't have the technical caliber to support those products."

If things do go sour, remember that an agent is almost impossible to fire in certain European countries unless the employer assumes responsibility for severance pay and about one year's lost commissions. European courts usually side with the employee. One American manufacturer protected himself by negotiating – with a handshake – a trial period before a contract was signed.

Reading 23

Lighting the way

Anon

Reprinted from *The Economist*, 16 October, 1990, p. 77.

This month our management page examines a company that comes close to many theorists' dream of what tomorrow's firm should look like. Does that make it a keener competitor?

Gurus love to talk of the firm of the future: networked, decentralised and customer-driven, its organisational structure flattened and inverted. Lithonia Lighting, a little-known company based in Conyers, Georgia, may be the closest any firm has got to that ideal. Owned by National Service Industries, a clothing-to-chemicals conglomerate, Lithonia is the world's biggest maker of lighting equipment. That means everything (except bulbs) from fluorescent office-lighting to lighting-control systems.

In America lighting equipment is usually sold through a web of contractors, distributors and agents. For a new building, "specifiers" draft the basic facts about the lighting system needed for the project, then put the job of installation out to tender. The winning contractor orders the system's components from an electrical distributor, which tends to sell several manufacturers' products. The distributor buys from an independent sales agent. These are usually linked to a single manufacturer: Lithonia follows industry practice by letting its agents stock complementary, but not competing products.

This network of relationships was the key to Lithonia's transformation into a guru's dream. At the start of the 1980s Lithonia was market leader, but its competitors were catching up. How could it remodel its business, become more competitive and turn itself into the world's lowest-cost, highest-quality maker of lighting equipment?

Mr Charles Darnell, a senior vice-president at Lithonia and architect of the firm's change, felt that exploiting the industry's dispersed structure and ditching Lithonia's conventional organisational hierarchy would give it an edge. He put Lithonia's independent agents at the hub of a spoked network. Grouped around the hub were the specifiers, contractors and distributors, plus Lithonia's various decentralised product divisions, its field warehouses and its headquarters team.

This process made Lithonia rethink its business links. It was not, as it had supposed, at the top of a hierarchy, with strong links only to its agents (the second tier of the hierarchical "pyramid"). In reality, the lighting-equipment business revolved around the agents. These had the local knowledge and customer relations necessary to get Lithonia's products chosen for lighting projects. A plan emerged: help make the agents more efficient and more profitable, break down the boundaries between Lithonia and its partners in the network, and business would boom. Lithonia has spent $20m turning that plan into practice.

Computers now link each bit of Lithonia's network, from specifiers to agents to Lithonia's own factories. Computer-aided design and artificial-intelligence systems help specifiers design a lighting layout to suit any project. Automated, flexible manufacturing systems (linked into the overall computer network) mean that Lithonia can swiftly modify its product lines; feedback from customers and agents helps design new products. Product catalogues can be tailored to show specific ranges and prices for individual customers.

Contractors, distributors and agents check the availability of products and order them from Lithonia on-line. The company's software automatically directs the various components of each order to the relevant Lithonia product division. The progress of each order can be tracked throughout the system. Even Lithonia's delivery trucks will eventually be linked into the computer network so that customers will know exactly when their orders will arrive.

All told, Lithonia's system has cut the lead-time on orders from up to nine days to under a day. None of the firm's competitors (principally Cooper Industries, Genlyte, Kidde and USI, the last two owned by Britain's Hanson) has such an integrated system. They also sell their products through specifiers, distributors and independent agents. Developing a Lithonia-like computerised information network would take them at least five years. But do they need one?

Lithonia reckons that its networked structure has contributed greatly to a close-to-doubling of sales (to $717m in the year to August) over the past six years, and a more-than-doubling of profits, to $59.5m. It also encourages agents to be loyal – and agents are at the hub of Mr Darnell's network. The efficiency of Lithonia's system increases the agents' profits, and ties them more closely to Lithonia by providing them with a plethora of computer systems and software to help them run their own businesses with fewer support staff. Defecting to another manufacturer would rob them of those benefits overnight.

A measure of Lithonia's faith in its strategy is its plan to take it a stage further. It hopes to bring its suppliers, too, into its burgeoning network by the end of 1991. They should then be able to help the firm design and develop new products. Lithonia sees no reason why its suppliers and customers should not talk to each other via Lithonia's network, if it means a better lighting fixture is eventually produced. But Lithonia's main aim in bringing its suppliers into its network is to eliminate the need for stocks. Not simply just-in-time, says Mr Darnell; if everyone in Lithonia's network is efficiently linked, there will be no need to carry stocks of either materials or finished products. And that, he believes, will give the company an unassailable lead.

Too optimistic? The weak bit of Lithonia's approach is the information on which its network feeds: if it is inaccurate or late, the system could grind to a halt. Worse, in such an integrated structure, a breakdown needs to occur at only one point in the network for havoc to be wrought. In traditional business hierarchies, the damage caused by such a breakdown tends to be limited to the nearby tiers of the pyramid. In networks, damage can spread more rapidly – and unpredictably. So far, Lithonia has got it right by ensuring that its computer systems make the lives of users easier – which means that it is in the users' interests to feed the system accurate, timely information. As Lithonia's network grows, that quality may be harder to control.

Part 6

Telemarketing and Trade Fairs

INTRODUCTION

Telemarketing and trade fairs now fulfil an important role in both generating new customers and communicating with existing customers in business-to-business markets. The extent of the development of telemarketing and trade shows varies enormously by country. For instance telemarketing is far more developed in the USA, whereas trade shows assume a far greater importance in continental Europe.

The term telemarketing is not well understood. The Teleculture 2000[1] report published by The Henley Centre in 1994 revealed that 50 per cent of those questioned thought that telemarketing was selling by telephone and 17 per cent thought it was cold selling. Michael Stevens[2] defines it as 'the planned and controlled use of telephone communication to build profitable long-term relationships with members of influential audiences who impact on an organization's success.' The Teleculture 2000 report found that 68 per cent of people would prefer not to deal with an organization again if *a single call* is badly handled.

Telemarketing in the USA[3] is growing at the rate of 25–30 per cent per annum and is used by over 250,000 businesses to generate annual sales revenue of $100 billion. The UK 'freephone' and 'local call' market is also growing very rapidly. Telemarketing is now used in very many industries from banking to builders merchants. Any organization that uses the telephone to contact customers is using some form of telemarketing. However, some see the uncontrolled use of the telephone as an unwarranted invasion of personal privacy especially when used to sell direct to the general public. Proposals to ban the use of the telephone for cold calling within the European Union without prior consent were rejected by the European Parliament in 1995.[4]

Telemarketing can be used to replace the traditional field sales force for low value items, and to support it as part of the response mechanism in direct response marketing. In inbound telemarketing customers call in response to a television advertisement or some other communication, usually using a free telephone number. The 1995 DRTV Channel 4/BT Joint Research study found that 19 per cent of all TV advertisements now carry a telephone number as a response mechanism. This was an increase of 46 per cent over the previous study conducted in 1993. In outbound telemarketing the organization calls out to existing or potential customers thus eliminating the need for a sales call.

There are many applications for telemarketing, but these can be grouped into four main headings:

- Lead generation
- Telesales
- Building and maintaining the database
- Customer service (including customer care lines and crisis management).

Setting up a telemarketing operation can be expensive as a substantial investment may be required in:

- Computer hardware, software and telecommunications equipment
- Recruitment, selection and in-depth training of telemarketing agents.

A company wishing to move into telemarketing might consider initially using a bureau until an in-house operation can be justified. Even some of the large telemarketing operators with their own in-house operations use a bureau for specific campaigns. When deciding to use telemarketing there are four basic options that can be considered.

- Set up an in-house operation to handle inbound and outbound calls
- Buy in all activities from a third party bureau
- Use a bureau to test the service and once the service has been identified as profitable then move it in-house
- Use a bureau to test before moving in-house, but still retain the bureau for specific tasks.

The first reading in this section by James S. Trager 'Balance: the cornerstone of telemarketing success' (Reading 24), outlines how telemarketing representatives can effectively perform both the marketing/prospecting and sales functions. Particular reference is made to 'upselling' and 'cross-selling'. However, short-term sales tactics to increase revenue should not be used if the company's mission is to build a partnership with its customers. Caution and restraint will be needed to ensure that customers are not sold either more items or more expensive items than they actually require or items that they don't actually need.

According to Michael Stevens new technology is transforming the use of the telephone in marketing and sales. He explains why this is so in Reading 25 entitled, 'A telephony revolution'. With the new digital networks calls can now be re-routed to remote sites. Inbound calls using an automatic call distributor (ACD) can be passed to a telemarketing person. It is possible for an incoming call to be identified (existing customer) and customer file details to be shown on screen as soon as the call is connected. A new development in outbound telemarketing is predictive dialling. Calls are made automatically from a list of numbers and then passed to an operator. Predictive dialling has been used particularly in credit collection. However, another potential use is for outbound customer service calls to check on, for instance, customer satisfaction with the product or service.

Trade fairs are another important element of the promotion mix in business-to-business marketing. While competitive pressure might influence a firm's decision to take part in a trade show other reasons[5] might include:

- *Managerial reasons* – to improve corporate image or employee morale.
- *Cost effectiveness* – to reach a large number of accounts quickly. It may be an economic way for a small firm to gain national or international exposure.
- *Reach new potential customers or distributors* – small accounts and distributors may visit trade shows to find new suppliers.
- *Gain direct contact with decision makers* – a trade show may be a better and easier way to meet key decision makers, which may not be possible on their own premises.
- *Product demonstration* – it may be a better place to demonstrate products that are too bulky for the sales representative to carry in a car, i.e. medical equipment or computer hardware.
- *Achieve sales-related objectives* – to generate sales leads, sales revenue.

Trade fairs provide an ideal opportunity to meet many existing and potential customers. In addition they can be a useful source of information on both competitor activity and competitors' products. Exhibitors can now get a list of visitors to their stand by 'swiping' the bar-code on their lapel badges. Follow-up calls or mailings can then be made.

An account of the European trade shows is provided in Reading 26 by Robin Cobb called 'Shows of force'. The importance of trade shows in Continental Europe is given a much higher priority compared to the UK. They are not only bigger, but attendance is regarded as mandatory rather than optional. International events can be used for locating new distributors and for breaking into new markets. Successful participation consists of three elements. First, the most influential events in any given market must be identified. Secondly, planning must be done well in advance including literature translated into the appropriate language. Thirdly, for European trade shows it is important to promote widely to potential customers as visitors often schedule their appointments in advance.

Exhibiting at trade fairs need not be as expensive as might be imagined. In 'Meet me at the fair' (Reading 27), Kerry Pechter explains the 'ins and outs' of how to get the most out of a foreign trade show. Attendance at trade shows can be done on a limited budget with some research and careful planning. Again, emphasis is made on selecting the right fair to attend. With a proliferation of trade fairs it is easy to pick the wrong one. The US and Foreign and Commercial Service (USFCS) or the equivalent such as the Department of Trade and Industry in the UK can usually help and advise. Agencies such as the USFCS often buy up blocks of booth space and then sell off at much less than the standard price. Again, the importance of pre-show marketing is stressed to ensure the right people turn up on the exhibition stand. It is also essential that a specialist freight forwarder is used to ensure all the exhibition equipment arrives safely and on time.

References

1 Teleculture 2000, The Henley Centre, 1994.
2 Stevens, M., *Telemarketing in Action*, McGraw-Hill, 1995.
3 Anderson, R., *Essentials of Personal Selling*, Prentice-Hall, 1995.
4 *Financial Times*, 14 December 1995.
5 Comer, J.M., *Sales Management*, Allyn and Bacon, 1991.

Reading 24

Balance: the cornerstone of telesales success

James S. Trager

Reprinted from *Telemarketing*, May 1992, Vol. 10, No. 11, pp. 18–23. Published by Technology Marketing Corporation, One Technology Plaza, Norwalk, CT06854 USA.

In discussing setting up a telesales department, let's start with what is meant by "telesales." For the business-to-business marketplace, "telesales" embraces both outbound and inbound, and can include any combination of the following telephone-based activities:

- Order taking
- Opening new accounts
- Increasing sales to existing accounts
- Customer service

Since orders (sales) are the lifeblood of any company, they almost always have first priority. Experience tells us that, in an inhouse department with several of these responsibilities, *order taking* can overwhelm all the others in terms of time spent on the telephone by telesales representatives. Therefore, to achieve the appropriate balance among these competing activities, the plan for the telesales department should include:

- Management's commitment to dedicate specific time and staff to *opening new accounts*.
- Telesales department management's responsibility for providing all representatives with training in sales techniques for *increasing the average order size* and *generating repeat business*.
- An evaluation of whether the *customer service function* will be more effective if maintained in the telesales or another department.

If the preceding steps are followed during the planning stage, the telesales activities will increase revenue, because telesales will be more than just an order *taking* department.

Telesales has the ability to perform many valuable functions in support of the four basic activities. Each telesales function is actually a different telemarketing application with a measurable economic benefit. The following aspects of telesales contribute to making one or more of the basic activities successful:

Marketing/prospecting functions –

- Gathering information needed to make sales,
- Building a direct marketing database,
- Qualifying businesses,
- Identifying decision makers,
- Generating leads.

Sales functions –

- Cross-selling,
- Upselling,
- Building customer relationships,
- Servicing regular customers,
- Following-up inactive accounts,
- Developing marginal accounts,
- Resolving problems and complaints.

Begin by reviewing this list to see which functions apply to your business. They are the underpinning of your telesales-department. We will discuss several of them in this article. Your representatives may need specific training, one function or application at a time, to effectively and consistently do each of the things that apply.

While there is some overlap, the first five functions are more marketing- or information-oriented, and the last seven are more directly sales-oriented. Another way to put it is that the first five functions are preliminary to the actual sales process. Let's look at how telesales representatives can effectively perform both the marketing/prospecting and the sales functions.

MARKETING/PROSPECTING FUNCTIONS

Unlike privacy-conscious consumers, business purchasing agents, office managers, controllers, personnel managers, telecommunications managers and many other decision makers will provide your representatives with all the information they need to qualify a business or make a sale. So will most small-business owners.

With every inbound call, the telesales representative has the opportunity to obtain information and build your database for direct marketing. The key to obtaining this information is to ask simple questions in a conversational tone of voice.

Outbound telesales representatives can learn the name of the decision maker for just about any product or service from the person answering the phone. The representative who has limited (or out-of-date) information about a prospect (which is often the case when working with rented lists and many house files) will be more effective proceeding from general questions to specific questions. For example, by asking to speak to "the person responsible for the phones," instead of the telecommunications manager, you overcome the hurdle of not understanding how the prospect company is organized and you will be directed to the person who can help you.

Some telesales representatives will be motivated enough – and appreciate a break from their routine – to devote a few hours every day or so to making calls like these. If they are "too busy," consider training other staff or part-timers to make your information-gathering, marketing and prospecting calls.

Purchased lists or house lists that need a lot of cleaning are prime candidates for this type of effort. Representatives can achieve a high rate of completed contacts per hour (16 to 22 listings can be completed). At relatively little cost, lists that representatives would normally avoid because they are perceived to be out-of-date or incomplete can yield valuable customers.

SALES FUNCTIONS

Cross-selling and upselling are frequently mentioned in the same breath, but they are really two very different techniques. In the industrial marketplace, upselling is usually easier and, therefore, should be taught first. Here's why.

There are two types of upselling: a larger quantity or a more expensive item. Telesales representatives should always go for the larger order quantity if there is a price break – and make purchasers feel they are making smart decisions by saving their company's money. Make your representatives aware of all the volume discounts – and monitor their performance to make sure they are using them.

The "smart decision" approach also applies to the more expensive item, and is especially appropriate for one-of-a-kind purchases. The representative should be helpful and emphasize the extra features or greater capacity. Positive answers can be solicited by asking questions about how the product will be used. Then, unless you know the customer is looking only at price, you are in a position to upsell successfully.

Other than straightforward add-ons, cross-selling usually requires a great deal more product training and product line knowledge. Add-ons are usually very obvious in the sales literature or on order forms – so train these first. Wait until the telesales representatives have mastered the add-ons and the quantity upsell before proceeding with the time-consuming training needed to learn the more numerous cross-selling combinations.

Servicing regular customers takes a great deal of the telesales representative's time. The proportion increases when you expect them to be more proactive and build customer relationships. Therefore, it is easy for following-up inactive accounts to become a secondary activity, and for representatives (especially commission representatives) to pay lip service to developing marginal accounts.

Reactivating dormant accounts requires knowledge of why they stopped buying. And marginal accounts may need to be screened and qualified, then sold. This type of call is part information-gathering, part prospecting. Here, we come to management's commitment to specific time and staff for opening accounts. Will the telesales representatives make these calls consistently and effectively? If not, these functions can be handled by a separate group, as described earlier.

COMBINING INBOUND AND OUTBOUND

Allocating resources is also an issue for operations that include a large inbound component coupled with some outbound applications, such as account servicing or prospecting. A rule of thumb is that reactive (inbound) always takes precedence over proactive (outbound).

To establish a balance, some companies ask their telesales representatives to continuously alternate between inbound and outbound, depending on the next available call. Here, another condition comes into play: if representatives have two primary tasks, most will be more comfortable with (and will, therefore, put more energy into) *the easier task*. In the case of telesales, handling inbound calls is usually perceived as the easier task. As a result, the outbound effort will be less productive, and this strategy will *not* achieve the desired balance.

Today, there are telephone systems that can alleviate that problem and help you avoid the twin difficulties inherent in inbound telemarketing – lost calls (during peak hours) and idle time (during slow periods). Using a PBX or telephone switch with ACD (automatic call distribution) software, you can establish separate telesales groups for inbound and outbound that can be managed efficiently.

My recommendation is to staff the inbound group at a level below peak, to reduce staff costs. Your telecommunications department or consultant can help you determine that number. I also recommend utilizing part-timers to make sure all business hours are covered. This way, inbound representatives will spend a large portion of their time taking calls.

Whenever a peak condition occurs, the telephone switch or the supervisor can temporarily transfer the required number of outbound representatives to inbound, until the peak passes. The outbound representatives realize that they are only handling overflow inbound, and most of their energy will still be devoted to their regular job, outbound telesales.

COMPENSATING TELESALES REPRESENTATIVES

A basic salary, plus commission based on revenue generated, is the standard way to compensate telesales representatives. Commission percentages may vary within a company by product sold, margin, territory quota and so forth. For successful representatives, commission can average as much as two times salary.

However, it is *not* in management's interest for revenue dollars to be the *only* basis for extra compensation. Since most businesses have parallel goals, i.e., opening new accounts and retaining satisfied customers, telesales compensation should be designed to reflect these goals as well. Here are some illustrations of performance criteria that can be used in planning compensation for representatives:

Quantity – For example, exceeding the standard for: number of calls received (inbound); number of calls made (outbound).

Service Level – For example, meeting or exceeding standards for: response time (inbound); promptness of follow-up (outbound); accuracy of information (prospecting).

Activity Level – For specific accomplishments, such as: opening new accounts (outbound); increasing order size (inbound).

Customer Satisfaction – (both inbound and outbound).

As long as the criterion is meaningful to the company, *and performance against that criterion can be measured,* it can be incorporated into the telesales representative's compensation.

SUMMARY AND CONCLUSIONS

- Planning is the key to managing competing activities within telesales.
- Both the marketing/prospecting and the sales functions can be accomplished successfully by telesales representatives.
- Extensive information capture on prospects is feasible, allowing you to employ otherwise unusable lists for telesales.
- Where necessary, dedicated individuals can be assigned to marketing/prospecting functions.

- The different techniques for increasing the size of the order should be taught to all telesales representatives.
- The proper telephone system can help you manage both inbound and outbound effectively.
- Telesales compensation is primarily base plus commission, but should also reflect other criteria important to the company.

James S. Trager is a partner in TeleSpectra Associates, a consulting firm that offers professional telemarketing and telecommunications services to companies interested in realizing opportunities created by combining new marketing concepts, telecommunications technology and management information systems.

Reading 25

A telephony revolution

Michael Stevens

Reprinted from *Marketing*, 16 September 1993, pp. 38.

New technology is transforming the use of the telephone in marketing and sales, but how does it work in practice? Michael Stevens offers a simple guide to the daunting techno-jargon.

The telephone has started to fulfil its promise as a strategic business tool, thanks to advances in two areas: telecommunications and data management. Telecoms can link departments, sites and even suppliers in a dynamic information network.

The digital network is only just beginning to yield its benefits, one of which is the seamless transfer of calls between remote sites.

For instance software corporation Microsoft and telemarketing agency Brann Contact 24 transfer calls between their respective offices. A request for literature answered at Microsoft's switchboard can be routed to Brann Contact 24 at Bristol for qualification and fulfilment. If that caller then asks for detailed technical information, the call can be routed back to the appropriate Microsoft department.

Andy McInally, sales and marketing director at the agency, explains the significance: "The technology allows agencies to take the majority of calls for a client and filter them, managing the simpler ones and forwarding the most heavily technical to the client. It takes the pressure off their switchboard and off their staff. Strategically that must be a large step forward."

Another feature of the network is the ability to reroute calls automatically. For example, telemarketing agency Merit Direct handles donation calls for the NSPCC. When all operators are busy, overflow calls are diverted to Legion's automated call-handling service.

High volume inbound traffic can be successfully handled using an automated call distributor (ACD). Some of these have an interactive voice response (IVR) facility. This allows callers to choose between a menu of options, using the touch tones on their phones. ECI Book and Record Club in Holland uses this system for automatically capturing orders.

Calls can also be answered automatically by dedicated IVR equipment. Leeds-based IMS claims to be the UK's largest automated call-handling facility, with a capacity of 20 million calls per week. One mail order company uses this regularly to download responses generated by its direct response TV commercials.

Direct dial-in (DDI) enables an ACD to identify which number has been dialled and route the call accordingly. Holiday Inn's Worldwide Reservations Centre in Amsterdam takes calls from all over Europe. Its ACD identifies the country of origin and sends the call to an operator who speaks the right language.

DDI also permits the synchronisation of call and data. Aspect's Application Bridge is one example of a kit which links the ACD and the database. Customers' phone numbers are linked to their file records. The file appears automatically on screen when a customer's call is connected.

This month BT is testing the Calling Line Identity service again. Similar automatic number identification is used widely in the US. It enables a company to identify the number of anyone calling in, search the database for a match, and deliver the customer's record to the operator's screen.

There are many ways of helping operators to meet individual callers' needs. Computerised scripts, for example, can hold a vast amount of information. Mailcom's mail order and telemarketing response centre uses software written in-house. "Clients want so many different things and off-the-shelf does not provide the scope we require," explains account director Lynn Gray. The system helps operators achieve maximum order value.

There is a trend towards establishing customer communication centres. Various corporate information systems are integrated at these sites so that agents can access whichever is appropriate to a call. NORWEB, the electricity utility, receives around three million calls a year across six sites, each with an Aspect Call Center. "Our main interface with our customers these days is the telephone," says NORWEB's supply projects manager Norman Nurney. Since introducing the new technology, calls handled per agent have risen by at least 25%.

A big headache for large operations is managing the unpredictable volume of inbound calls. NORWEB is introducing the Employee Management Planning System, a Cybernetics product distributed by Call Centre Logistics. EMPS analyses historical call traffic flow and predicts future staffing requirements in half-hour time bands.

Technology can also help non-specialist operators to deliver expert advice using an expert system. The operator is prompted to answer a series of questions on screen and the system deduces the appropriate response using its computerised store of knowledge.

One of the most recent developments in outbound calling in the UK is predictive dialling. This automatically dials numbers from a list, keeping operators fully occupied. Records appear on screen as the calls connect. One credit card processor has achieved a 380% productivity gain, on cash collection calls.

TDS, the database and marketing services company, installed a 24-station EIS call processing system, with integral predictive dialler, earlier this year. The company is using it to update and develop the TDS Business File, its database of UK businesses, as well as for building client databases and telemarketing. "The cost of telephone updating is so huge, we felt we had to commit to it," says managing director Adrian Gregory. "It has improved productivity quite significantly and we have been able to reduce our hourly cost to clients by a third."

One of the UK's leading mail order companies uses three Davox predictive diallers, supplied by Datapoint UK, in applications such as cash collection, customer recruitment and sales promotion.

The company also uses the Davox Smart Management Centre (SMC), which gives a further 20% productivity gain. The SMC provides real-time graphic monitoring of call activity and more flexible, dynamic control over dialling across multiple applications.

This is just a glimpse of how technology is changing the face of telemarketing and giving it a higher profile in business strategy. Continuous developments in telecommunications and data management will give it further impetus.

Reading 26

Shows of force

Robin Cobb

Reprinted from *Marketing*, 26 April 1990, pp. 44–5.

UK trade shows fare badly in comparison to those in Europe. Not only are venues far smaller and less numerous here, but companies' attitudes to exhibitions are more conservative than their continental competition.

Although many UK-based trade shows and exhibitions include "international" in their titles, this is often just wishful thinking. Only a sprinkle of exhibitors and visitors actually journey in from continental Europe and beyond.

The fact is that one equally has to look across the Channel for any truly international events, and particularly to Germany and France.

Major exhibitions complexes – such as those in Hanover, Frankfurt, Düsseldorf, Cologne and Paris – house events up to twice the size of anything that can be accommodated at the UK's largest venue, the National Exhibition Centre (NEC).

Paris alone is said to contain as much specialist exhibition space as the whole UK.

Trade shows are accorded a higher marketing priority on the Continent. Shows that UK manufacturers regard as an optional extra in their marketing budgets, their continental competitors see as virtually mandatory.

Experienced exporters are well aware of this. But manufacturers exploring the promise of the Single Market have only just discovered the potential of trade shows.

Of course exhibitors are essentially for the promotion of sales. However, beyond that, international events can be used for market research and to make contact with potential new agents and distributions in hitherto untapped third markets.

According to the annual survey into exhibition expenditure by the incorporated Society of British Advertising (ISBA), UK companies spent about £700m on show participation in 1988 (the latest figures available). This represents nearly 10% of advertising budgets and is an increase of about 40% on the previous year.

But Reg Best, assistant director of ISBA, points out that the UK spend on shows is dwarfed by that in some of other European countries. In Germany, for instance, it is equal to about 20% or more of companies' advertising budgets.

Nevertheless, it is significant that UK companies have sharply increased their spend on shows outside the UK, again by about 40%, indicating an increased awareness of the importance of these events in the European marketing scene.

A marked trend in the major European shows is burgeoning participation from the Far East. About one in eight exhibitors at the main German shows are from Japan, South Korea and Taiwan, spearheading a challenge for European markets.

"They have come in on a very serious level and are investing large sums of money," Best warns. "UK companies ought to take heed."

Adopting the principle "if you can't beat 'em, join 'em," several UK exhibition organising companies have been developing continental interests. The Blenheim group has acquired companies in Germany, France, Switzerland and Belgium and set up an office in Spain.

Together, these companies stage about 120 shows, enabling Blenheim to claim that it is the biggest independent exhibition organiser in Europe. But, "independent" is an important qualifier. Unlike those in the UK, virtually all of Germany's major events are organised by the venue owners, with independents using their facilities only on sufferance.

"If they decide they want to run their own show, they can freeze you out," admits Deborah Carlton, director of Blenheim's European development group. Perhaps this is why the group's two biggest events are in Paris rather than in Germany – Equip-Hotel and Batimat, respectively the main European shows for the hotel and construction industries.

Carlton has seen a growth of interest by UK companies in exhibitions on the Continent. But many are hesitating.

"It is a fear of the unknown," she says. "They are concerned about the lack of knowledge of the market, language difficulties, how to get their exhibits there and where to stay. One of the reasons this department was set up was to help such first-time exhibitors."

Interestingly, although Reed Exhibitions has large-scale interests in the US and the Far East, it is relatively small in continental Europe, a situation that it intends to change.

Reed now has companies in Italy and France together with 14 events on the Continent and in Scandinavia organised from the UK. The French company is Midem, responsible for the main international exhibitions of the television and music industries.

"I spend a fair amount of my time looking at opportunities for Reed to do more in Europe," says Nick Forster, European commercial development director.

He admits, however, that Germany is a difficult nut to crack. "We have to accept that the Germans are very well organised. It doesn't preclude the possibility of niche shows but we wouldn't want to fall out with the hall owners as some have done by acquiring shows in Germany."

Some of the medium to small sized UK organisers have for many years been making successful forays into Europe. Mack-Brooks Exhibitions, for example, launched its first European event in Basle in 1972.

"Germany was a closed shop to foreign organisers in those days and we found the Swiss more receptive," explains chairman Ken Brooks. Today the situation is a little more relaxed and Brooks' company's portfolio includes the International Sheet Metalworking Exhibition in Essen.

It is indicative of the comparative scale of shows. In Germany this event is considered to be a moderately-sized niche exhibition, even though it attracts nearly 60,000 visitors and would occupy about half of the NEC.

World Trade Promotions has organised shows in such diverse locations as the US, Singapore and Saudi Arabia. It is now setting up an ambitious Eurofreight exhibition in Brussels.

Chief executive Dermot Graham says:

> It has become increasingly necessary to go to mainland Europe if you wish to establish a genuinely international event. It is a sad fact that shows in the UK are often regarded by the rest of Europe as being domestic, suitable only for the UK market. Similarly, UK exhibitors are realising that they have to cross the Channel to show to a full European audience rather than relying on visitors coming in significant numbers to UK-based exhibitions.

This is borne out by the findings of Exhibition Surveys, of Melton Mowbray. Visitors to UK exhibitions make it a day-trip, while on the Continent, business people will typically spend a day-and-a-half at shows in their market.

Veteran exhibitors say that the secret of successful participation consists of three main elements.

The first is research into which events are the most influential in any given market. European organisers will usually supply on request an independently audited visitor profile, showing their buying interests, and in addition a catalogue of the previous event, indicating clearly the products or services displayed.

The second element is to plan well in advance – and in fine detail. For many major shows it is necessary to book as much as a year ahead to obtain a well-located stand and accommodation within reasonable travelling distance of the venue.

Be aware of the nationalities of visitors so that literature can be translated into the appropriate languages of target markets and interpreting services arranged.

Post-1992 exhibits can get to European Community destinations with a minimum of difficulty, but in the meantime the unversed can find their products delayed because of incomplete documentation.

Insurance, including third party liability, is a must and firms must check whether their standard cover includes literal and not just insurance jargon "all risks".

Third, remember that it is increasingly the case in European shows for visitors to schedule most or even all of their appointments in advance, especially with the exhibitors they wish to see. It is therefore vital to promote widely to potential customers, inviting them to the stand.

Many continental organisers generally distribute their catalogues in advance of the event rather than – as is more usually the case in the UK – holding them back until the show opens. This means, of course, that the copy date for catalogue entries is well before the show.

Some large companies have specialist exhibition managers to take care of organisational detail. Most, however, do not have these executive resources. Fortunately, there are specialist firms which will take on this burden.

Many stand design and construction companies now tailor service packages to include, as desired, the ancillary details of the design and translation of literature, transport and documentation, insurance arrangements and even the booking of travel and accommodation.

"There aren't many company exhibition managers any more and we tend to work for marketing managers, who don't have time for all the details," says Bryan Hayes, marketing director of the Firbank Kempster Group. "What often happens is that the client gives us a brief and a total budget and we do the complete package."

HP: ICM's background in audio-visual presentations enables it to offer such eye-catching techniques as video walls and multi-language programmes.

"UK companies presenting themselves in Europe in greater numbers," says director Richard Cuthbertson. "We have noticed that as well as employing exhibitions they are also using the techniques of their own company presentations and roadshows. It is an area where we have seen a tremendous surge in activity."

Robert Tracy, managing director of SGL Presentation, points out that exhibiting in continental Europe need not be significantly more expensive than a domestic UK show. Although both transport and travel costs have to be taken into account, stand building tends to be cheaper on the Continent.

But while UK exhibitors average three days' duration, European ones are often longer, increasing demands on staff time and the costs of accommodation.

In order to compete for attention in large-scale events, the stands have become larger and more spectacular. Designers, such as those mentioned, are consequently called upon to defray initial costs by producing modular constructions which can be dismantled and re-used.

Design flexibility is absolutely necessary to enable the units to be assembled in various configurations to meet different space sizes and shapes.

These days, the exhibitor should not be surprised if the designer asks what nationality style is required.

Tracy points out that he can usually identify which country an exhibit is from by whether it is one-off, flimsy and flamboyant French; solid, well-finished and durable German; or crowded-with-products Italian.

He qualifies this: "But at the top end of the scale, good design is good design the world over."

Reading 27

Meet me at the fair

Getting the most out of a foreign trade show is more of a challenge than ever

Kerry Pechter

Reprinted from *International Business*, May 1992, Vol. 5, No. 5, pp. 32–9.

A reporter for a Japanese fashion magazine strolled up to James Kaitery's booth at the start of the Fur and Fashion trade fair in Tokyo last February and advised the furrier to pack up his samples and go back to his shop on New York's Seventh Avenue. Japanese women, the reporter said, had little interest in paying up to $300 for Mr. Kaitery's sable hats, chinchilla-lined gloves or mink-trimmed berets.

The reporter, however, was wrong. During and after the fair, Mr. Kaitery, the junior member of a $6 million father-and-son business, scribbled down orders for more than a half million dollars worth of fur accessories. He easily earned back the $15,000 he'd spent to attend the fair, as one of a contingent of New York furriers who'd been fleeced in their own country by the recession and by guilt-mongering animal rights advocates.

At virtually every moment of every year, at least one colossal commercial trade show is underway somewhere outside the U.S. These lavish and exotic corporate coming-out parties, often mammoth by U.S. standards, offer companies of every size an annual or biennial opportunity to showcase their wares and press the flesh of distributors and agents from dozens of countries.

Each year, American exporters wonder whether to gamble a large chunk of their marketing dollars on a five-day fling in a foreign city. On the one hand, who can afford to spend thousands of dollars a day on a single show? On the other hand, with demand in the U.S. so weak, who can afford to miss the biggest show of the year?

Fortunately, it is possible to attend a foreign trade show on a limited budget. Conversations with fair-goers show that, with a little research, a company can rent a booth for as little as $3,000, find comfortable lodging for $60 a night, and fly to Europe and back for less than $500 – prices that even a startup could afford. While there's still an element of risk, most companies say foreign shows are well worth the price of admission. And some even hit the jackpot on their first or second try. "My father is still in shock," says Mr. Kaitery.

When attending a foreign trade show, there are several pointers to keep in mind.

Companies, especially those on a limited budget, can't afford to pick the wrong trade show. But with the recent proliferation of new shows (they are highly profitable for the organizers), picking the wrong show is becoming easier to do. As a first step, company execs should contact one of the government agencies that leads delegations of small to medium-sized companies to foreign trade shows. These agencies are often criticized, but they can be very helpful and their prices are usually unbeatable.

PICKING THE RIGHT SHOW

For instance, the U.S. and Foreign Commercial Service (USFCS), a branch of the U.S. Commerce Department, leads delegations of small companies to trade fairs all over the world. Anyone can go to one of the 67 USFCS branch offices in the U.S. and find out which trade fairs have been targeted. Similarly, state agencies such as the California State World Trade Commission or the Port Authority of New York & New Jersey also lead trips to certain shows. Often, they or the organizer of the show will create a "U.S.A." or "Made in America" pavilion, which attracts agents and distributors who are looking specifically for U.S. goods.

These agencies can save a company thousands of dollars in booth rentals alone. They typically buy up large blocks of booth space and sell booths or half-booths at much less than the standard minimum price. At a recent show in Singapore, for instance, the Indianapolis office of the USFCS provided a standard nine-square-meter booth for only $3,700. California's export office rents half-booths for as little as $3,000.

U.S. representatives of foreign shows can also help steer exporters to the right show. The Japan External Trade Organization (JETRO), for instance, offers information on dozens of shows in Japan. The major German fairs have representatives in the U.S. Consultants such as Glahé International of Washington, D.C., can help companies find the optimal show, too, as can the international edition of the Tradeshow Week Data Book. One exporter offers this additional rule of thumb: find out which show your competitors attend year after year and go there.

PRE-SHOW MARKETING

The best way to ensure a successful show, experienced fair-goers say, is to tell your potential customers you'll be there. Smart companies send out hundreds of letters and press releases prior to the show to make sure the right people come to their booths.

One such company is Omnicomp Graphics Corp., a private Houston company with sales of $5 million to $8 million. Omnicomp makes devices that connect computers to monitors and turn digital information into graphic displays. Before a show, Omnicomp's CEO and president, Tony Masraff, sends announcements to foreign trade magazines, hoping for – and often receiving – free notices. Then he raids his database for old contacts and sends thousands of letters telling people where to meet him. "If people know that you're going to be there," says one fair-goer, "it doesn't matter where your booth is. They'll find you even if you're in a closet."

Ironically, most companies fail to send out letters. "Most people get so caught up in their underwear – that is, they worry so much about the logistics – that they forget that a show is a marketing event," says Jane Lorimer, president of Trade Show Bureau, a nonprofit group in Denver that compiles data on trade shows in the U.S. and Canada.

But logistics can make or break a trip. The process of moving people and equipment to and from a foreign show is, aside from the cost of the booth, the biggest expense. Companies on a tight budget can minimize this expense by doing their own legwork or by joining an organized group.

For instance, Carolyn Randall, a chemist and chief marketer for Ionetics Inc., a Costa Mesa, Calif., maker of medical diagnostic equipment, handled her own travel arrangements. When she and her boss decided to attend Medica, the big medical fair in Dusseldorf, last fall, they joined a California State World Trade expedition, paying about $3,000 for their booth. But they did the rest themselves.

HANDLING THE LOGISTICS

Five months before the show, Ms. Randall opened her Michelin Guide and started calling hotels in Dusseldorf. By then, most hotels had been filled, but she eventually found a small place for $60 a night about 45 minutes by train from the fair. "Some people need an atrium lobby and a private balcony," she says, "but I just wanted a clean, quiet, comfortable room." She purchased a 21-day advance ticket for $700, and saved an estimated $800 in freight-forwarding costs by taking her product, an electrolyte analyzer, on the plane with her.

Those who use a freight forwarder are advised to pick a specialist in trade shows. Ben Rosenthal, president of Rosenthal Manufacturing in Chicago, says he once chose a shipper who didn't have an office at the fair, and his equipment, a high-tech cutting machine, got stuck in customs. That can spell disaster. "I've seen people at trade shows holding signs that say, 'My exhibit is in Hamburg,' or 'My merchandise is in

Customs,'" says Jerry Kallman of Kallman Associates, a Waldwick, N.J., firm that represents the Munich fairs in the U.S.

If you plan to carry product samples in and out of several foreign countries, you can avoid a lot of paperwork by obtaining an ATA Carnet before your trip. The Carnet indicates that you have posted a bond of 40 percent of the value of your samples with the U.S. Council for International Business, which has offices in New York and seven other large U.S. cities. Typically, the council charges a fee of $120 to $250. Carnets aren't accepted in China, Taiwan, Russia, the Philippines or South America. Korea and Israel require a 100 percent surety bond.

GOOD BOOTHSMANSHIP

At their first overseas fair, many Americans are too dazzled to do much selling. With thousands of exhibitors and hundreds of thousands of attendees, the big foreign shows are grander, splashier and more festive than most U.S. shows. Europeans, for instance, can't tolerate the tacky pipe-and-drape booths that are so common in the U.S. "European trade shows are centuries more mature than ours," says John Wakely, an exhibit design manager at Glahé International.

If only one or two people represent your company at a fair, they should include a decision-maker or someone who will form a relationship with the customer. Companies that send only one person should consider going with a group or taking part in a U.S.A. pavilion, where interpreters, trade specialists and hospitality room are furnished for free.

Good "boothsmanship" is vital. "The friendlier you are, the friendlier they are," says Mr. Kaitery. Some exhibitors attract attention by conducting a prize drawing, or by giving away key chains or pens. (In Russia or China, attendees and others will stampede a booth that offers freebies.) And a good gimmick never hurts. Mr. Masraff, a Texan of Armenian extraction, has worn a cowboy hat, and Ms. Randall, red, white and blue clothes. Mr. Rosenthal's secret weapon was always his elderly mother. She would circulate the hall, arm-hooking people and not letting go until they'd seen her son's fabulous machine.

Not everyone is a natural boothsperson. "Some people don't know how to conduct themselves," says Franc Manzolillo, a Commerce Department trade specialist. "They sit in the back of the booth talking to the pretty interpreters, or they've got overflowing ashtrays, or they stand in front of their booths with their arms folded like Mr. Clean, daring people to come in. You've got to say, 'Can I show you how this widget works?' And you've got to talk loudly. The only way to attract people to the booth is to speak loudly."

THE BOTTOM LINE

What do people do when they close the booth at the end of a 10-hour day? "There were times when I went back to my hotel and said, 'I'm just going to take a short nap,' and I woke up the next morning with my clothes still on," says Mr. Masraff. Ed James, president of Zical Ltd., a $250,000 Santa Ana, Calif., exporter of pregnancy test kits, spends his free moments prowling around whatever city he's in, observing the local folk, watching them shop and even noting what colors they seem to prefer. "The Germans are very fond of blue," he says.

Interestingly, recent fair-goers say their American-made products are much sought after by foreign distributors. Despite the supposed decline in U.S. competitiveness, the quality of goods displayed by U.S. manufacturers was never questioned. Indeed, the U.S.A. pavilion at foreign fairs always seems to attract crowds as well as respect. In furs, says Mr. Kaitery, "the Japanese go to Hong Kong for price but America for quality."

Making money, of course, is the point of the trip, and some people do very well. Zical Ltd.'s Ed James picked up 73 leads at Dusseldorf's Medica show in 1989. Twenty placed orders and a dozen became regular customers. The next year was unremarkable for him, but after the 1991 show he received more than 120 leads. Zical was just one of 200 small California companies that collectively sold more than $50 million worth of merchandise last year on trips arranged by the state Office of Export Development.

But others say that expectations should be kept low. "People expect to make a million dollars overnight, but I don't necessarily look for sales right away," says one exporter. In fact, some people don't even cover their expenses. Mr. Rosenthal has sold as much as 13 times his expenses at past European fairs, but last fall he spent $25,000 to attend the Protronics show in Munich and sold only one machine. "It's also expensive because my wife shops," he quips. Success often depends on aggressive post-show follow-up.

The cardinal rule of international fair-going seems to be that whether you sell anything or not, you should keep going back. "Patience is my competitive edge," says Mr. Masraff. "I love it when I hear my competitors say, 'It's been three months since the show and I haven't heard from a single customer. We're not going back.'" Others agree. "Once you decide which show you're going to, you've got to go regularly," says Mr. James. It might take three or four trips to convince the industry that you're for real. And by that time, you will be. "There's a certain jauntiness you notice about the guy who comes back a second year," says Mr. Kallman. "Going to a trade show is like opening a fresh bottle of olives. The hardest part is getting out the first one."

The Basics: How Uncle Sam Can Help

American exporters and the U.S. Commerce Department have mixed emotions about each other. Some businesspeople think that Commerce's International Trade Administration and U.S. and Foreign Commercial Service do a great job of export promotion. Others call their efforts inconsistent. Commerce officials are merely puzzled that more people don't use their programs.

"We have a hell of a lot of services,' says Franc Manzolillo, a specialist in the ITA's Office of Microelectronics and Instrumentation. "But people don't know how to take advantage of them."

Here are some of Commerce's programs:

- Catalog Shows. For a fee of $200 to $300, an ITA official will display your printed or video catalog at a foreign trade show. To discourage idle inquiries, agents and distributors are required to order one.
- Matchmaker Trade Delegations. For a price ranging from $500 to $1,800, U.S. officials will arrange a two-to seven-day spree of overseas meetings between U.S. companies and prospective agents, distributors or joint venture partners. In the past, the first 10 small businesses to sign up for these programs have been eligible for a $500 to $750 rebate. That policy is under review.
- Trade Fairs, Solo Exhibitions and Trade Center Shows. If you can pay about $3,000, Commerce can arrange a booth for you in a small, exclusively American exhibition at a foreign trade center or fit you into the U.S.A. pavillion at a foreign trade show.
- Trade and Executive Missions. For $2,000 to $5,000, U.S. executives can participate in overseas meetings or technical seminars with senior government officials, as well as selected agents and distributors.

More information about these programs is available at local Commerce Department offices.

Resources

Trade Information Center, U.S. Department of Commerce, Room 7424, Herbert C. Hoover Bldg., 14th St. and Constitution Ave. N.W., Washington, DC 20230, (800) USA-TRADE.

Tradeshow Week Data Book, International Division, 12233 W. Olympic Blvd., Suite 236, Los Angeles, CA 90064 (800) 521–8110.

U.S. Council for International Trade, 1212 Avenue of the Americas, New York, NY 10036, (212) 354480.

Japan External Trade Organization, McGraw-Hill Building, 1221 Avenue of the Americas, New York, NY 10020, (212) 997–0400.

Trade Show Bureau, 1660 Lincoln St., Suite 2080, Denver, CO 80264, (303) 860–7626.

Ten of the World's Largest Trade Shows in 1993

SHOW: Toronto International Boat and Marine Trade Show
LOCATION: Toronto
WHEN: Jan. 8–17, 1993
DESCRIPTION: Marine products. 450 exhibitors, 120,000 attendees.
CONTACT: Outdoor Canada/Sportsmen's Shows, (416) 695–0311.

SHOW: MACEF
LOCATION: Milan
WHEN: February and September 1993
DESCRIPTION: Gifts, fine jewelry and household products. 3,200 exhibitors, 150,00 attendees.
CONTACT: Michael Delia Associates, (800) 524–2193.

SHOW: CeBIT
LOCATION: Hannover, Germany
WHEN: March 24–31, 1993
DESCRIPTION: Computer and communications equipment. 5,000 exhibitors, 570,000 attendees.
CONTACT: Hannover Fairs USA Inc. (609) 987–1202.

SHOW: Hannover Industrie Fair
LOCATION: Hannover, Germany
WHEN: April 21–28, 1993
DESCRIPTION: Industrial machinery and electronics. 6,300 exhibitors, 400,000 attendees.
CONTACT: Hannover Fairs USA Inc., (609) 987–1202.

SHOW: INTERPACK
LOCATION: Dusseldorf, Germany
WHEN: May 6–12, 1993
DESCRIPTION: Packaging machinery and materials. 2,100 exhibitors, 179,000 attendees.
CONTACT: Dusseldorf Trade Shows Inc., (312) 781–5180

SHOW: Business Show Osaka
LOCATION: Osaka, Japan
WHEN: May 1993
DESCRIPTION: Office and data processing equipment. 149 exhibitors, 252,000 attendees.
CONTACT: Nippon Omni Management Association, 011–34–03–3403–1331.

SHOW: SMAU
LOCATION: Milan, Italy
WHEN: October 1993
DESCRIPTION: Computers, office machinery and furnishings. 2,600 exhibitors, 175,000 attendees.
CONTACT: Michael Delia Associates, (800) 524–2193.

SHOW: BATIMAT
LOCATION: Paris
WHEN: November 1993
DESCRIPTION: Building and construction materials and machinery. 3,800 exhibitors, 600,000 attendees.
CONTACT: Batimat Glenheim, 011–33–1–47–56–5000.

SHOW: COMDEX
LOCATION: Las Vegas
WHEN: Nov. 15–19, 1993
DESCRIPTION: Computer hardware and software. 1,850 exhibitors, 98,000 attendees.
CONTACT: Interface Group, (617) 449–6600.

SHOW: MEDICA
LOCATION: Dusseldorf
WHEN: Nov. 17–20, 1993
DESCRIPTION: Medical instrumentation; diagnostic, technical and therapeutic health care products. 1,336 exhibitors, 107,000 attendees.
CONTACT: Dusseldorf Trade Shows Inc., (312) 781–5180.

Index